Fantastic Four
THE INHUMANS

INHUMANS
Writers: Carlos Pacheco & Rafael Marin
Art: Ladrönn with Jorge Pereira Lucas
Colors: Studio F's Francisco Ruiz-Velasco & Raul Trevino
Letters: Richard Starkings & Comicraft's Wes Abbott
Editor: Mark Powers

FANTASTIC FOUR
Plot: Carlos Pacheco & Rafael Marin
Dialogue: Karl Kesel
Pencils: Mark Bagley
Inks: Karl Kesel, Al Vey & Scott Koblish
Colors: Liquid! Graphics
Letters: Richard Starkings & Comicraft's Saida Temofonte & Albert Deschesne
Assistant Editors: Marc Sumerak & Jeff Youngquist
Editor: Tom Brevoort

Cover Art: Mike Wieringo, Karl Kesel & Paul Mounts
Research: Stuart Vandal
Recap text: Michael Hoskin

Senior Editor, Special Projects: Jeff Youngquist
Associate Editors: Jennifer Grünwald & Mark D. Beazley
Assistant Editors: Michael Short & Cory Levine
Senior Vice President of Sales: David Gabriel
Production: Jerron Quality Color
Vice President of Creative: Tom Marvelli

Editor in Chief: Joe Quesada
Publisher: Dan Buckley

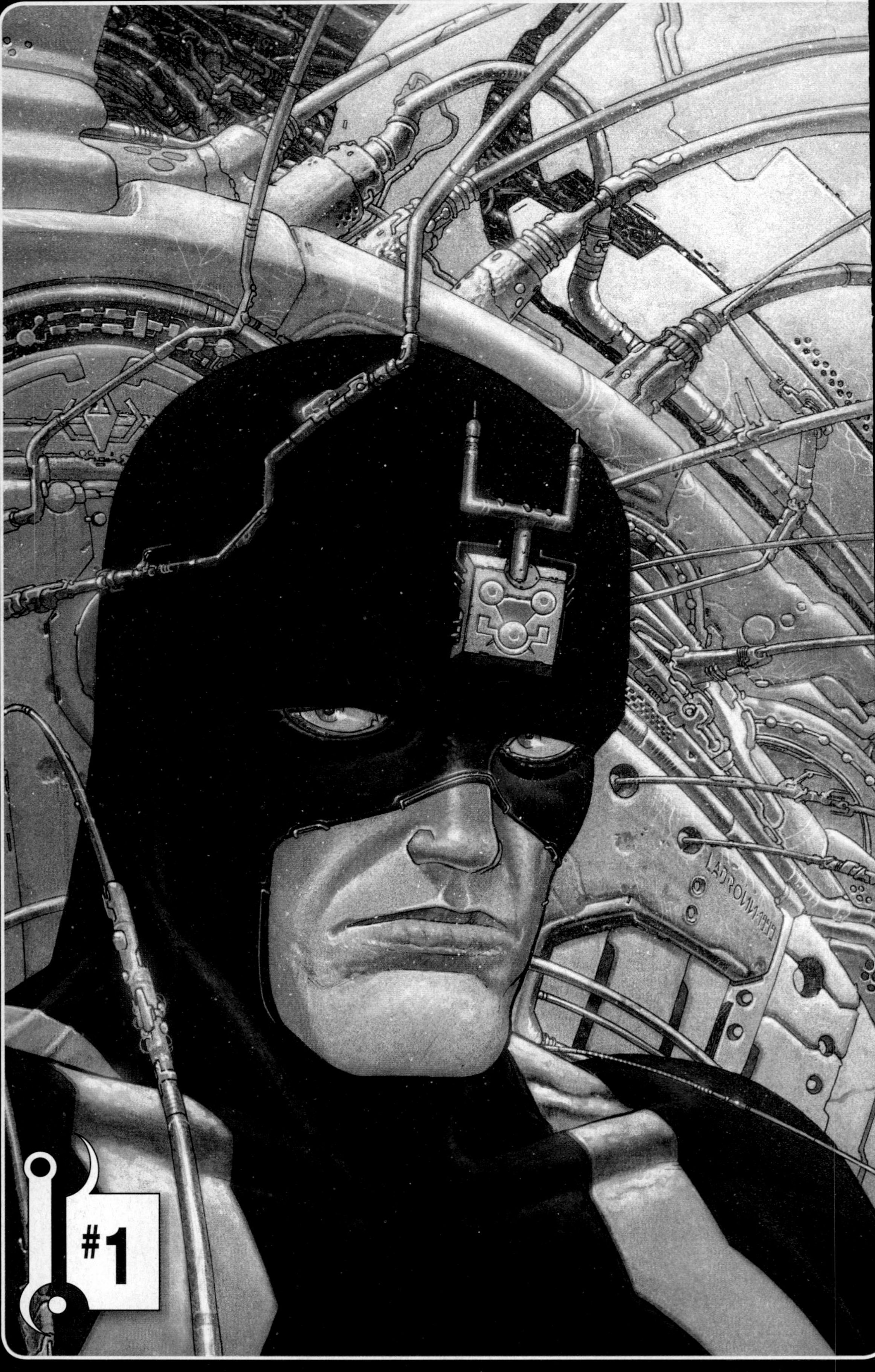
#1

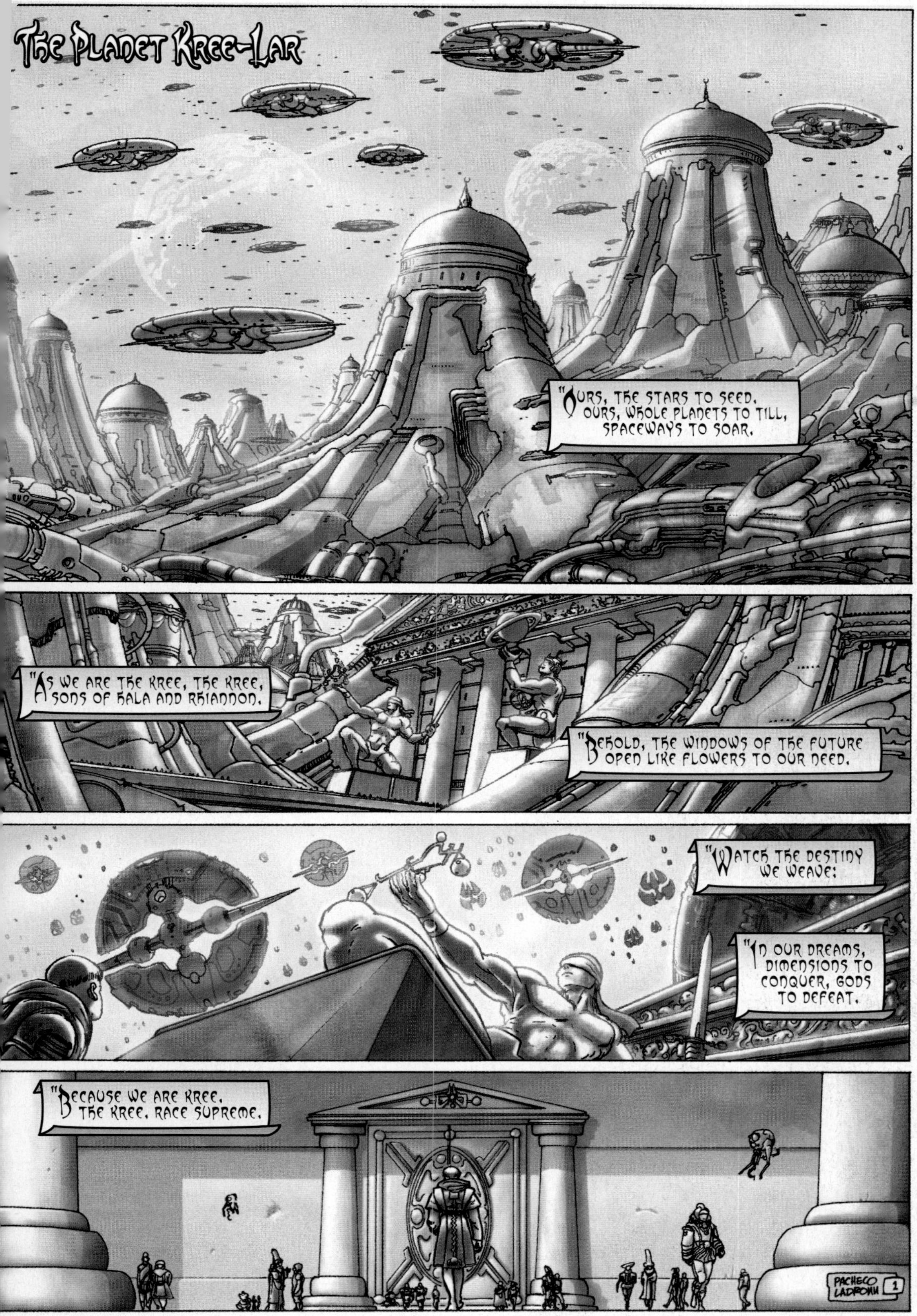

THE PLANET KREE-LAR
"OURS, THE STARS TO SEED. OURS, WHOLE PLANETS TO TILL, SPACEWAYS TO SOAR.
"AS WE ARE THE KREE, THE KREE, SONS OF HALA AND RHIANNON.
"BEHOLD, THE WINDOWS OF THE FUTURE OPEN LIKE FLOWERS TO OUR NEED.
"WATCH THE DESTINY WE WEAVE:
"IN OUR DREAMS, DIMENSIONS TO CONQUER, GODS TO DEFEAT.
"BECAUSE WE ARE KREE. THE KREE, RACE SUPREME.
PACHECO LADRONN
1

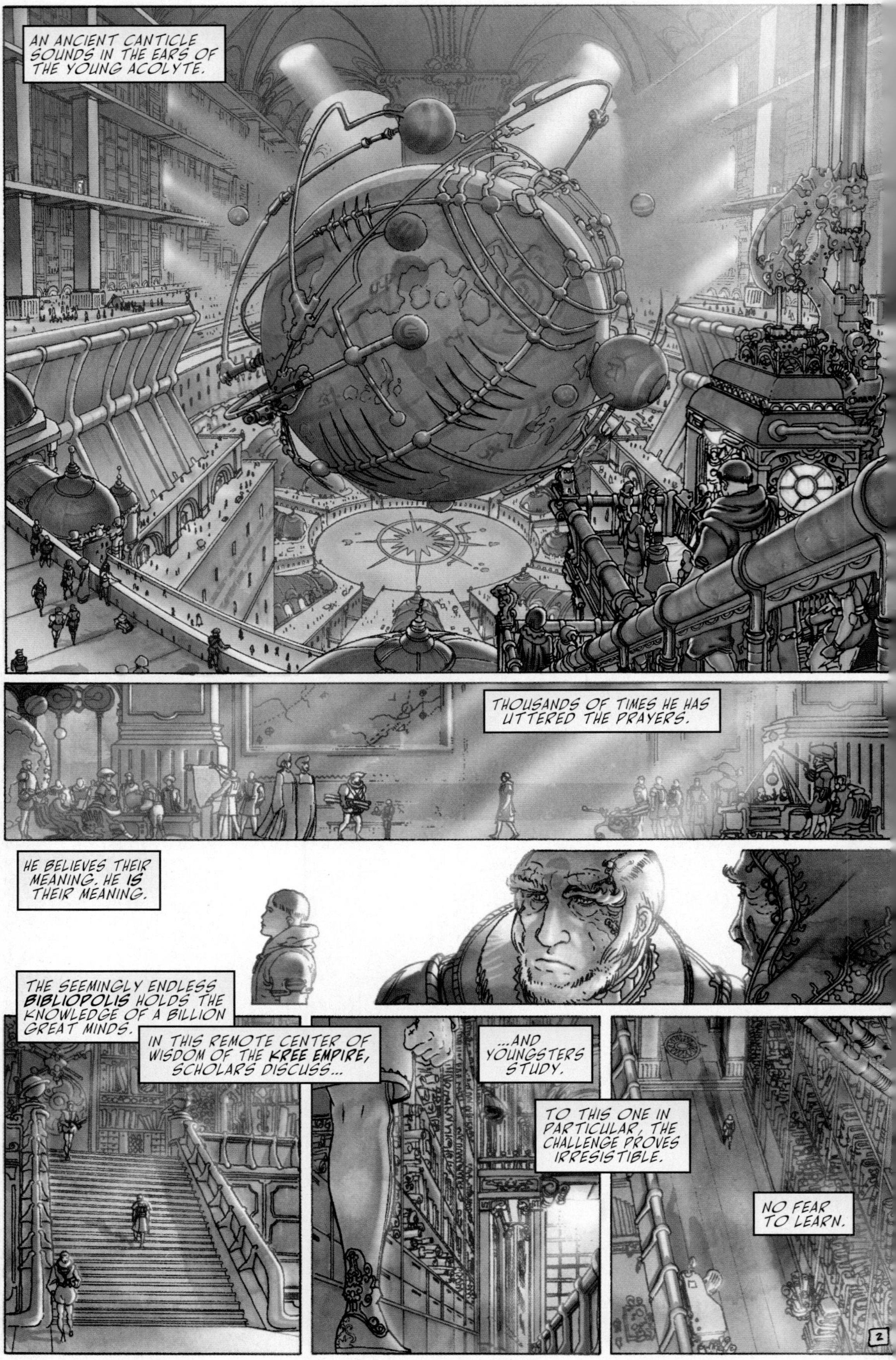

AN ANCIENT CANTICLE SOUNDS IN THE EARS OF THE YOUNG ACOLYTE.
THOUSANDS OF TIMES HE HAS UTTERED THE PRAYERS.
HE BELIEVES THEIR MEANING. HE **IS** THEIR MEANING.
THE SEEMINGLY ENDLESS **BIBLIOPOLIS** HOLDS THE KNOWLEDGE OF A BILLION GREAT MINDS.
IN THIS REMOTE CENTER OF WISDOM OF THE **KREE EMPIRE,** SCHOLARS DISCUSS...
...AND YOUNGSTERS STUDY.
TO THIS ONE IN PARTICULAR, THE CHALLENGE PROVES IRRESISTIBLE.
NO FEAR TO LEARN.

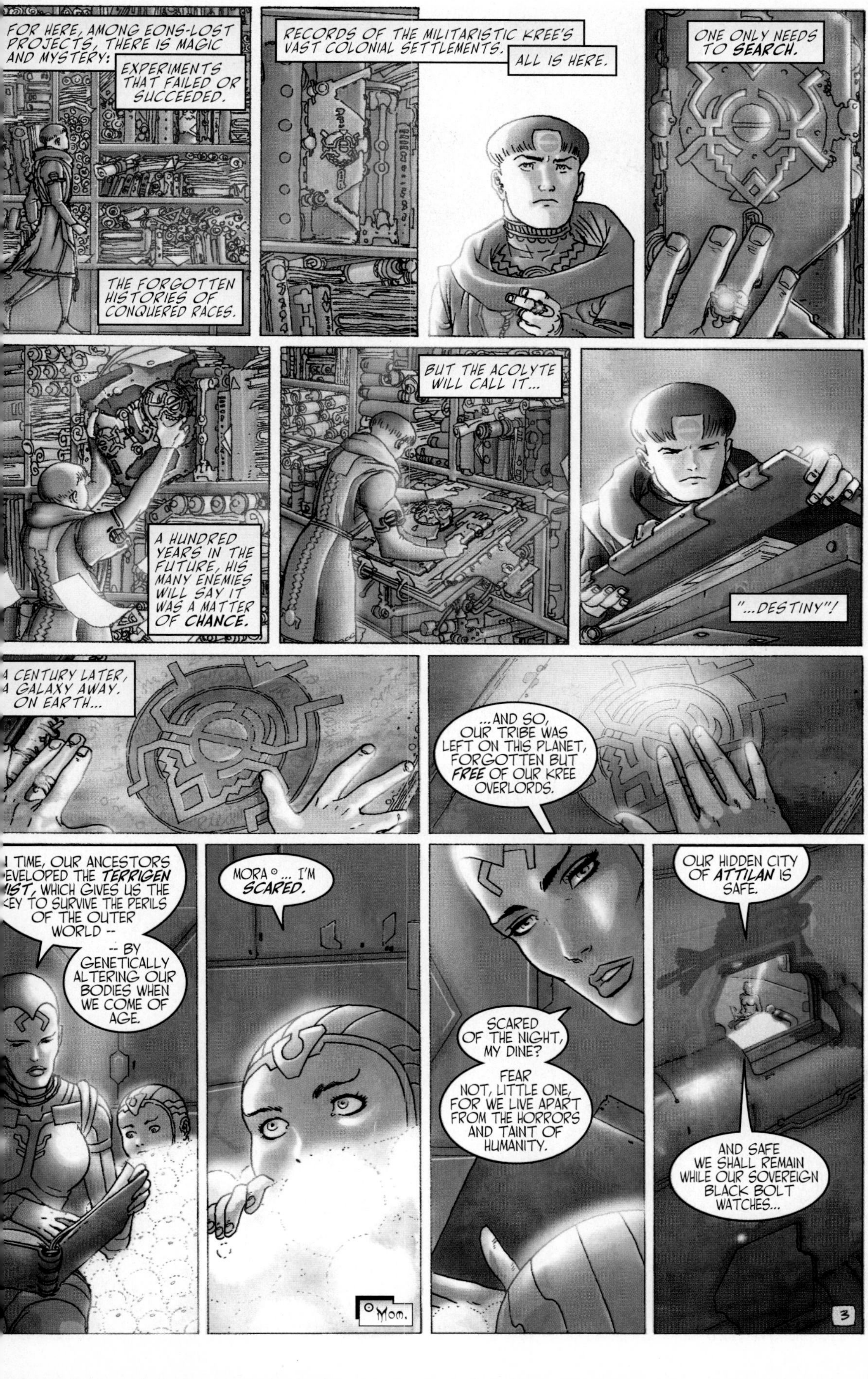
FOR HERE, AMONG EONS-LOST PROJECTS, THERE IS MAGIC AND MYSTERY:
EXPERIMENTS THAT FAILED OR SUCCEEDED.
THE FORGOTTEN HISTORIES OF CONQUERED RACES.
RECORDS OF THE MILITARISTIC KREE'S VAST COLONIAL SETTLEMENTS.
ALL IS HERE.
ONE ONLY NEEDS TO SEARCH.
A HUNDRED YEARS IN THE FUTURE, HIS MANY ENEMIES WILL SAY IT WAS A MATTER OF CHANCE.
BUT THE ACOLYTE WILL CALL IT...
"...DESTINY"!
A CENTURY LATER, A GALAXY AWAY. ON EARTH...
...AND SO, OUR TRIBE WAS LEFT ON THIS PLANET, FORGOTTEN BUT FREE OF OUR KREE OVERLORDS.
I TIME, OUR ANCESTORS EVELOPED THE TERRIGEN IIST, WHICH GIVES US THE KEY TO SURVIVE THE PERILS OF THE OUTER WORLD --
-- BY GENETICALLY ALTERING OUR BODIES WHEN WE COME OF AGE.
MORA ° ... I'M SCARED.
° MOM.
SCARED OF THE NIGHT, MY DINE?
FEAR NOT, LITTLE ONE, FOR WE LIVE APART FROM THE HORRORS AND TAINT OF HUMANITY.
OUR HIDDEN CITY OF ATTILAN IS SAFE.
AND SAFE WE SHALL REMAIN WHILE OUR SOVEREIGN BLACK BOLT WATCHES...

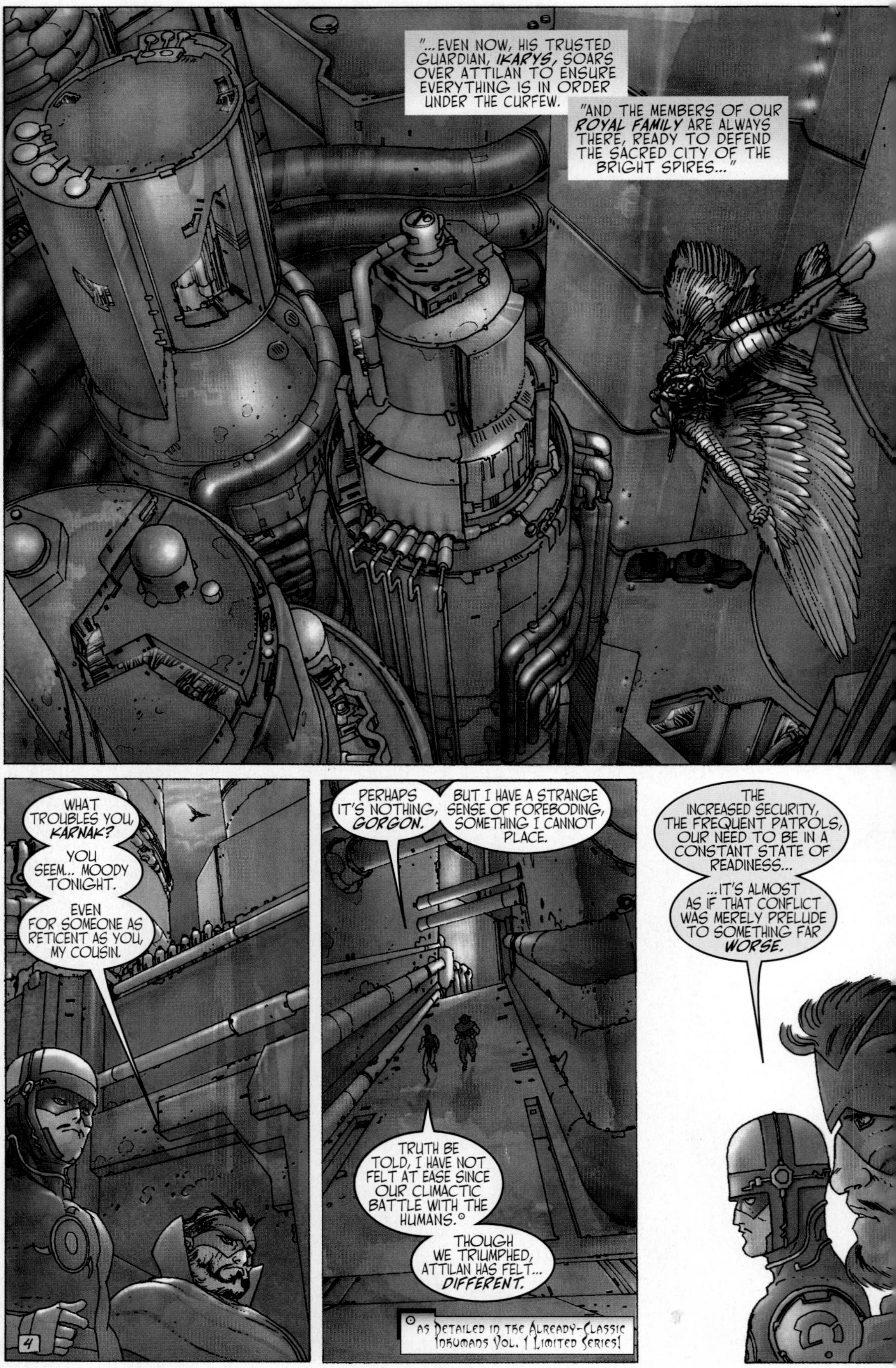
"...EVEN NOW, HIS TRUSTED GUARDIAN, IKARYS, SOARS OVER ATTILAN TO ENSURE EVERYTHING IS IN ORDER UNDER THE CURFEW.
"AND THE MEMBERS OF OUR ROYAL FAMILY ARE ALWAYS THERE, READY TO DEFEND THE SACRED CITY OF THE BRIGHT SPIRES..."
WHAT TROUBLES YOU, KARNAK?
YOU SEEM... MOODY TONIGHT.
EVEN FOR SOMEONE AS RETICENT AS YOU, MY COUSIN.
4
PERHAPS IT'S NOTHING, GORGON.
BUT I HAVE A STRANGE SENSE OF FOREBODING, SOMETHING I CANNOT PLACE.
TRUTH BE TOLD, I HAVE NOT FELT AT EASE SINCE OUR CLIMACTIC BATTLE WITH THE HUMANS.°
THOUGH WE TRIUMPHED, ATTILAN HAS FELT... DIFFERENT.
° AS DETAILED IN THE ALREADY-CLASSIC INHUMANS VOL. 1 LIMITED SERIES!
THE INCREASED SECURITY, THE FREQUENT PATROLS, OUR NEED TO BE IN A CONSTANT STATE OF READINESS...
...IT'S ALMOST AS IF THAT CONFLICT WAS MERELY PRELUDE TO SOMETHING FAR WORSE.

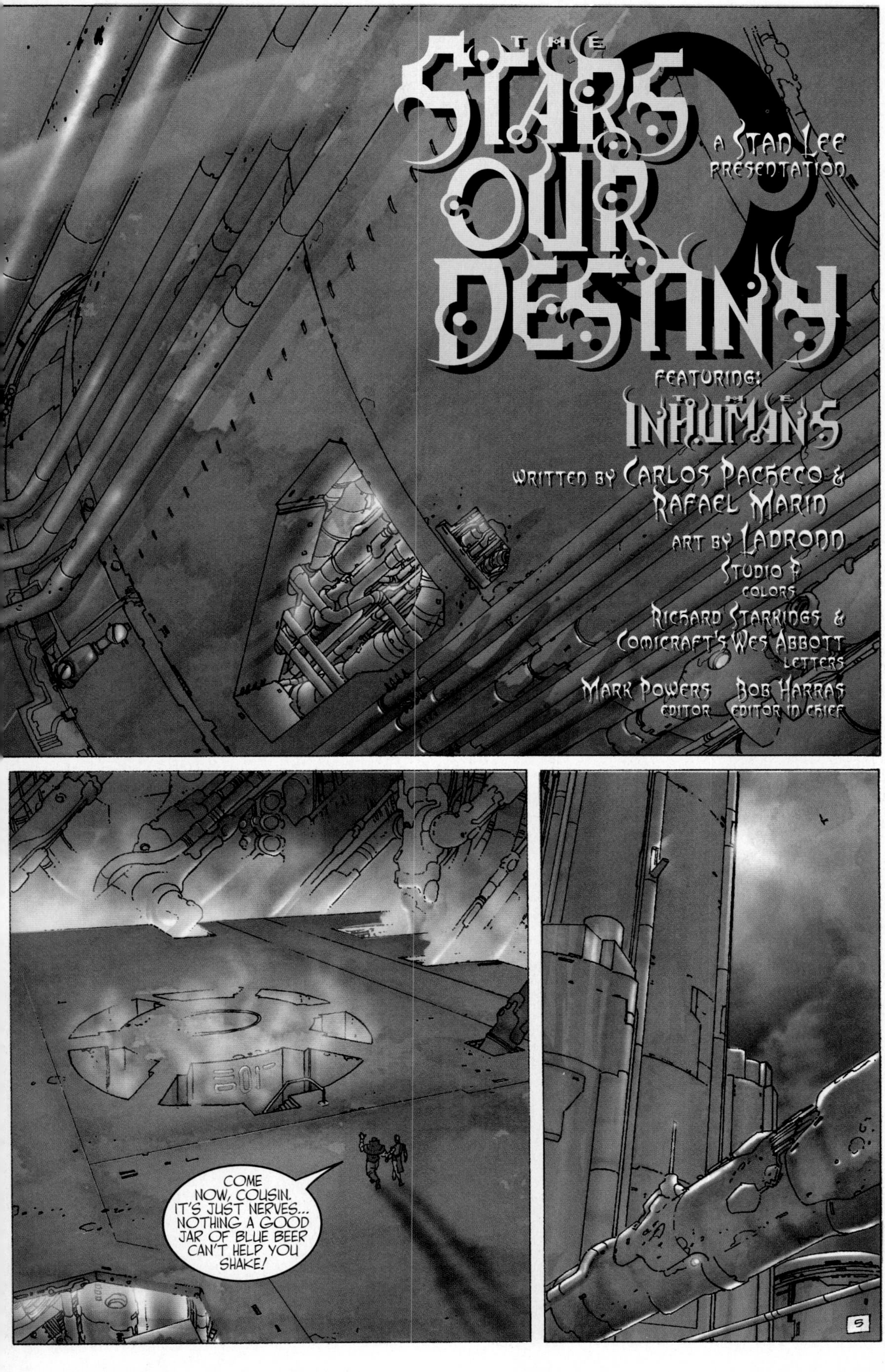
THE STARS OUR DESTINY
A STAN LEE PRESENTATION
FEATURING: THE INHUMANS
WRITTEN BY CARLOS PACHECO & RAFAEL MARIN
ART BY LADRONN
STUDIO F COLORS
RICHARD STARKINGS & COMICRAFT'S WES ABBOTT LETTERS
MARK POWERS EDITOR
BOB HARRAS EDITOR IN CHIEF
COME NOW, COUSIN. IT'S JUST NERVES... NOTHING A GOOD JAR OF BLUE BEER CAN'T HELP YOU SHAKE!

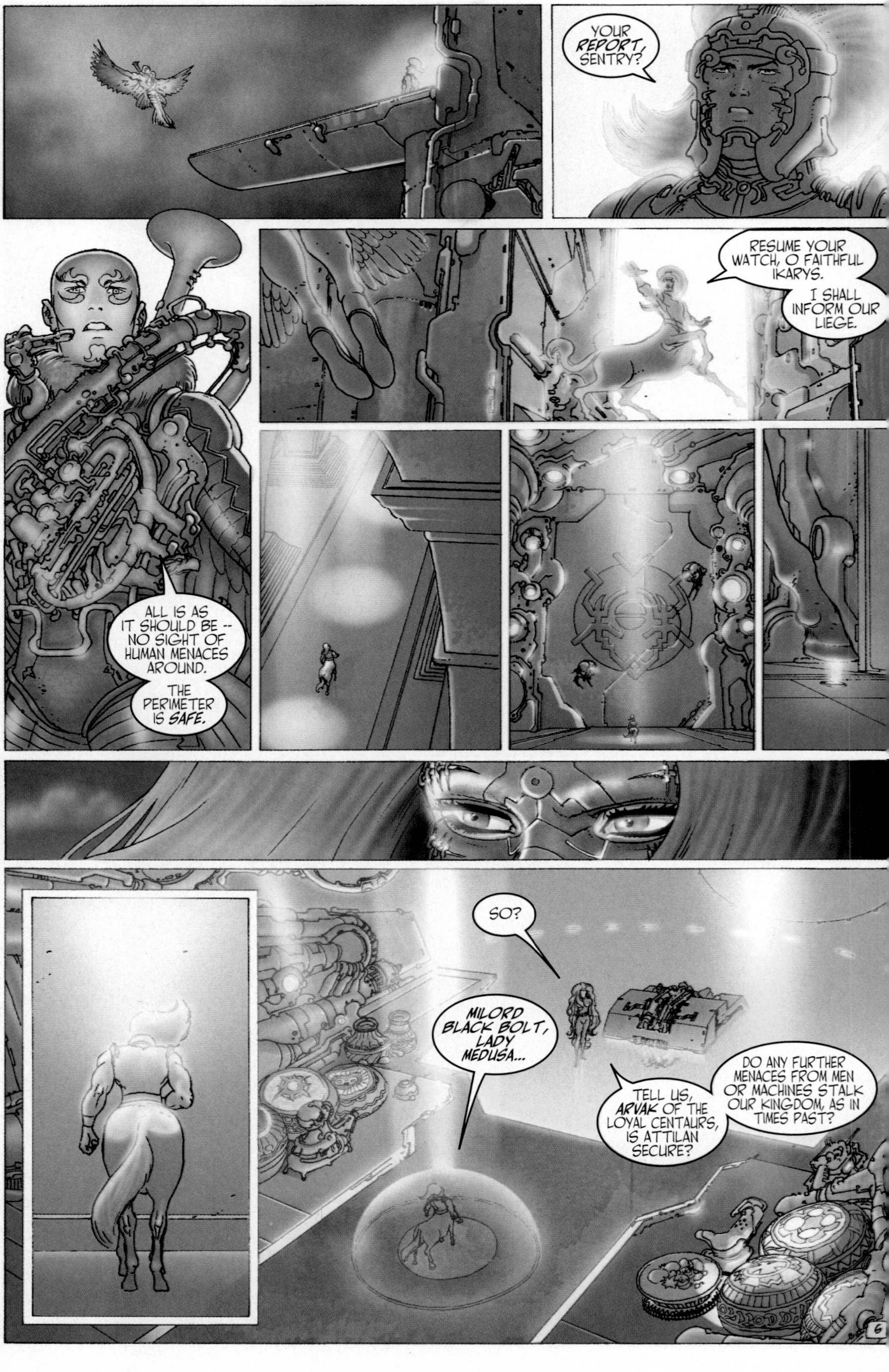
YOUR REPORT, SENTRY?
ALL IS AS IT SHOULD BE -- NO SIGHT OF HUMAN MENACES AROUND.
THE PERIMETER IS SAFE.
RESUME YOUR WATCH, O FAITHFUL IKARYS.
I SHALL INFORM OUR LIEGE.
SO?
MILORD BLACK BOLT, LADY MEDUSA...
TELL US, ARVAK OF THE LOYAL CENTAURS, IS ATTILAN SECURE?
DO ANY FURTHER MENACES FROM MEN OR MACHINES STALK OUR KINGDOM, AS IN TIMES PAST?
6

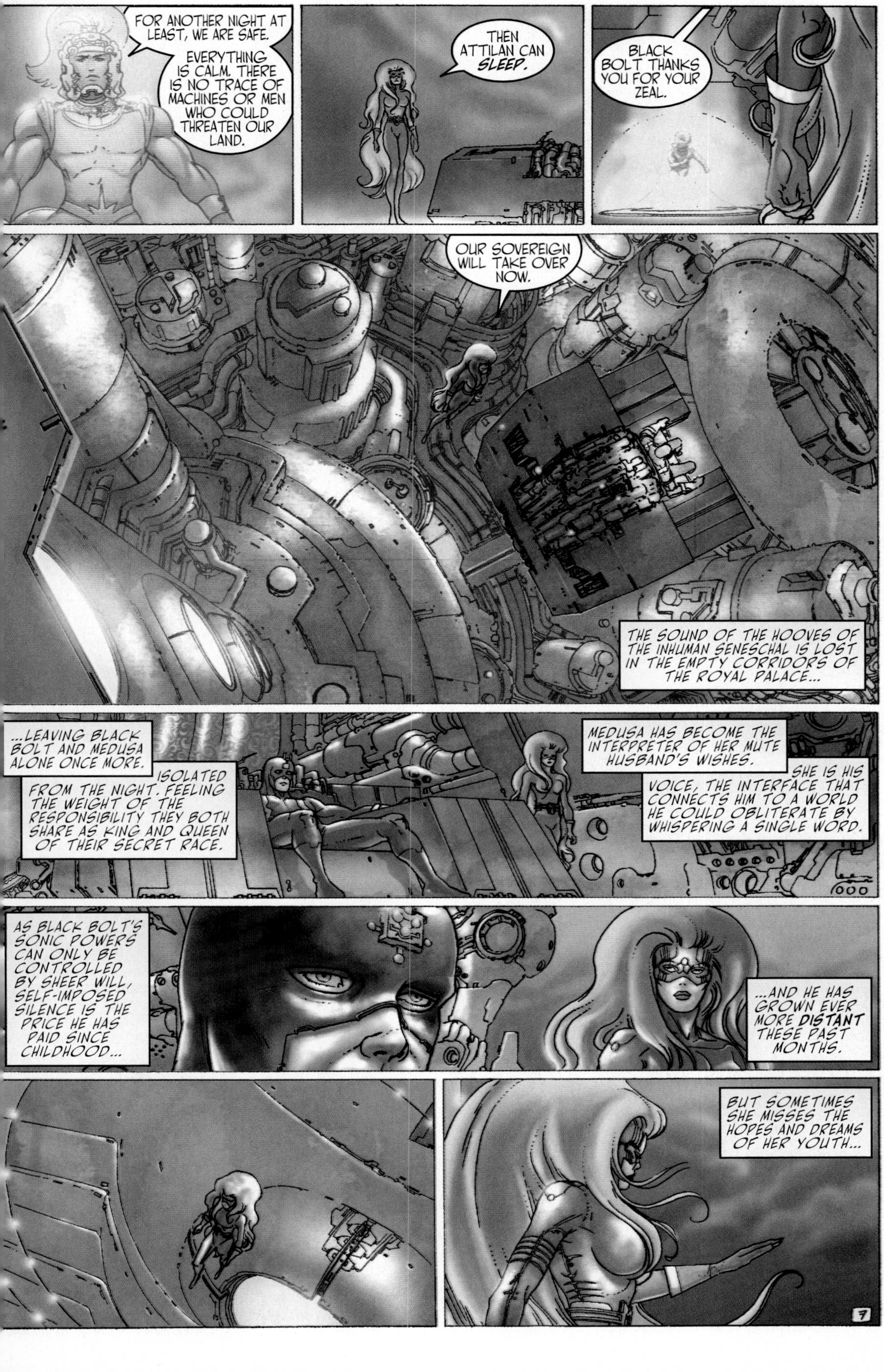

FOR ANOTHER NIGHT AT LEAST, WE ARE SAFE.
EVERYTHING IS CALM. THERE IS NO TRACE OF MACHINES OR MEN WHO COULD THREATEN OUR LAND.
THEN ATTILAN CAN SLEEP.
BLACK BOLT THANKS YOU FOR YOUR ZEAL.
OUR SOVEREIGN WILL TAKE OVER NOW.
THE SOUND OF THE HOOVES OF THE INHUMAN SENESCHAL IS LOST IN THE EMPTY CORRIDORS OF THE ROYAL PALACE...
...LEAVING BLACK BOLT AND MEDUSA ALONE ONCE MORE.
ISOLATED FROM THE NIGHT. FEELING THE WEIGHT OF THE RESPONSIBILITY THEY BOTH SHARE AS KING AND QUEEN OF THEIR SECRET RACE.
MEDUSA HAS BECOME THE INTERPRETER OF HER MUTE HUSBAND'S WISHES.
SHE IS HIS VOICE, THE INTERFACE THAT CONNECTS HIM TO A WORLD HE COULD OBLITERATE BY WHISPERING A SINGLE WORD.
AS BLACK BOLT'S SONIC POWERS CAN ONLY BE CONTROLLED BY SHEER WILL, SELF-IMPOSED SILENCE IS THE PRICE HE HAS PAID SINCE CHILDHOOD...
...AND HE HAS GROWN EVER MORE DISTANT THESE PAST MONTHS.
BUT SOMETIMES SHE MISSES THE HOPES AND DREAMS OF HER YOUTH...

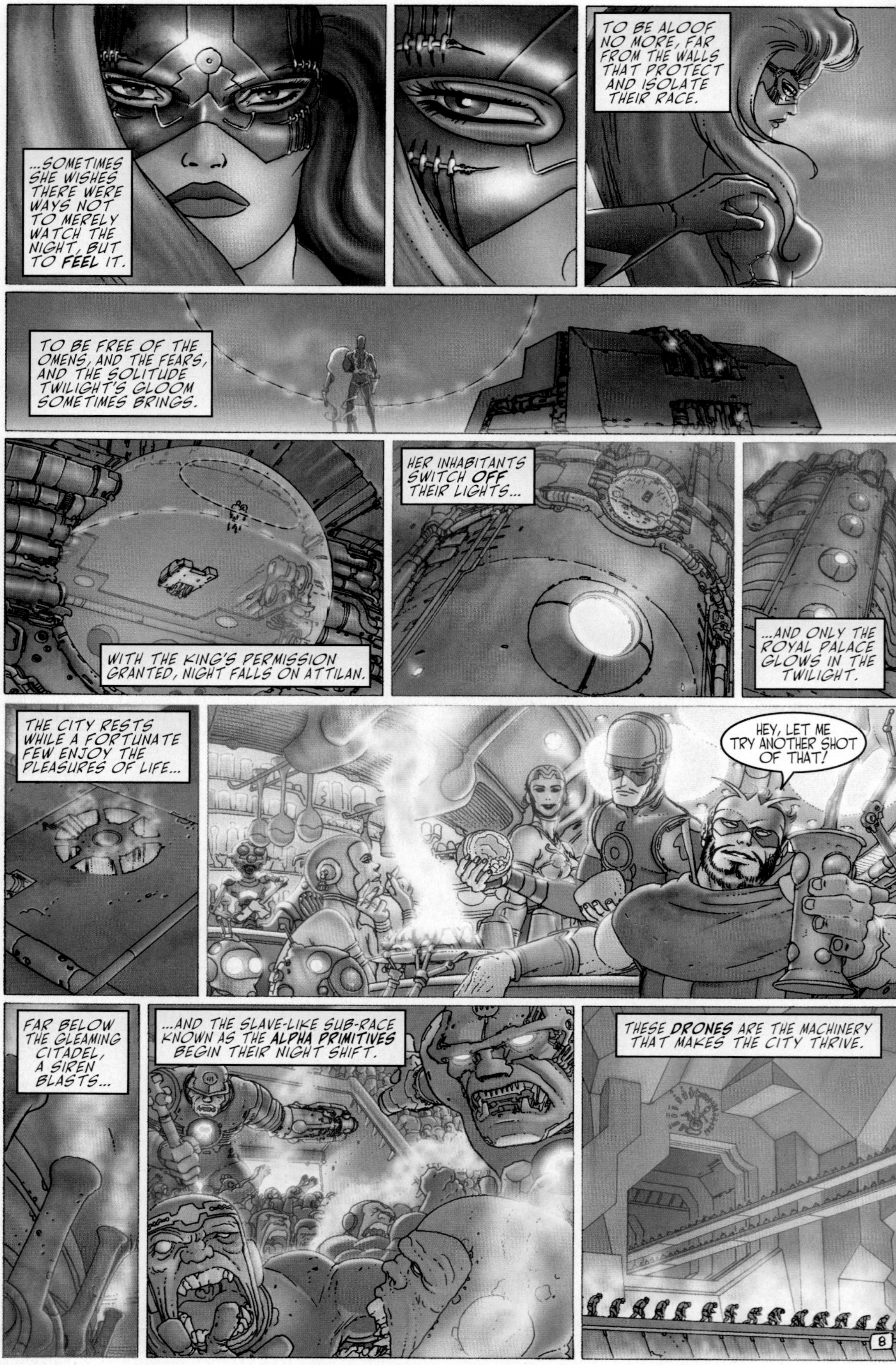
...SOMETIMES SHE WISHES THERE WERE WAYS NOT TO MERELY WATCH THE NIGHT, BUT TO FEEL IT.
TO BE ALOOF NO MORE, FAR FROM THE WALLS THAT PROTECT AND ISOLATE THEIR RACE.
TO BE FREE OF THE OMENS, AND THE FEARS, AND THE SOLITUDE TWILIGHT'S GLOOM SOMETIMES BRINGS.
WITH THE KING'S PERMISSION GRANTED, NIGHT FALLS ON ATTILAN.
HER INHABITANTS SWITCH OFF THEIR LIGHTS...
...AND ONLY THE ROYAL PALACE GLOWS IN THE TWILIGHT.
THE CITY RESTS WHILE A FORTUNATE FEW ENJOY THE PLEASURES OF LIFE...
HEY, LET ME TRY ANOTHER SHOT OF THAT!
FAR BELOW THE GLEAMING CITADEL, A SIREN BLASTS...
...AND THE SLAVE-LIKE SUB-RACE KNOWN AS THE ALPHA PRIMITIVES BEGIN THEIR NIGHT SHIFT.
THESE DRONES ARE THE MACHINERY THAT MAKES THE CITY THRIVE.

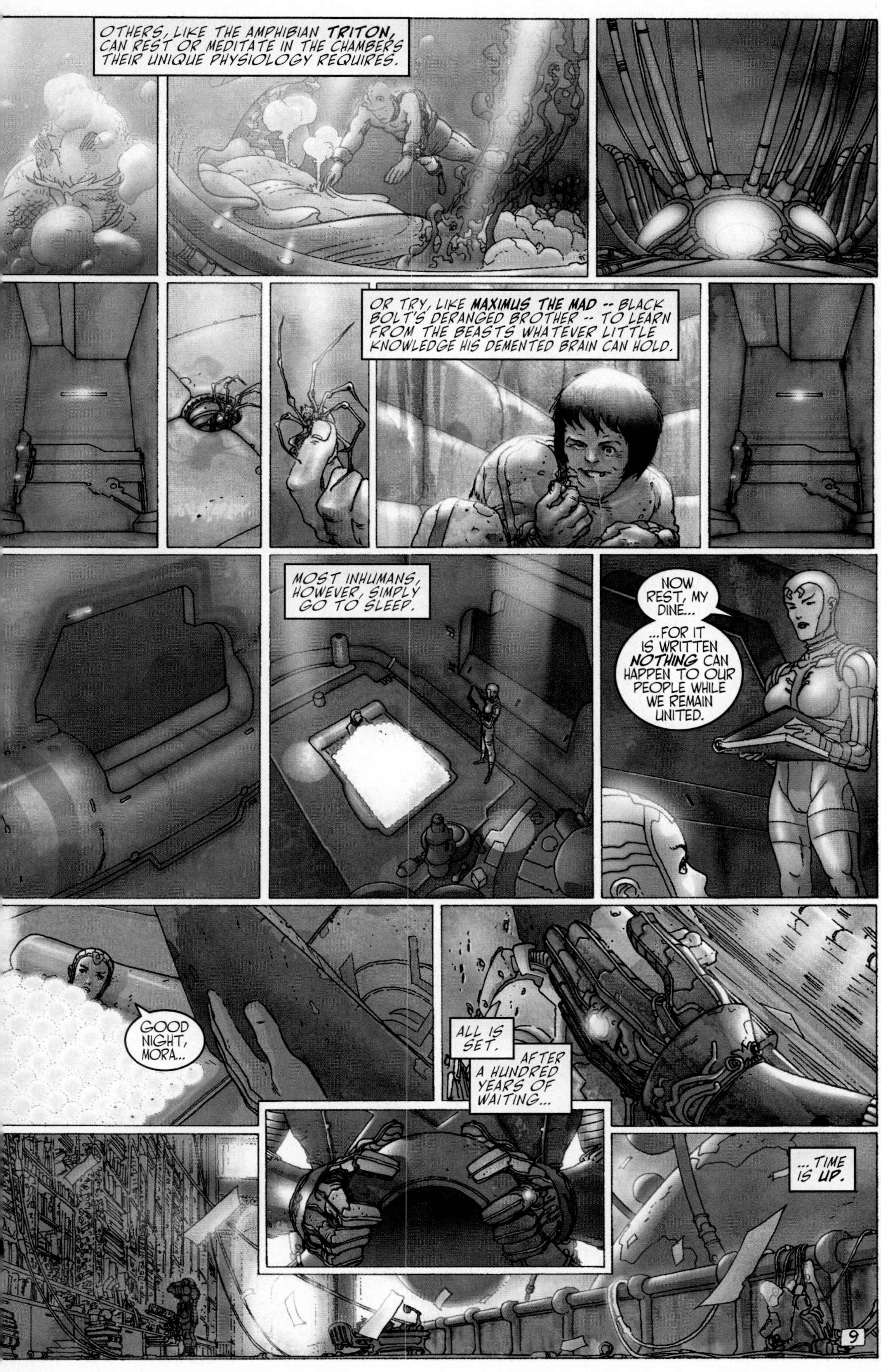
OTHERS, LIKE THE AMPHIBIAN TRITON, CAN REST OR MEDITATE IN THE CHAMBERS THEIR UNIQUE PHYSIOLOGY REQUIRES.
OR TRY, LIKE MAXIMUS THE MAD -- BLACK BOLT'S DERANGED BROTHER -- TO LEARN FROM THE BEASTS WHATEVER LITTLE KNOWLEDGE HIS DEMENTED BRAIN CAN HOLD.
MOST INHUMANS, HOWEVER, SIMPLY GO TO SLEEP.
NOW REST, MY DINE...
...FOR IT IS WRITTEN NOTHING CAN HAPPEN TO OUR PEOPLE WHILE WE REMAIN UNITED.
GOOD NIGHT, MORA...
ALL IS SET.
AFTER A HUNDRED YEARS OF WAITING...
...TIME IS UP.

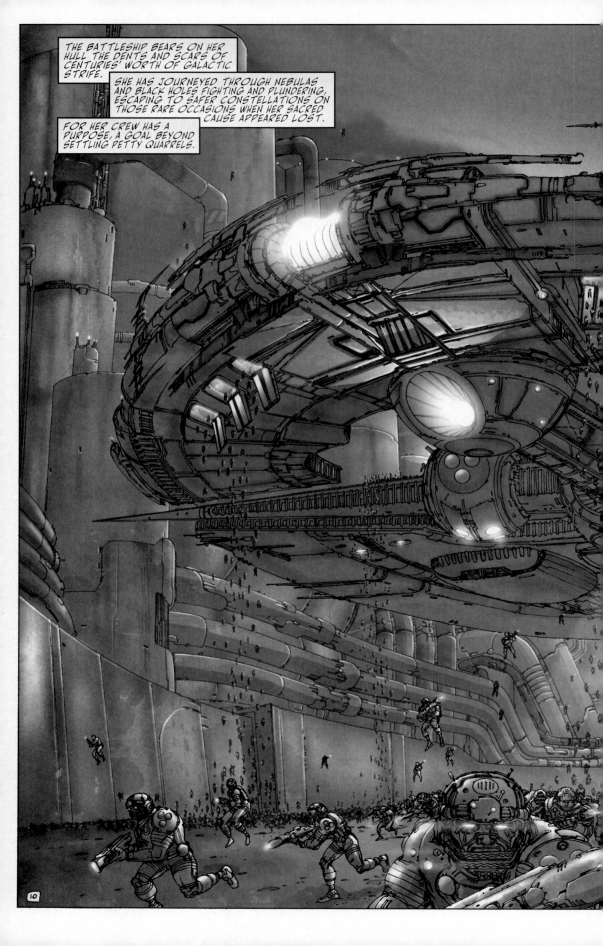

THE BATTLESHIP BEARS ON HER HULL THE DENTS AND SCARS OF CENTURIES' WORTH OF GALACTIC STRIFE.

SHE HAS JOURNEYED THROUGH NEBULAS AND BLACK HOLES FIGHTING AND PLUNDERING, ESCAPING TO SAFER CONSTELLATIONS ON THOSE RARE OCCASIONS WHEN HER SACRED CAUSE APPEARED LOST.

FOR HER CREW HAS A PURPOSE, A GOAL BEYOND SETTLING PETTY QUARRELS.

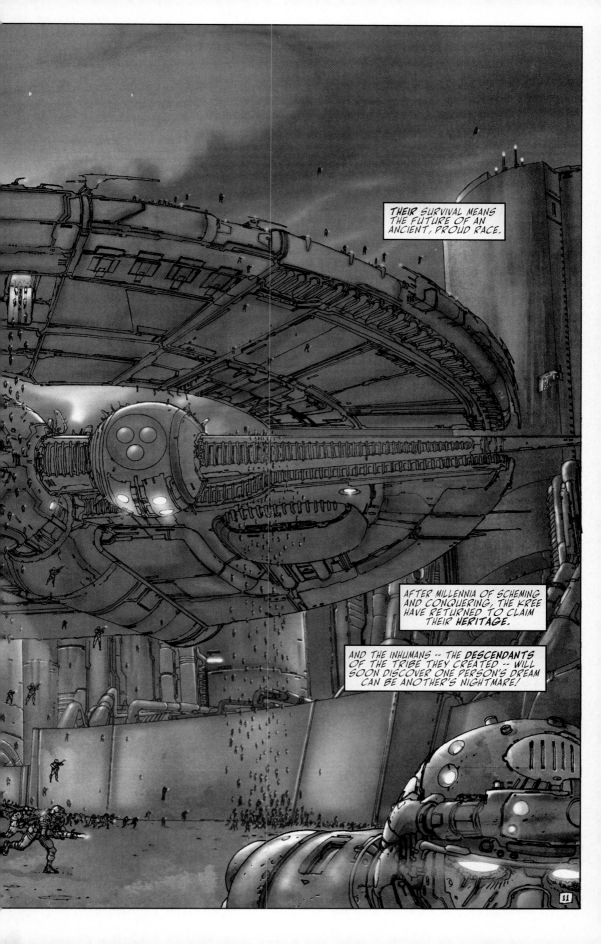

THEIR SURVIVAL MEANS THE FUTURE OF AN ANCIENT, PROUD RACE.

AFTER MILLENNIA OF SCHEMING AND CONQUERING, THE KREE HAVE RETURNED TO CLAIM THEIR **HERITAGE**.

AND THE INHUMANS -- THE **DESCENDANTS** OF THE TRIBE THEY CREATED -- WILL SOON DISCOVER ONE PERSON'S DREAM CAN BE ANOTHER'S NIGHTMARE!

11

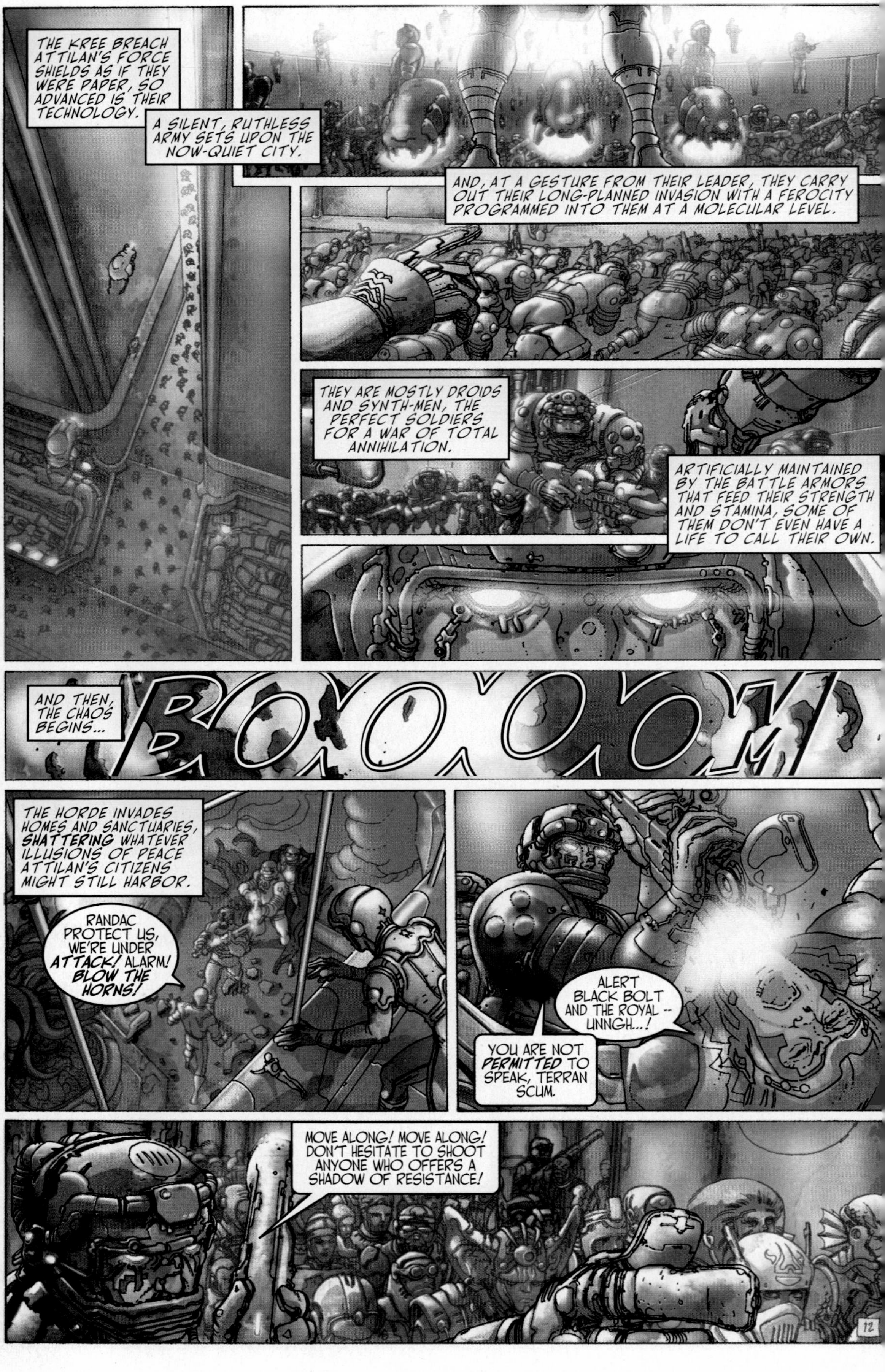
THE KREE BREACH ATTILAN'S FORCE SHIELDS AS IF THEY WERE PAPER, SO ADVANCED IS THEIR TECHNOLOGY.
A SILENT, RUTHLESS ARMY SETS UPON THE NOW-QUIET CITY.
AND, AT A GESTURE FROM THEIR LEADER, THEY CARRY OUT THEIR LONG-PLANNED INVASION WITH A FEROCITY PROGRAMMED INTO THEM AT A MOLECULAR LEVEL.
THEY ARE MOSTLY DROIDS AND SYNTH-MEN, THE PERFECT SOLDIERS FOR A WAR OF TOTAL ANNIHILATION.
ARTIFICIALLY MAINTAINED BY THE BATTLE ARMORS THAT FEED THEIR STRENGTH AND STAMINA, SOME OF THEM DON'T EVEN HAVE A LIFE TO CALL THEIR OWN.
AND THEN, THE CHAOS BEGINS...
BOOOOM
THE HORDE INVADES HOMES AND SANCTUARIES, SHATTERING WHATEVER ILLUSIONS OF PEACE ATTILAN'S CITIZENS MIGHT STILL HARBOR.
RANDAC PROTECT US, WE'RE UNDER ATTACK! ALARM! BLOW THE HORNS!
ALERT BLACK BOLT AND THE ROYAL -- UNNGH...!
YOU ARE NOT PERMITTED TO SPEAK, TERRAN SCUM.
MOVE ALONG! MOVE ALONG! DON'T HESITATE TO SHOOT ANYONE WHO OFFERS A SHADOW OF RESISTANCE!
12

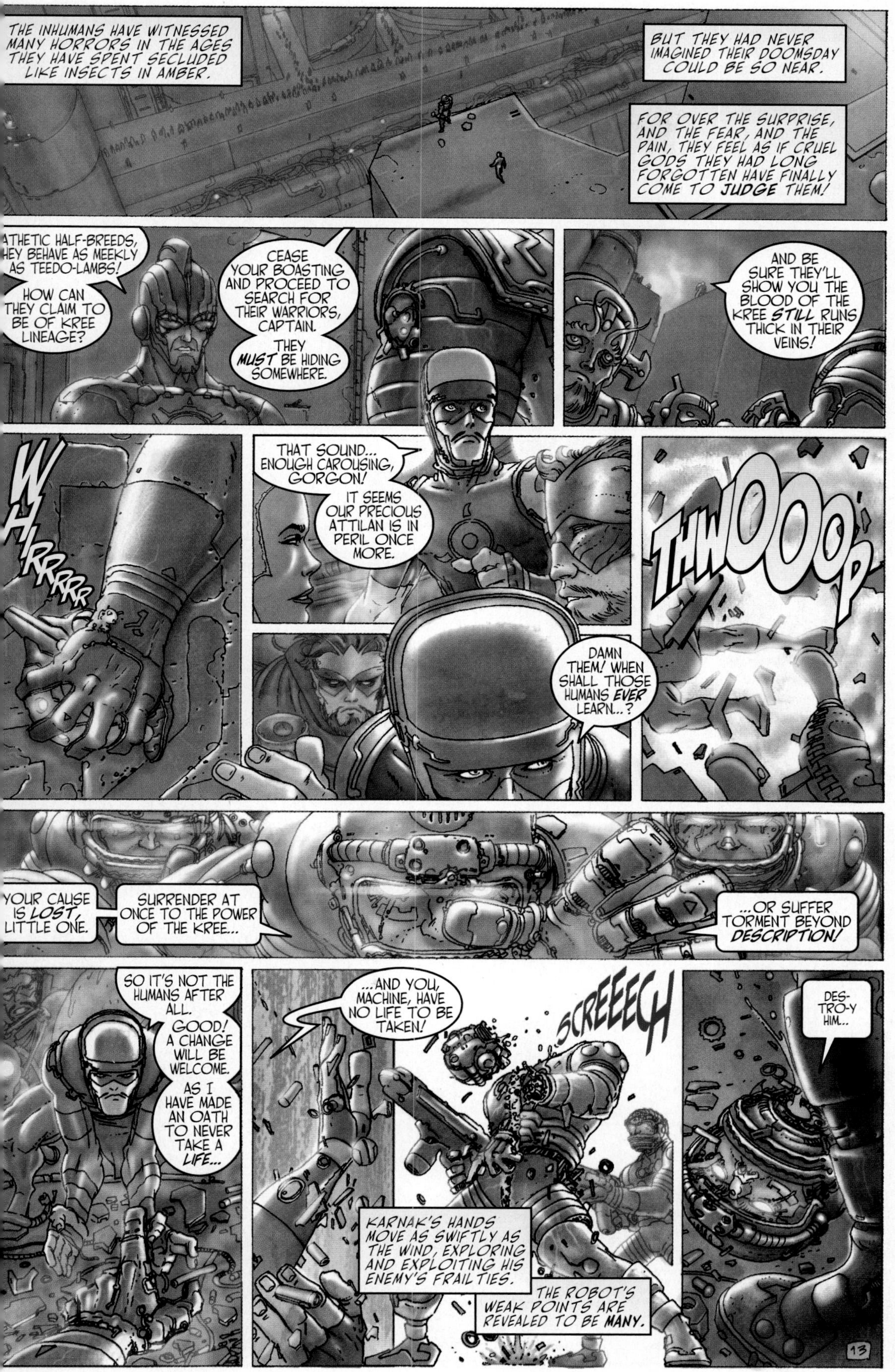
THE INHUMANS HAVE WITNESSED MANY HORRORS IN THE AGES THEY HAVE SPENT SECLUDED LIKE INSECTS IN AMBER.
BUT THEY HAD NEVER IMAGINED THEIR DOOMSDAY COULD BE SO NEAR.
FOR OVER THE SURPRISE, AND THE FEAR, AND THE PAIN, THEY FEEL AS IF CRUEL GODS THEY HAD LONG FORGOTTEN HAVE FINALLY COME TO JUDGE THEM!
ATHETIC HALF-BREEDS, HEY BEHAVE AS MEEKLY AS TEEDO-LAMBS!
HOW CAN THEY CLAIM TO BE OF KREE LINEAGE?
CEASE YOUR BOASTING AND PROCEED TO SEARCH FOR THEIR WARRIORS, CAPTAIN.
THEY MUST BE HIDING SOMEWHERE.
AND BE SURE THEY'LL SHOW YOU THE BLOOD OF THE KREE STILL RUNS THICK IN THEIR VEINS!
WHIRRRRR
THAT SOUND... ENOUGH CAROUSING, GORGON!
IT SEEMS OUR PRECIOUS ATTILAN IS IN PERIL ONCE MORE.
DAMN THEM! WHEN SHALL THOSE HUMANS EVER LEARN...?
THWOOOOP
YOUR CAUSE IS LOST, LITTLE ONE.
SURRENDER AT ONCE TO THE POWER OF THE KREE...
...OR SUFFER TORMENT BEYOND DESCRIPTION!
SO IT'S NOT THE HUMANS AFTER ALL.
GOOD! A CHANGE WILL BE WELCOME.
AS I HAVE MADE AN OATH TO NEVER TAKE A LIFE...
...AND YOU, MACHINE, HAVE NO LIFE TO BE TAKEN!
SCREEECH
DES-TRO-Y HIM...
KARNAK'S HANDS MOVE AS SWIFTLY AS THE WIND, EXPLORING AND EXPLOITING HIS ENEMY'S FRAILTIES.
THE ROBOT'S WEAK POINTS ARE REVEALED TO BE MANY.

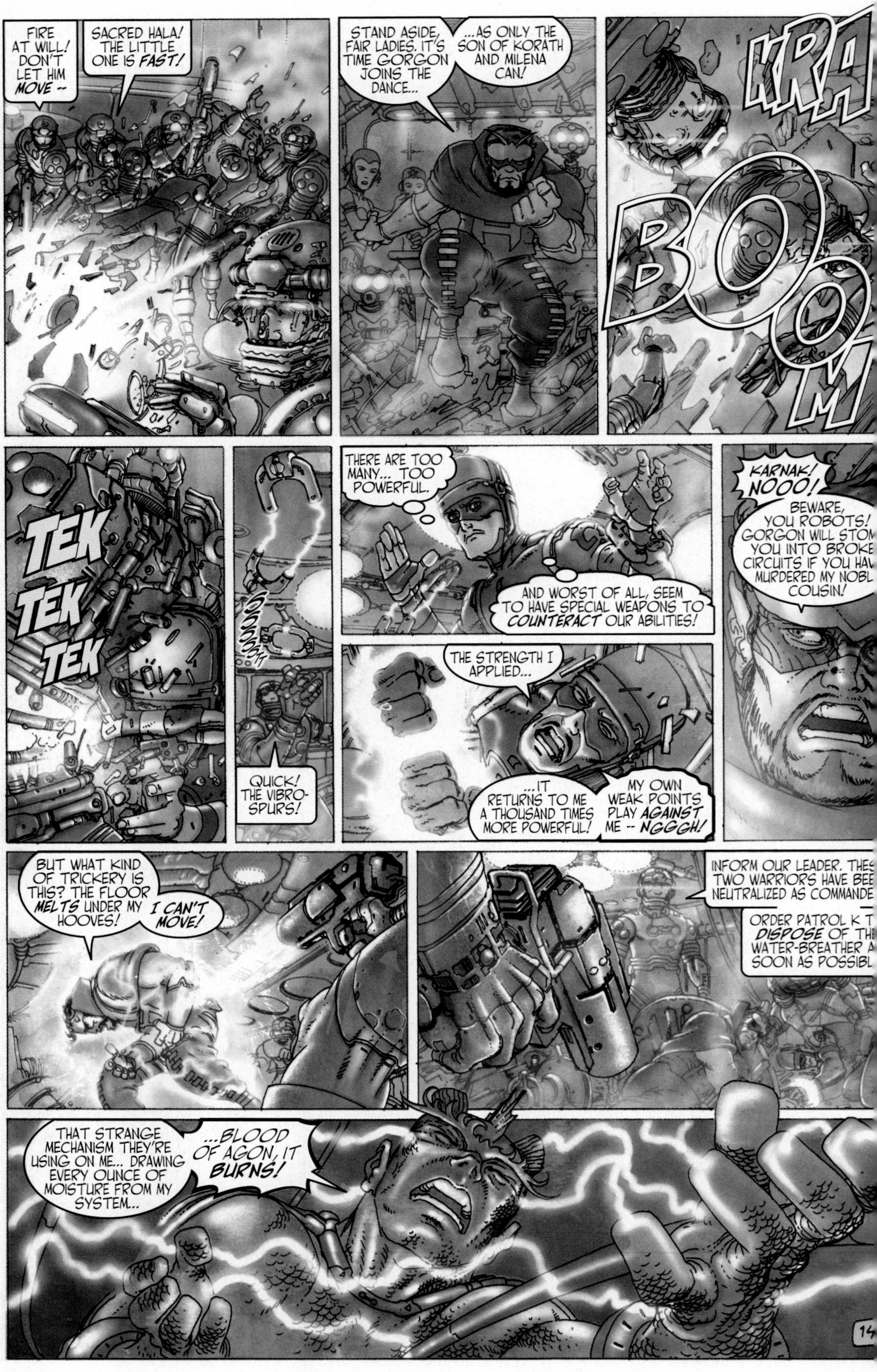

FIRE AT WILL! DON'T LET HIM *MOVE* --
SACRED HALA! THE LITTLE ONE IS *FAST!*
STAND ASIDE, FAIR LADIES. IT'S TIME GORGON JOINS THE DANCE...
...AS ONLY THE SON OF KORATH AND MILENA CAN!
KRA
BOOOM
TEK
TEK
TEK
SKREEEEK
QUICK! THE VIBRO-SPURS!
THERE ARE TOO MANY... TOO POWERFUL.
AND WORST OF ALL, SEEM TO HAVE SPECIAL WEAPONS TO *COUNTERACT* OUR ABILITIES!
THE STRENGTH I APPLIED...
...IT RETURNS TO ME A THOUSAND TIMES MORE POWERFUL!
MY OWN WEAK POINTS PLAY *AGAINST* ME -- *NGGGH!*
KARNAK! NOOO!
BEWARE, YOU ROBOTS! GORGON WILL STOM YOU INTO BROKE CIRCUITS IF YOU HAV MURDERED MY NOBL COUSIN!
BUT WHAT KIND OF TRICKERY IS THIS? THE FLOOR *MELTS* UNDER MY HOOVES!
I CAN'T MOVE!
INFORM OUR LEADER. THES TWO WARRIORS HAVE BEE NEUTRALIZED AS COMMANDE
ORDER PATROL K T *DISPOSE* OF TH WATER-BREATHER A SOON AS POSSIBL
THAT STRANGE MECHANISM THEY'RE USING ON ME... DRAWING EVERY OUNCE OF MOISTURE FROM MY SYSTEM...
...*BLOOD OF AGON, IT BURNS!*
14

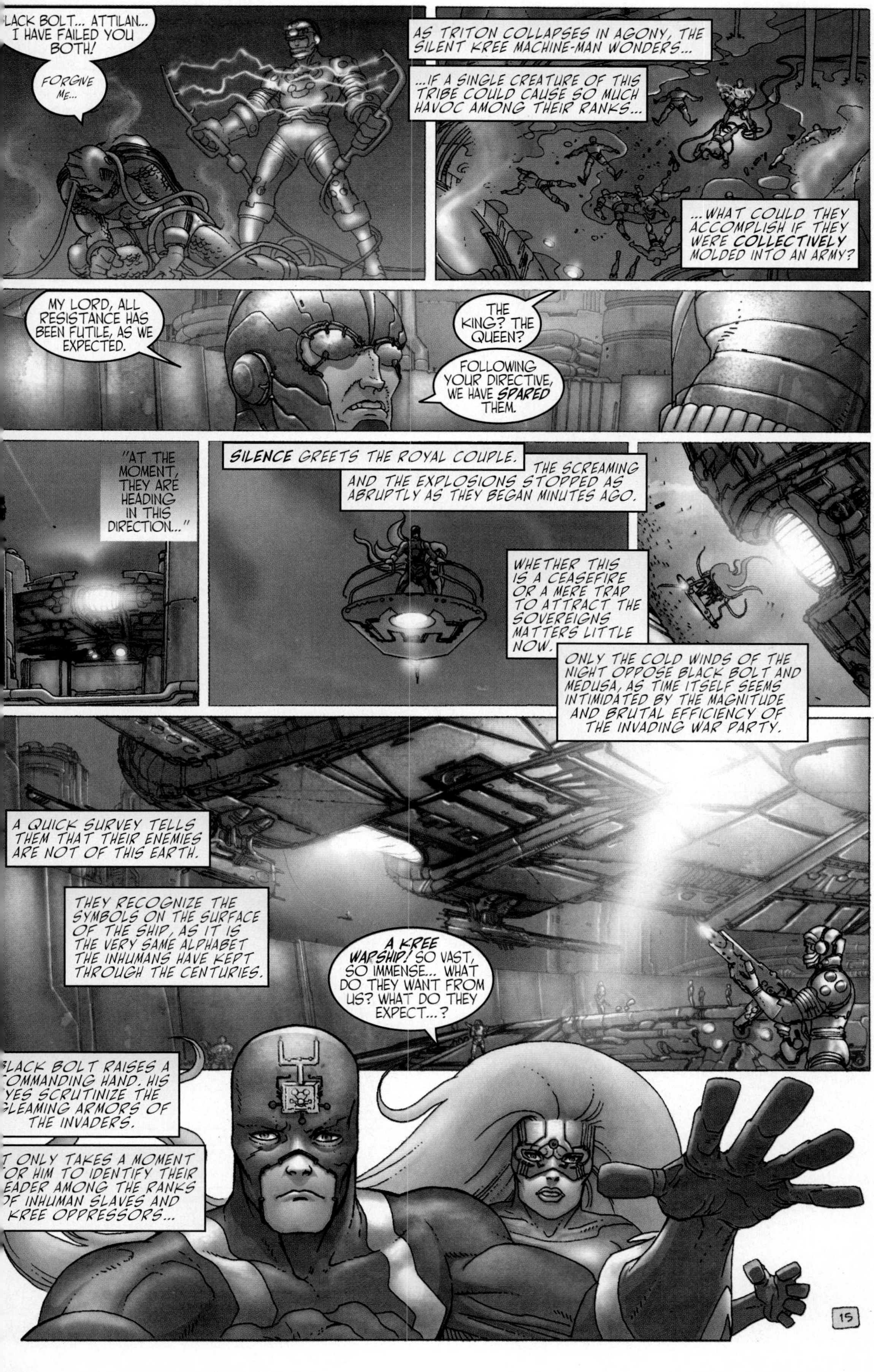

LACK BOLT... ATTILAN... I HAVE FAILED YOU BOTH!
FORGIVE ME...
AS TRITON COLLAPSES IN AGONY, THE SILENT KREE MACHINE-MAN WONDERS...
...IF A SINGLE CREATURE OF THIS TRIBE COULD CAUSE SO MUCH HAVOC AMONG THEIR RANKS...
...WHAT COULD THEY ACCOMPLISH IF THEY WERE COLLECTIVELY MOLDED INTO AN ARMY?
MY LORD, ALL RESISTANCE HAS BEEN FUTILE, AS WE EXPECTED.
THE KING? THE QUEEN?
FOLLOWING YOUR DIRECTIVE, WE HAVE SPARED THEM.
"AT THE MOMENT, THEY ARE HEADING IN THIS DIRECTION..."
SILENCE GREETS THE ROYAL COUPLE.
THE SCREAMING AND THE EXPLOSIONS STOPPED AS ABRUPTLY AS THEY BEGAN MINUTES AGO.
WHETHER THIS IS A CEASEFIRE OR A MERE TRAP TO ATTRACT THE SOVEREIGNS MATTERS LITTLE NOW.
ONLY THE COLD WINDS OF THE NIGHT OPPOSE BLACK BOLT AND MEDUSA, AS TIME ITSELF SEEMS INTIMIDATED BY THE MAGNITUDE AND BRUTAL EFFICIENCY OF THE INVADING WAR PARTY.
A QUICK SURVEY TELLS THEM THAT THEIR ENEMIES ARE NOT OF THIS EARTH.
THEY RECOGNIZE THE SYMBOLS ON THE SURFACE OF THE SHIP, AS IT IS THE VERY SAME ALPHABET THE INHUMANS HAVE KEPT THROUGH THE CENTURIES.
A KREE WARSHIP! SO VAST, SO IMMENSE... WHAT DO THEY WANT FROM US? WHAT DO THEY EXPECT...?
LACK BOLT RAISES A COMMANDING HAND. HIS EYES SCRUTINIZE THE GLEAMING ARMORS OF THE INVADERS.
T ONLY TAKES A MOMENT FOR HIM TO IDENTIFY THEIR LEADER AMONG THE RANKS OF INHUMAN SLAVES AND KREE OPPRESSORS...

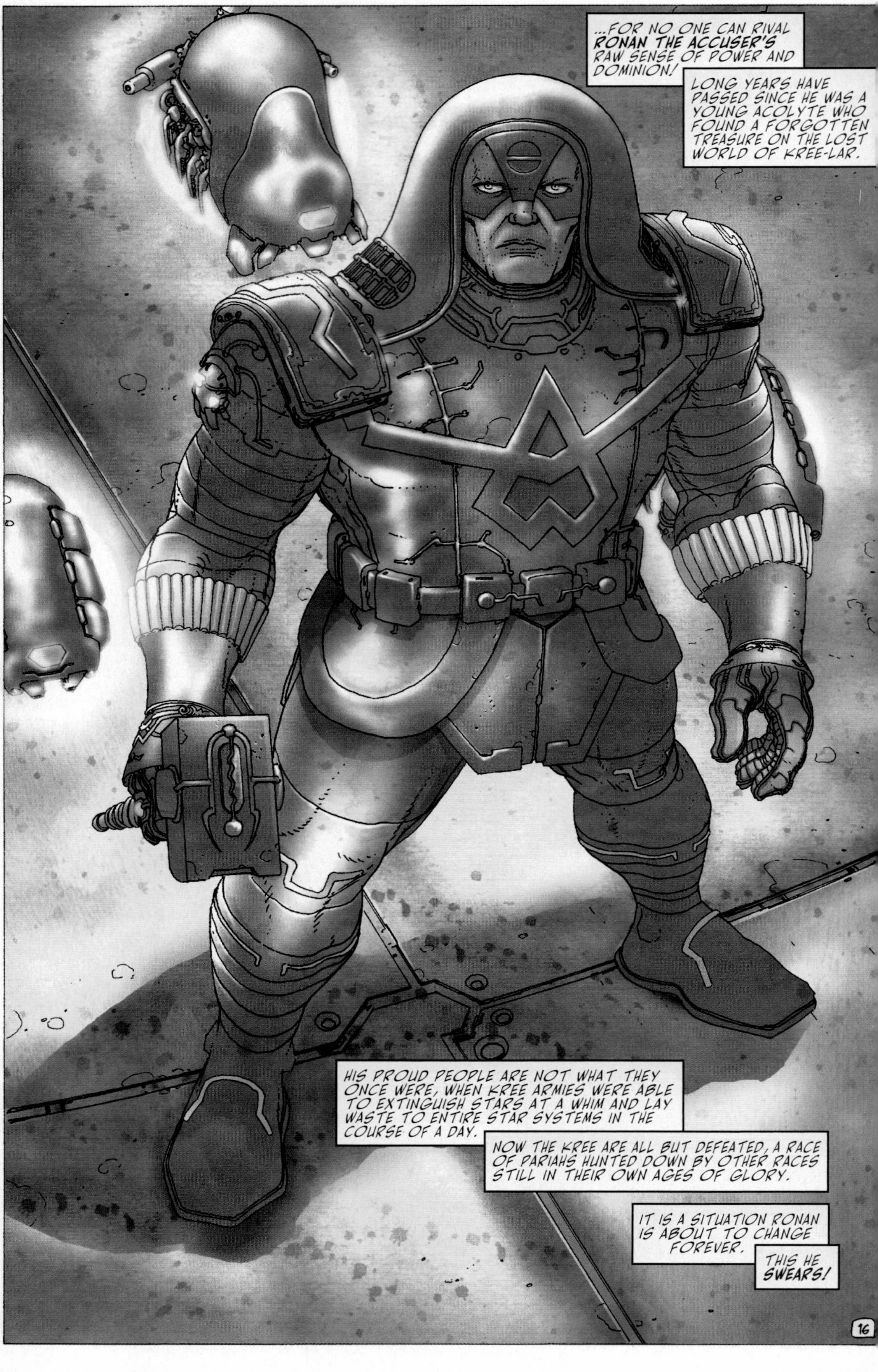
...FOR NO ONE CAN RIVAL RONAN THE ACCUSER'S RAW SENSE OF POWER AND DOMINION!
LONG YEARS HAVE PASSED SINCE HE WAS A YOUNG ACOLYTE WHO FOUND A FORGOTTEN TREASURE ON THE LOST WORLD OF KREE-LAR.
HIS PROUD PEOPLE ARE NOT WHAT THEY ONCE WERE, WHEN KREE ARMIES WERE ABLE TO EXTINGUISH STARS AT A WHIM AND LAY WASTE TO ENTIRE STAR SYSTEMS IN THE COURSE OF A DAY.
NOW THE KREE ARE ALL BUT DEFEATED, A RACE OF PARIAHS HUNTED DOWN BY OTHER RACES STILL IN THEIR OWN AGES OF GLORY.
IT IS A SITUATION RONAN IS ABOUT TO CHANGE FOREVER.
THIS HE SWEARS!
16

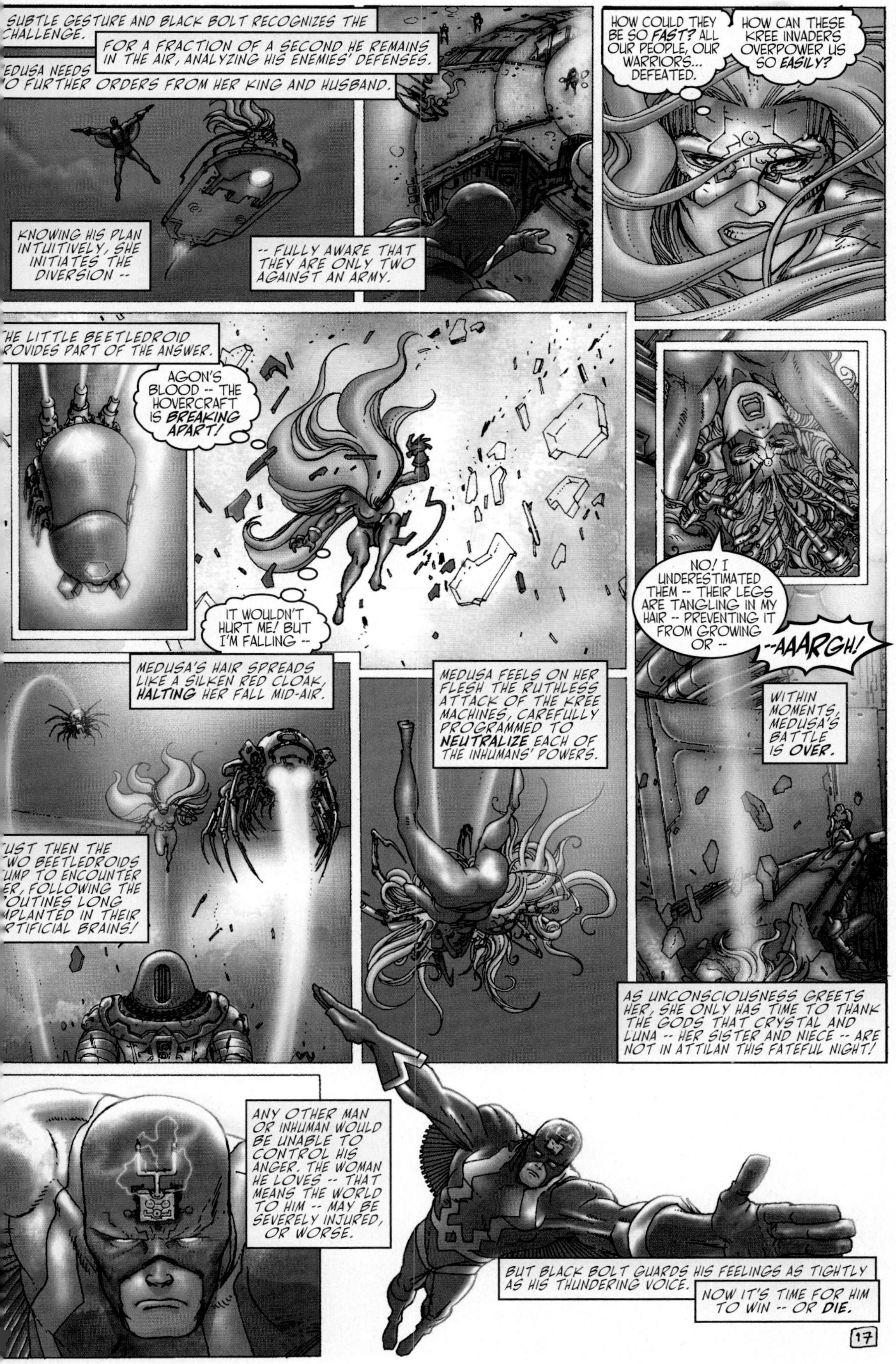
SUBTLE GESTURE AND BLACK BOLT RECOGNIZES THE CHALLENGE.
FOR A FRACTION OF A SECOND HE REMAINS IN THE AIR, ANALYZING HIS ENEMIES' DEFENSES.
EDUSA NEEDS O FURTHER ORDERS FROM HER KING AND HUSBAND.
KNOWING HIS PLAN INTUITIVELY, SHE INITIATES THE DIVERSION --
-- FULLY AWARE THAT THEY ARE ONLY TWO AGAINST AN ARMY.
HOW COULD THEY BE SO FAST? ALL OUR PEOPLE, OUR WARRIORS... DEFEATED.
HOW CAN THESE KREE INVADERS OVERPOWER US SO EASILY?
HE LITTLE BEETLEDROID ROVIDES PART OF THE ANSWER.
AGON'S BLOOD -- THE HOVERCRAFT IS BREAKING APART!
IT WOULDN'T HURT ME! BUT I'M FALLING --
NO! I UNDERESTIMATED THEM -- THEIR LEGS ARE TANGLING IN MY HAIR -- PREVENTING IT FROM GROWING OR --
--AAARGH!
MEDUSA'S HAIR SPREADS LIKE A SILKEN RED CLOAK, HALTING HER FALL MID-AIR.
UST THEN THE WO BEETLEDROIDS UMP TO ENCOUNTER ER, FOLLOWING THE OUTINES LONG MPLANTED IN THEIR RTIFICIAL BRAINS!
MEDUSA FEELS ON HER FLESH THE RUTHLESS ATTACK OF THE KREE MACHINES, CAREFULLY PROGRAMMED TO NEUTRALIZE EACH OF THE INHUMANS' POWERS.
WITHIN MOMENTS, MEDUSA'S BATTLE IS OVER.
AS UNCONSCIOUSNESS GREETS HER, SHE ONLY HAS TIME TO THANK THE GODS THAT CRYSTAL AND LUNA -- HER SISTER AND NIECE -- ARE NOT IN ATTILAN THIS FATEFUL NIGHT!
ANY OTHER MAN OR INHUMAN WOULD BE UNABLE TO CONTROL HIS ANGER. THE WOMAN HE LOVES -- THAT MEANS THE WORLD TO HIM -- MAY BE SEVERELY INJURED, OR WORSE.
BUT BLACK BOLT GUARDS HIS FEELINGS AS TIGHTLY AS HIS THUNDERING VOICE.
NOW IT'S TIME FOR HIM TO WIN -- OR DIE.

THE AIR VIBRATES WITH THE SPEED OF BLACK BOLT'S APPROACH --

-- BUT RONAN DOESN'T EVEN BLINK.

HE KNOWS ALL RESISTANCE TO HIS POWER IS, IN THE END, IMPOSSIBLE.

FOR HIS ANCESTORS SCULPTED HIS RACE FROM THE WEAK CLAY OF HUMANITY --

-- AND THE KNOWLEDGE OF THEIR VAST INFERIORITY IS DEEPLY HARDWIRED INTO THEIR BRAINS.

CAN A FIGHTING DOG ATTACK ITS TRAINER? CAN A MERE CUB HOWL AGAINST THE NATURAL LEADER OF THE PACK?

BLACK BOLT'S POWER IS TURNED AGAINST HIMSELF INSIDE THE STASIS FIELD.

HIS SUFFERING DEFIES COMPARISON...

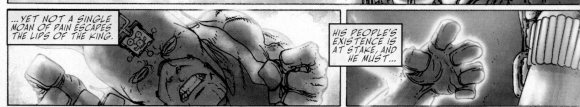

...YET NOT A SINGLE MOAN OF PAIN ESCAPES THE LIPS OF THE KING.

HIS PEOPLE'S EXISTENCE IS AT STAKE, AND HE MUST...

HE MUST...

EXCELLENT. EXCELLENT. SO SOME OF THE FIRE OF MY RACE RAGES STILL IN YOUR BLOOD.

HAD YOU *CHOSEN* IT, EARTH WOULD BE YOUR KINGDOM, NOT A HOSTILE WORLD FROM WHICH TO HIDE.

DON'T FRET, MY HOUND. THINGS ARE GOING TO CHANGE.

FOREVER.

18

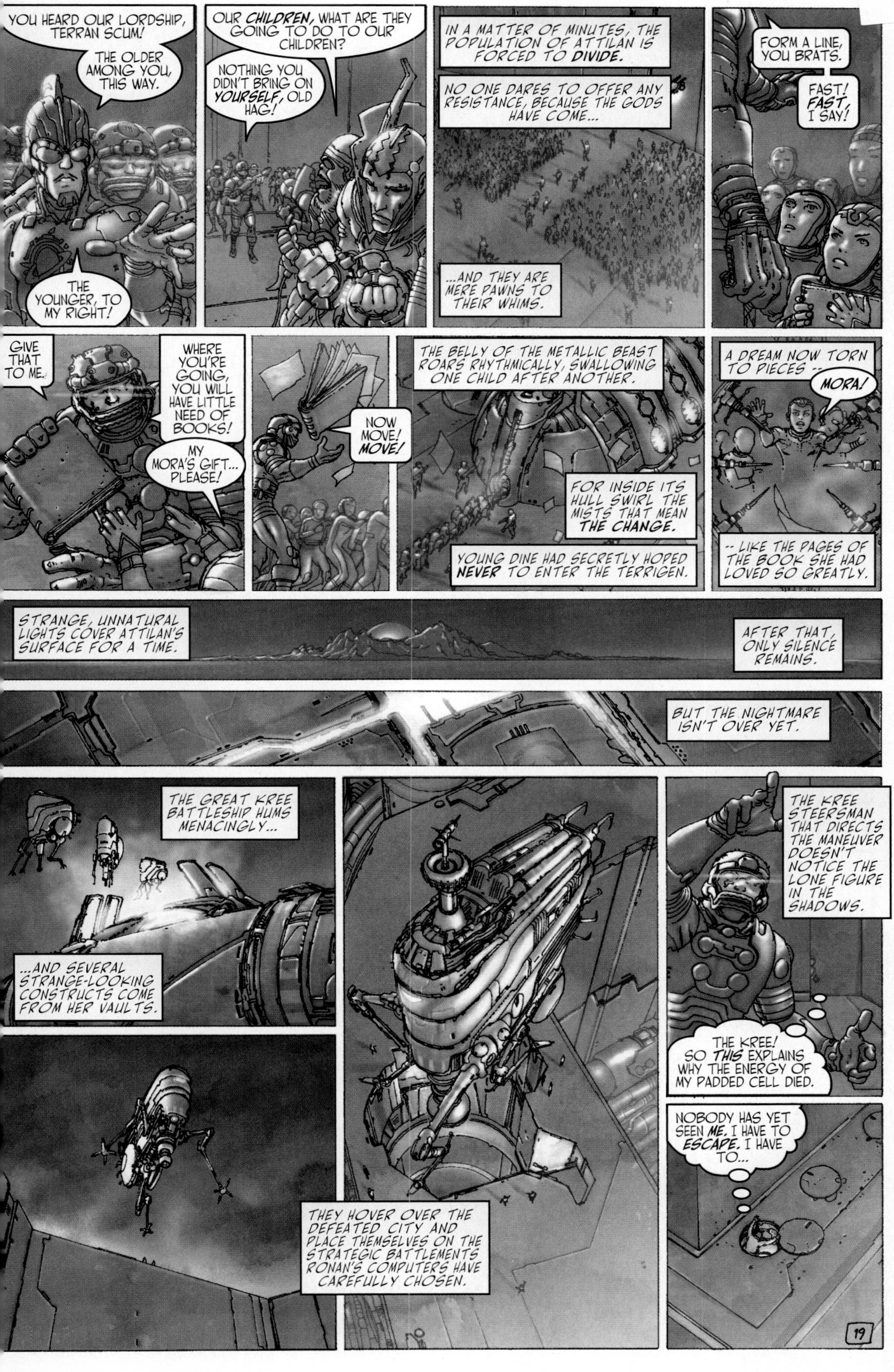
YOU HEARD OUR LORDSHIP, TERRAN SCUM!
THE OLDER AMONG YOU, THIS WAY.
THE YOUNGER, TO MY RIGHT!
OUR CHILDREN, WHAT ARE THEY GOING TO DO TO OUR CHILDREN?
NOTHING YOU DIDN'T BRING ON YOURSELF, OLD HAG!
IN A MATTER OF MINUTES, THE POPULATION OF ATTILAN IS FORCED TO DIVIDE.
NO ONE DARES TO OFFER ANY RESISTANCE, BECAUSE THE GODS HAVE COME...
...AND THEY ARE MERE PAWNS TO THEIR WHIMS.
FORM A LINE, YOU BRATS.
FAST! FAST, I SAY!
GIVE THAT TO ME.
WHERE YOU'RE GOING, YOU WILL HAVE LITTLE NEED OF BOOKS!
MY MORA'S GIFT... PLEASE!
NOW MOVE! MOVE!
THE BELLY OF THE METALLIC BEAST ROARS RHYTHMICALLY, SWALLOWING ONE CHILD AFTER ANOTHER.
FOR INSIDE ITS HULL SWIRL THE MISTS THAT MEAN THE CHANGE.
YOUNG DINE HAD SECRETLY HOPED NEVER TO ENTER THE TERRIGEN.
A DREAM NOW TORN TO PIECES --
MORA!
-- LIKE THE PAGES OF THE BOOK SHE HAD LOVED SO GREATLY.
STRANGE, UNNATURAL LIGHTS COVER ATTILAN'S SURFACE FOR A TIME.
AFTER THAT, ONLY SILENCE REMAINS.
BUT THE NIGHTMARE ISN'T OVER YET.
THE GREAT KREE BATTLESHIP HUMS MENACINGLY...
...AND SEVERAL STRANGE-LOOKING CONSTRUCTS COME FROM HER VAULTS.
THEY HOVER OVER THE DEFEATED CITY AND PLACE THEMSELVES ON THE STRATEGIC BATTLEMENTS RONAN'S COMPUTERS HAVE CAREFULLY CHOSEN.
THE KREE STEERSMAN THAT DIRECTS THE MANEUVER DOESN'T NOTICE THE LONE FIGURE IN THE SHADOWS.
THE KREE! SO THIS EXPLAINS WHY THE ENERGY OF MY PADDED CELL DIED.
NOBODY HAS YET SEEN ME. I HAVE TO ESCAPE. I HAVE TO...
19

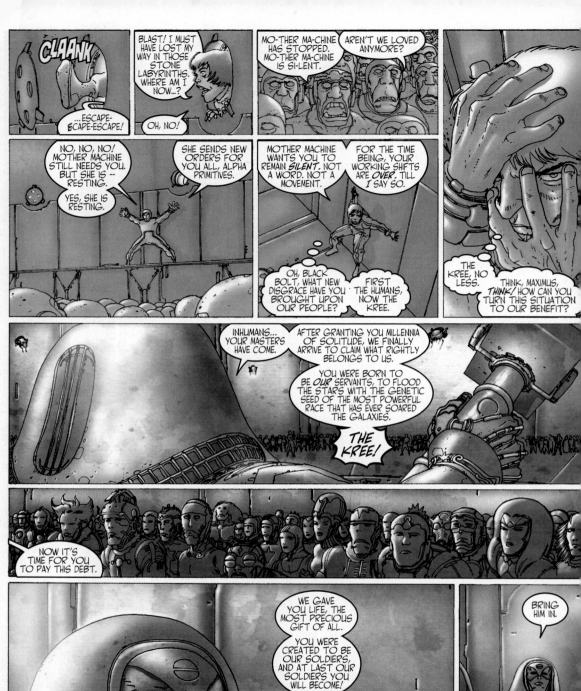

CLAANK

...ESCAPE-ESCAPE-ESCAPE!

BLAST! I MUST HAVE LOST MY WAY IN THOSE STONE LABYRINTHS. WHERE AM I NOW...?

OH, NO!

MO-THER MA-CHINE HAS STOPPED. MO-THER MA-CHINE IS SI-LENT.

AREN'T WE LOVED ANYMORE?

NO, NO, NO! MOTHER MACHINE STILL NEEDS YOU. BUT SHE IS -- RESTING.

YES, SHE IS RESTING.

SHE SENDS NEW ORDERS FOR YOU ALL, ALPHA PRIMITIVES.

MOTHER MACHINE WANTS YOU TO REMAIN *SILENT*. NOT A WORD. NOT A MOVEMENT.

FOR THE TIME BEING, YOUR WORKING SHIFTS ARE *OVER*. TILL I SAY SO.

OH, BLACK BOLT, WHAT NEW DISGRACE HAVE YOU BROUGHT UPON OUR PEOPLE?

FIRST THE HUMANS, NOW THE KREE.

THE KREE, NO LESS.

THINK, MAXIMUS, *THINK!* HOW CAN YOU TURN THIS SITUATION TO OUR BENEFIT?

INHUMANS... YOUR MASTERS HAVE COME.

AFTER GRANTING YOU MILLENNIA OF SOLITUDE, WE FINALLY ARRIVE TO CLAIM WHAT RIGHTLY BELONGS TO US.

YOU WERE BORN TO BE *OUR* SERVANTS, TO FLOOD THE STARS WITH THE GENETIC SEED OF THE MOST POWERFUL RACE THAT HAS EVER SOARED THE GALAXIES.

THE KREE!

NOW IT'S TIME FOR YOU TO PAY THIS DEBT.

WE GAVE YOU LIFE, THE MOST PRECIOUS GIFT OF ALL.

YOU WERE CREATED TO BE OUR SOLDIERS, AND AT LAST OUR SOLDIERS YOU WILL BECOME!

BRING HIM IN.

20

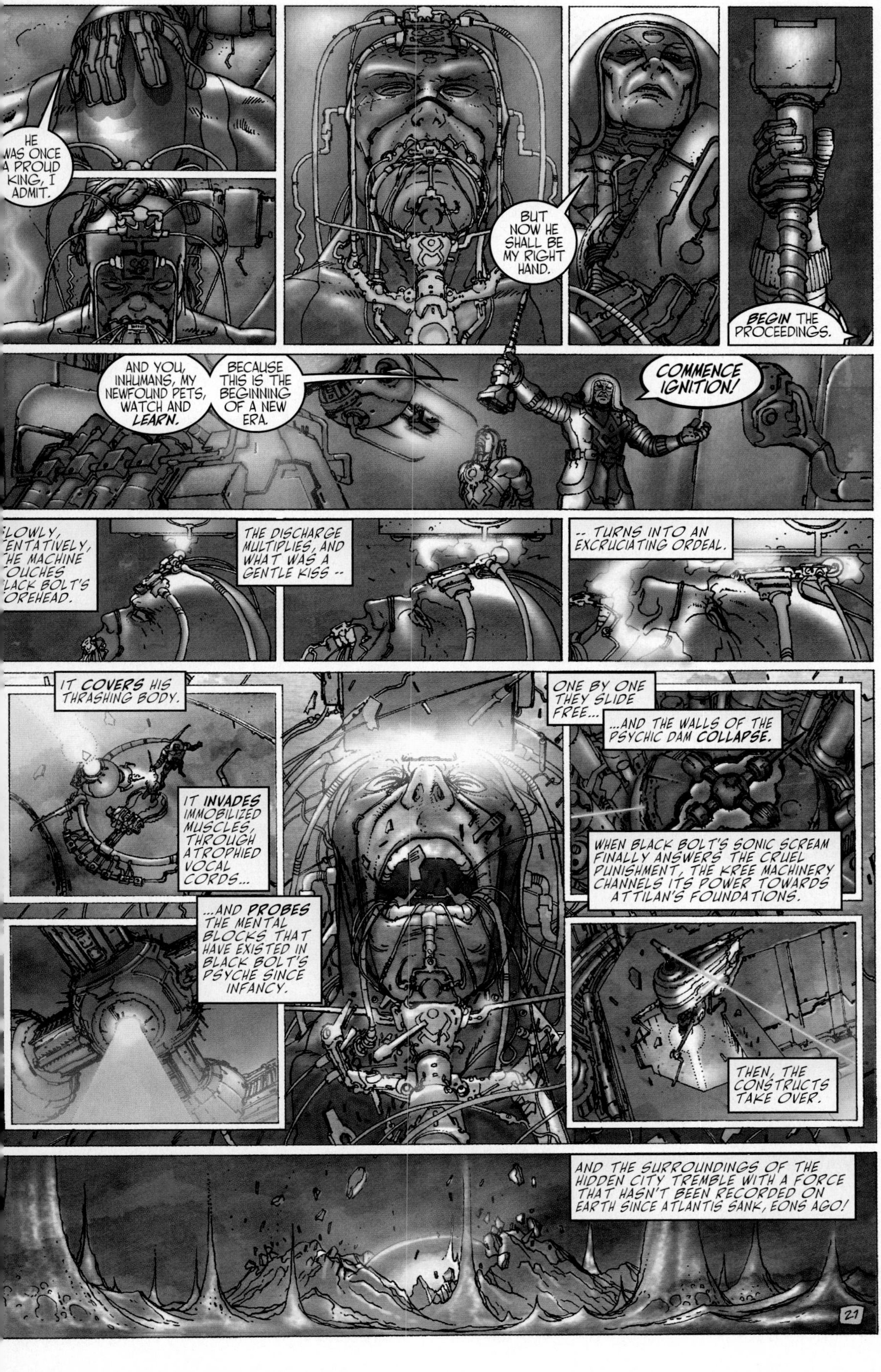
HE WAS ONCE A PROUD KING, I ADMIT.
BUT NOW HE SHALL BE MY RIGHT HAND.
BEGIN THE PROCEEDINGS.
AND YOU, INHUMANS, MY NEWFOUND PETS, WATCH AND LEARN.
BECAUSE THIS IS THE BEGINNING OF A NEW ERA.
COMMENCE IGNITION!
SLOWLY, TENTATIVELY, THE MACHINE TOUCHES BLACK BOLT'S FOREHEAD.
THE DISCHARGE MULTIPLIES, AND WHAT WAS A GENTLE KISS --
-- TURNS INTO AN EXCRUCIATING ORDEAL.
IT COVERS HIS THRASHING BODY.
IT INVADES IMMOBILIZED MUSCLES, THROUGH ATROPHIED VOCAL CORDS...
...AND PROBES THE MENTAL BLOCKS THAT HAVE EXISTED IN BLACK BOLT'S PSYCHE SINCE INFANCY.
ONE BY ONE THEY SLIDE FREE...
...AND THE WALLS OF THE PSYCHIC DAM COLLAPSE.
WHEN BLACK BOLT'S SONIC SCREAM FINALLY ANSWERS THE CRUEL PUNISHMENT, THE KREE MACHINERY CHANNELS ITS POWER TOWARDS ATTILAN'S FOUNDATIONS.
THEN, THE CONSTRUCTS TAKE OVER.
AND THE SURROUNDINGS OF THE HIDDEN CITY TREMBLE WITH A FORCE THAT HASN'T BEEN RECORDED ON EARTH SINCE ATLANTIS SANK, EONS AGO!

OURS, UNIVERSES TO EXPLORE. OURS, CIVILIZATIONS TO CRUSH, EMPIRES TO SACK.

BLACK BOLT'S UNLEASHED POWERS ROCK THE ISLAND WHERE ATTILAN STANDS...

...AND THE REPEATED DISCHARGES OF PURE IONIC ENERGY FREE THE CITY FROM ITS FOUNDATIONS.

BEWARE, ENEMIES OF MY FATHERLAND. NEVER CONSIDER WE HAVE LOST OUR HAND. IF OUR FATHERS DIE, OUR SONS WILL FIGHT BACK.

DEFYING GRAVITY, ADDING THE KREE TECHNOLOGY TO THE PECULIARITIES OF THE HIDDEN CITY, ATTILAN PARTS FROM THE LOCATION IT COULD NEVER CALL HOME.

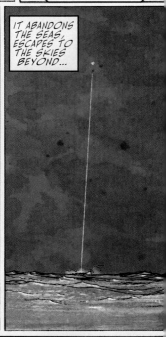

IT ABANDONS THE SEAS, ESCAPES TO THE SKIES BEYOND...

...AND SOON LEAVES THE BLUE PLANET, PERHAPS NEVER TO RETURN.

RONAN THE ACCUSER SMILES. THE FIRST STEPS OF HIS GRAND PLAN HAVE SUCCESSFULLY BEEN TAKEN.

BECAUSE WE ARE THE KREE. THE KREE, HEIRS TO THE STARS!

NEXT STOP, THE SHI'AR EMPIRE, HOME TO THOSE WHO THOUGHT TO BEND THE KREE TO THEIR WILL.

NEXT STOP, VICTORY!

TO BE CONTINUED

T
NHUMAN
ntastic Fou
E
T
NHUMAN
antastic Fou
E
T
NHUMAN
antastic Fou
E

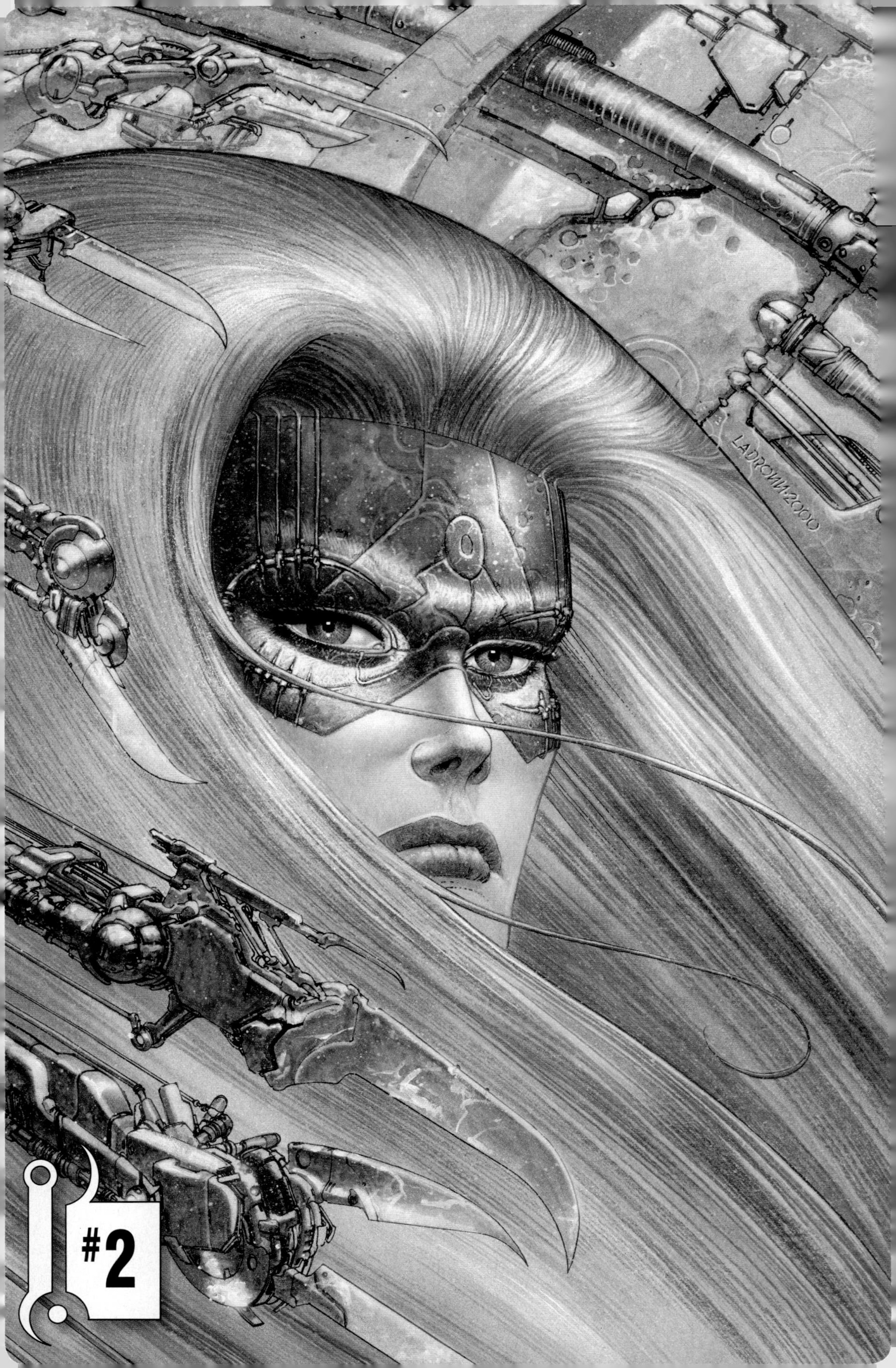
LADRONN 2000
#2

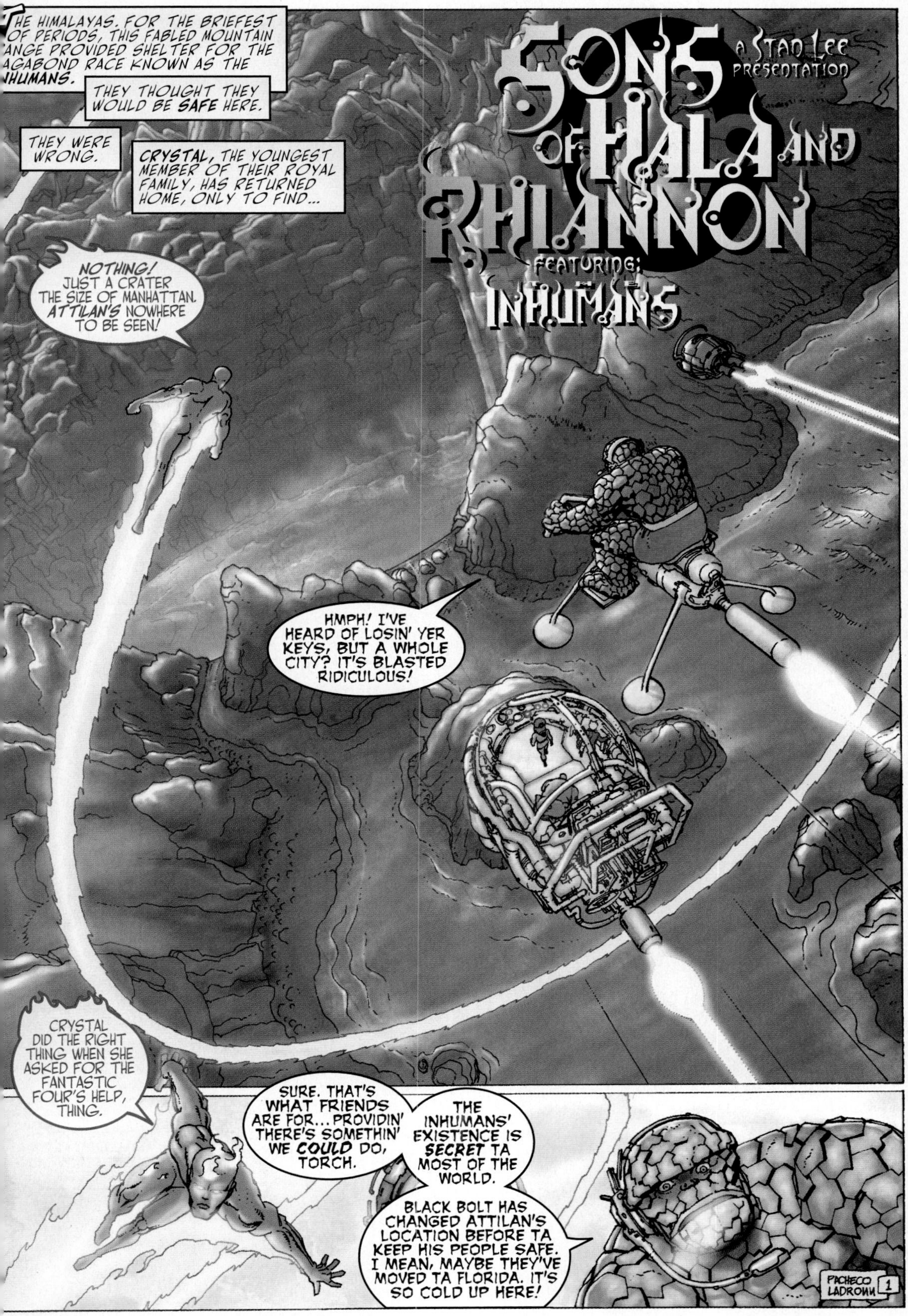
THE HIMALAYAS. FOR THE BRIEFEST OF PERIODS, THIS FABLED MOUNTAIN RANGE PROVIDED SHELTER FOR THE VAGABOND RACE KNOWN AS THE INHUMANS.
THEY THOUGHT THEY WOULD BE SAFE HERE.
THEY WERE WRONG.
CRYSTAL, THE YOUNGEST MEMBER OF THEIR ROYAL FAMILY, HAS RETURNED HOME, ONLY TO FIND...
SONS OF HALA AND RHIANNON
A STAN LEE PRESENTATION
FEATURING: INHUMANS
NOTHING! JUST A CRATER THE SIZE OF MANHATTAN. ATTILAN'S NOWHERE TO BE SEEN!
HMPH! I'VE HEARD OF LOSIN' YER KEYS, BUT A WHOLE CITY? IT'S BLASTED RIDICULOUS!
CRYSTAL DID THE RIGHT THING WHEN SHE ASKED FOR THE FANTASTIC FOUR'S HELP, THING.
SURE. THAT'S WHAT FRIENDS ARE FOR... PROVIDIN' THERE'S SOMETHIN' WE COULD DO, TORCH.
THE INHUMANS' EXISTENCE IS SECRET TA MOST OF THE WORLD.
BLACK BOLT HAS CHANGED ATTILAN'S LOCATION BEFORE TA KEEP HIS PEOPLE SAFE. I MEAN, MAYBE THEY'VE MOVED TA FLORIDA. IT'S SO COLD UP HERE!
PACHECO LADRONN
1

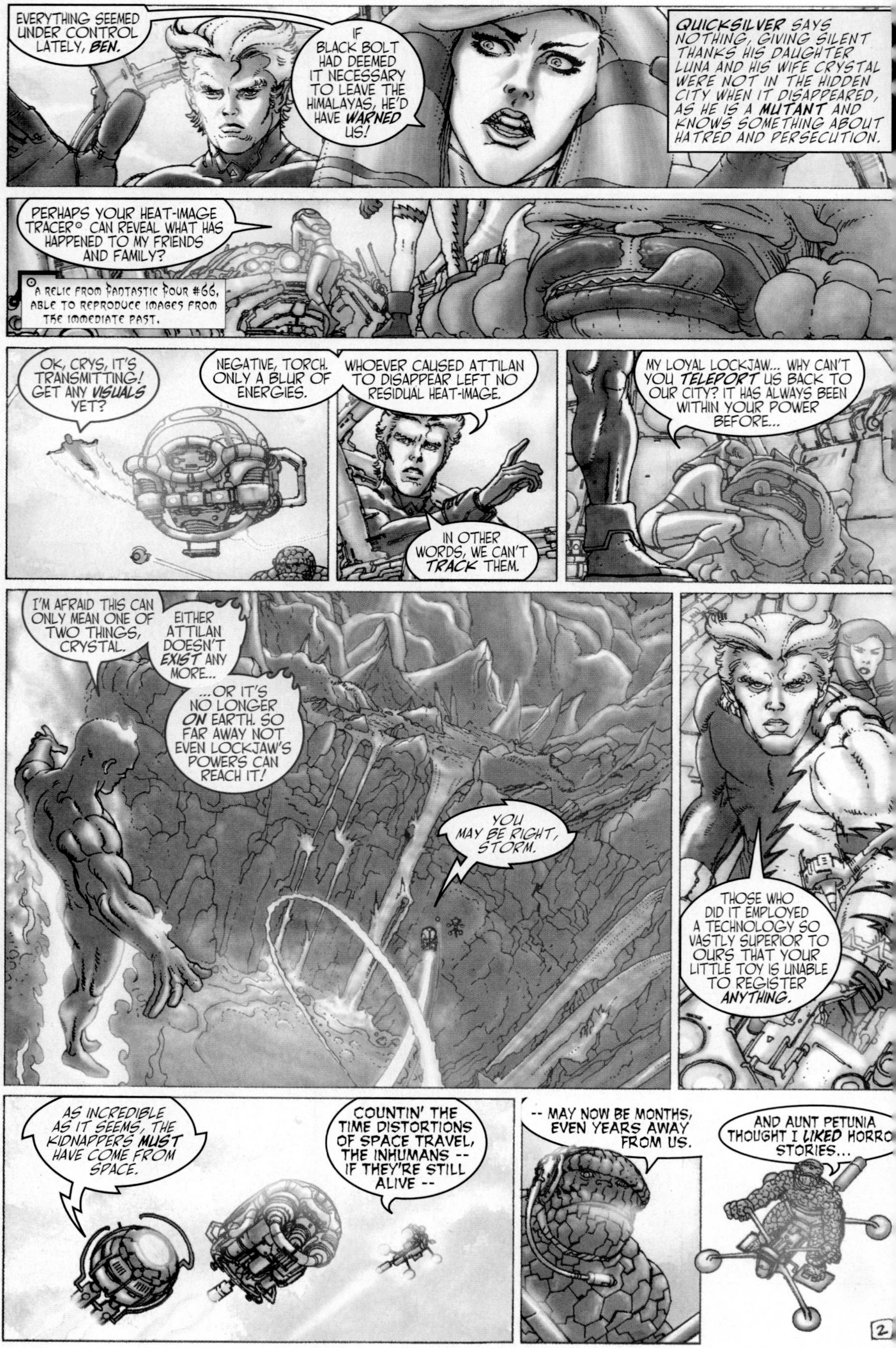
EVERYTHING SEEMED UNDER CONTROL LATELY, BEN.
IF BLACK BOLT HAD DEEMED IT NECESSARY TO LEAVE THE HIMALAYAS, HE'D HAVE WARNED US!
QUICKSILVER SAYS NOTHING, GIVING SILENT THANKS HIS DAUGHTER LUNA AND HIS WIFE CRYSTAL WERE NOT IN THE HIDDEN CITY WHEN IT DISAPPEARED, AS HE IS A MUTANT AND KNOWS SOMETHING ABOUT HATRED AND PERSECUTION.
PERHAPS YOUR HEAT-IMAGE TRACER CAN REVEAL WHAT HAS HAPPENED TO MY FRIENDS AND FAMILY?
A RELIC FROM FANTASTIC FOUR #66, ABLE TO REPRODUCE IMAGES FROM THE IMMEDIATE PAST.
OK, CRYS, IT'S TRANSMITTING! GET ANY VISUALS YET?
NEGATIVE, TORCH. ONLY A BLUR OF ENERGIES.
WHOEVER CAUSED ATTILAN TO DISAPPEAR LEFT NO RESIDUAL HEAT-IMAGE.
IN OTHER WORDS, WE CAN'T TRACK THEM.
MY LOYAL LOCKJAW... WHY CAN'T YOU TELEPORT US BACK TO OUR CITY? IT HAS ALWAYS BEEN WITHIN YOUR POWER BEFORE...
I'M AFRAID THIS CAN ONLY MEAN ONE OF TWO THINGS, CRYSTAL.
EITHER ATTILAN DOESN'T EXIST ANY MORE...
...OR IT'S NO LONGER ON EARTH. SO FAR AWAY NOT EVEN LOCKJAW'S POWERS CAN REACH IT!
YOU MAY BE RIGHT, STORM.
THOSE WHO DID IT EMPLOYED A TECHNOLOGY SO VASTLY SUPERIOR TO OURS THAT YOUR LITTLE TOY IS UNABLE TO REGISTER ANYTHING.
AS INCREDIBLE AS IT SEEMS, THE KIDNAPPERS MUST HAVE COME FROM SPACE.
COUNTIN' THE TIME DISTORTIONS OF SPACE TRAVEL, THE INHUMANS -- IF THEY'RE STILL ALIVE --
-- MAY NOW BE MONTHS, EVEN YEARS AWAY FROM US.
AND AUNT PETUNIA THOUGHT I LIKED HORRO STORIES...

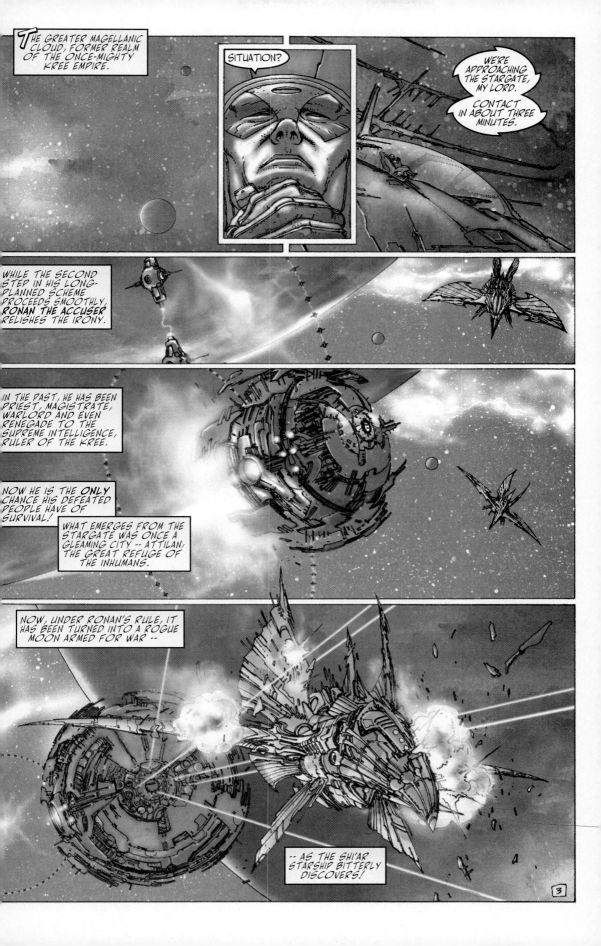

THE GREATER MAGELLANIC CLOUD, FORMER REALM OF THE ONCE-MIGHTY KREE EMPIRE.

SITUATION?

WE'RE APPROACHING THE STARGATE, MY LORD.

CONTACT IN ABOUT THREE MINUTES.

WHILE THE SECOND STEP IN HIS LONG-PLANNED SCHEME PROCEEDS SMOOTHLY, **RONAN THE ACCUSER** RELISHES THE IRONY.

IN THE PAST, HE HAS BEEN PRIEST, MAGISTRATE, WARLORD AND EVEN RENEGADE TO THE SUPREME INTELLIGENCE, RULER OF THE KREE.

NOW HE IS THE **ONLY** CHANCE HIS DEFEATED PEOPLE HAVE OF SURVIVAL!

WHAT EMERGES FROM THE STARGATE WAS ONCE A GLEAMING CITY -- ATTILAN, THE GREAT REFUGE OF THE INHUMANS.

NOW, UNDER RONAN'S RULE, IT HAS BEEN TURNED INTO A ROGUE MOON ARMED FOR WAR --

-- AS THE SHI'AR STARSHIP BITTERLY DISCOVERS!

3

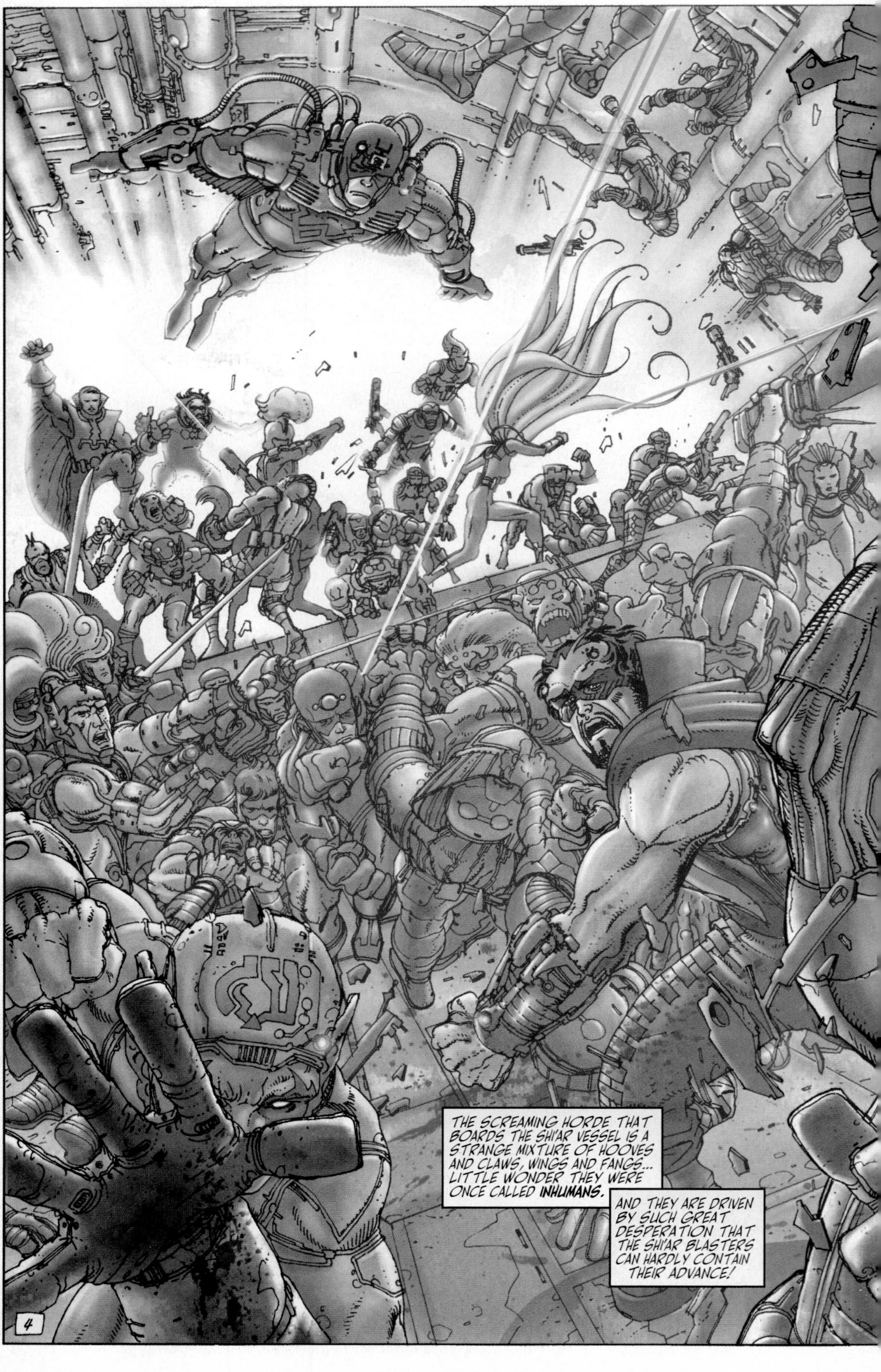
THE SCREAMING HORDE THAT BOARDS THE SHI'AR VESSEL IS A STRANGE MIXTURE OF HOOVES AND CLAWS, WINGS AND FANGS... LITTLE WONDER THEY WERE ONCE CALLED **INHUMANS.**
AND THEY ARE DRIVEN BY SUCH GREAT DESPERATION THAT THE SHI'AR BLASTERS CAN HARDLY CONTAIN THEIR ADVANCE!
4

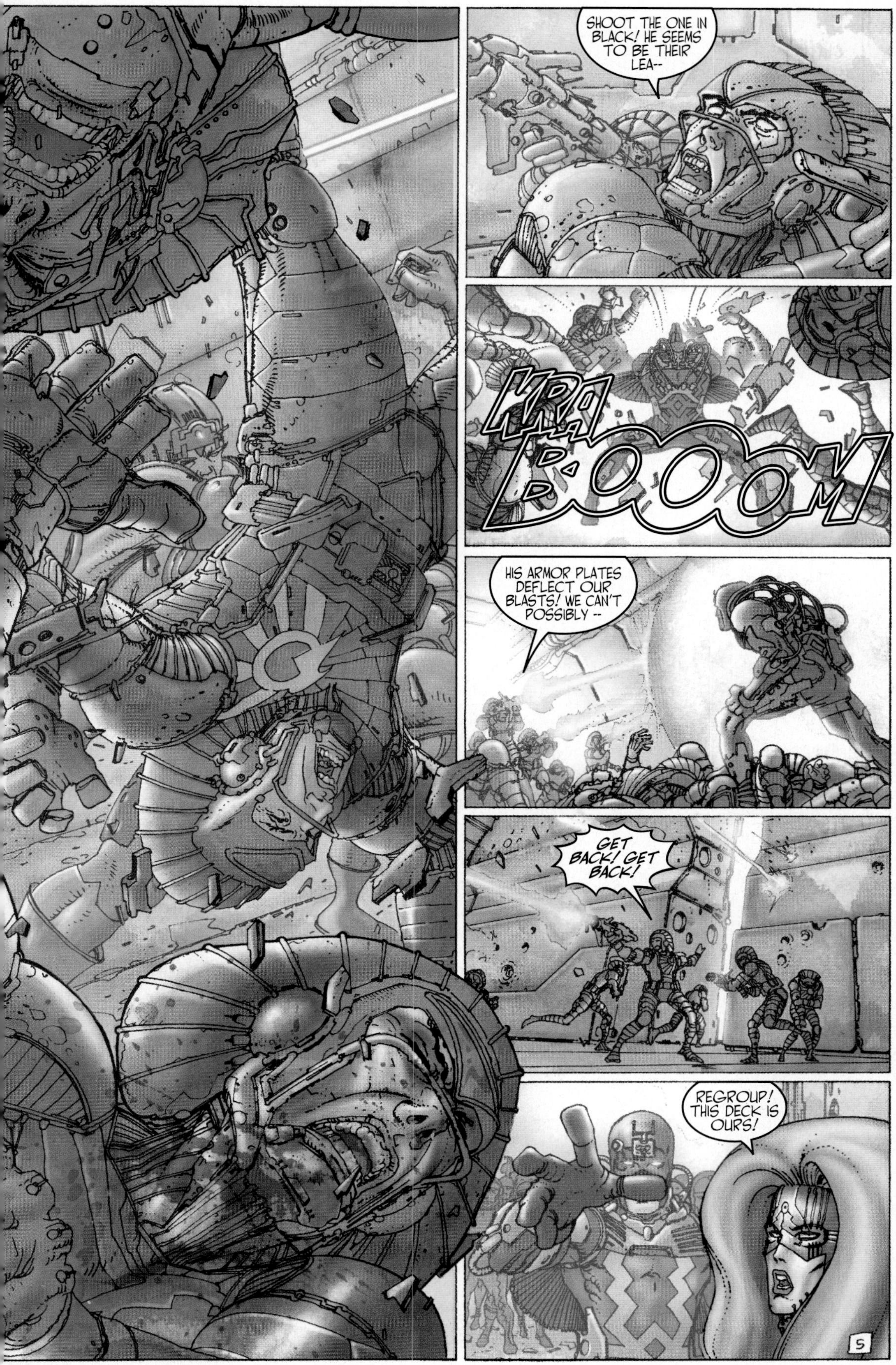

SHOOT THE ONE IN BLACK! HE SEEMS TO BE THEIR LEA--
KRA-BOOOM
HIS ARMOR PLATES DEFLECT OUR BLASTS! WE CAN'T POSSIBLY --
GET BACK! GET BACK!
REGROUP! THIS DECK IS OURS!

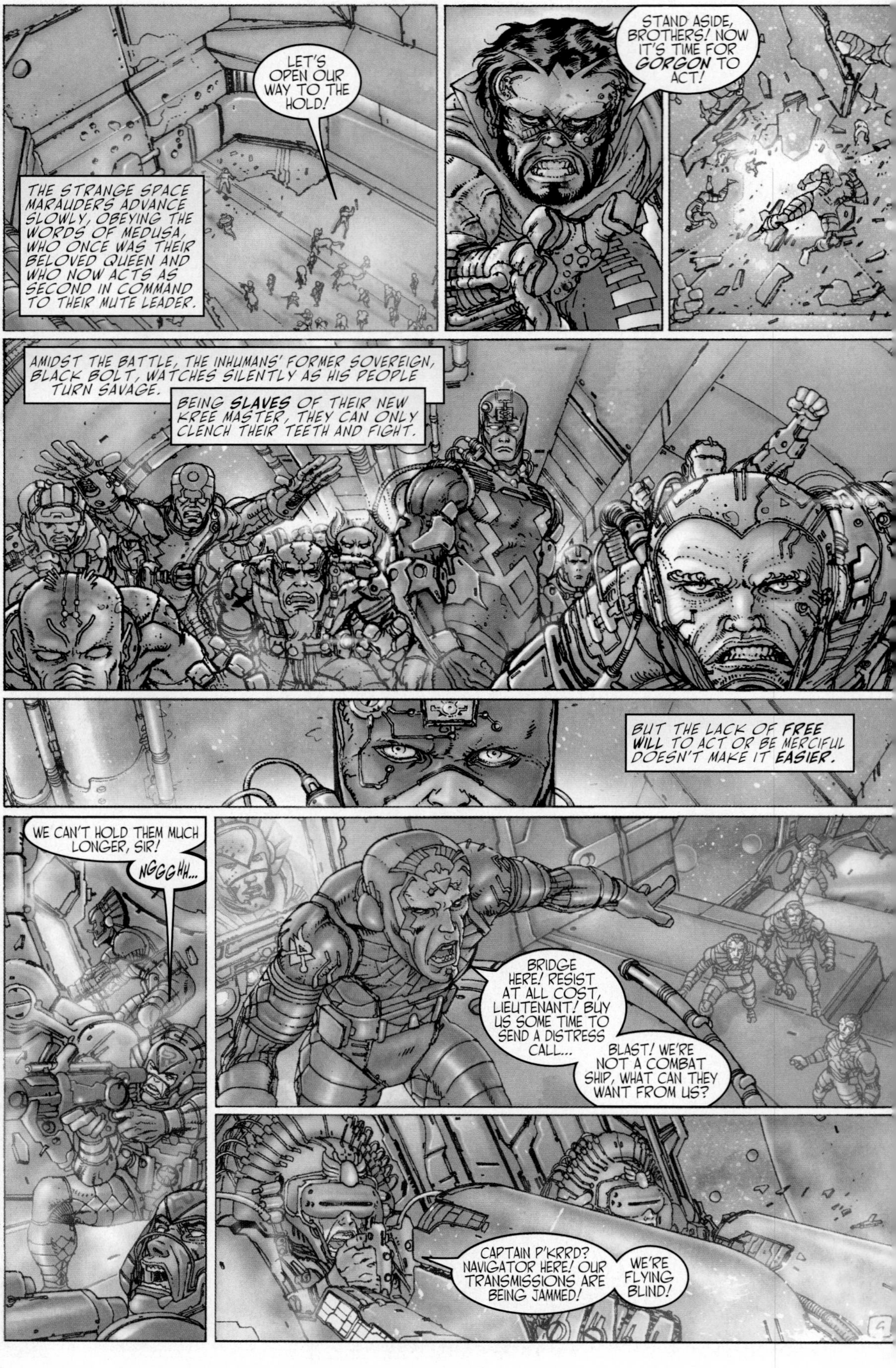
LET'S OPEN OUR WAY TO THE HOLD!
THE STRANGE SPACE MARAUDERS ADVANCE SLOWLY, OBEYING THE WORDS OF MEDUSA, WHO ONCE WAS THEIR BELOVED QUEEN AND WHO NOW ACTS AS SECOND IN COMMAND TO THEIR MUTE LEADER.
STAND ASIDE, BROTHERS! NOW IT'S TIME FOR GORGON TO ACT!
AMIDST THE BATTLE, THE INHUMANS' FORMER SOVEREIGN, BLACK BOLT, WATCHES SILENTLY AS HIS PEOPLE TURN SAVAGE.
BEING SLAVES OF THEIR NEW KREE MASTER, THEY CAN ONLY CLENCH THEIR TEETH AND FIGHT.
BUT THE LACK OF FREE WILL TO ACT OR BE MERCIFUL DOESN'T MAKE IT EASIER.
WE CAN'T HOLD THEM MUCH LONGER, SIR!
NGGGHH...
BRIDGE HERE! RESIST AT ALL COST, LIEUTENANT! BUY US SOME TIME TO SEND A DISTRESS CALL...
BLAST! WE'RE NOT A COMBAT SHIP, WHAT CAN THEY WANT FROM US?
CAPTAIN P'KRRD? NAVIGATOR HERE! OUR TRANSMISSIONS ARE BEING JAMMED!
WE'RE FLYING BLIND!
9

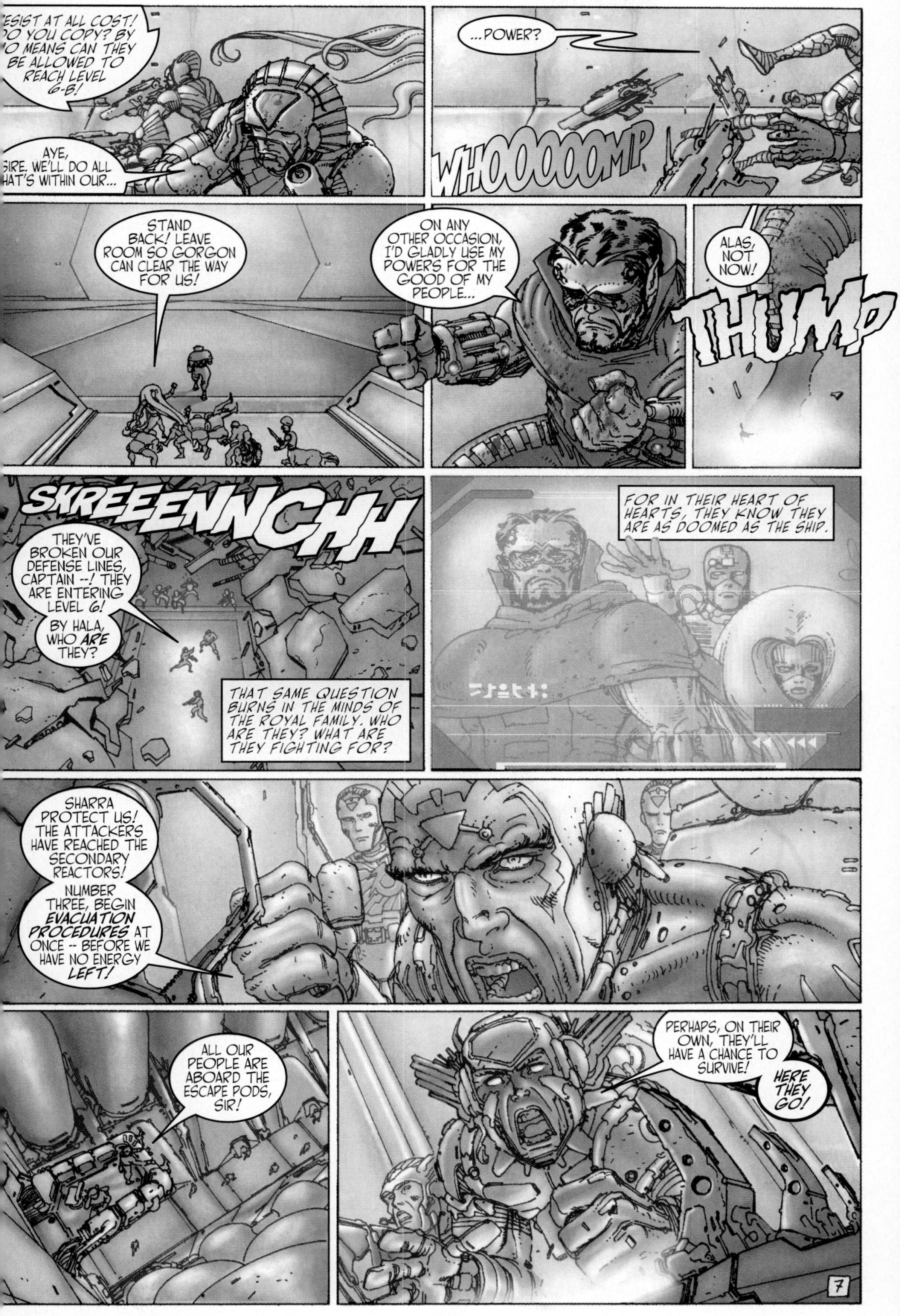

RESIST AT ALL COST! DO YOU COPY? BY NO MEANS CAN THEY BE ALLOWED TO REACH LEVEL 6-B!
AYE, SIRE. WE'LL DO ALL THAT'S WITHIN OUR...
...POWER?
WHOOOOOOMP
STAND BACK! LEAVE ROOM SO GORGON CAN CLEAR THE WAY FOR US!
ON ANY OTHER OCCASION, I'D GLADLY USE MY POWERS FOR THE GOOD OF MY PEOPLE...
ALAS, NOT NOW!
THUMP
SKREEENNCHH
THEY'VE BROKEN OUR DEFENSE LINES, CAPTAIN --! THEY ARE ENTERING LEVEL 6!
BY HALA, WHO ARE THEY?
THAT SAME QUESTION BURNS IN THE MINDS OF THE ROYAL FAMILY. WHO ARE THEY? WHAT ARE THEY FIGHTING FOR?
FOR IN THEIR HEART OF HEARTS, THEY KNOW THEY ARE AS DOOMED AS THE SHIP.
SHARRA PROTECT US! THE ATTACKERS HAVE REACHED THE SECONDARY REACTORS!
NUMBER THREE, BEGIN EVACUATION PROCEDURES AT ONCE -- BEFORE WE HAVE NO ENERGY LEFT!
ALL OUR PEOPLE ARE ABOARD THE ESCAPE PODS, SIR!
PERHAPS, ON THEIR OWN, THEY'LL HAVE A CHANCE TO SURVIVE!
HERE THEY GO!

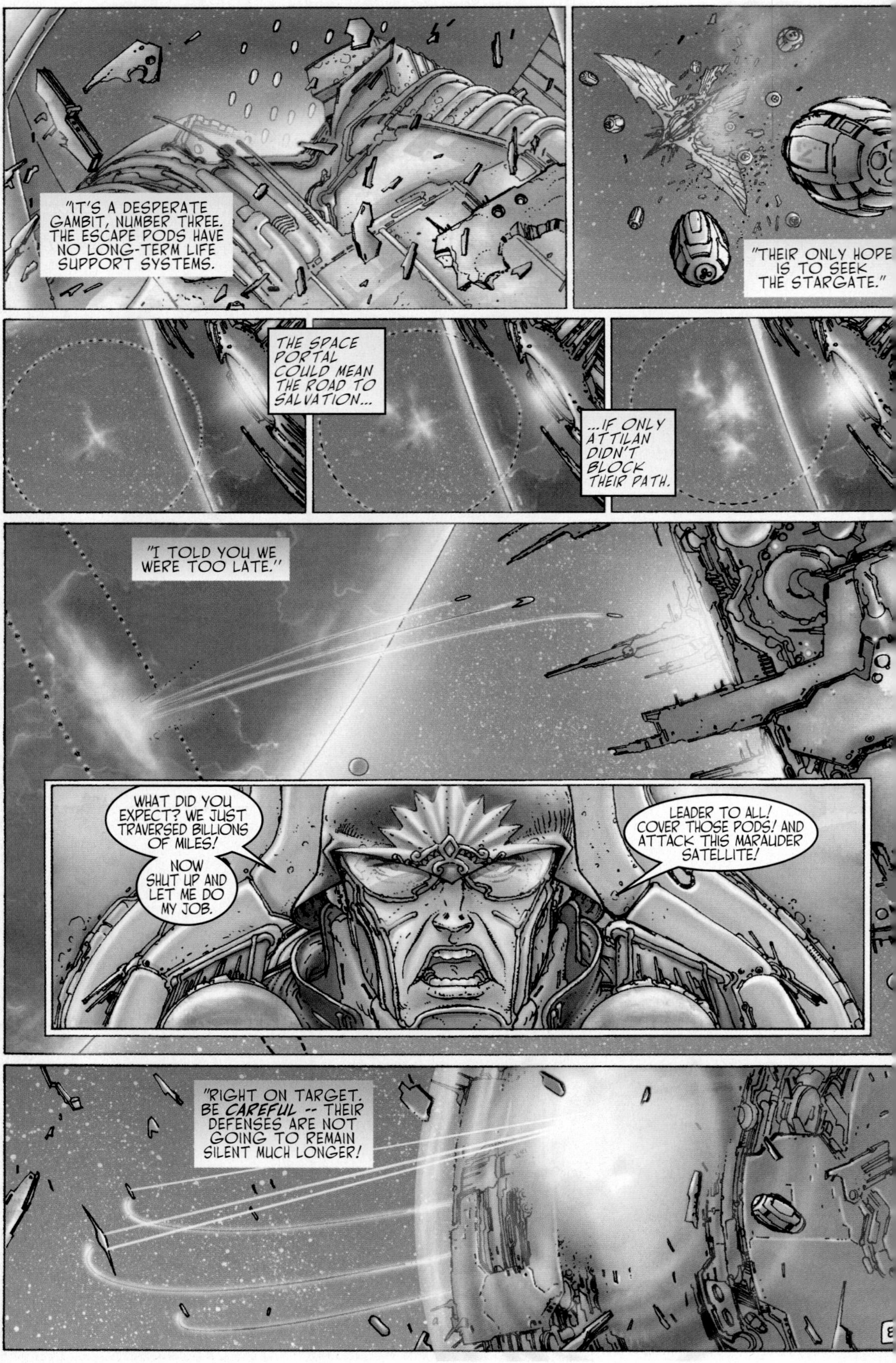
"IT'S A DESPERATE GAMBIT, NUMBER THREE. THE ESCAPE PODS HAVE NO LONG-TERM LIFE SUPPORT SYSTEMS.
"THEIR ONLY HOPE IS TO SEEK THE STARGATE."
THE SPACE PORTAL COULD MEAN THE ROAD TO SALVATION...
...IF ONLY ATTILAN DIDN'T BLOCK THEIR PATH.
"I TOLD YOU WE WERE TOO LATE."
WHAT DID YOU EXPECT? WE JUST TRAVERSED BILLIONS OF MILES!
NOW SHUT UP AND LET ME DO MY JOB.
LEADER TO ALL! COVER THOSE PODS! AND ATTACK THIS MARAUDER SATELLITE!
"RIGHT ON TARGET. BE CAREFUL -- THEIR DEFENSES ARE NOT GOING TO REMAIN SILENT MUCH LONGER!
8

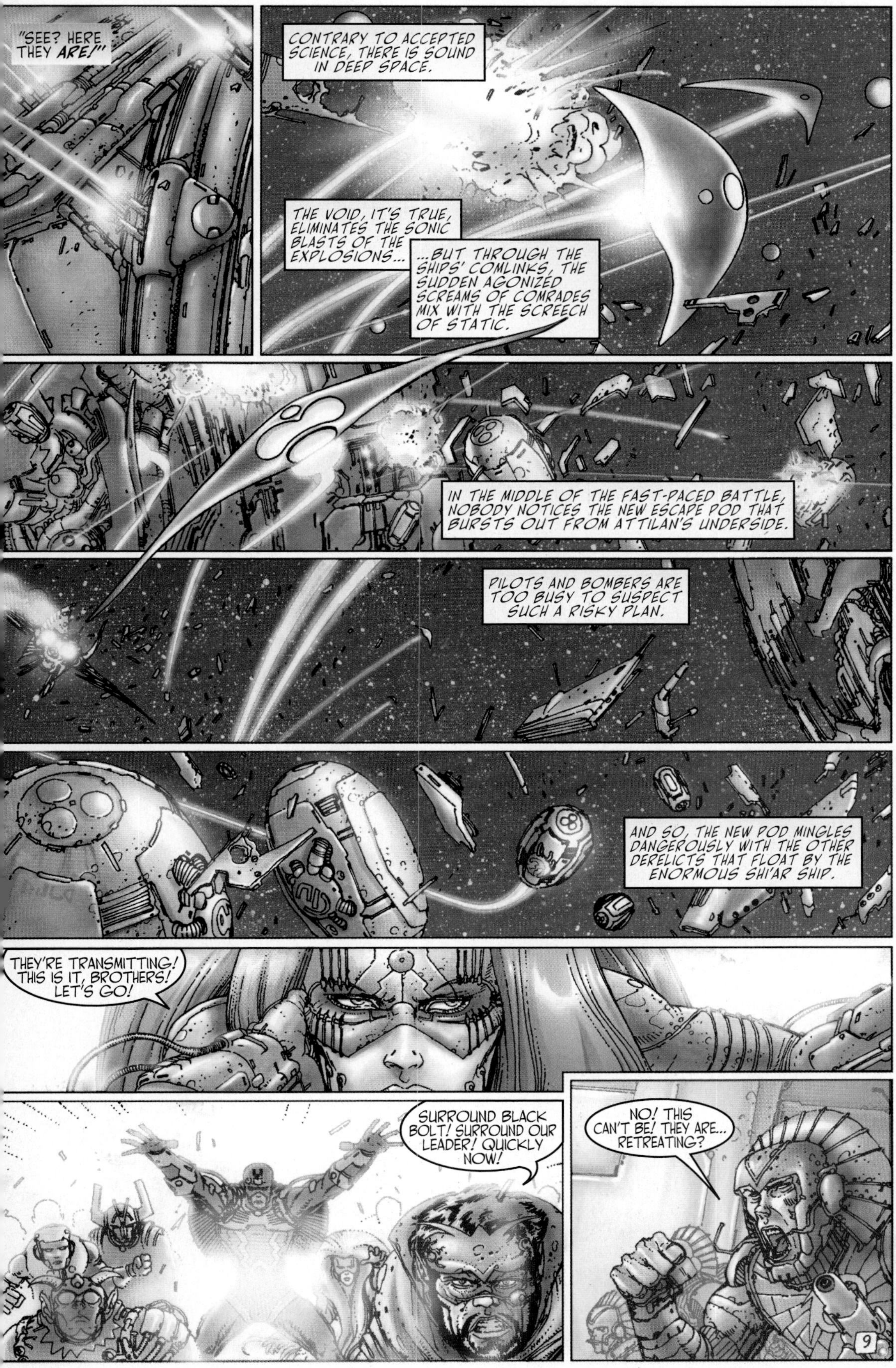
"SEE? HERE THEY ARE!"
CONTRARY TO ACCEPTED SCIENCE, THERE IS SOUND IN DEEP SPACE.
THE VOID, IT'S TRUE, ELIMINATES THE SONIC BLASTS OF THE EXPLOSIONS...
...BUT THROUGH THE SHIPS' COMLINKS, THE SUDDEN AGONIZED SCREAMS OF COMRADES MIX WITH THE SCREECH OF STATIC.
IN THE MIDDLE OF THE FAST-PACED BATTLE, NOBODY NOTICES THE NEW ESCAPE POD THAT BURSTS OUT FROM ATTILAN'S UNDERSIDE.
PILOTS AND BOMBERS ARE TOO BUSY TO SUSPECT SUCH A RISKY PLAN.
AND SO, THE NEW POD MINGLES DANGEROUSLY WITH THE OTHER DERELICTS THAT FLOAT BY THE ENORMOUS SHI'AR SHIP.
THEY'RE TRANSMITTING! THIS IS IT, BROTHERS! LET'S GO!
SURROUND BLACK BOLT! SURROUND OUR LEADER! QUICKLY NOW!
NO! THIS CAN'T BE! THEY ARE... RETREATING?
9

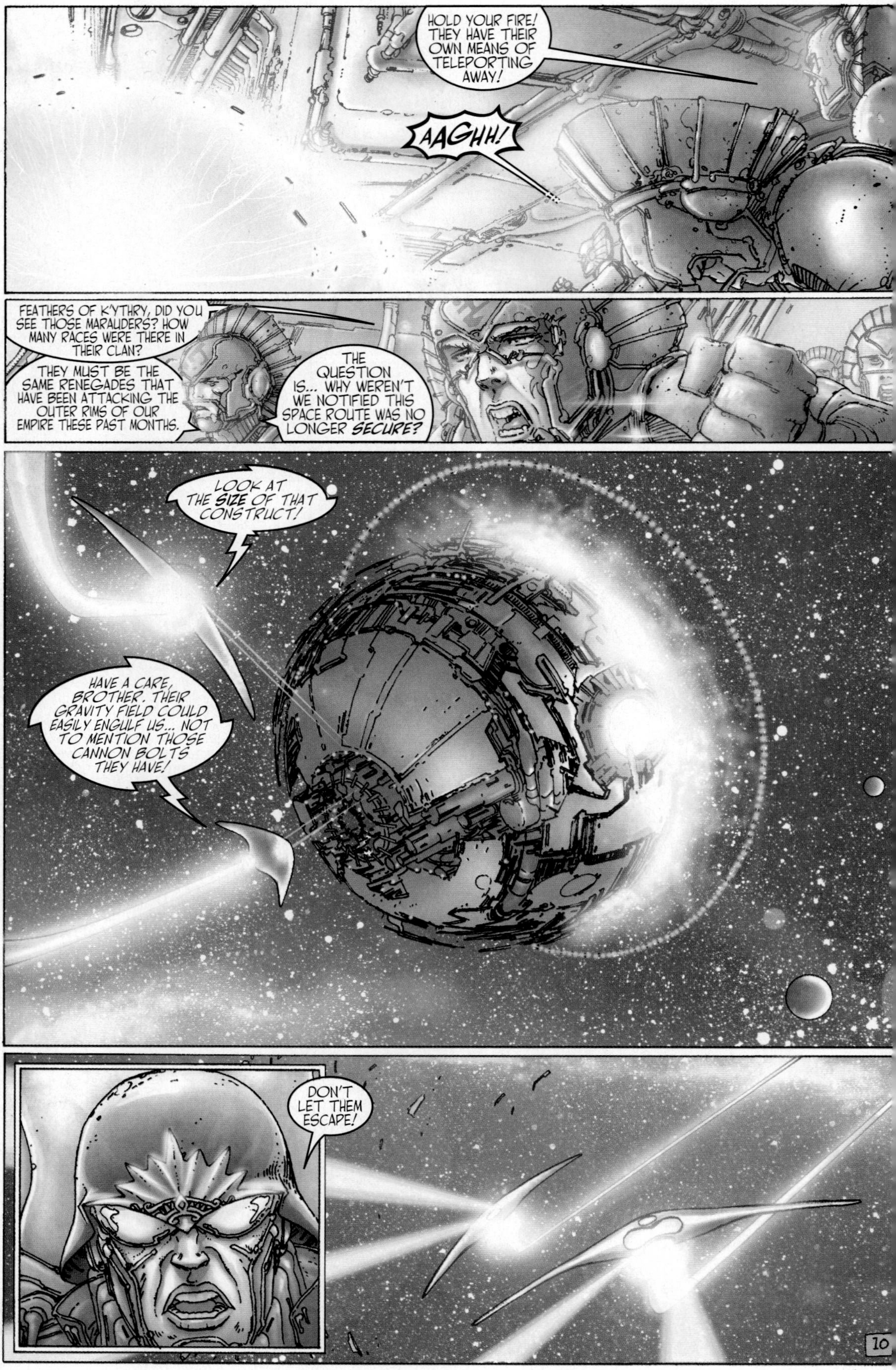
HOLD YOUR FIRE! THEY HAVE THEIR OWN MEANS OF TELEPORTING AWAY!
AAGHH!
FEATHERS OF K'YTHRY, DID YOU SEE THOSE MARAUDERS? HOW MANY RACES WERE THERE IN THEIR CLAN?
THEY MUST BE THE SAME RENEGADES THAT HAVE BEEN ATTACKING THE OUTER RIMS OF OUR EMPIRE THESE PAST MONTHS.
THE QUESTION IS... WHY WEREN'T WE NOTIFIED THIS SPACE ROUTE WAS NO LONGER SECURE?
LOOK AT THE SIZE OF THAT CONSTRUCT!
HAVE A CARE, BROTHER. THEIR GRAVITY FIELD COULD EASILY ENGULF US... NOT TO MENTION THOSE CANNON BOLTS THEY HAVE!
DON'T LET THEM ESCAPE!

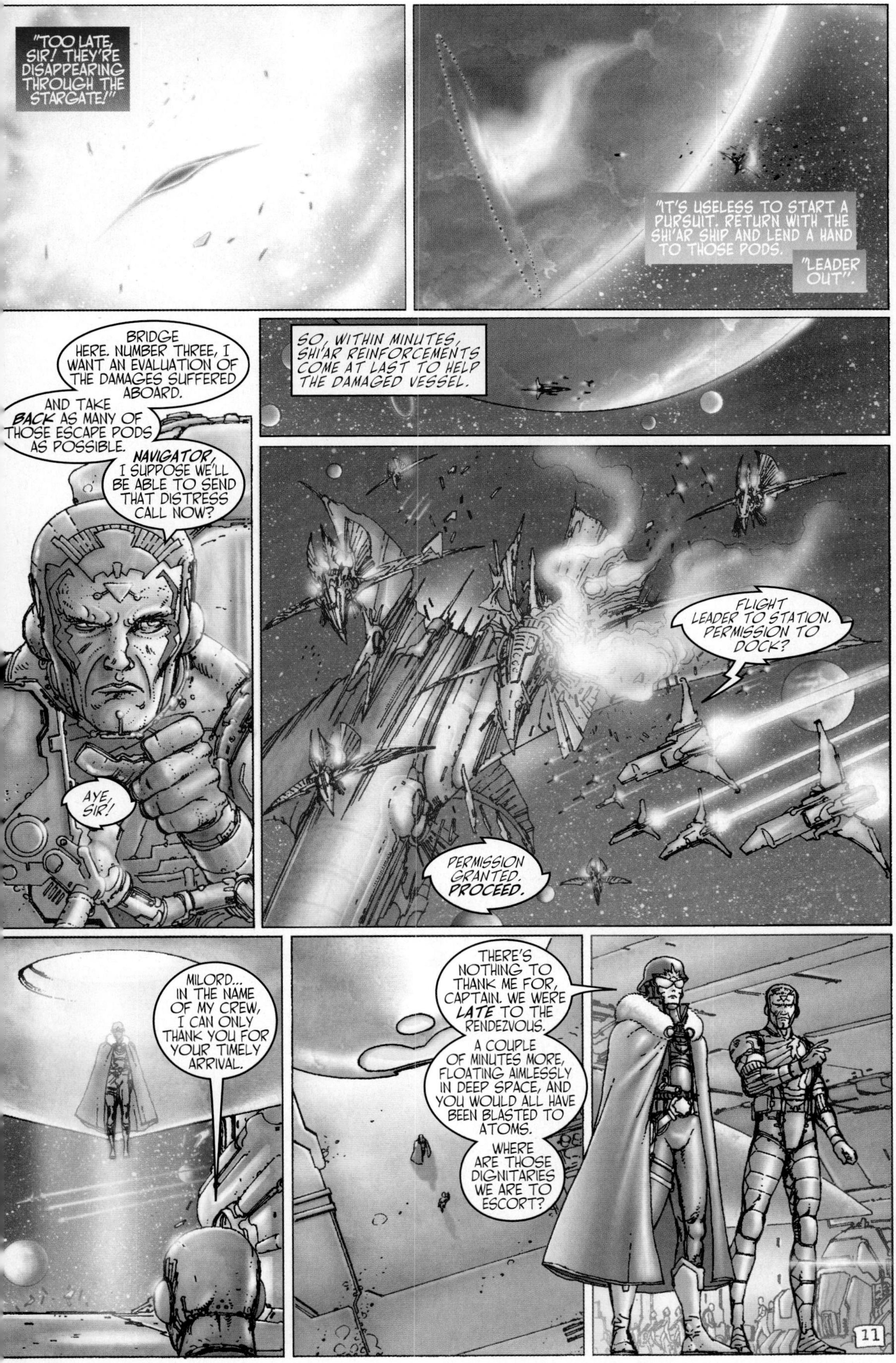
"TOO LATE, SIR! THEY'RE DISAPPEARING THROUGH THE STARGATE!"
"IT'S USELESS TO START A PURSUIT. RETURN WITH THE SHI'AR SHIP AND LEND A HAND TO THOSE PODS.
"LEADER OUT".
BRIDGE HERE. NUMBER THREE, I WANT AN EVALUATION OF THE DAMAGES SUFFERED ABOARD.
AND TAKE BACK AS MANY OF THOSE ESCAPE PODS AS POSSIBLE.
NAVIGATOR, I SUPPOSE WE'LL BE ABLE TO SEND THAT DISTRESS CALL NOW?
AYE, SIR!
SO, WITHIN MINUTES, SHI'AR REINFORCEMENTS COME AT LAST TO HELP THE DAMAGED VESSEL.
FLIGHT LEADER TO STATION. PERMISSION TO DOCK?
PERMISSION GRANTED. PROCEED.
MILORD... IN THE NAME OF MY CREW, I CAN ONLY THANK YOU FOR YOUR TIMELY ARRIVAL.
THERE'S NOTHING TO THANK ME FOR, CAPTAIN. WE WERE LATE TO THE RENDEZVOUS.
A COUPLE OF MINUTES MORE, FLOATING AIMLESSLY IN DEEP SPACE, AND YOU WOULD ALL HAVE BEEN BLASTED TO ATOMS.
WHERE ARE THOSE DIGNITARIES WE ARE TO ESCORT?
11

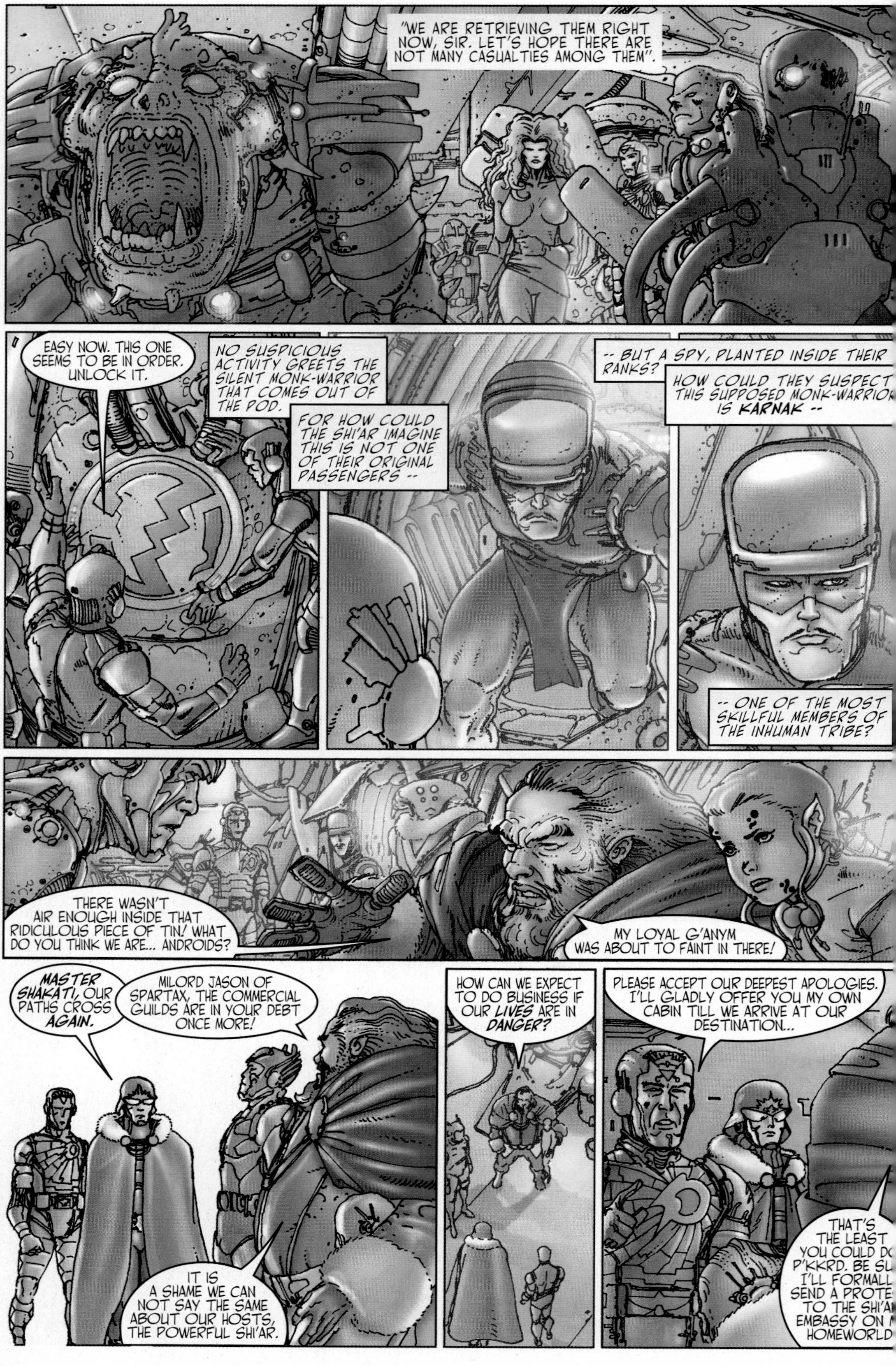
"WE ARE RETRIEVING THEM RIGHT NOW, SIR. LET'S HOPE THERE ARE NOT MANY CASUALTIES AMONG THEM".
EASY NOW. THIS ONE SEEMS TO BE IN ORDER. UNLOCK IT.
NO SUSPICIOUS ACTIVITY GREETS THE SILENT MONK-WARRIOR THAT COMES OUT OF THE POD.
FOR HOW COULD THE SHI'AR IMAGINE THIS IS NOT ONE OF THEIR ORIGINAL PASSENGERS --
-- BUT A SPY, PLANTED INSIDE THEIR RANKS?
HOW COULD THEY SUSPECT THIS SUPPOSED MONK-WARRIOR IS KARNAK --
-- ONE OF THE MOST SKILLFUL MEMBERS OF THE INHUMAN TRIBE?
THERE WASN'T AIR ENOUGH INSIDE THAT RIDICULOUS PIECE OF TIN! WHAT DO YOU THINK WE ARE... ANDROIDS?
MY LOYAL G'ANYM WAS ABOUT TO FAINT IN THERE!
MASTER SHAKATI, OUR PATHS CROSS AGAIN.
MILORD JASON OF SPARTAX, THE COMMERCIAL GUILDS ARE IN YOUR DEBT ONCE MORE!
IT IS A SHAME WE CAN NOT SAY THE SAME ABOUT OUR HOSTS, THE POWERFUL SHI'AR.
HOW CAN WE EXPECT TO DO BUSINESS IF OUR LIVES ARE IN DANGER?
PLEASE ACCEPT OUR DEEPEST APOLOGIES. I'LL GLADLY OFFER YOU MY OWN CABIN TILL WE ARRIVE AT OUR DESTINATION...

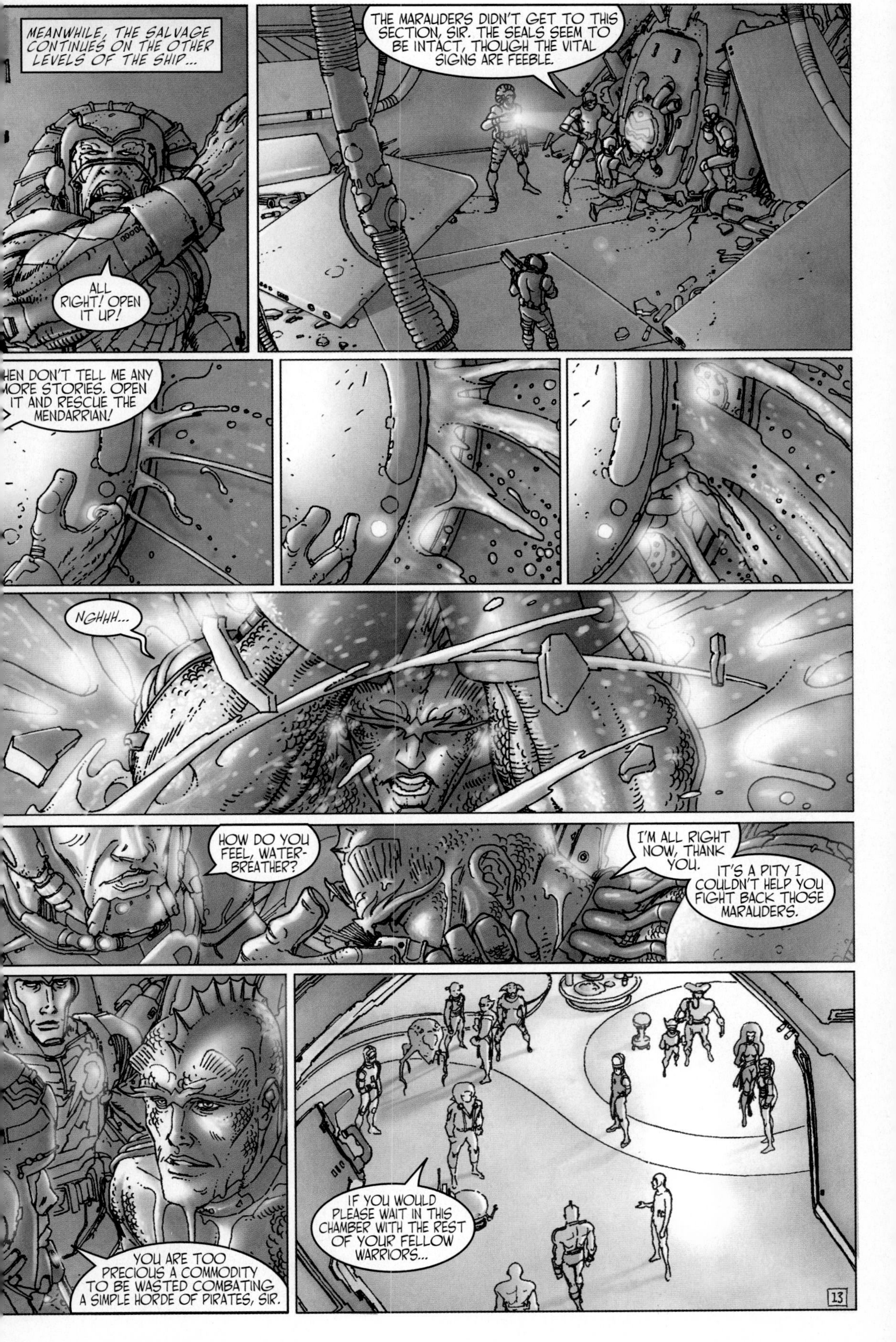
MEANWHILE, THE SALVAGE CONTINUES ON THE OTHER LEVELS OF THE SHIP...
THE MARAUDERS DIDN'T GET TO THIS SECTION, SIR. THE SEALS SEEM TO BE INTACT, THOUGH THE VITAL SIGNS ARE FEEBLE.
ALL RIGHT! OPEN IT UP!
HEN DON'T TELL ME ANY MORE STORIES. OPEN IT AND RESCUE THE MENDARRIAN!
NGHHH...
HOW DO YOU FEEL, WATER-BREATHER?
I'M ALL RIGHT NOW, THANK YOU.
IT'S A PITY I COULDN'T HELP YOU FIGHT BACK THOSE MARAUDERS.
YOU ARE TOO PRECIOUS A COMMODITY TO BE WASTED COMBATING A SIMPLE HORDE OF PIRATES, SIR.
IF YOU WOULD PLEASE WAIT IN THIS CHAMBER WITH THE REST OF YOUR FELLOW WARRIORS...
13

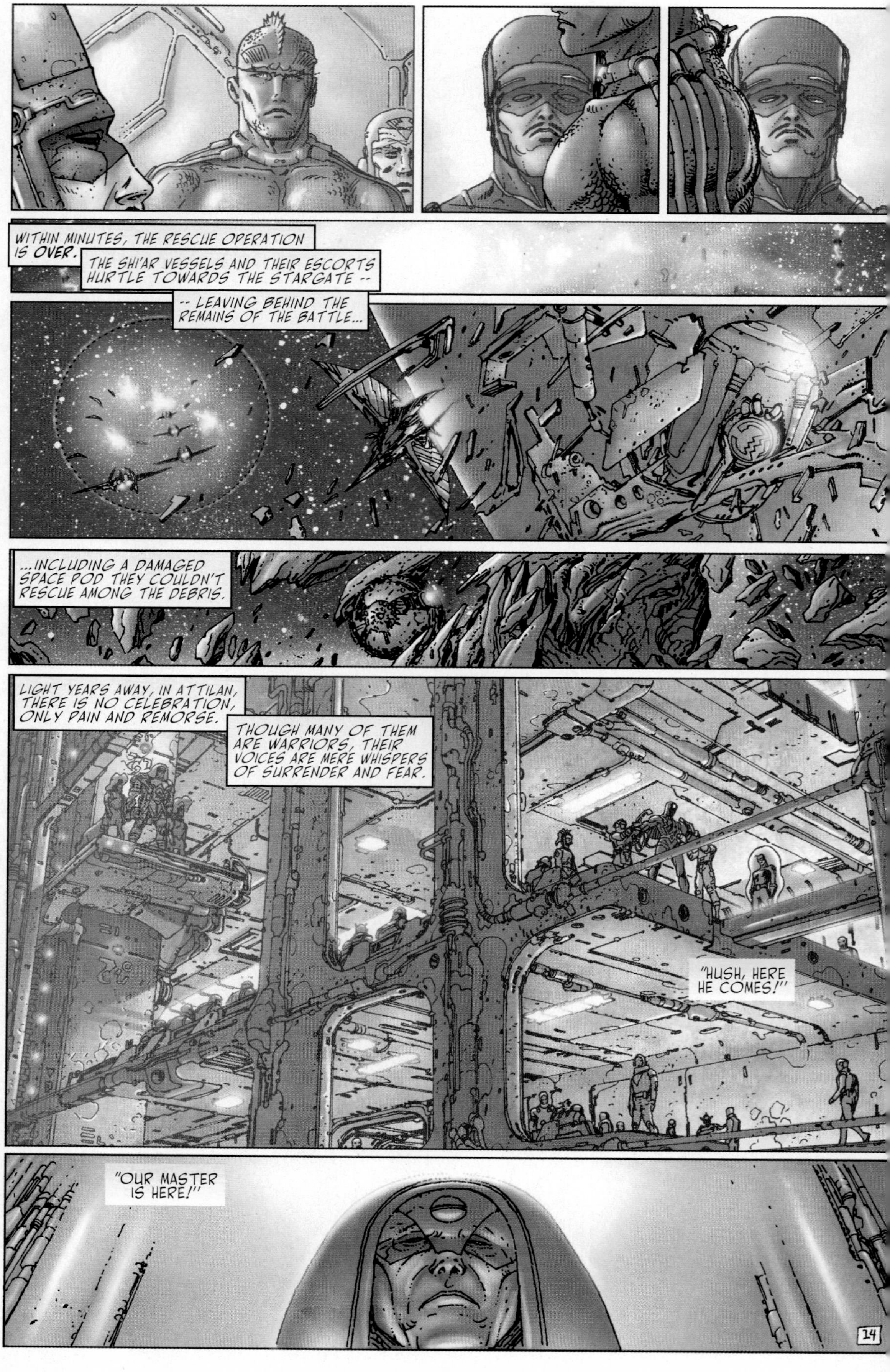

WITHIN MINUTES, THE RESCUE OPERATION IS OVER.
THE SHI'AR VESSELS AND THEIR ESCORTS HURTLE TOWARDS THE STARGATE --
-- LEAVING BEHIND THE REMAINS OF THE BATTLE...
...INCLUDING A DAMAGED SPACE POD THEY COULDN'T RESCUE AMONG THE DEBRIS.
LIGHT YEARS AWAY, IN ATTILAN, THERE IS NO CELEBRATION, ONLY PAIN AND REMORSE.
THOUGH MANY OF THEM ARE WARRIORS, THEIR VOICES ARE MERE WHISPERS OF SURRENDER AND FEAR.
"HUSH, HERE HE COMES!"
"OUR MASTER IS HERE!"

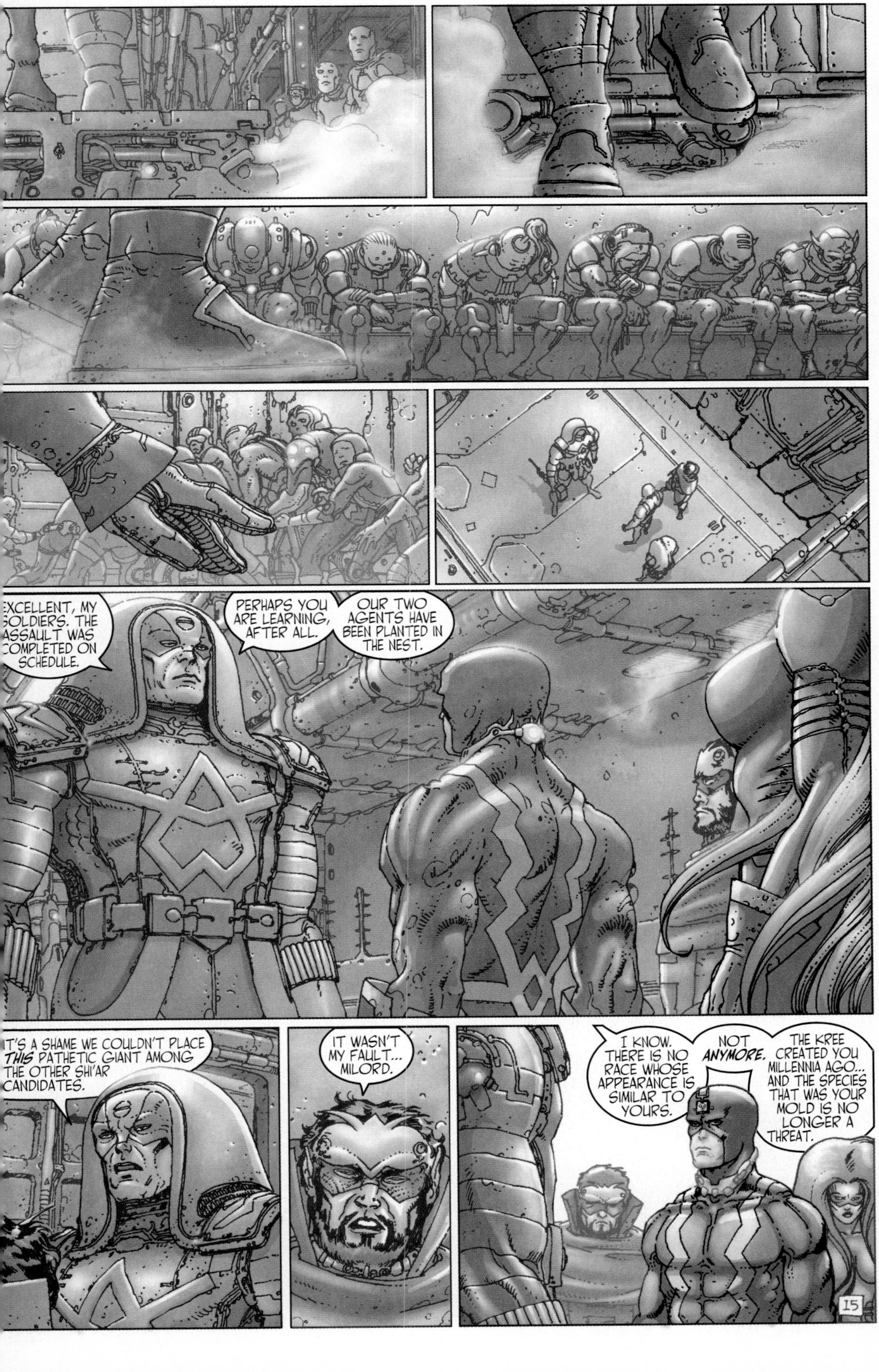

EXCELLENT, MY SOLDIERS. THE ASSAULT WAS COMPLETED ON SCHEDULE.
PERHAPS YOU ARE LEARNING, AFTER ALL.
OUR TWO AGENTS HAVE BEEN PLANTED IN THE NEST.
IT'S A SHAME WE COULDN'T PLACE THIS PATHETIC GIANT AMONG THE OTHER SHI'AR CANDIDATES.
IT WASN'T MY FAULT... MILORD.
I KNOW. THERE IS NO RACE WHOSE APPEARANCE IS SIMILAR TO YOURS.
NOT ANYMORE.
THE KREE CREATED YOU MILLENNIA AGO... AND THE SPECIES THAT WAS YOUR MOLD IS NO LONGER A THREAT.

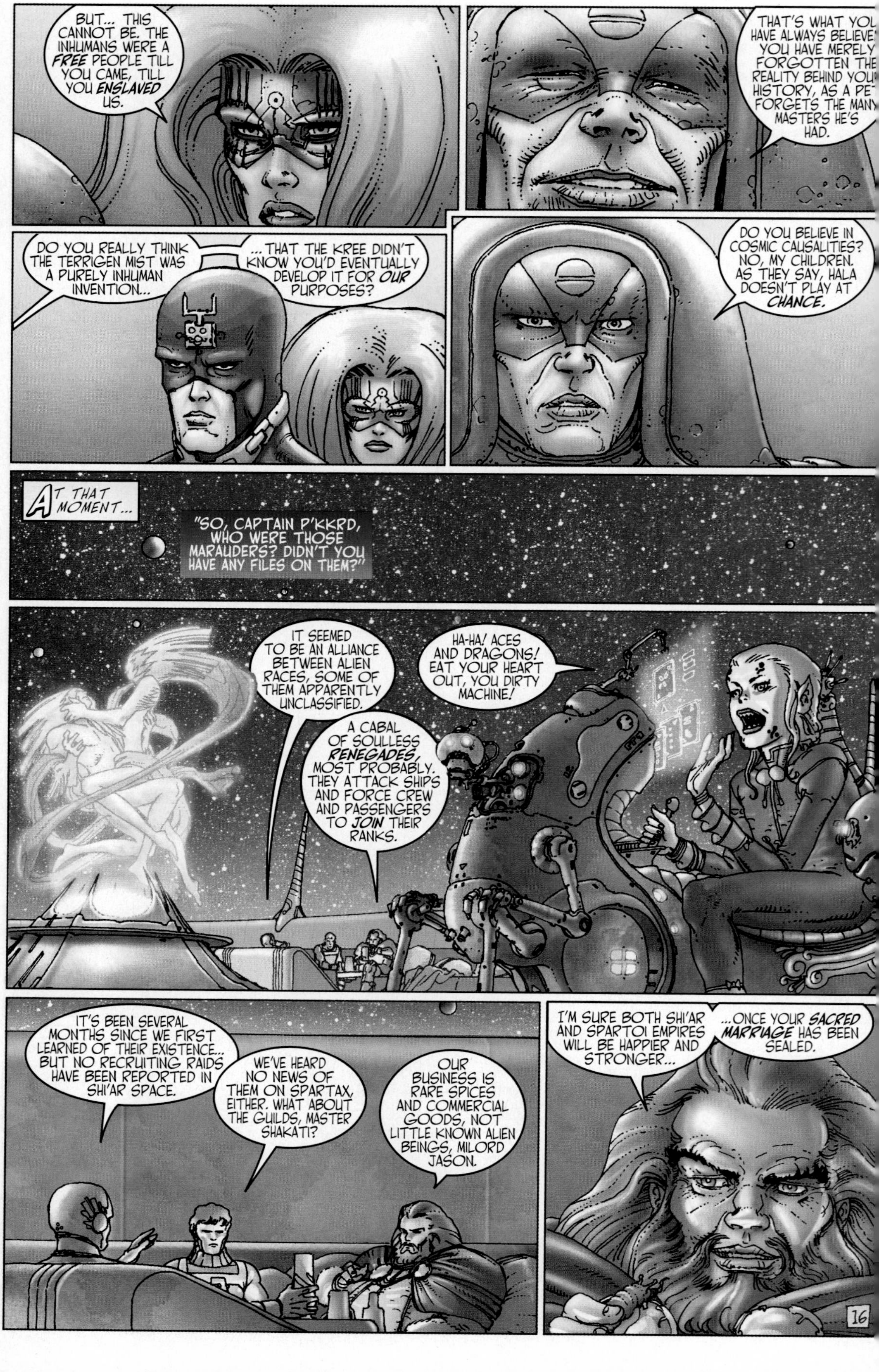

BUT... THIS CANNOT BE. THE INHUMANS WERE A FREE PEOPLE TILL YOU CAME, TILL YOU ENSLAVED US.
THAT'S WHAT YOU HAVE ALWAYS BELIEVED. YOU HAVE MERELY FORGOTTEN THE REALITY BEHIND YOUR HISTORY, AS A PET FORGETS THE MANY MASTERS HE'S HAD.
DO YOU REALLY THINK THE TERRIGEN MIST WAS A PURELY INHUMAN INVENTION...
...THAT THE KREE DIDN'T KNOW YOU'D EVENTUALLY DEVELOP IT FOR OUR PURPOSES?
DO YOU BELIEVE IN COSMIC CAUSALITIES? NO, MY CHILDREN. AS THEY SAY, HALA DOESN'T PLAY AT CHANCE.
AT THAT MOMENT...
"SO, CAPTAIN P'KKRD, WHO WERE THOSE MARAUDERS? DIDN'T YOU HAVE ANY FILES ON THEM?"
IT SEEMED TO BE AN ALLIANCE BETWEEN ALIEN RACES, SOME OF THEM APPARENTLY UNCLASSIFIED.
A CABAL OF SOULLESS RENEGADES, MOST PROBABLY. THEY ATTACK SHIPS AND FORCE CREW AND PASSENGERS TO JOIN THEIR RANKS.
HA-HA! ACES AND DRAGONS! EAT YOUR HEART OUT, YOU DIRTY MACHINE!
IT'S BEEN SEVERAL MONTHS SINCE WE FIRST LEARNED OF THEIR EXISTENCE... BUT NO RECRUITING RAIDS HAVE BEEN REPORTED IN SHI'AR SPACE.
WE'VE HEARD NO NEWS OF THEM ON SPARTAX, EITHER. WHAT ABOUT THE GUILDS, MASTER SHAKATI?
OUR BUSINESS IS RARE SPICES AND COMMERCIAL GOODS, NOT LITTLE KNOWN ALIEN BEINGS, MILORD JASON.
I'M SURE BOTH SHI'AR AND SPARTOI EMPIRES WILL BE HAPPIER AND STRONGER...
...ONCE YOUR SACRED MARRIAGE HAS BEEN SEALED.

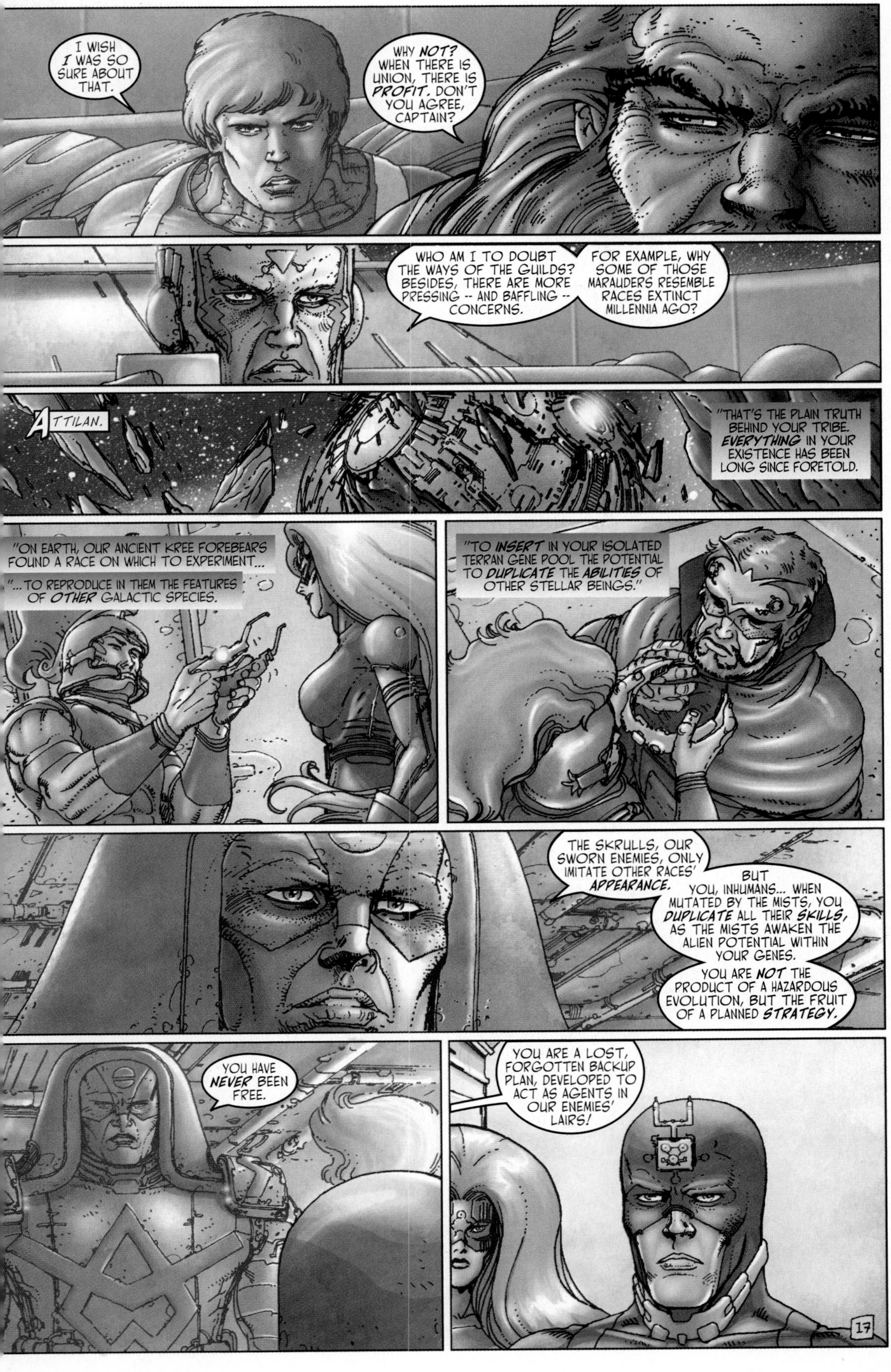

I WISH I WAS SO SURE ABOUT THAT.
WHY NOT? WHEN THERE IS UNION, THERE IS PROFIT. DON'T YOU AGREE, CAPTAIN?
WHO AM I TO DOUBT THE WAYS OF THE GUILDS? BESIDES, THERE ARE MORE PRESSING -- AND BAFFLING -- CONCERNS.
FOR EXAMPLE, WHY SOME OF THOSE MARAUDERS RESEMBLE RACES EXTINCT MILLENNIA AGO?
ATTILAN.
"THAT'S THE PLAIN TRUTH BEHIND YOUR TRIBE. EVERYTHING IN YOUR EXISTENCE HAS BEEN LONG SINCE FORETOLD.
"ON EARTH, OUR ANCIENT KREE FOREBEARS FOUND A RACE ON WHICH TO EXPERIMENT...
"...TO REPRODUCE IN THEM THE FEATURES OF OTHER GALACTIC SPECIES.
"TO INSERT IN YOUR ISOLATED TERRAN GENE POOL THE POTENTIAL TO DUPLICATE THE ABILITIES OF OTHER STELLAR BEINGS."
THE SKRULLS, OUR SWORN ENEMIES, ONLY IMITATE OTHER RACES' APPEARANCE.
BUT YOU, INHUMANS... WHEN MUTATED BY THE MISTS, YOU DUPLICATE ALL THEIR SKILLS, AS THE MISTS AWAKEN THE ALIEN POTENTIAL WITHIN YOUR GENES.
YOU ARE NOT THE PRODUCT OF A HAZARDOUS EVOLUTION, BUT THE FRUIT OF A PLANNED STRATEGY.
YOU HAVE NEVER BEEN FREE.
YOU ARE A LOST, FORGOTTEN BACKUP PLAN, DEVELOPED TO ACT AS AGENTS IN OUR ENEMIES' LAIRS!
17

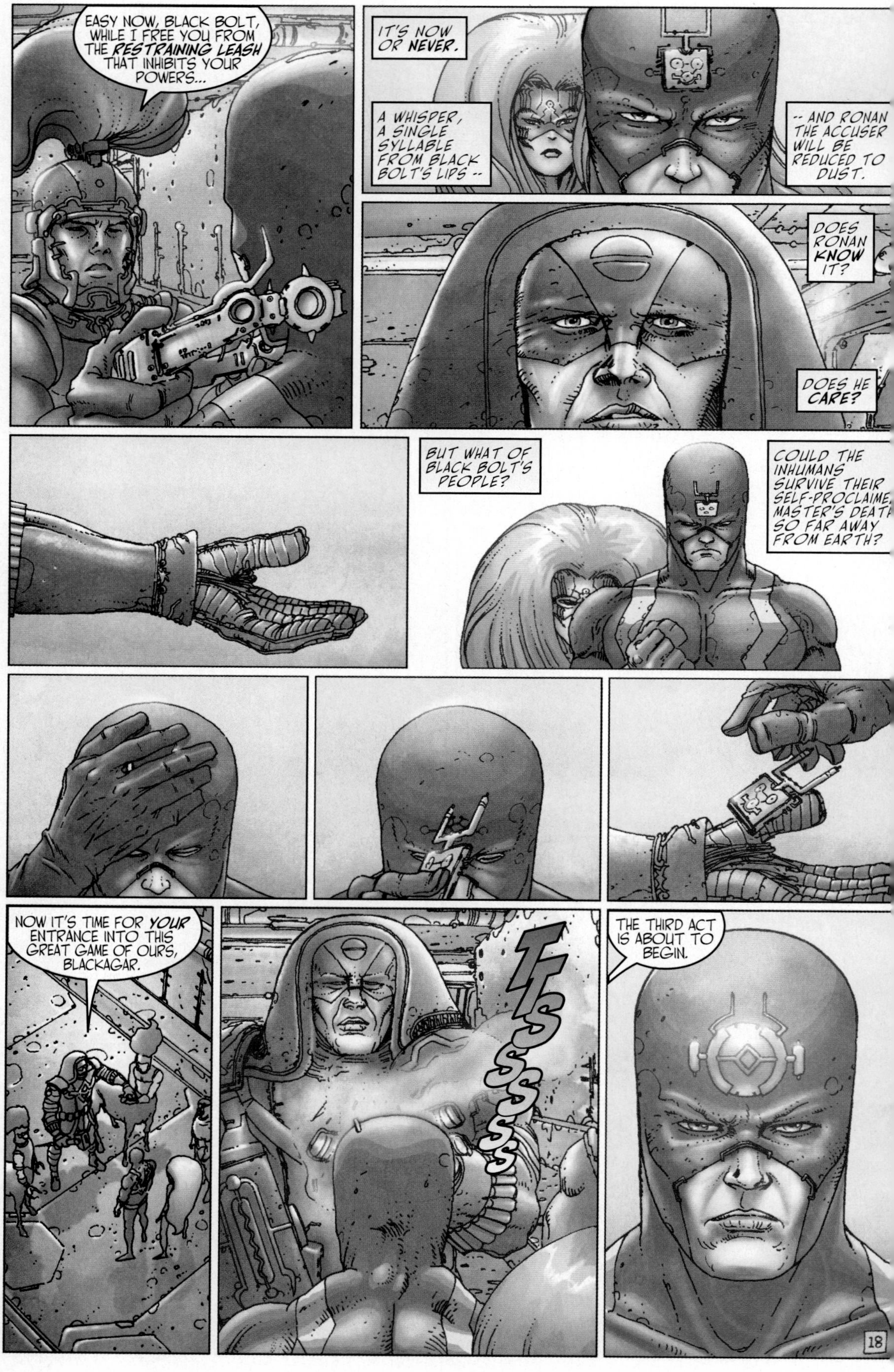

EASY NOW, BLACK BOLT, WHILE I FREE YOU FROM THE RESTRAINING LEASH THAT INHIBITS YOUR POWERS...
IT'S NOW OR NEVER.
A WHISPER, A SINGLE SYLLABLE FROM BLACK BOLT'S LIPS --
-- AND RONAN THE ACCUSER WILL BE REDUCED TO DUST.
DOES RONAN KNOW IT?
DOES HE CARE?
BUT WHAT OF BLACK BOLT'S PEOPLE?
COULD THE INHUMANS SURVIVE THEIR SELF-PROCLAIME MASTER'S DEAT SO FAR AWAY FROM EARTH?
NOW IT'S TIME FOR YOUR ENTRANCE INTO THIS GREAT GAME OF OURS, BLACKAGAR.
TTSSSSS
THE THIRD ACT IS ABOUT TO BEGIN.
18

MAKE THE NECESSARY CALCULATIONS FOR ANOTHER SPACE JUMP, AVRAK...

...AND PREPARE MY SHIP FOR THEM.

INHUMANS -- DO WHAT YOU MUST.

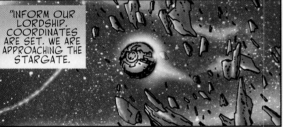

"INFORM OUR LORDSHIP. COORDINATES ARE SET. WE ARE APPROACHING THE STARGATE.

"SEAL ALL HATCHES. ALL SYSTEMS ON-LINE. HERE WE GO!"

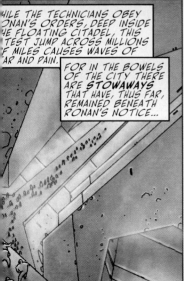

WHILE THE TECHNICIANS OBEY RONAN'S ORDERS, DEEP INSIDE THE FLOATING CITADEL, THIS TEST JUMP ACROSS MILLIONS OF MILES CAUSES WAVES OF FEAR AND PAIN.

FOR IN THE BOWELS OF THE CITY THERE ARE STOWAWAYS THAT HAVE, THUS FAR, REMAINED BENEATH RONAN'S NOTICE...

DO NOT BE AFRAID, MY ALPHA PRIMITIVES. THIS TREMBLING WILL PASS, AS ON OTHER OCCASIONS.

MOTHER MACHINE IS RECOVERING, THAT IS ALL.

WE WILL FIGHT TO SEE THE LIGHT AGAIN SOON ENOUGH.

TRUST THE WORDS OF MAXIMUS -- TRUST MY PROMISES!

19

HE'S BEEN SITTING HERE FOR HOURS, MEDITATING.

TO ACT MEANS TO BETRAY -- HIS BELIEFS, HIS IDEALS, EVERYTHING THAT TRULY **MATTERS** TO HIM.

BY NOT ACTING, HE WOULD **CONDEMN** HIS PEOPLE, THE ONES HE **LOVES**, THOSE HE HAS SWORN TO **PROTECT**.

MY HUSBAND...

*T*WO WEEKS LATER, IN SHI'AR SPACE... THE TRANSIT STATION HAS A THOUSAND NAMES, AS IT SERVES A THOUSAND DIFFERENT PEOPLES.

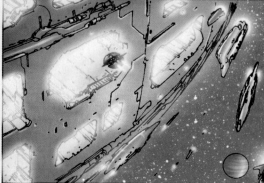

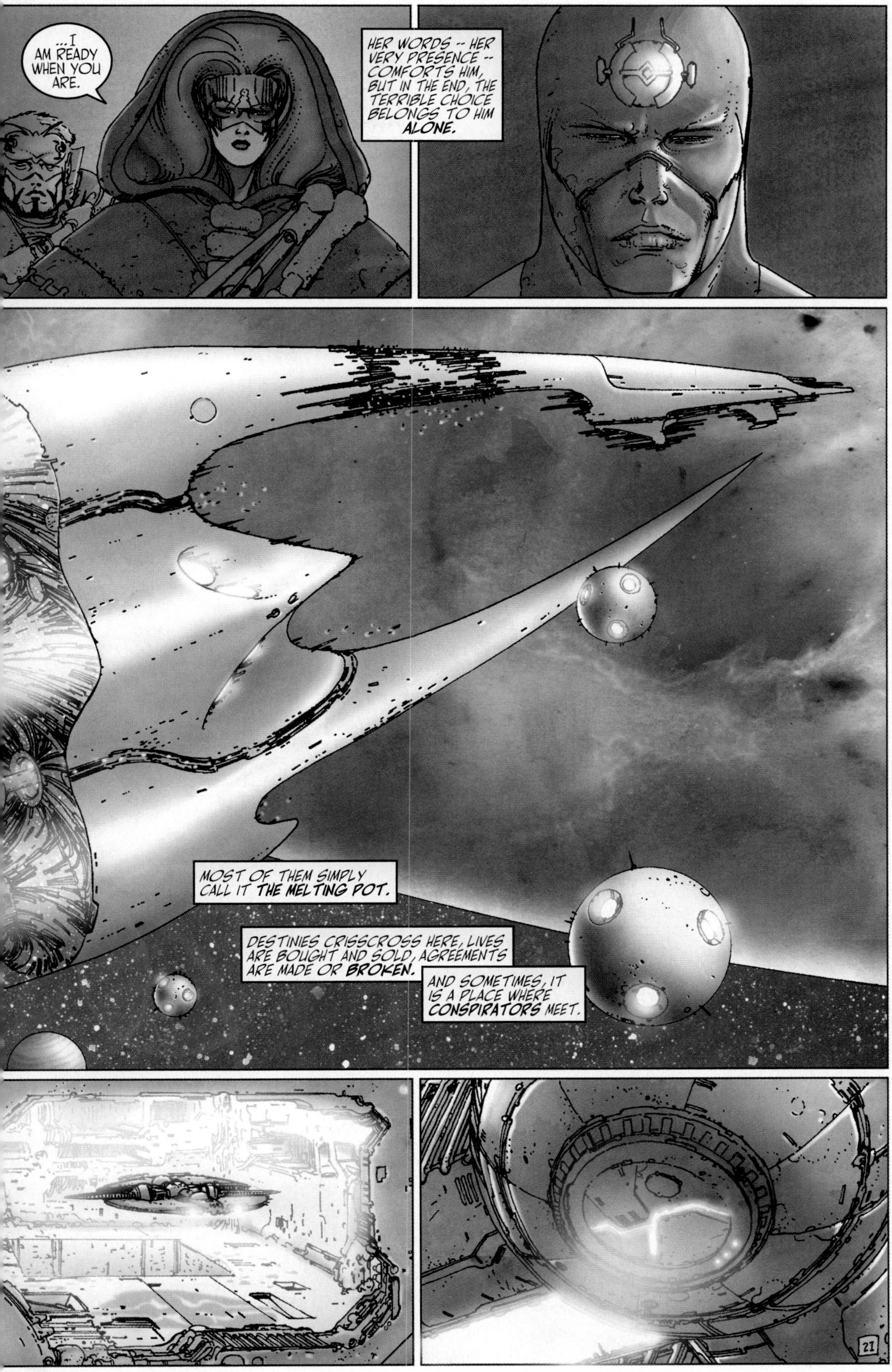
...I AM READY WHEN YOU ARE.
HER WORDS -- HER VERY PRESENCE -- COMFORTS HIM, BUT IN THE END, THE TERRIBLE CHOICE BELONGS TO HIM ALONE.
MOST OF THEM SIMPLY CALL IT THE MELTING POT.
DESTINIES CRISSCROSS HERE, LIVES ARE BOUGHT AND SOLD, AGREEMENTS ARE MADE OR BROKEN.
AND SOMETIMES, IT IS A PLACE WHERE CONSPIRATORS MEET.

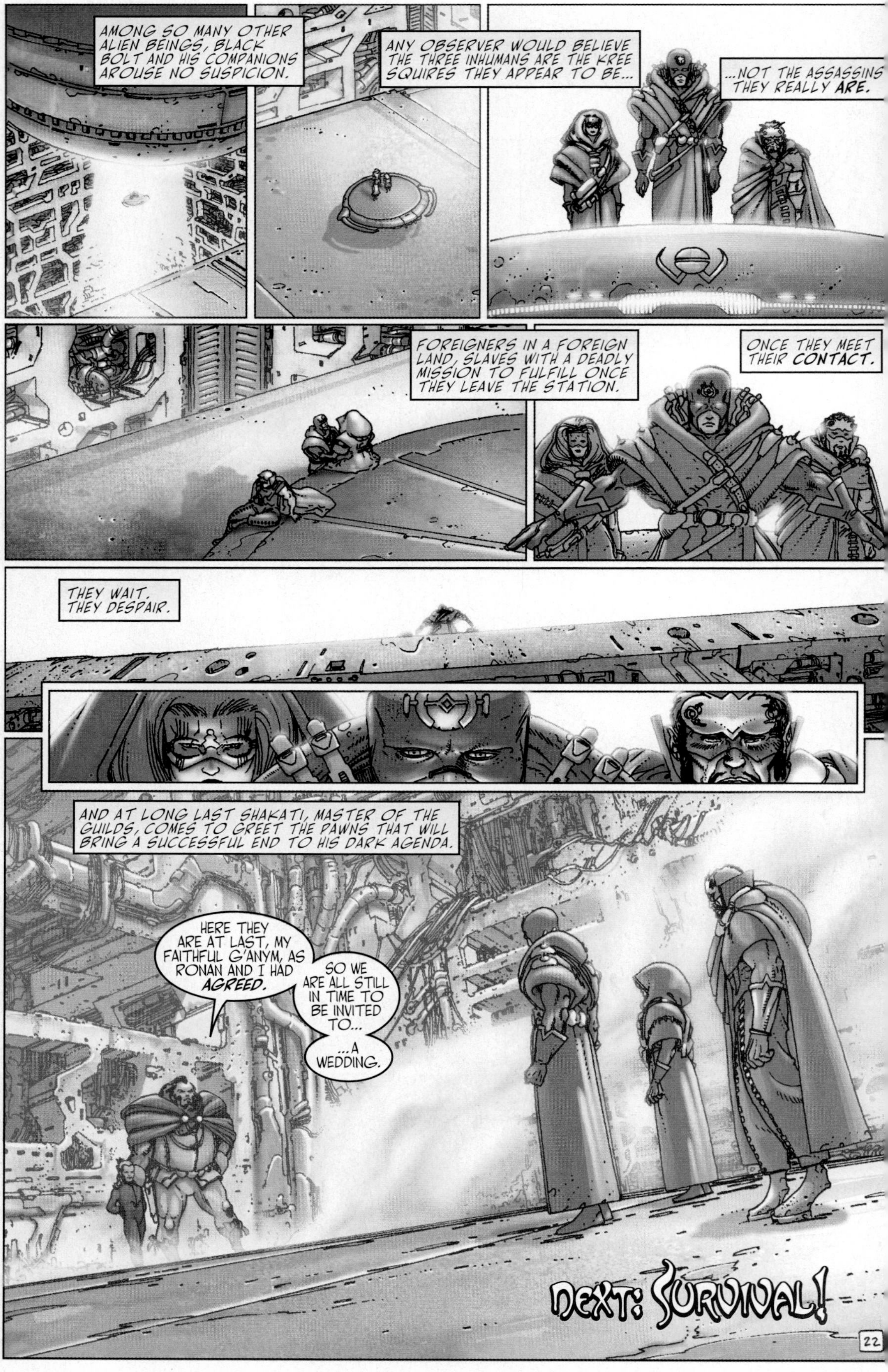
AMONG SO MANY OTHER ALIEN BEINGS, BLACK BOLT AND HIS COMPANIONS AROUSE NO SUSPICION.
ANY OBSERVER WOULD BELIEVE THE THREE INHUMANS ARE THE KREE SQUIRES THEY APPEAR TO BE...
...NOT THE ASSASSINS THEY REALLY ARE.
FOREIGNERS IN A FOREIGN LAND, SLAVES WITH A DEADLY MISSION TO FULFILL ONCE THEY LEAVE THE STATION.
ONCE THEY MEET THEIR CONTACT.
THEY WAIT. THEY DESPAIR.
AND AT LONG LAST SHAKATI, MASTER OF THE GUILDS, COMES TO GREET THE PAWNS THAT WILL BRING A SUCCESSFUL END TO HIS DARK AGENDA.
HERE THEY ARE AT LAST, MY FAITHFUL G'ANYM, AS RONAN AND I HAD AGREED.
SO WE ARE ALL STILL IN TIME TO BE INVITED TO...
...A WEDDING.
NEXT: SURVIVAL!

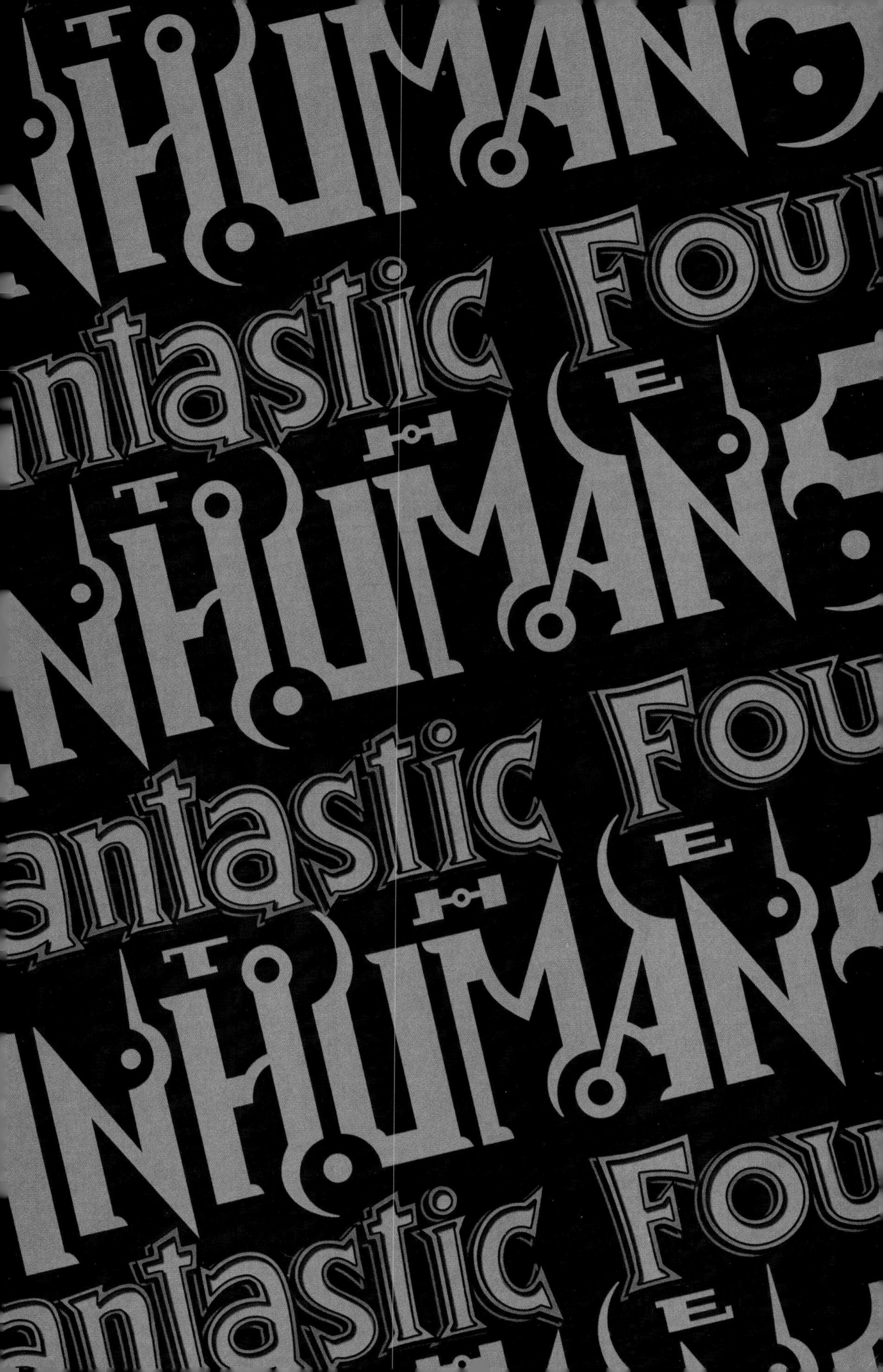

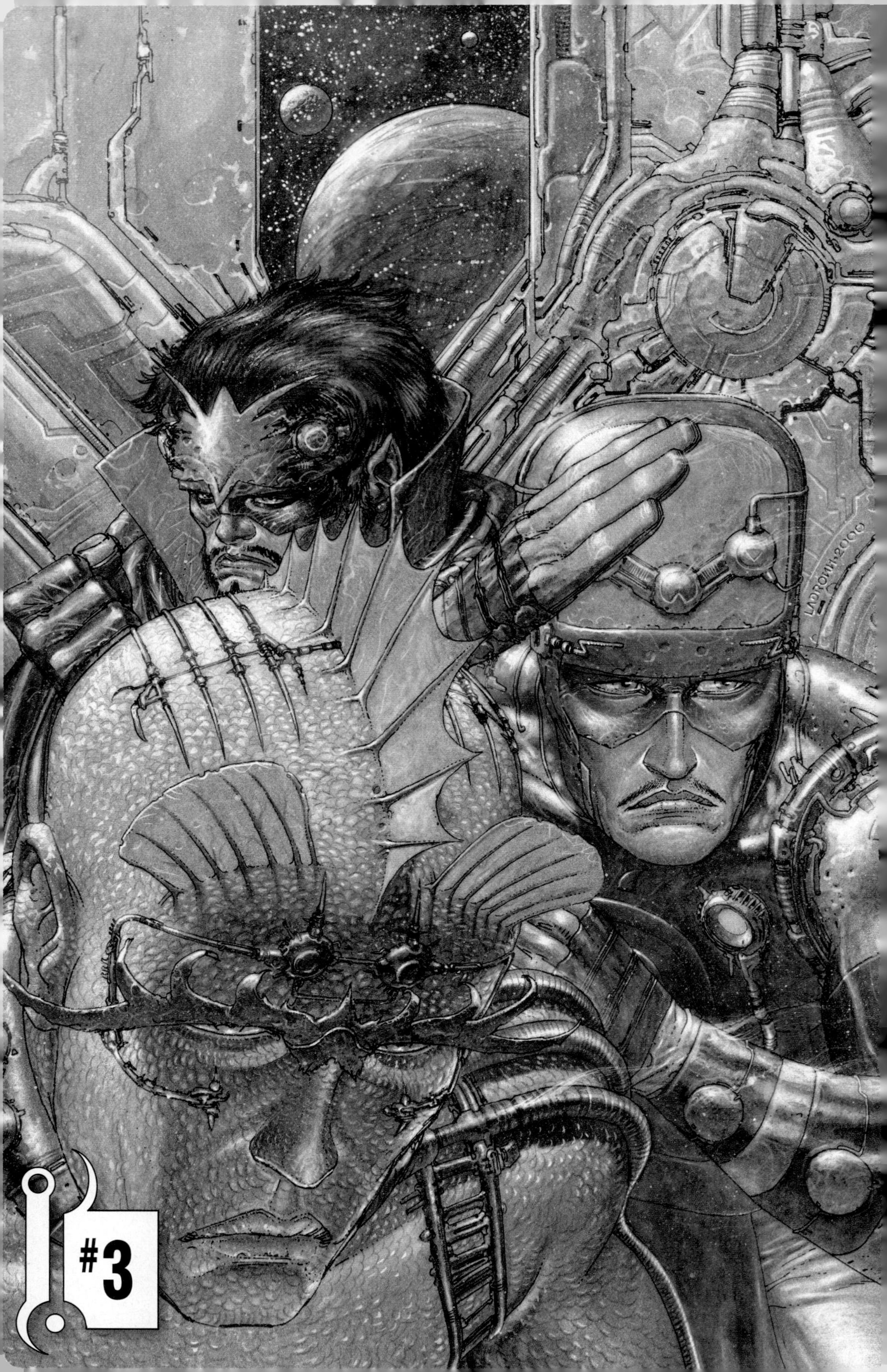
#3

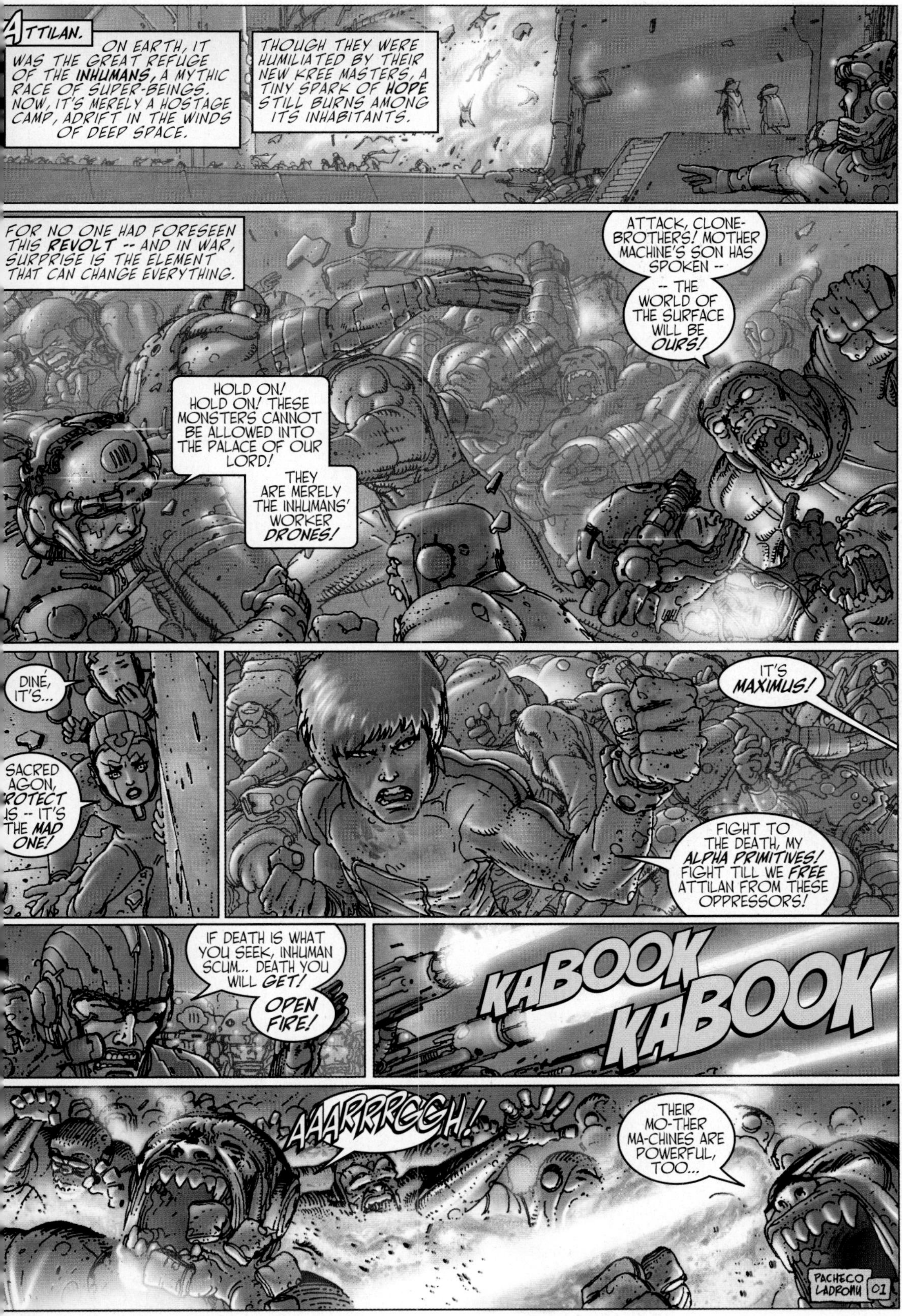
ATTILAN.
ON EARTH, IT WAS THE GREAT REFUGE OF THE INHUMANS, A MYTHIC RACE OF SUPER-BEINGS. NOW, IT'S MERELY A HOSTAGE CAMP, ADRIFT IN THE WINDS OF DEEP SPACE.
THOUGH THEY WERE HUMILIATED BY THEIR NEW KREE MASTERS, A TINY SPARK OF HOPE STILL BURNS AMONG ITS INHABITANTS.
FOR NO ONE HAD FORESEEN THIS REVOLT -- AND IN WAR, SURPRISE IS THE ELEMENT THAT CAN CHANGE EVERYTHING.
ATTACK, CLONE-BROTHERS! MOTHER MACHINE'S SON HAS SPOKEN --
-- THE WORLD OF THE SURFACE WILL BE OURS!
HOLD ON! HOLD ON! THESE MONSTERS CANNOT BE ALLOWED INTO THE PALACE OF OUR LORD!
THEY ARE MERELY THE INHUMANS' WORKER DRONES!
DINÉ, IT'S...
SACRED AGON, ROTECT IS -- IT'S THE MAD ONE!
IT'S MAXIMUS!
FIGHT TO THE DEATH, MY ALPHA PRIMITIVES! FIGHT TILL WE FREE ATTILAN FROM THESE OPPRESSORS!
IF DEATH IS WHAT YOU SEEK, INHUMAN SCUM... DEATH YOU WILL GET!
OPEN FIRE!
KABOOK
KABOOK
AAARRRGGH!
THEIR MO-THER MA-CHINES ARE POWERFUL, TOO...
PACHECO LADRONN 01

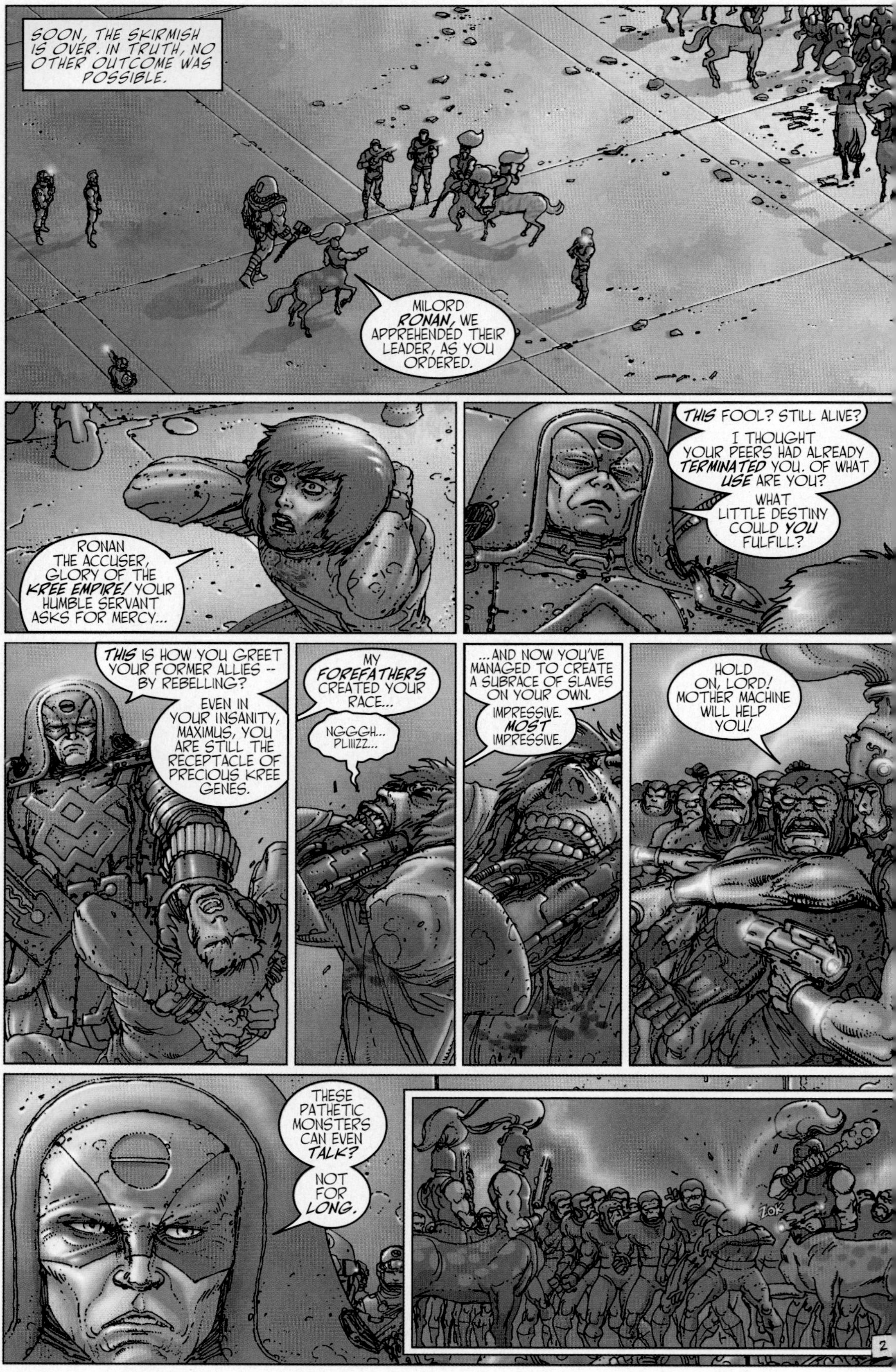
SOON, THE SKIRMISH IS OVER. IN TRUTH, NO OTHER OUTCOME WAS POSSIBLE.
MILORD RONAN, WE APPREHENDED THEIR LEADER, AS YOU ORDERED.
RONAN THE ACCUSER, GLORY OF THE KREE EMPIRE! YOUR HUMBLE SERVANT ASKS FOR MERCY...
THIS FOOL? STILL ALIVE?
I THOUGHT YOUR PEERS HAD ALREADY TERMINATED YOU. OF WHAT USE ARE YOU?
WHAT LITTLE DESTINY COULD YOU FULFILL?
THIS IS HOW YOU GREET YOUR FORMER ALLIES -- BY REBELLING?
EVEN IN YOUR INSANITY, MAXIMUS, YOU ARE STILL THE RECEPTACLE OF PRECIOUS KREE GENES.
MY FOREFATHERS CREATED YOUR RACE...
NGGGH... PLIIIZZ...
...AND NOW YOU'VE MANAGED TO CREATE A SUBRACE OF SLAVES ON YOUR OWN.
IMPRESSIVE. MOST IMPRESSIVE.
HOLD ON, LORD! MOTHER MACHINE WILL HELP YOU!
THESE PATHETIC MONSTERS CAN EVEN TALK?
NOT FOR LONG.
ZOK

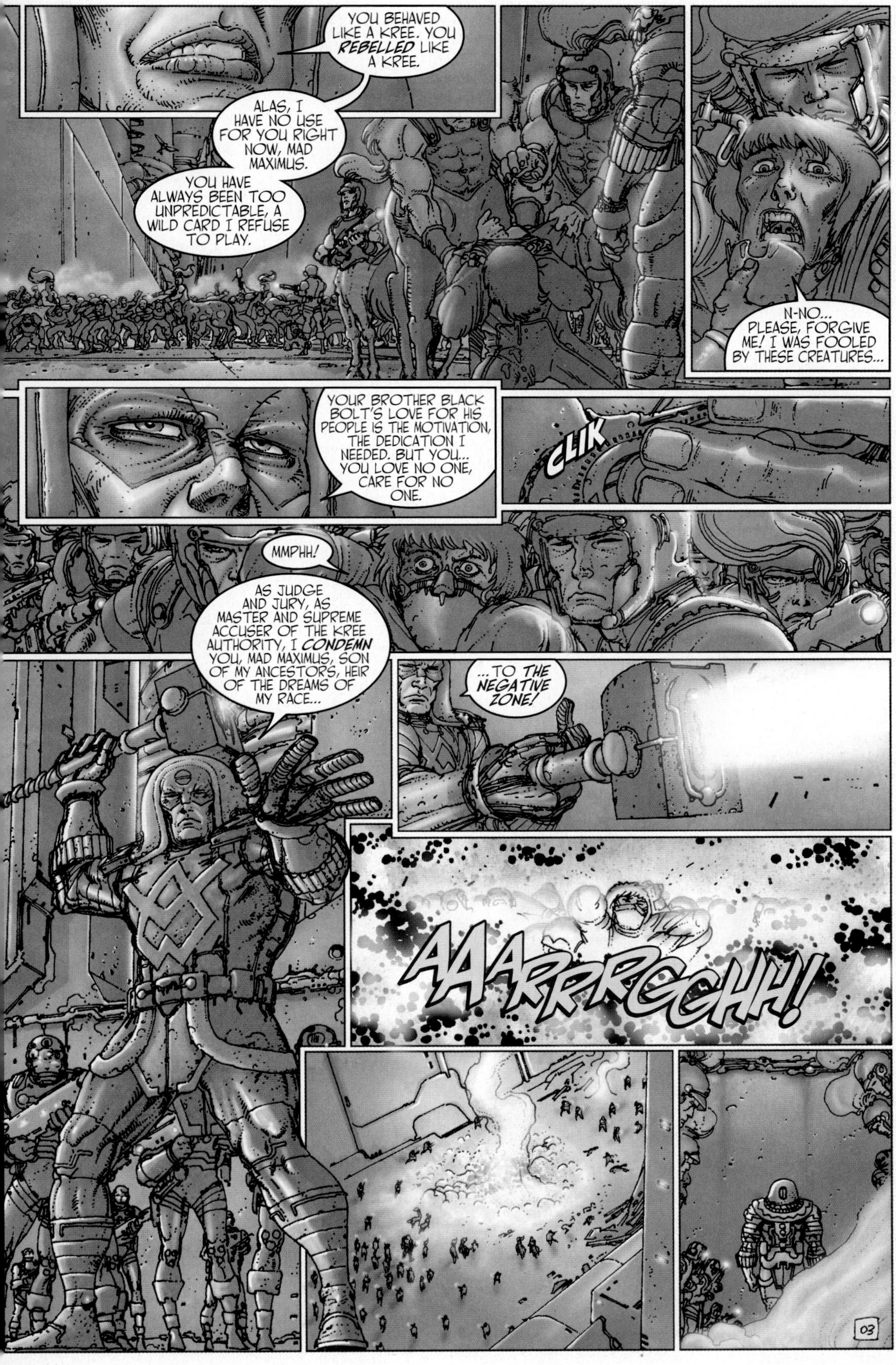

YOU BEHAVED LIKE A KREE. YOU REBELLED LIKE A KREE.
ALAS, I HAVE NO USE FOR YOU RIGHT NOW, MAD MAXIMUS.
YOU HAVE ALWAYS BEEN TOO UNPREDICTABLE, A WILD CARD I REFUSE TO PLAY.
N-NO... PLEASE, FORGIVE ME! I WAS FOOLED BY THESE CREATURES...
YOUR BROTHER BLACK BOLT'S LOVE FOR HIS PEOPLE IS THE MOTIVATION, THE DEDICATION I NEEDED. BUT YOU... YOU LOVE NO ONE, CARE FOR NO ONE.
CLIK
MMPHH!
AS JUDGE AND JURY, AS MASTER AND SUPREME ACCUSER OF THE KREE AUTHORITY, I CONDEMN YOU, MAD MAXIMUS, SON OF MY ANCESTORS, HEIR OF THE DREAMS OF MY RACE...
...TO THE NEGATIVE ZONE!
AAARRRGGHH!

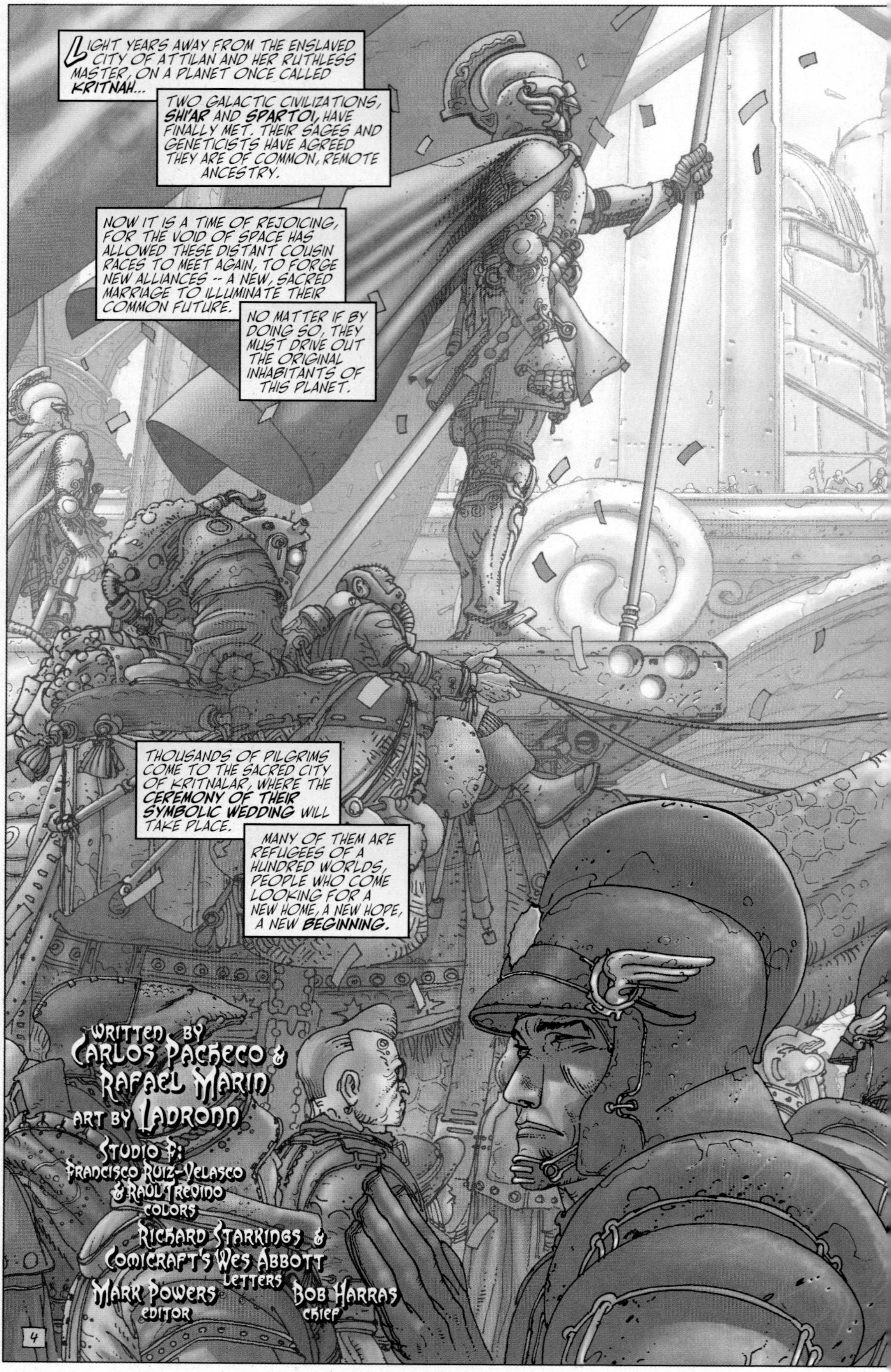
LIGHT YEARS AWAY FROM THE ENSLAVED CITY OF ATTILAN AND HER RUTHLESS MASTER, ON A PLANET ONCE CALLED KRITNAH...
TWO GALACTIC CIVILIZATIONS, SHI'AR AND SPARTOI, HAVE FINALLY MET. THEIR SAGES AND GENETICISTS HAVE AGREED THEY ARE OF COMMON, REMOTE ANCESTRY.
NOW IT IS A TIME OF REJOICING, FOR THE VOID OF SPACE HAS ALLOWED THESE DISTANT COUSIN RACES TO MEET AGAIN, TO FORGE NEW ALLIANCES -- A NEW, SACRED MARRIAGE TO ILLUMINATE THEIR COMMON FUTURE.
NO MATTER IF BY DOING SO, THEY MUST DRIVE OUT THE ORIGINAL INHABITANTS OF THIS PLANET.
THOUSANDS OF PILGRIMS COME TO THE SACRED CITY OF KRITNALAR, WHERE THE CEREMONY OF THEIR SYMBOLIC WEDDING WILL TAKE PLACE.
MANY OF THEM ARE REFUGEES OF A HUNDRED WORLDS, PEOPLE WHO COME LOOKING FOR A NEW HOME, A NEW HOPE, A NEW BEGINNING.
WRITTEN BY CARLOS PACHECO & RAFAEL MARIN
ART BY LADRONN
STUDIO F: FRANCISCO RUIZ-VELASCO & RAUL TREVINO COLORS
RICHARD STARKINGS & COMICRAFT'S WES ABBOTT LETTERS
MARK POWERS EDITOR
BOB HARRAS CHIEF
4

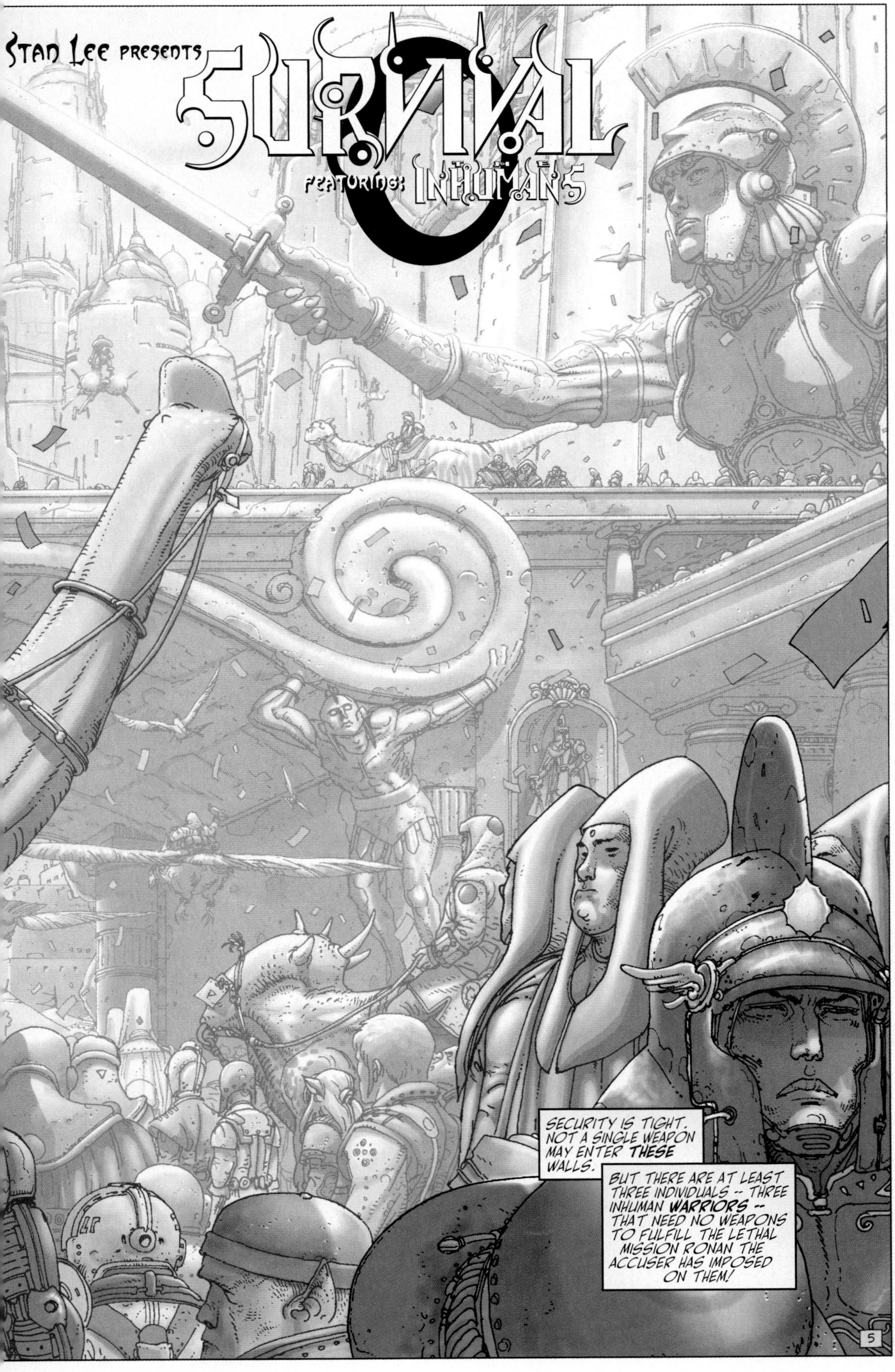
STAN LEE PRESENTS
SURVIVAL
FEATURING: THE INHUMANS
SECURITY IS TIGHT. NOT A SINGLE WEAPON MAY ENTER THESE WALLS.
BUT THERE ARE AT LEAST THREE INDIVIDUALS -- THREE INHUMAN WARRIORS -- THAT NEED NO WEAPONS TO FULFILL THE LETHAL MISSION RONAN THE ACCUSER HAS IMPOSED ON THEM!

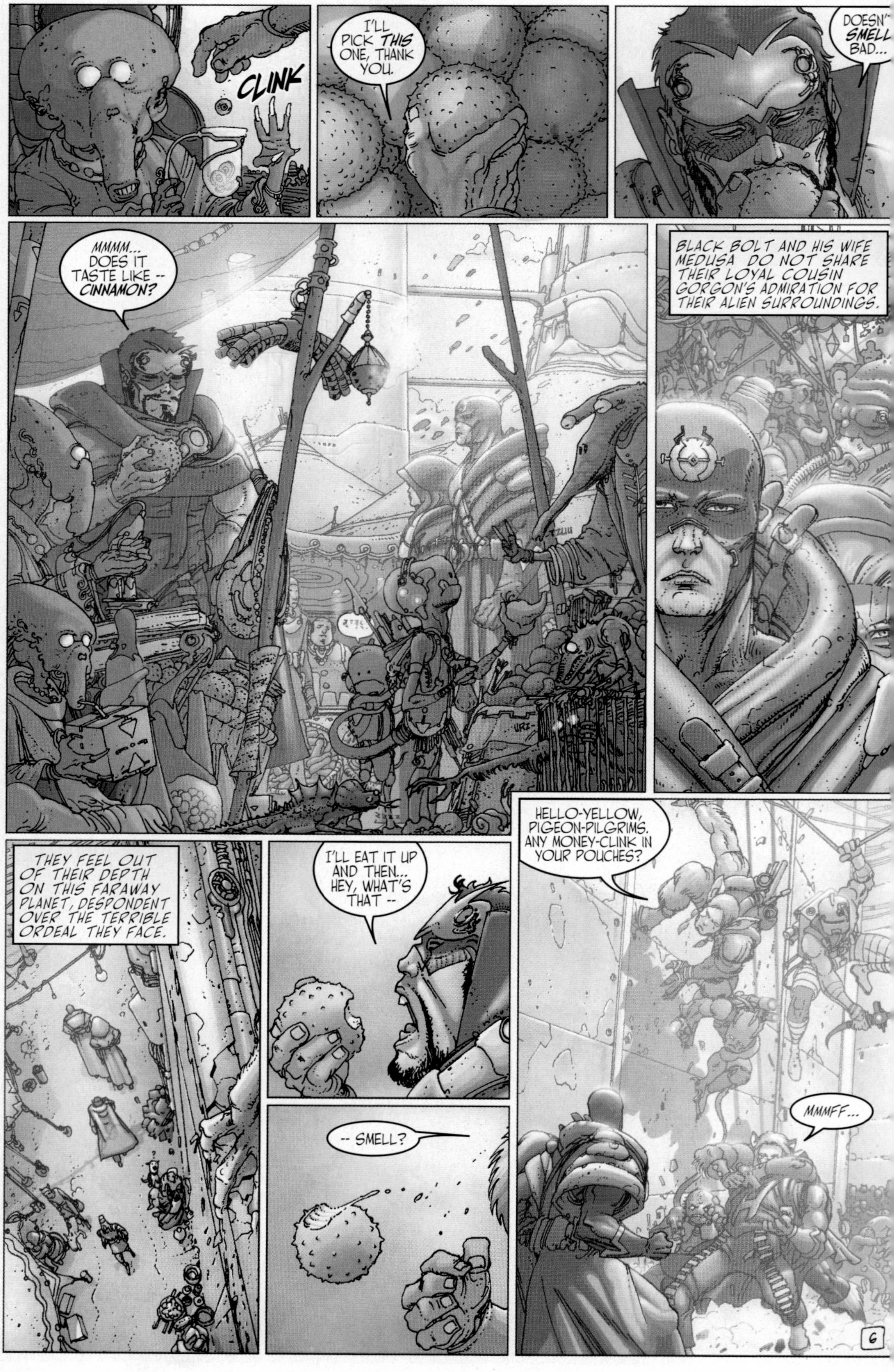
CLINK
I'LL PICK THIS ONE, THANK YOU.
DOESN'T SMELL BAD...
MMMM... DOES IT TASTE LIKE -- CINNAMON?
BLACK BOLT AND HIS WIFE MEDUSA DO NOT SHARE THEIR LOYAL COUSIN GORGON'S ADMIRATION FOR THEIR ALIEN SURROUNDINGS.
THEY FEEL OUT OF THEIR DEPTH ON THIS FARAWAY PLANET, DESPONDENT OVER THE TERRIBLE ORDEAL THEY FACE.
I'LL EAT IT UP AND THEN... HEY, WHAT'S THAT --
-- SMELL?
HELLO-YELLOW, PIGEON-PILGRIMS. ANY MONEY-CLINK IN YOUR POUCHES?
MMMFF...

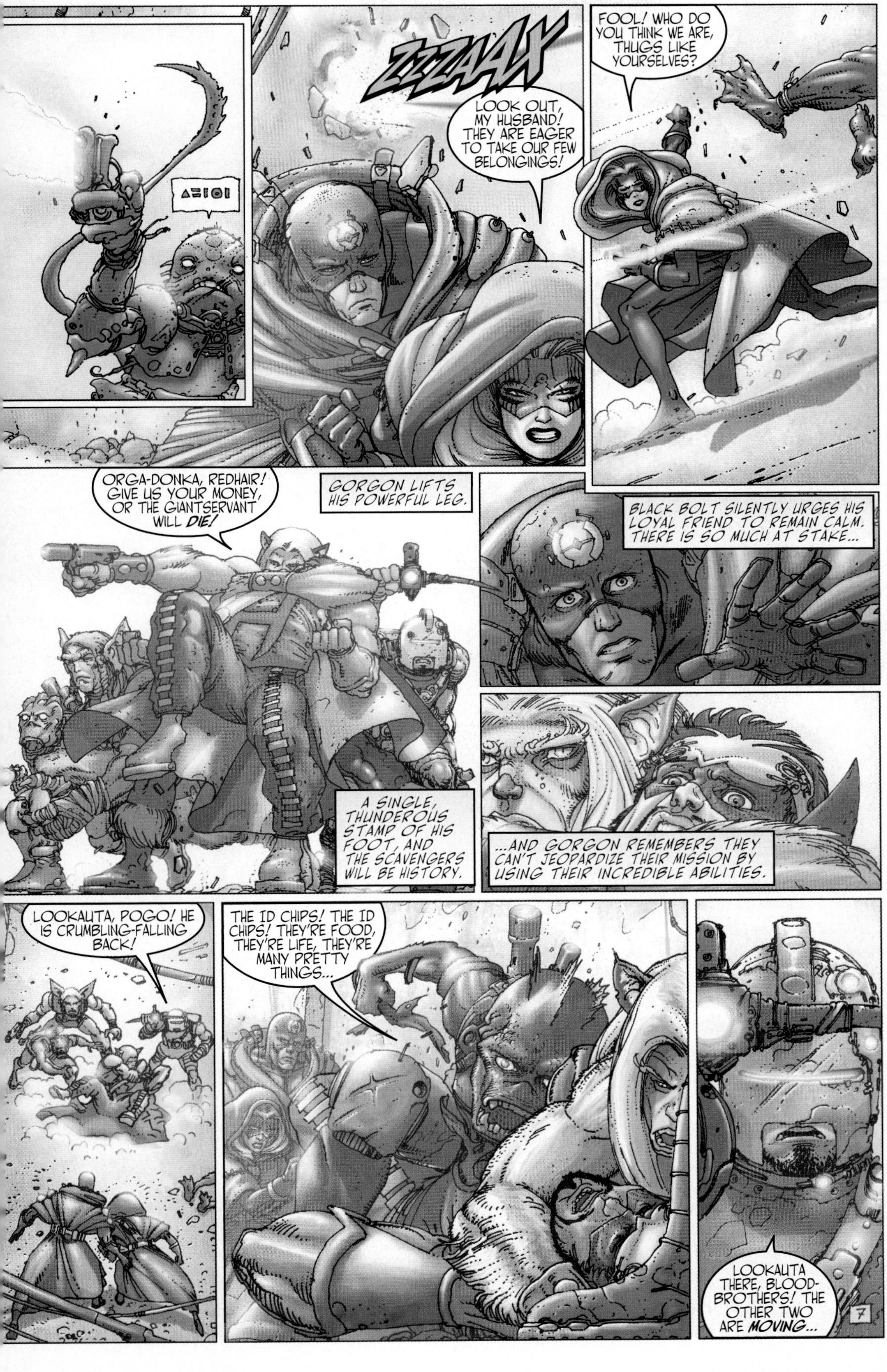
ZZZAAAX
LOOK OUT, MY HUSBAND! THEY ARE EAGER TO TAKE OUR FEW BELONGINGS!
FOOL! WHO DO YOU THINK WE ARE, THUGS LIKE YOURSELVES?
ORGA-DONKA, REDHAIR! GIVE US YOUR MONEY, OR THE GIANTSERVANT WILL DIE!
GORGON LIFTS HIS POWERFUL LEG.
A SINGLE, THUNDEROUS STAMP OF HIS FOOT, AND THE SCAVENGERS WILL BE HISTORY.
BLACK BOLT SILENTLY URGES HIS LOYAL FRIEND TO REMAIN CALM. THERE IS SO MUCH AT STAKE...
...AND GORGON REMEMBERS THEY CAN'T JEOPARDIZE THEIR MISSION BY USING THEIR INCREDIBLE ABILITIES.
LOOKAUTA, POGO! HE IS CRUMBLING-FALLING BACK!
THE ID CHIPS! THE ID CHIPS! THEY'RE FOOD, THEY'RE LIFE, THEY'RE MANY PRETTY THINGS...
LOOKAUTA THERE, BLOOD-BROTHERS! THE OTHER TWO ARE MOVING...
7

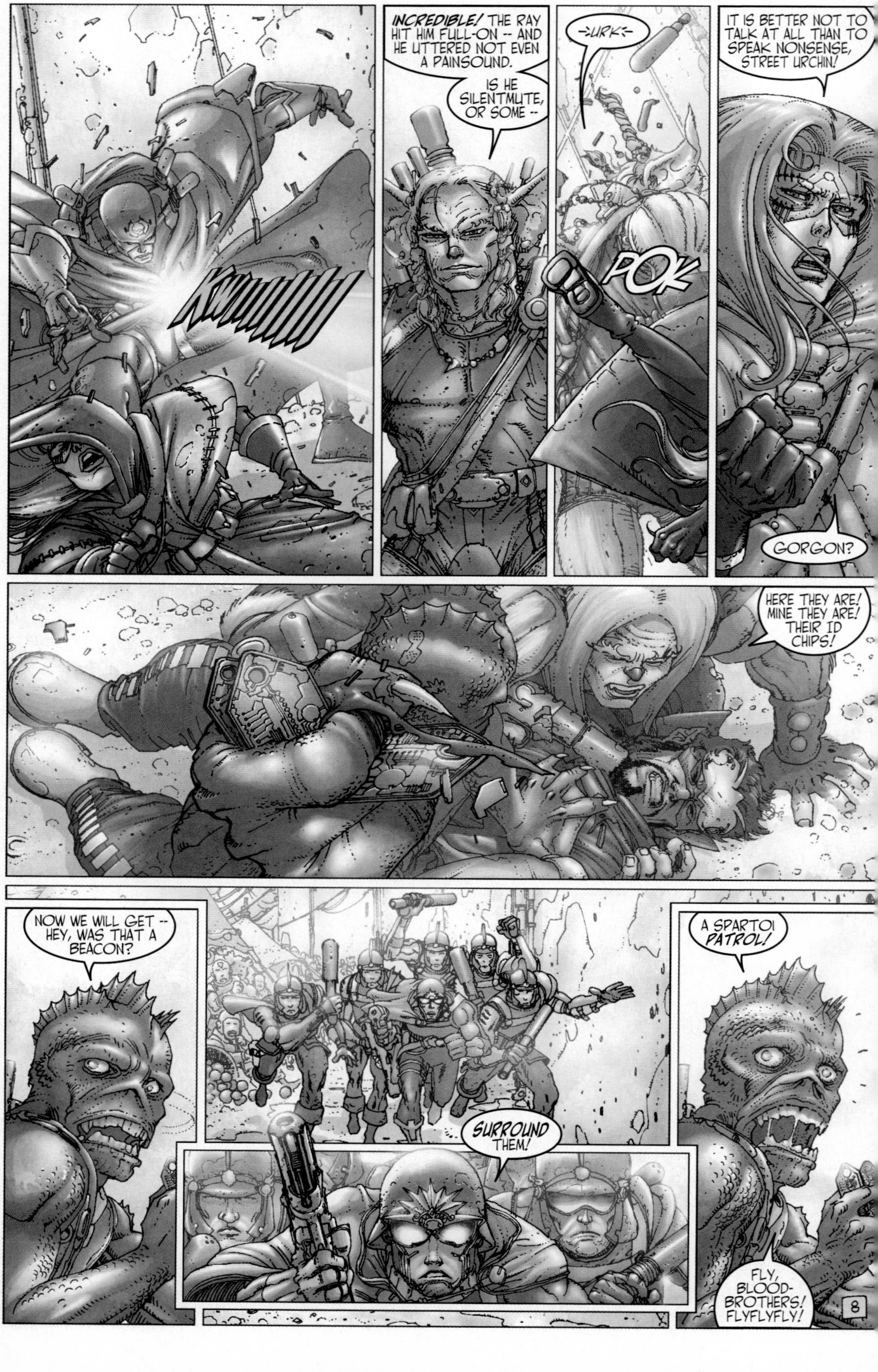

KWUUUUUU
INCREDIBLE! THE RAY HIT HIM FULL-ON -- AND HE UTTERED NOT EVEN A PAINSOUND.
IS HE SILENTMUTE, OR SOME --
-URK-
POK
IT IS BETTER NOT TO TALK AT ALL THAN TO SPEAK NONSENSE, STREET URCHIN!
GORGON?
HERE THEY ARE! MINE THEY ARE! THEIR ID CHIPS!
NOW WE WILL GET -- HEY, WAS THAT A BEACON?
SURROUND THEM!
A SPARTOI PATROL!
FLY, BLOOD-BROTHERS! FLYFLYFLYFLY!

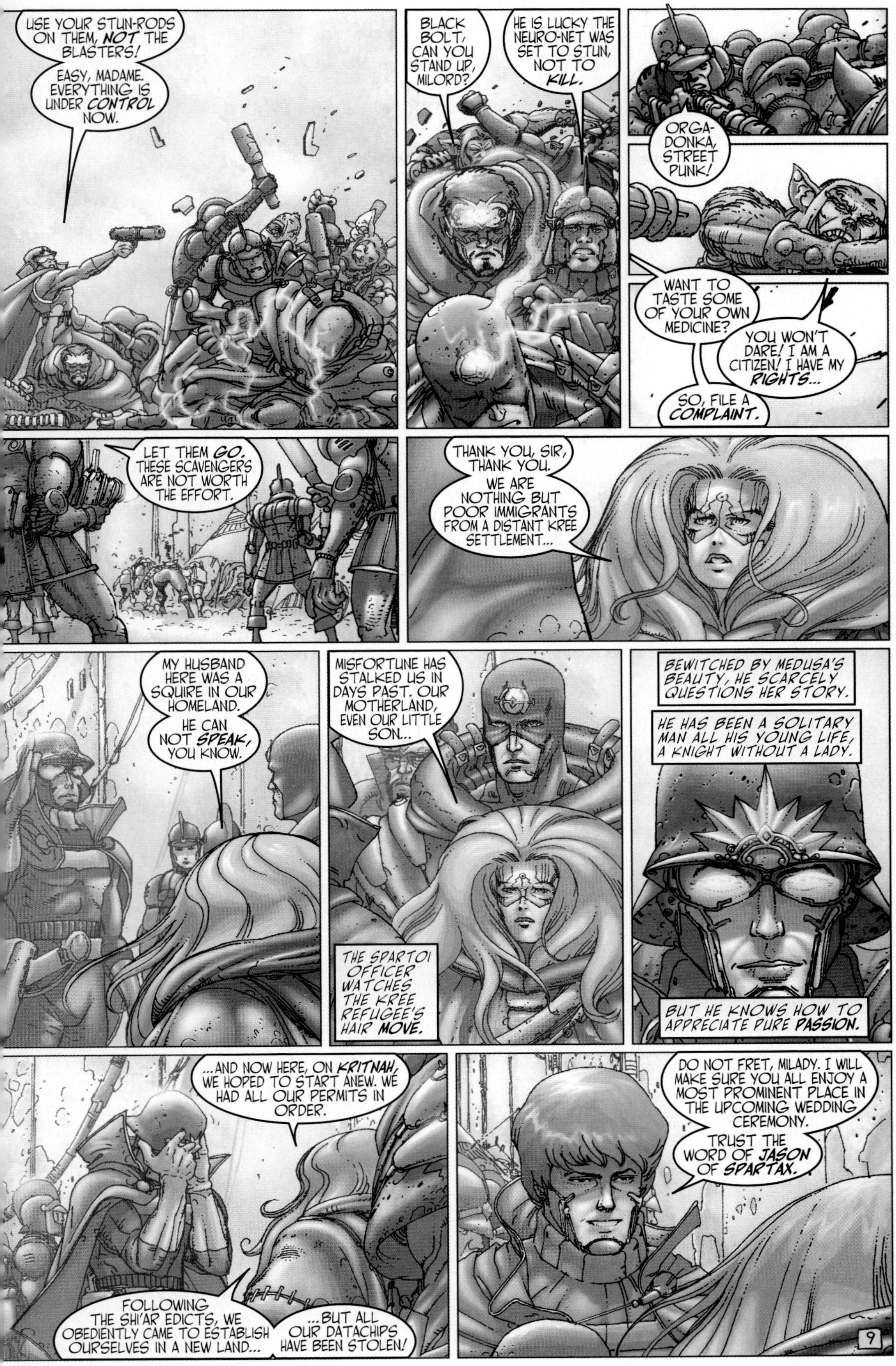
USE YOUR STUN-RODS ON THEM, *NOT* THE BLASTERS!
EASY, MADAME. EVERYTHING IS UNDER *CONTROL* NOW.
BLACK BOLT, CAN YOU STAND UP, MILORD?
HE IS LUCKY THE NEURO-NET WAS SET TO STUN, NOT TO *KILL.*
ORGA-DONKA, STREET PUNK!
WANT TO TASTE SOME OF YOUR OWN MEDICINE?
YOU WON'T DARE! I AM A CITIZEN! I HAVE MY *RIGHTS...*
SO, FILE A *COMPLAINT.*
LET THEM *GO.* THESE SCAVENGERS ARE NOT WORTH THE EFFORT.
THANK YOU, SIR, THANK YOU.
WE ARE NOTHING BUT POOR IMMIGRANTS FROM A DISTANT KREE SETTLEMENT...
MY HUSBAND HERE WAS A SQUIRE IN OUR HOMELAND.
HE CAN NOT *SPEAK,* YOU KNOW.
MISFORTUNE HAS STALKED US IN DAYS PAST. OUR MOTHERLAND, EVEN OUR LITTLE SON...
THE SPARTOI OFFICER WATCHES THE KREE REFUGEE'S HAIR *MOVE.*
BEWITCHED BY MEDUSA'S BEAUTY, HE SCARCELY QUESTIONS HER STORY.
HE HAS BEEN A SOLITARY MAN ALL HIS YOUNG LIFE, A KNIGHT WITHOUT A LADY.
BUT HE KNOWS HOW TO APPRECIATE PURE *PASSION.*
...AND NOW HERE, ON *KRITNAH,* WE HOPED TO START ANEW. WE HAD ALL OUR PERMITS IN ORDER.
FOLLOWING THE SHI'AR EDICTS, WE OBEDIENTLY CAME TO ESTABLISH OURSELVES IN A NEW LAND...
...BUT ALL OUR DATACHIPS HAVE BEEN STOLEN!
DO NOT FRET, MILADY. I WILL MAKE SURE YOU ALL ENJOY A MOST PROMINENT PLACE IN THE UPCOMING WEDDING CEREMONY.
TRUST THE WORD OF *JASON* OF *SPARTAX.*

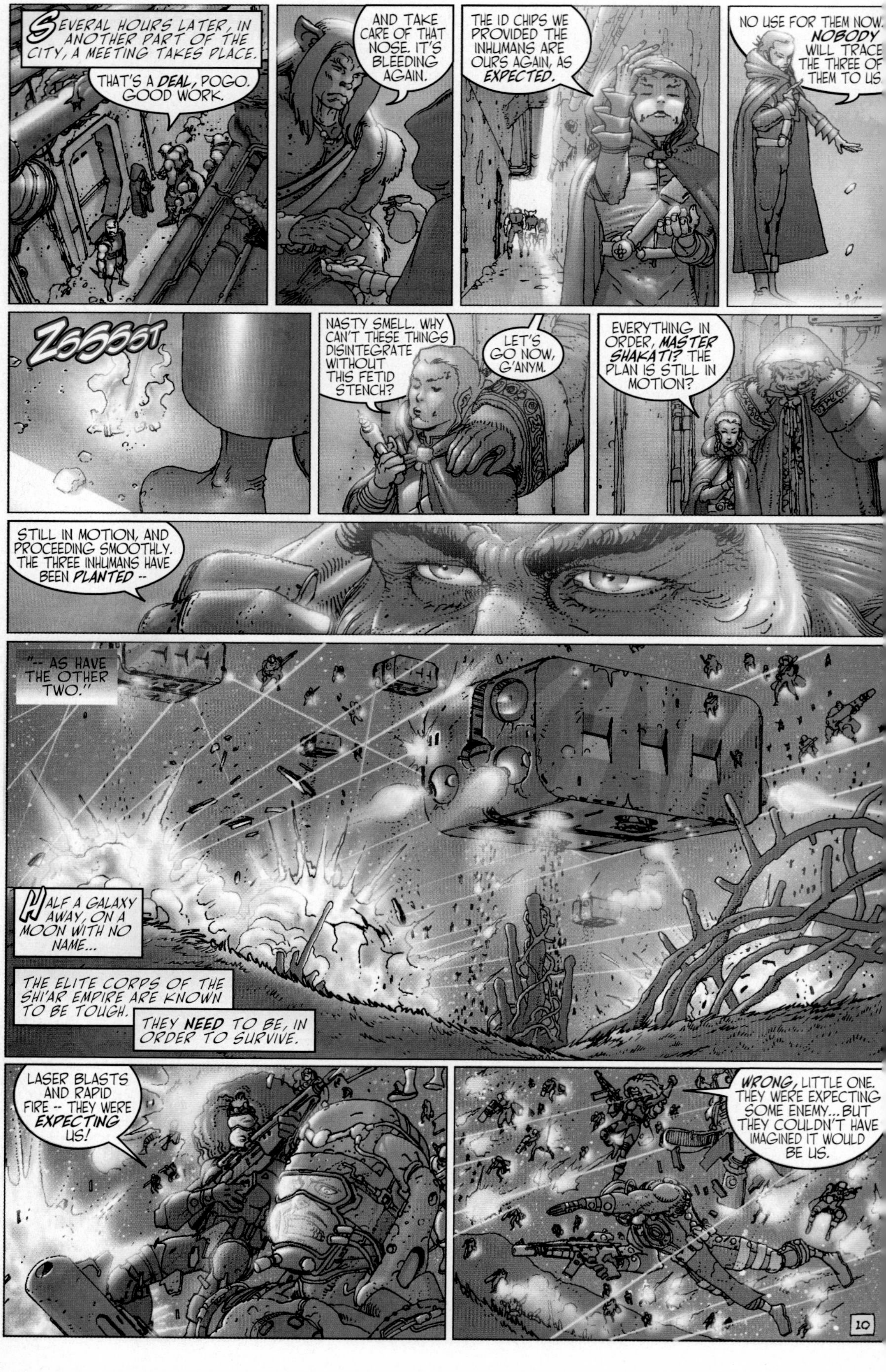

SEVERAL HOURS LATER, IN ANOTHER PART OF THE CITY, A MEETING TAKES PLACE.
THAT'S A DEAL, POGO. GOOD WORK.
AND TAKE CARE OF THAT NOSE. IT'S BLEEDING AGAIN.
THE ID CHIPS WE PROVIDED THE INHUMANS ARE OURS AGAIN, AS EXPECTED.
NO USE FOR THEM NOW. NOBODY WILL TRACE THE THREE OF THEM TO US.
ZSSSST
NASTY SMELL. WHY CAN'T THESE THINGS DISINTEGRATE WITHOUT THIS FETID STENCH?
LET'S GO NOW, G'ANYM.
EVERYTHING IN ORDER, MASTER SHAKATI? THE PLAN IS STILL IN MOTION?
STILL IN MOTION, AND PROCEEDING SMOOTHLY. THE THREE INHUMANS HAVE BEEN PLANTED --
"-- AS HAVE THE OTHER TWO."
HALF A GALAXY AWAY, ON A MOON WITH NO NAME...
THE ELITE CORPS OF THE SHI'AR EMPIRE ARE KNOWN TO BE TOUGH.
THEY NEED TO BE, IN ORDER TO SURVIVE.
LASER BLASTS AND RAPID FIRE -- THEY WERE EXPECTING US!
WRONG, LITTLE ONE. THEY WERE EXPECTING SOME ENEMY... BUT THEY COULDN'T HAVE IMAGINED IT WOULD BE US.

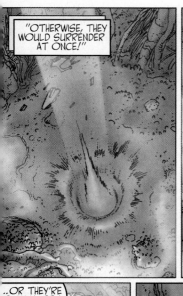

"OTHERWISE, THEY WOULD SURRENDER AT ONCE!"

THE WARRIOR WOMAN'S NAME IS **DELPHOS.** HER COMRADE IS **KARNAK,** MEMBER OF THE **INHUMAN** ROYAL FAMILY.

AS IS THE CASE WITH **BLACK BOLT** AND HIS COMPANIONS, KARNAK IS WORKING **UNDERCOVER,** FORCED TO BE PART OF AN INVASION FOR LOVE OF HIS IMPRISONED PEOPLE.

THEY'VE CEASED FIRE, LITTLE ONE! EITHER WE FELL TOO FAR AWAY FROM THE CENTER OF THE BATTLE...

..OR THEY'RE GONNA **FRY** US IN AN **AMBUSH!**

LOOK! IN THE MIDDLE OF THOSE MUDDY WATERS -- THE **AMPHIBIAN!**

WHERE IS THE **REST** OF THE PLATOON?

WHAT'S HAPPENING TO THE FISH-MAN? WHY DOESN'T HE SWIM ASHORE? HAVE THEY **HIT** HIM?

NO. BUT KNOWING HIS WEAK POINTS AS NO OTHER BEING ALIVE, I WOULD GUESS THE SWAMP IS **POISONED.**

HIS BEING AN AMPHIBIAN IS NOW NOT AN ADVANTAGE, BUT A **LIABILITY.**

HOLD ON -- WE'LL TRY TO RESCUE YOU!

?

FOR A MOMENT, DELPHOS HESITATES. SHE IS USED TO WITNESSING HER COMRADES FALL IN BATTLE, AND HAS NEVER SHED A TEAR FOR THEM.

WAR HAS MADE HER CALLOUS.

HOW COULD SHE KNOW THE AMPHIBIAN IS **TRITON,** KARNAK'S OWN BROTHER?

LIKE THE REST OF HIS TRIBE, TRITON IS A WARRIOR WHOSE SKILLS HAVE BEEN AWAKENED BY THE **TERRIGEN MIST**...

...TO ALLOW HIM TO THRIVE IN HOSTILE ENVIRONMENTS AND CONDITIONS WHERE OTHERS COULD NOT SURVIVE.

BUT ALAS, NOT IN THIS PARTICULAR ENVIRONMENT.

BUDDA BUDDA BUDDA

WE'RE UNDER **ATTACK!**

11

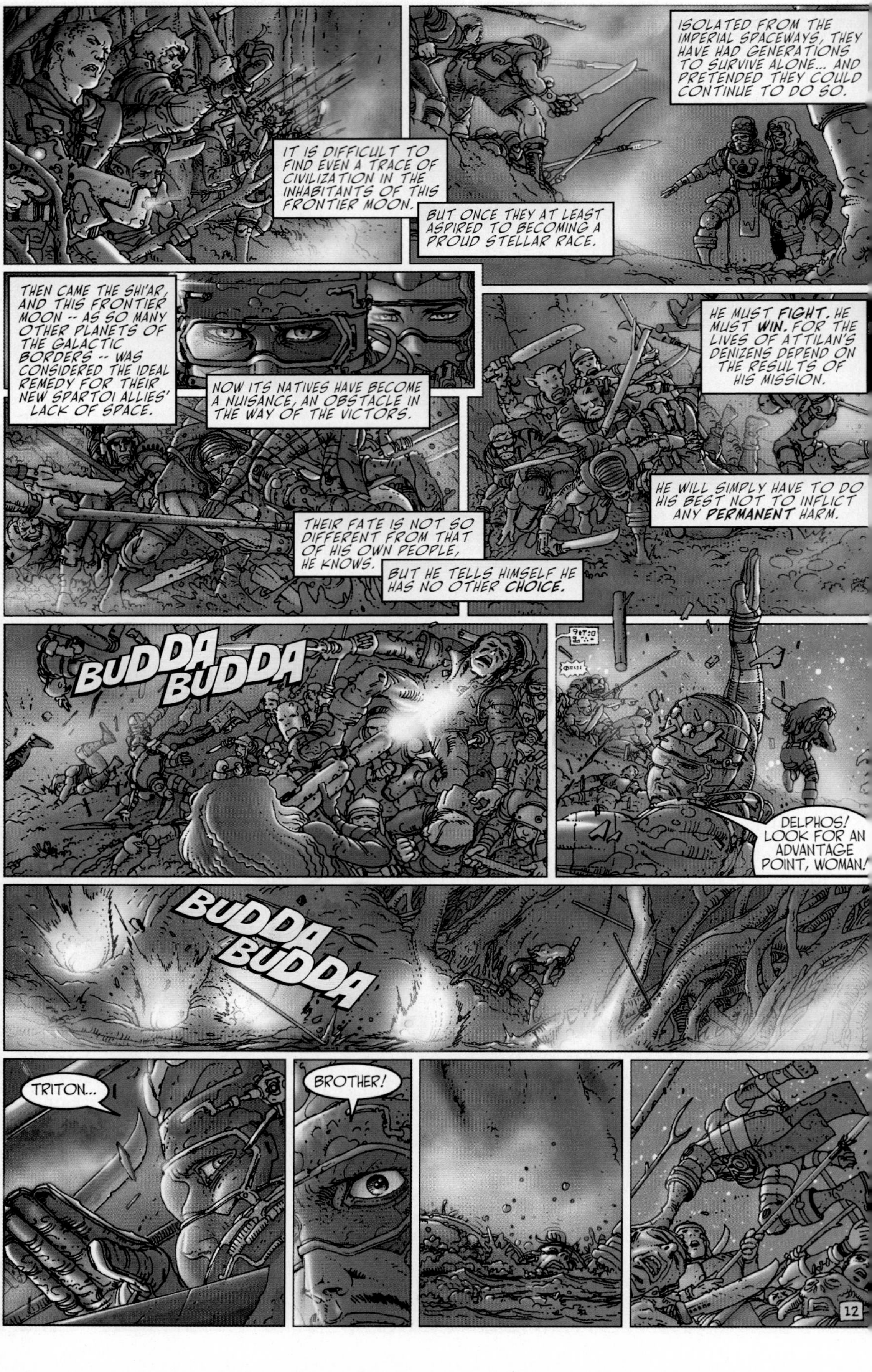
IT IS DIFFICULT TO FIND EVEN A TRACE OF CIVILIZATION IN THE INHABITANTS OF THIS FRONTIER MOON.
BUT ONCE THEY AT LEAST ASPIRED TO BECOMING A PROUD STELLAR RACE.
ISOLATED FROM THE IMPERIAL SPACEWAYS, THEY HAVE HAD GENERATIONS TO SURVIVE ALONE... AND PRETENDED THEY COULD CONTINUE TO DO SO.
THEN CAME THE SHI'AR, AND THIS FRONTIER MOON -- AS SO MANY OTHER PLANETS OF THE GALACTIC BORDERS -- WAS CONSIDERED THE IDEAL REMEDY FOR THEIR NEW SPARTOI ALLIES' LACK OF SPACE.
NOW ITS NATIVES HAVE BECOME A NUISANCE, AN OBSTACLE IN THE WAY OF THE VICTORS.
THEIR FATE IS NOT SO DIFFERENT FROM THAT OF HIS OWN PEOPLE, HE KNOWS.
BUT HE TELLS HIMSELF HE HAS NO OTHER CHOICE.
HE MUST FIGHT. HE MUST WIN. FOR THE LIVES OF ATTILAN'S DENIZENS DEPEND ON THE RESULTS OF HIS MISSION.
HE WILL SIMPLY HAVE TO DO HIS BEST NOT TO INFLICT ANY PERMANENT HARM.
BUDDA BUDDA
DELPHOS! LOOK FOR AN ADVANTAGE POINT, WOMAN!
BUDDA BUDDA
TRITON...
BROTHER!

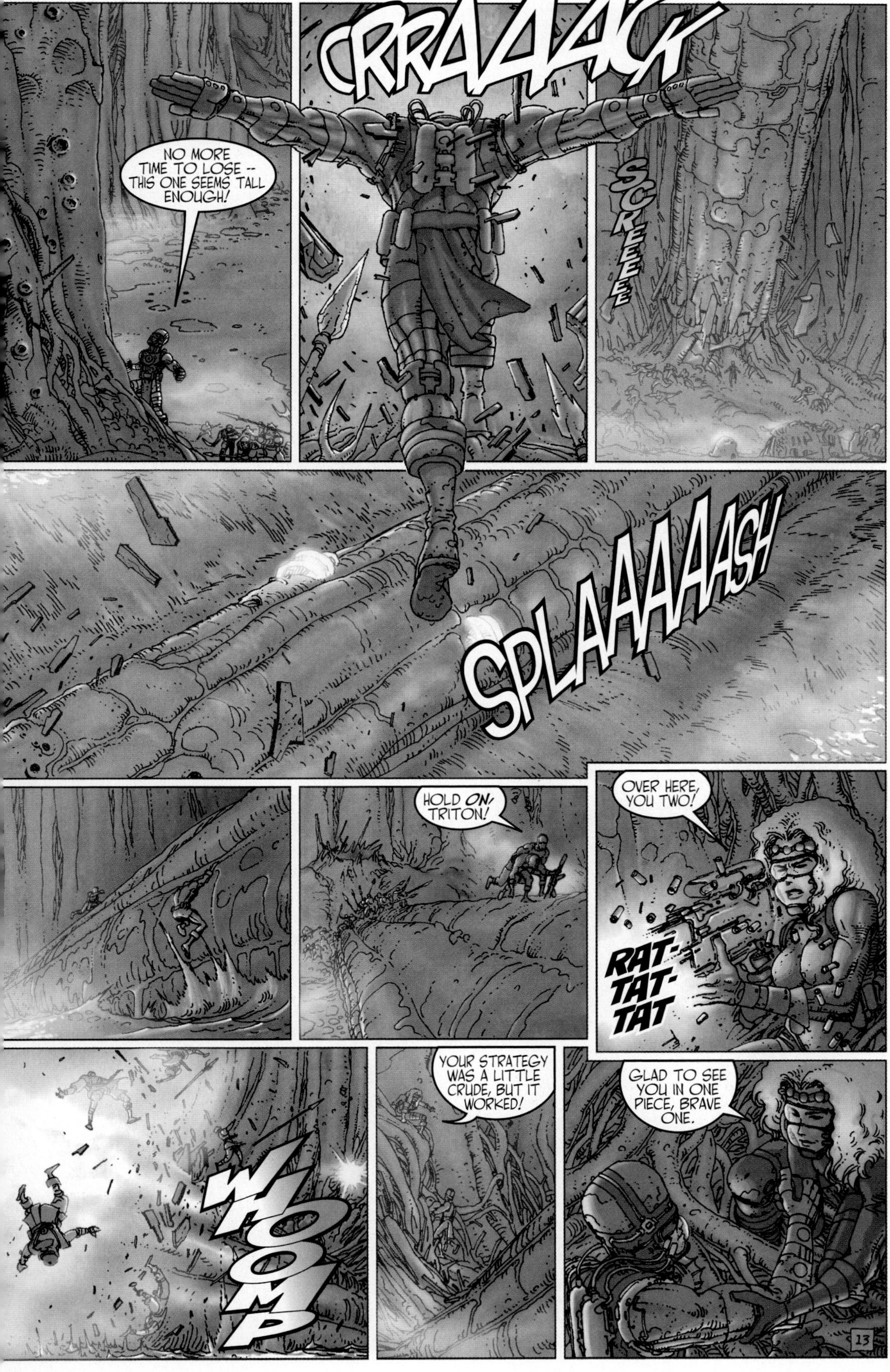
NO MORE TIME TO LOSE -- THIS ONE SEEMS TALL ENOUGH!
CRRAAACK
SCREEEE
SPLAAAAASH
HOLD ON, TRITON!
OVER HERE, YOU TWO!
RAT-TAT-TAT
WHOOMP
YOUR STRATEGY WAS A LITTLE CRUDE, BUT IT WORKED!
GLAD TO SEE YOU IN ONE PIECE, BRAVE ONE.
13

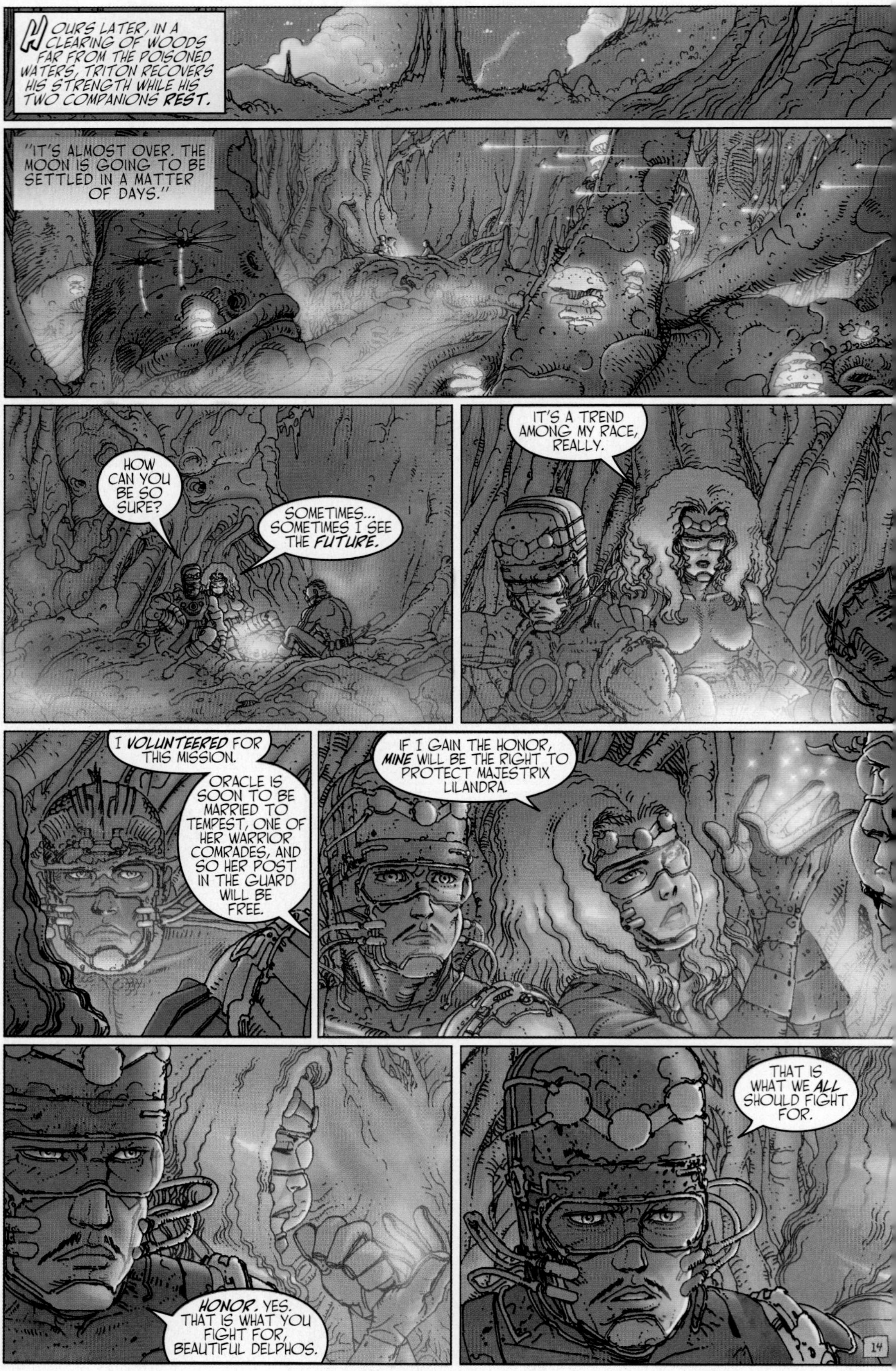
HOURS LATER, IN A CLEARING OF WOODS FAR FROM THE POISONED WATERS, TRITON RECOVERS HIS STRENGTH WHILE HIS TWO COMPANIONS REST.
"IT'S ALMOST OVER. THE MOON IS GOING TO BE SETTLED IN A MATTER OF DAYS."
HOW CAN YOU BE SO SURE?
SOMETIMES... SOMETIMES I SEE THE FUTURE.
IT'S A TREND AMONG MY RACE, REALLY.
I VOLUNTEERED FOR THIS MISSION.
ORACLE IS SOON TO BE MARRIED TO TEMPEST, ONE OF HER WARRIOR COMRADES, AND SO HER POST IN THE GUARD WILL BE FREE.
IF I GAIN THE HONOR, MINE WILL BE THE RIGHT TO PROTECT MAJESTRIX LILANDRA.
HONOR. YES. THAT IS WHAT YOU FIGHT FOR, BEAUTIFUL DELPHOS.
THAT IS WHAT WE ALL SHOULD FIGHT FOR.

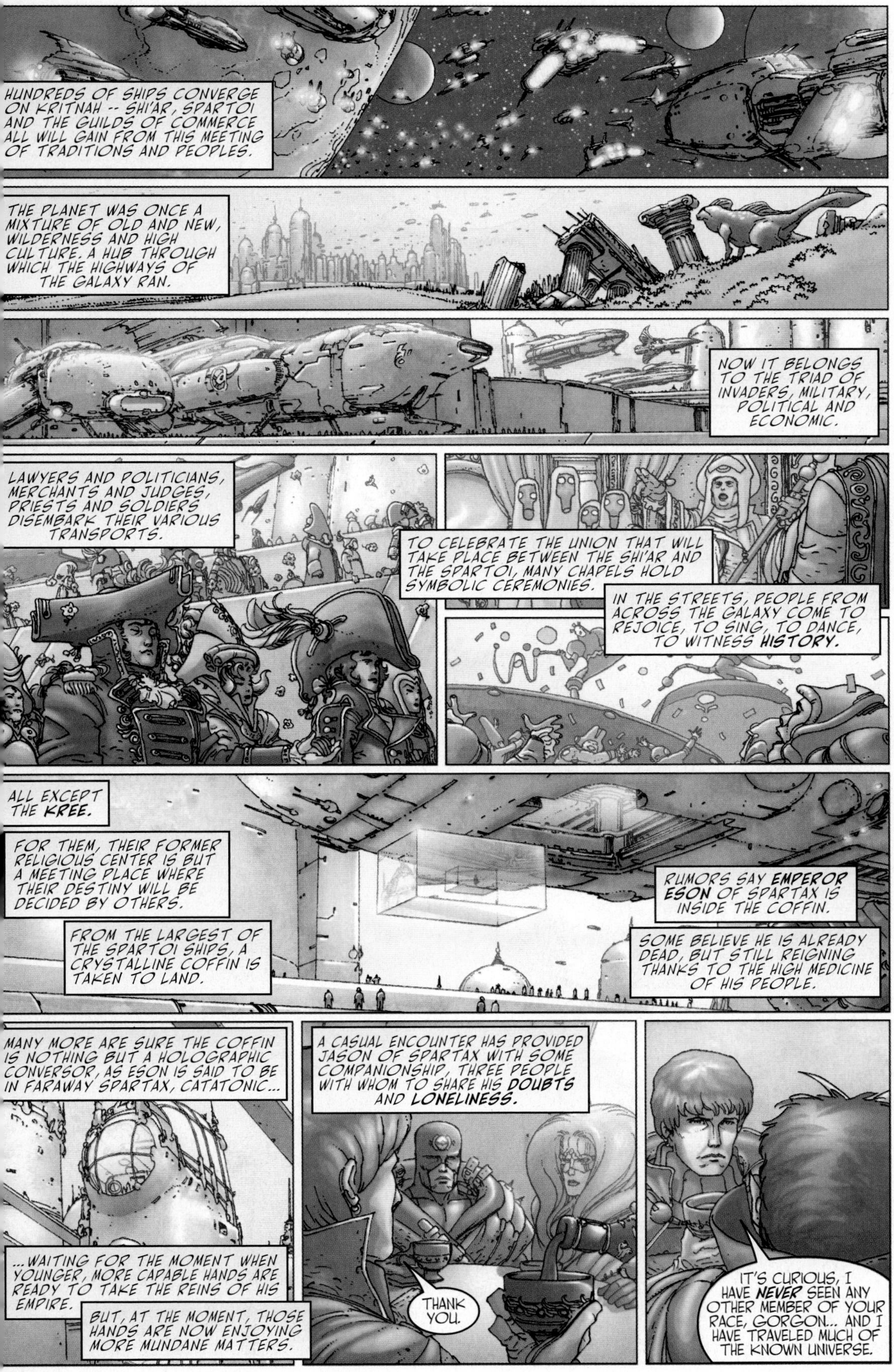
HUNDREDS OF SHIPS CONVERGE ON KRITNAH -- SHI'AR, SPARTOI AND THE GUILDS OF COMMERCE ALL WILL GAIN FROM THIS MEETING OF TRADITIONS AND PEOPLES.
THE PLANET WAS ONCE A MIXTURE OF OLD AND NEW, WILDERNESS AND HIGH CULTURE. A HUB THROUGH WHICH THE HIGHWAYS OF THE GALAXY RAN.
NOW IT BELONGS TO THE TRIAD OF INVADERS, MILITARY, POLITICAL AND ECONOMIC.
LAWYERS AND POLITICIANS, MERCHANTS AND JUDGES, PRIESTS AND SOLDIERS DISEMBARK THEIR VARIOUS TRANSPORTS.
TO CELEBRATE THE UNION THAT WILL TAKE PLACE BETWEEN THE SHI'AR AND THE SPARTOI, MANY CHAPELS HOLD SYMBOLIC CEREMONIES.
IN THE STREETS, PEOPLE FROM ACROSS THE GALAXY COME TO REJOICE, TO SING, TO DANCE, TO WITNESS **HISTORY.**
ALL EXCEPT THE **KREE.**
FOR THEM, THEIR FORMER RELIGIOUS CENTER IS BUT A MEETING PLACE WHERE THEIR DESTINY WILL BE DECIDED BY OTHERS.
FROM THE LARGEST OF THE SPARTOI SHIPS, A CRYSTALLINE COFFIN IS TAKEN TO LAND.
RUMORS SAY **EMPEROR ESON** OF SPARTAX IS INSIDE THE COFFIN.
SOME BELIEVE HE IS ALREADY DEAD, BUT STILL REIGNING THANKS TO THE HIGH MEDICINE OF HIS PEOPLE.
MANY MORE ARE SURE THE COFFIN IS NOTHING BUT A HOLOGRAPHIC CONVERSOR, AS ESON IS SAID TO BE IN FARAWAY SPARTAX, CATATONIC...
...WAITING FOR THE MOMENT WHEN YOUNGER, MORE CAPABLE HANDS ARE READY TO TAKE THE REINS OF HIS EMPIRE.
BUT, AT THE MOMENT, THOSE HANDS ARE NOW ENJOYING MORE MUNDANE MATTERS.
A CASUAL ENCOUNTER HAS PROVIDED JASON OF SPARTAX WITH SOME COMPANIONSHIP, THREE PEOPLE WITH WHOM TO SHARE HIS **DOUBTS** AND **LONELINESS.**
THANK YOU.
IT'S CURIOUS, I HAVE **NEVER** SEEN ANY OTHER MEMBER OF YOUR RACE, GORGON... AND I HAVE TRAVELED MUCH OF THE KNOWN UNIVERSE.

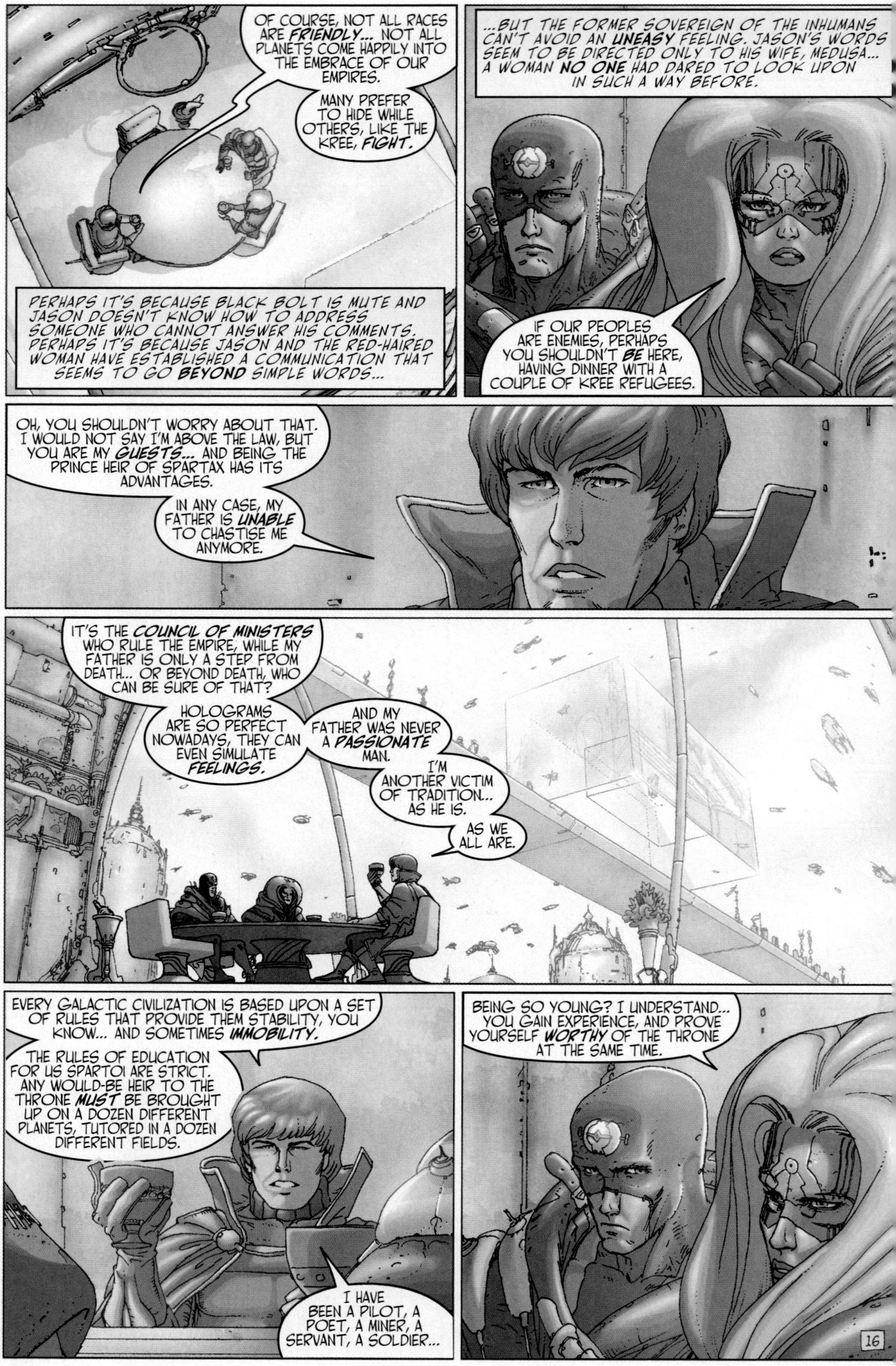

OF COURSE, NOT ALL RACES ARE FRIENDLY... NOT ALL PLANETS COME HAPPILY INTO THE EMBRACE OF OUR EMPIRES.
MANY PREFER TO HIDE WHILE OTHERS, LIKE THE KREE, FIGHT.
PERHAPS IT'S BECAUSE BLACK BOLT IS MUTE AND JASON DOESN'T KNOW HOW TO ADDRESS SOMEONE WHO CANNOT ANSWER HIS COMMENTS. PERHAPS IT'S BECAUSE JASON AND THE RED-HAIRED WOMAN HAVE ESTABLISHED A COMMUNICATION THAT SEEMS TO GO BEYOND SIMPLE WORDS...
...BUT THE FORMER SOVEREIGN OF THE INHUMANS CAN'T AVOID AN UNEASY FEELING. JASON'S WORDS SEEM TO BE DIRECTED ONLY TO HIS WIFE, MEDUSA... A WOMAN NO ONE HAD DARED TO LOOK UPON IN SUCH A WAY BEFORE.
IF OUR PEOPLES ARE ENEMIES, PERHAPS YOU SHOULDN'T BE HERE, HAVING DINNER WITH A COUPLE OF KREE REFUGEES.
OH, YOU SHOULDN'T WORRY ABOUT THAT. I WOULD NOT SAY I'M ABOVE THE LAW, BUT YOU ARE MY GUESTS... AND BEING THE PRINCE HEIR OF SPARTAX HAS ITS ADVANTAGES.
IN ANY CASE, MY FATHER IS UNABLE TO CHASTISE ME ANYMORE.
IT'S THE COUNCIL OF MINISTERS WHO RULE THE EMPIRE, WHILE MY FATHER IS ONLY A STEP FROM DEATH... OR BEYOND DEATH, WHO CAN BE SURE OF THAT?
HOLOGRAMS ARE SO PERFECT NOWADAYS, THEY CAN EVEN SIMULATE FEELINGS.
AND MY FATHER WAS NEVER A PASSIONATE MAN.
I'M ANOTHER VICTIM OF TRADITION... AS HE IS.
AS WE ALL ARE.
EVERY GALACTIC CIVILIZATION IS BASED UPON A SET OF RULES THAT PROVIDE THEM STABILITY, YOU KNOW... AND SOMETIMES IMMOBILITY.
THE RULES OF EDUCATION FOR US SPARTOI ARE STRICT. ANY WOULD-BE HEIR TO THE THRONE MUST BE BROUGHT UP ON A DOZEN DIFFERENT PLANETS, TUTORED IN A DOZEN DIFFERENT FIELDS.
I HAVE BEEN A PILOT, A POET, A MINER, A SERVANT, A SOLDIER...
BEING SO YOUNG? I UNDERSTAND... YOU GAIN EXPERIENCE, AND PROVE YOURSELF WORTHY OF THE THRONE AT THE SAME TIME.

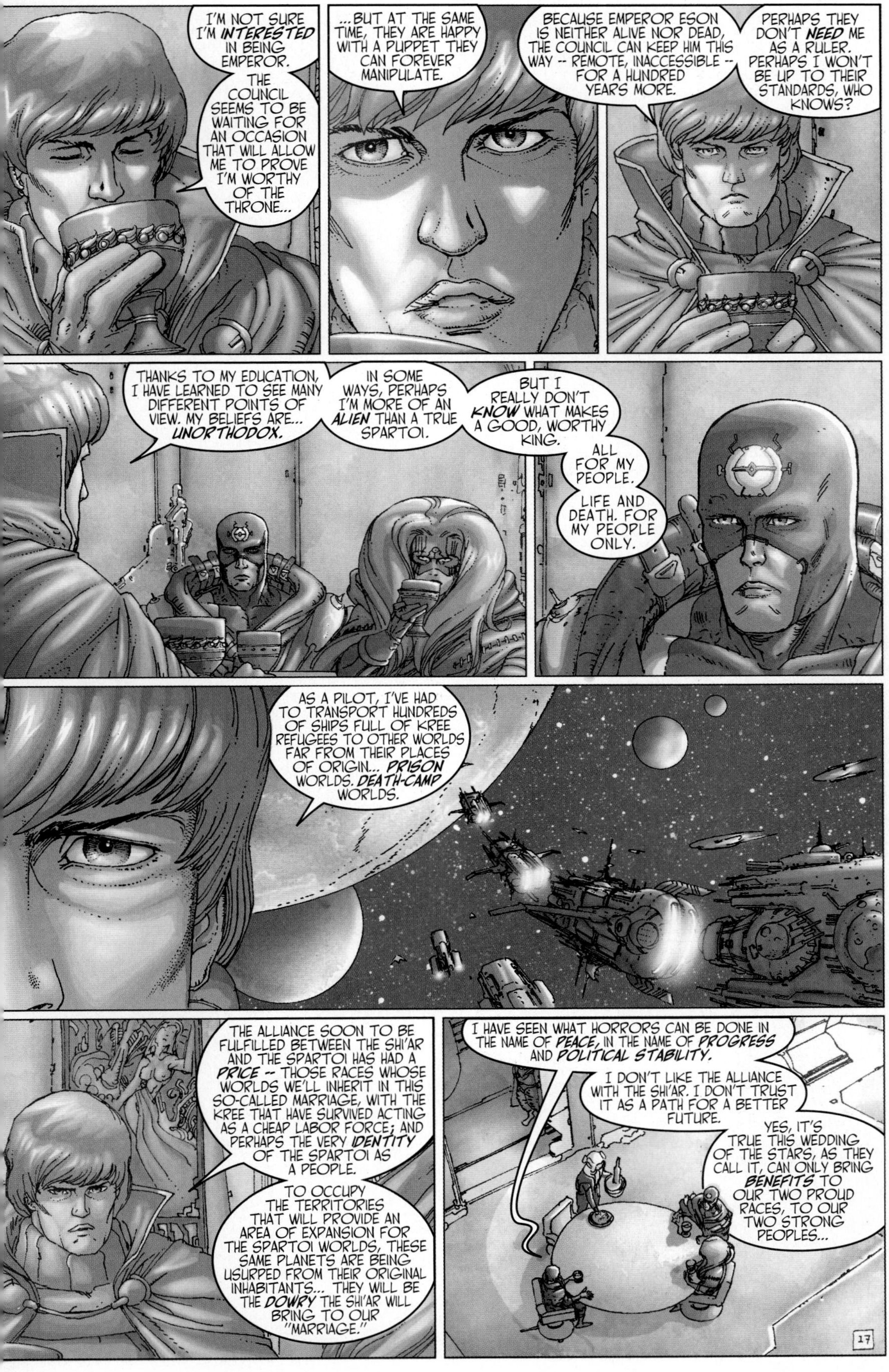
I'M NOT SURE I'M INTERESTED IN BEING EMPEROR.
THE COUNCIL SEEMS TO BE WAITING FOR AN OCCASION THAT WILL ALLOW ME TO PROVE I'M WORTHY OF THE THRONE...
...BUT AT THE SAME TIME, THEY ARE HAPPY WITH A PUPPET THEY CAN FOREVER MANIPULATE.
BECAUSE EMPEROR ESON IS NEITHER ALIVE NOR DEAD, THE COUNCIL CAN KEEP HIM THIS WAY -- REMOTE, INACCESSIBLE -- FOR A HUNDRED YEARS MORE.
PERHAPS THEY DON'T NEED ME AS A RULER. PERHAPS I WON'T BE UP TO THEIR STANDARDS, WHO KNOWS?
THANKS TO MY EDUCATION, I HAVE LEARNED TO SEE MANY DIFFERENT POINTS OF VIEW. MY BELIEFS ARE... UNORTHODOX.
IN SOME WAYS, PERHAPS I'M MORE OF AN ALIEN THAN A TRUE SPARTOI.
BUT I REALLY DON'T KNOW WHAT MAKES A GOOD, WORTHY KING.
ALL FOR MY PEOPLE.
LIFE AND DEATH. FOR MY PEOPLE ONLY.
AS A PILOT, I'VE HAD TO TRANSPORT HUNDREDS OF SHIPS FULL OF KREE REFUGEES TO OTHER WORLDS FAR FROM THEIR PLACES OF ORIGIN... PRISON WORLDS. DEATH-CAMP WORLDS.
THE ALLIANCE SOON TO BE FULFILLED BETWEEN THE SHI'AR AND THE SPARTOI HAS HAD A PRICE -- THOSE RACES WHOSE WORLDS WE'LL INHERIT IN THIS SO-CALLED MARRIAGE, WITH THE KREE THAT HAVE SURVIVED ACTING AS A CHEAP LABOR FORCE; AND PERHAPS THE VERY IDENTITY OF THE SPARTOI AS A PEOPLE.
TO OCCUPY THE TERRITORIES THAT WILL PROVIDE AN AREA OF EXPANSION FOR THE SPARTOI WORLDS, THESE SAME PLANETS ARE BEING USURPED FROM THEIR ORIGINAL INHABITANTS... THEY WILL BE THE DOWRY THE SHI'AR WILL BRING TO OUR "MARRIAGE."
I HAVE SEEN WHAT HORRORS CAN BE DONE IN THE NAME OF PEACE, IN THE NAME OF PROGRESS AND POLITICAL STABILITY.
I DON'T LIKE THE ALLIANCE WITH THE SHI'AR. I DON'T TRUST IT AS A PATH FOR A BETTER FUTURE.
YES, IT'S TRUE THIS WEDDING OF THE STARS, AS THEY CALL IT, CAN ONLY BRING BENEFITS TO OUR TWO PROUD RACES, TO OUR TWO STRONG PEOPLES...
17

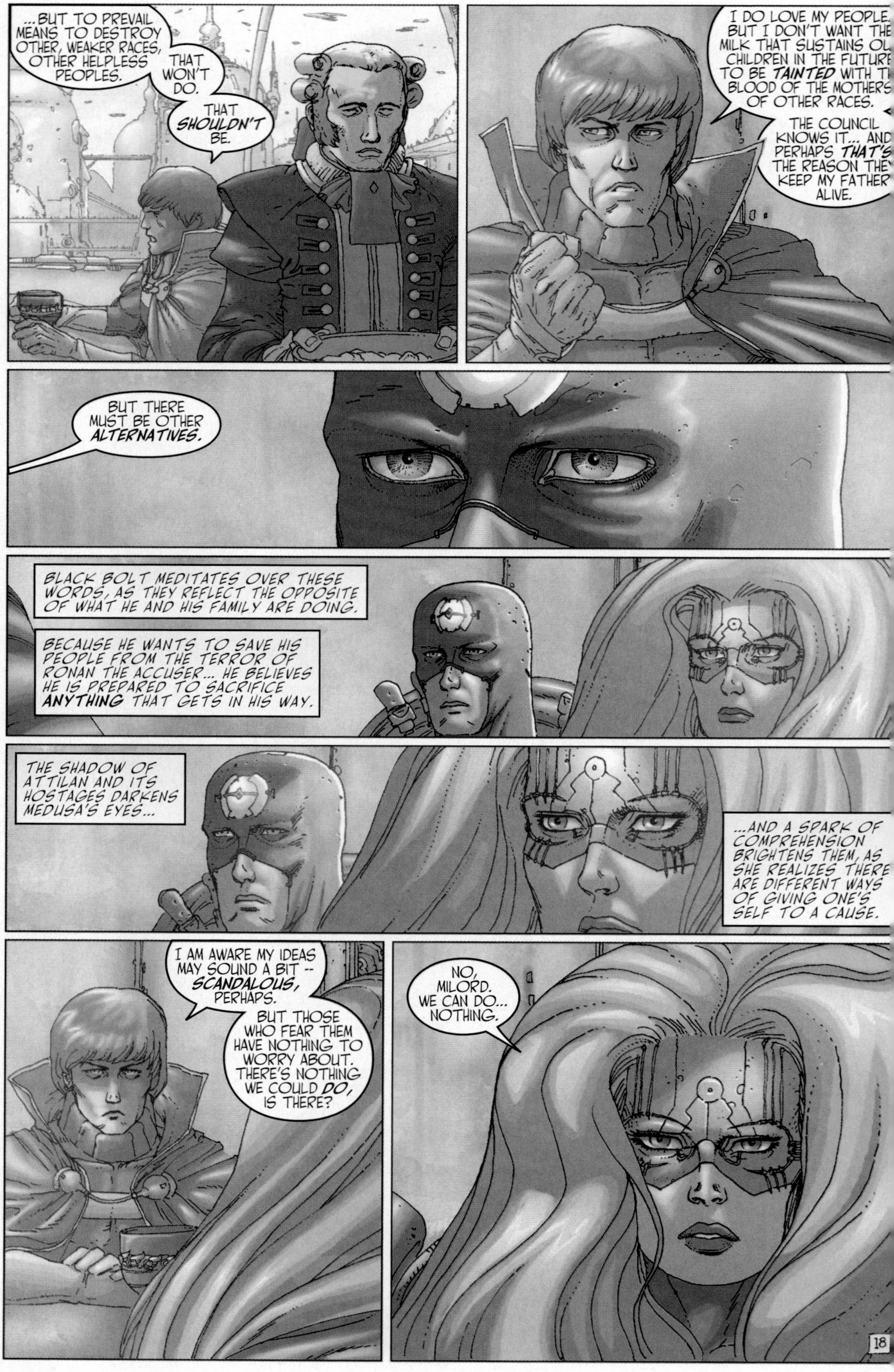

...BUT TO PREVAIL MEANS TO DESTROY OTHER, WEAKER RACES, OTHER HELPLESS PEOPLES.
THAT WON'T DO.
THAT SHOULDN'T BE.
I DO LOVE MY PEOPLE. BUT I DON'T WANT THE MILK THAT SUSTAINS OUR CHILDREN IN THE FUTURE TO BE TAINTED WITH THE BLOOD OF THE MOTHERS OF OTHER RACES.
THE COUNCIL KNOWS IT... AND PERHAPS THAT'S THE REASON THEY KEEP MY FATHER ALIVE.
BUT THERE MUST BE OTHER ALTERNATIVES.
BLACK BOLT MEDITATES OVER THESE WORDS, AS THEY REFLECT THE OPPOSITE OF WHAT HE AND HIS FAMILY ARE DOING.
BECAUSE HE WANTS TO SAVE HIS PEOPLE FROM THE TERROR OF RONAN THE ACCUSER... HE BELIEVES HE IS PREPARED TO SACRIFICE ANYTHING THAT GETS IN HIS WAY.
THE SHADOW OF ATTILAN AND ITS HOSTAGES DARKENS MEDUSA'S EYES...
...AND A SPARK OF COMPREHENSION BRIGHTENS THEM, AS SHE REALIZES THERE ARE DIFFERENT WAYS OF GIVING ONE'S SELF TO A CAUSE.
I AM AWARE MY IDEAS MAY SOUND A BIT -- SCANDALOUS, PERHAPS.
BUT THOSE WHO FEAR THEM HAVE NOTHING TO WORRY ABOUT. THERE'S NOTHING WE COULD DO, IS THERE?
NO, MILORD. WE CAN DO... NOTHING.

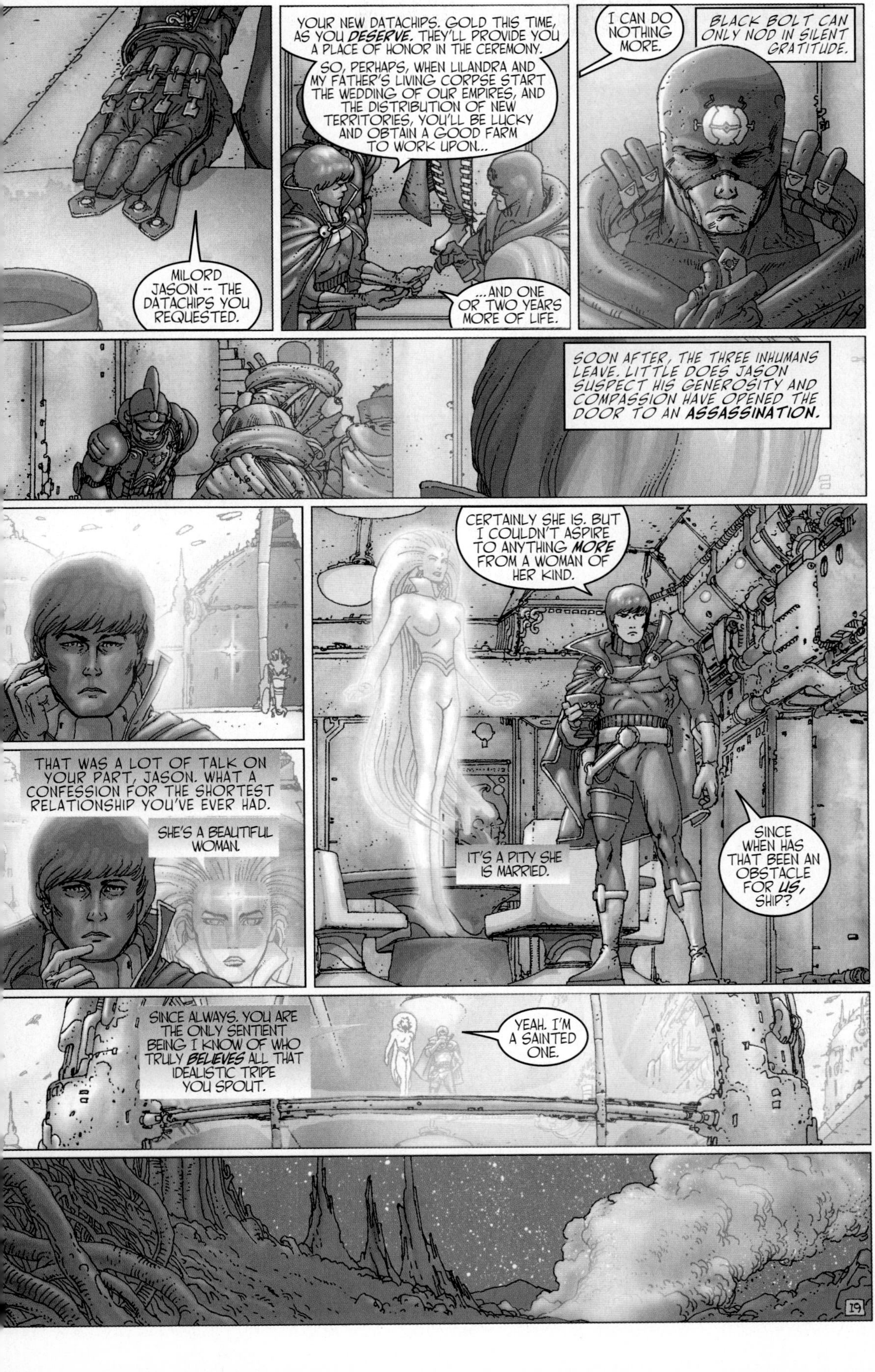
MILORD JASON -- THE DATACHIPS YOU REQUESTED.
YOUR NEW DATACHIPS. GOLD THIS TIME, AS YOU DESERVE. THEY'LL PROVIDE YOU A PLACE OF HONOR IN THE CEREMONY.
SO, PERHAPS, WHEN LILANDRA AND MY FATHER'S LIVING CORPSE START THE WEDDING OF OUR EMPIRES, AND THE DISTRIBUTION OF NEW TERRITORIES, YOU'LL BE LUCKY AND OBTAIN A GOOD FARM TO WORK UPON...
...AND ONE OR TWO YEARS MORE OF LIFE.
I CAN DO NOTHING MORE.
BLACK BOLT CAN ONLY NOD IN SILENT GRATITUDE.
SOON AFTER, THE THREE INHUMANS LEAVE. LITTLE DOES JASON SUSPECT HIS GENEROSITY AND COMPASSION HAVE OPENED THE DOOR TO AN ASSASSINATION.
THAT WAS A LOT OF TALK ON YOUR PART, JASON. WHAT A CONFESSION FOR THE SHORTEST RELATIONSHIP YOU'VE EVER HAD.
SHE'S A BEAUTIFUL WOMAN.
CERTAINLY SHE IS. BUT I COULDN'T ASPIRE TO ANYTHING MORE FROM A WOMAN OF HER KIND.
IT'S A PITY SHE IS MARRIED.
SINCE WHEN HAS THAT BEEN AN OBSTACLE FOR US, SHIP?
SINCE ALWAYS. YOU ARE THE ONLY SENTIENT BEING I KNOW OF WHO TRULY BELIEVES ALL THAT IDEALISTIC TRIPE YOU SPOUT.
YEAH. I'M A SAINTED ONE.
19

THE BATTLE IS OVER. AS DELPHOS HAD PREDICTED, ALL RESISTANCE ON THE BORDER MOON HAS BEEN SWEPT AWAY.

AND TWO INHUMANS BROTHERS BITTERLY REFLECT THAT IN THEIR CASE, THE ONLY DIFFERENCE BETWEEN VICTORY AND DEFEAT IS THAT THE DEAD FEEL NO REMORSE.

IT IS A FEELING THEY ENVY.

HEY! LOOK UP, GUYS! I KNOW THIS SHIP!

A SHI'AR SCOUT FIGHTER -- AND THOSE SYMBOLS... THEY CAN ONLY MEAN...

...IT'S HOBGOBLIN THE SHAPE-SHIFTER'S PERSONAL VESSEL!

I SEE THE ZONE HAS BEEN CLEARED IN LESS TIME THAN EXPECTED.

THE THREE OF YOU WHO LED THE ATTACK... YOUR PRESENCE IS AWAITED IN PLACE CALLED KRITNAH.

IT SEEMS YOU'RE GOING TO BE MADE MEMBER OF THE IMPERIAL GUARD.

IT'S BEEN AN HONOR TO MAKE WAR BY YOUR SIDE, LITTLE ONE.

IN THE FUTURE, WE'LL SURELY MINGLE OUR BLOOD AGAIN.

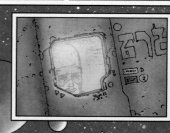

WITH THEIR MISSION ACCOMPLISHED, THE HEROES RETURN TO MORE CIVILIZED WORLDS. OTHER HANDS WILL INHERIT THE MOON'S RESOURCES, NOW THAT THERE IS NO OPPOSITION TO FIGHT BACK.

SO YOUR DREAM CAME TRUE, DELPHOS.

AND OUR NIGHTMARES, TOO.

20

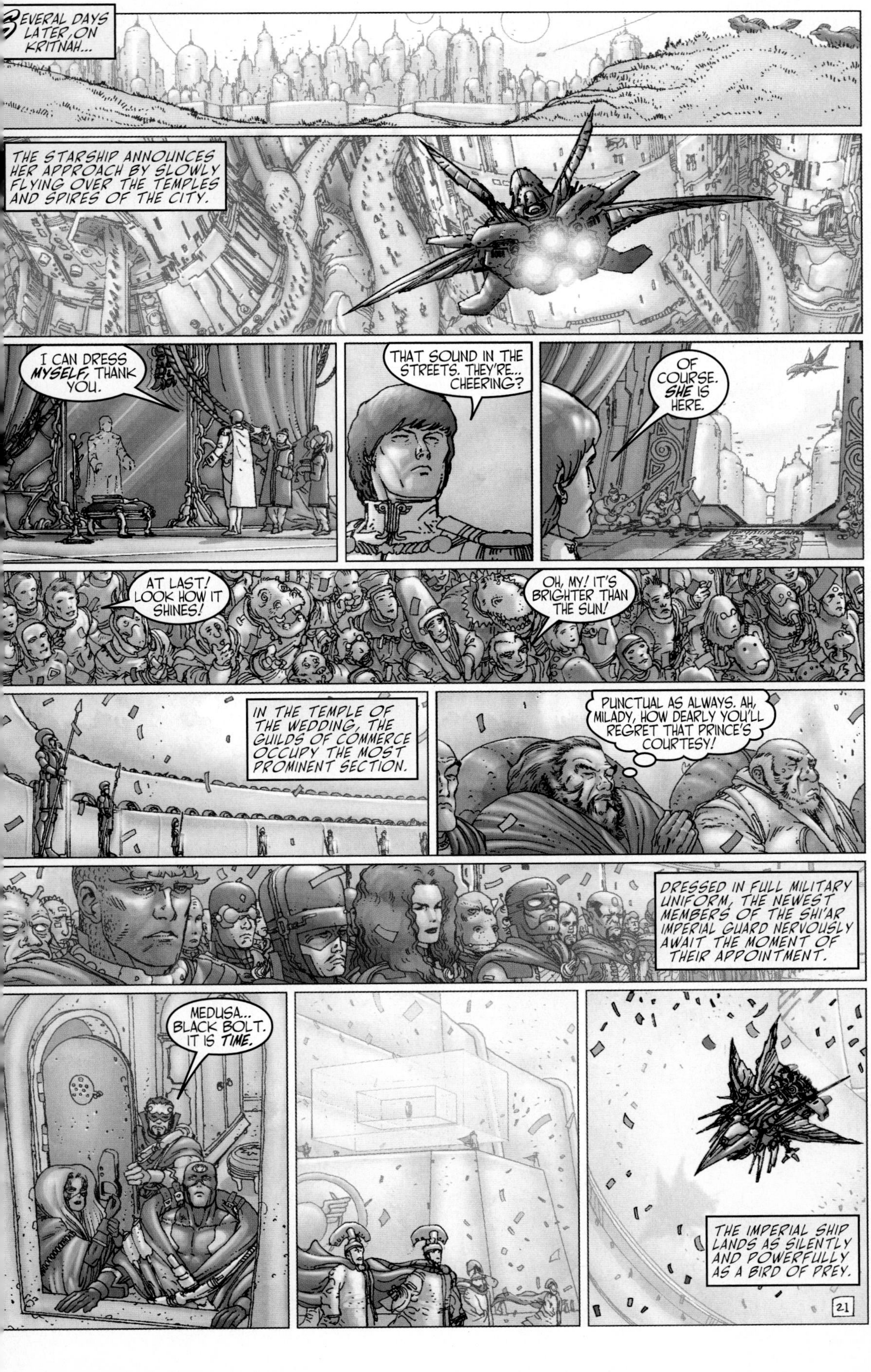

SEVERAL DAYS LATER, ON KRITNAH...
THE STARSHIP ANNOUNCES HER APPROACH BY SLOWLY FLYING OVER THE TEMPLES AND SPIRES OF THE CITY.
I CAN DRESS MYSELF, THANK YOU.
THAT SOUND IN THE STREETS. THEY'RE... CHEERING?
OF COURSE. SHE IS HERE.
AT LAST! LOOK HOW IT SHINES!
OH, MY! IT'S BRIGHTER THAN THE SUN!
IN THE TEMPLE OF THE WEDDING, THE GUILDS OF COMMERCE OCCUPY THE MOST PROMINENT SECTION.
PUNCTUAL AS ALWAYS. AH, MILADY, HOW DEARLY YOU'LL REGRET THAT PRINCE'S COURTESY!
DRESSED IN FULL MILITARY UNIFORM, THE NEWEST MEMBERS OF THE SHI'AR IMPERIAL GUARD NERVOUSLY AWAIT THE MOMENT OF THEIR APPOINTMENT.
MEDUSA... BLACK BOLT. IT IS TIME.
THE IMPERIAL SHIP LANDS AS SILENTLY AND POWERFULLY AS A BIRD OF PREY.

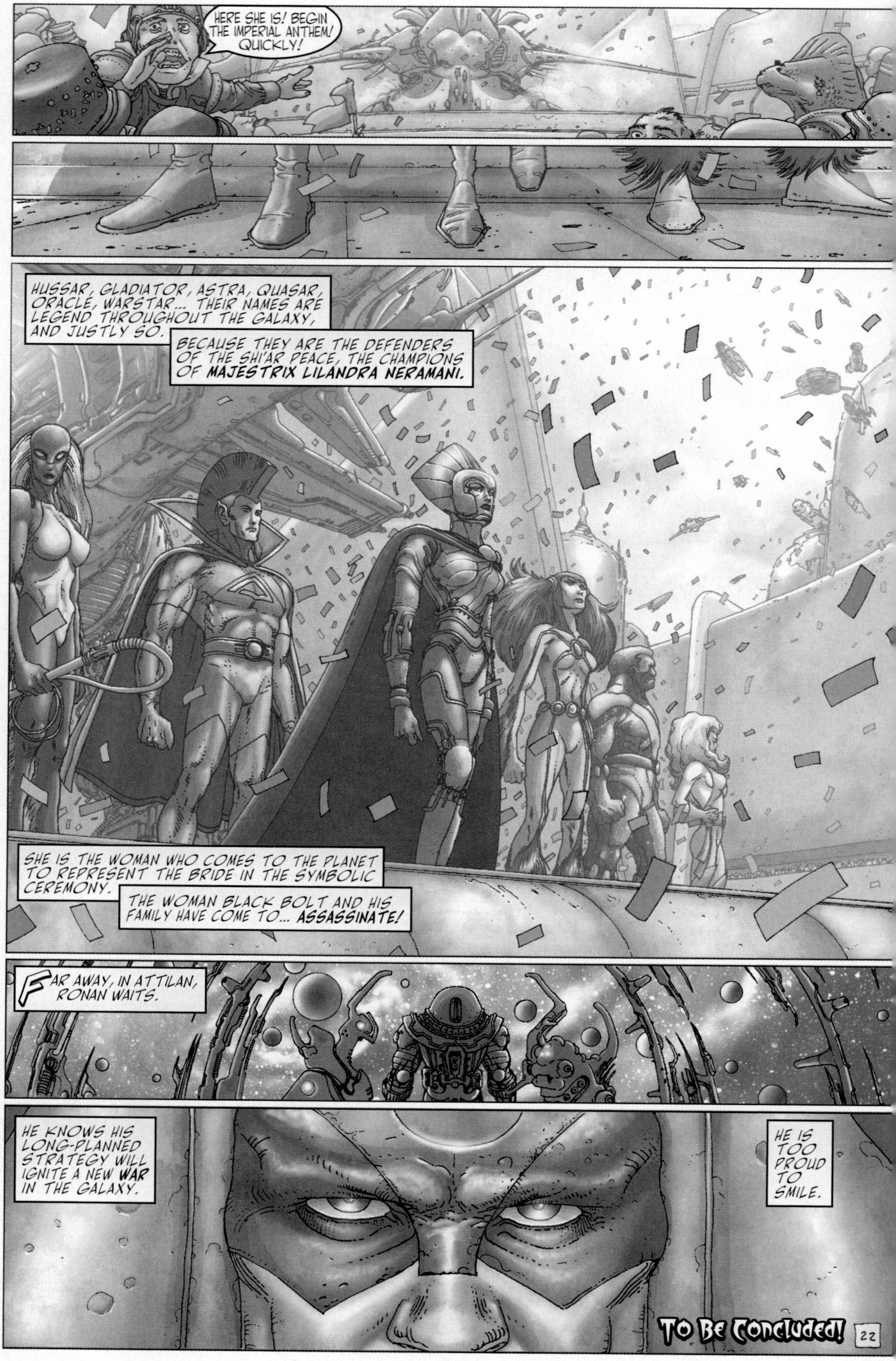
HERE SHE IS! BEGIN THE IMPERIAL ANTHEM! QUICKLY!
HUSSAR, GLADIATOR, ASTRA, QUASAR, ORACLE, WARSTAR... THEIR NAMES ARE LEGEND THROUGHOUT THE GALAXY, AND JUSTLY SO.
BECAUSE THEY ARE THE DEFENDERS OF THE SHI'AR PEACE, THE CHAMPIONS OF MAJESTRIX LILANDRA NERAMANI.
SHE IS THE WOMAN WHO COMES TO THE PLANET TO REPRESENT THE BRIDE IN THE SYMBOLIC CEREMONY.
THE WOMAN BLACK BOLT AND HIS FAMILY HAVE COME TO... ASSASSINATE!
FAR AWAY, IN ATTILAN, RONAN WAITS.
HE KNOWS HIS LONG-PLANNED STRATEGY WILL IGNITE A NEW WAR IN THE GALAXY.
HE IS TOO PROUD TO SMILE.
TO BE CONCLUDED!
22

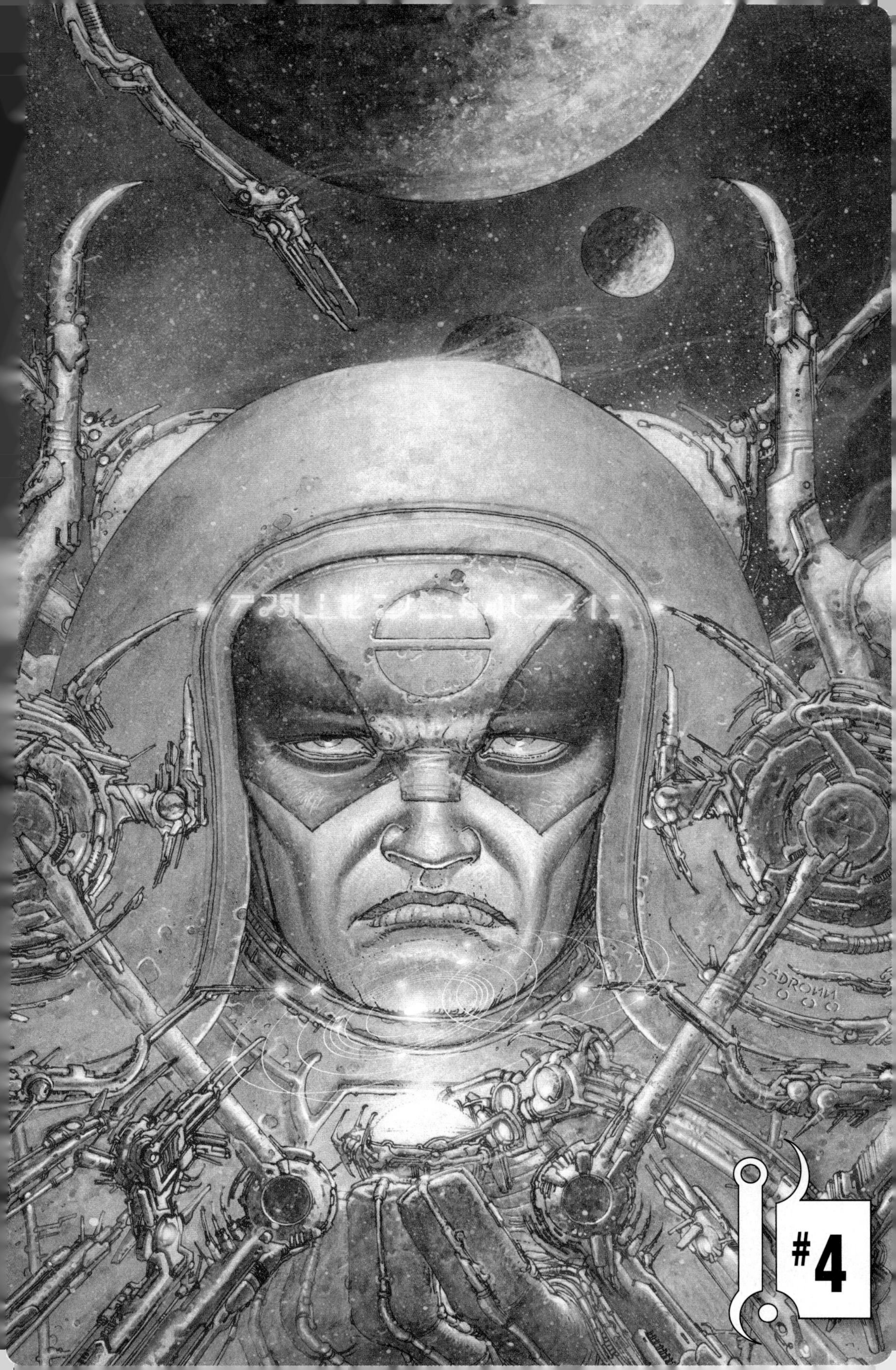
LADRONN
2000
#4

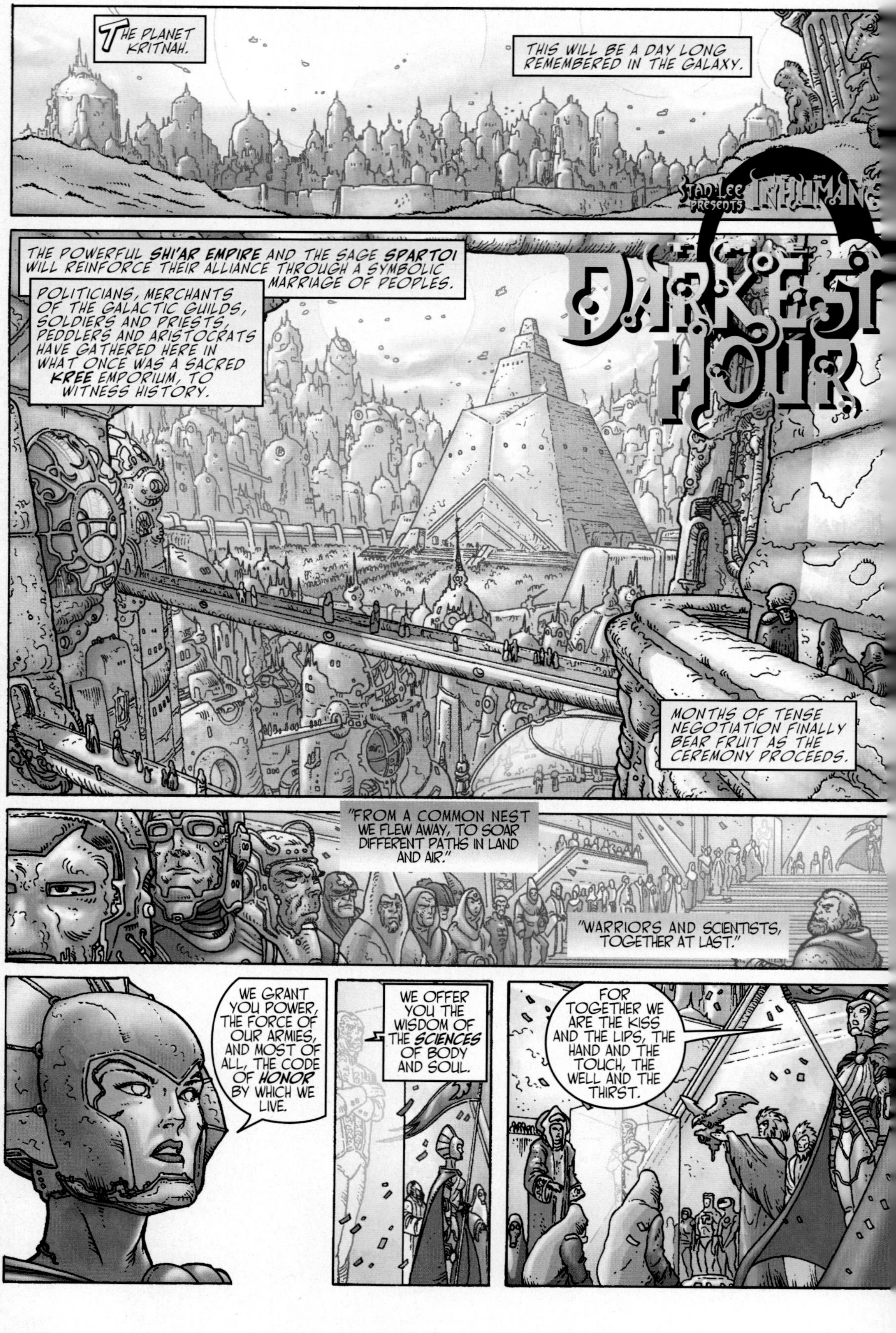
THE PLANET KRITNAH.
THIS WILL BE A DAY LONG REMEMBERED IN THE GALAXY.
STAN LEE PRESENTS INHUMANS
THE DARKEST HOUR
THE POWERFUL SHI'AR EMPIRE AND THE SAGE SPARTOI WILL REINFORCE THEIR ALLIANCE THROUGH A SYMBOLIC MARRIAGE OF PEOPLES.
POLITICIANS, MERCHANTS OF THE GALACTIC GUILDS, SOLDIERS AND PRIESTS, PEDDLERS AND ARISTOCRATS HAVE GATHERED HERE IN WHAT ONCE WAS A SACRED KREE EMPORIUM, TO WITNESS HISTORY.
MONTHS OF TENSE NEGOTIATION FINALLY BEAR FRUIT AS THE CEREMONY PROCEEDS.
"FROM A COMMON NEST WE FLEW AWAY, TO SOAR DIFFERENT PATHS IN LAND AND AIR."
"WARRIORS AND SCIENTISTS, TOGETHER AT LAST."
WE GRANT YOU POWER, THE FORCE OF OUR ARMIES, AND MOST OF ALL, THE CODE OF HONOR BY WHICH WE LIVE.
WE OFFER YOU THE WISDOM OF THE SCIENCES OF BODY AND SOUL.
FOR TOGETHER WE ARE THE KISS AND THE LIPS, THE HAND AND THE TOUCH, THE WELL AND THE THIRST.

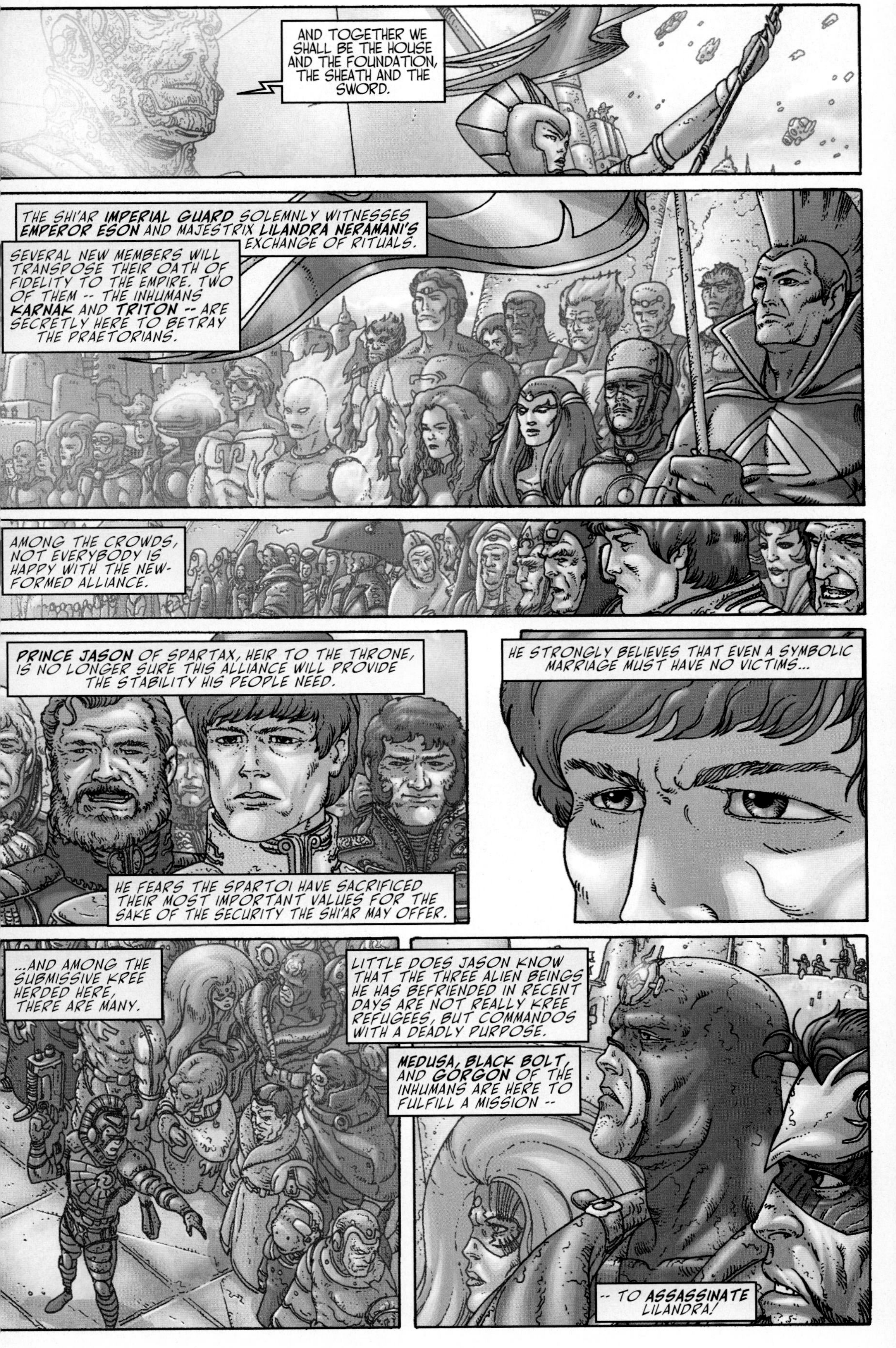
AND TOGETHER WE SHALL BE THE HOUSE AND THE FOUNDATION, THE SHEATH AND THE SWORD.
THE SHI'AR IMPERIAL GUARD SOLEMNLY WITNESSES EMPEROR ESON AND MAJESTRIX LILANDRA NERAMANI'S EXCHANGE OF RITUALS.
SEVERAL NEW MEMBERS WILL TRANSPOSE THEIR OATH OF FIDELITY TO THE EMPIRE. TWO OF THEM -- THE INHUMANS KARNAK AND TRITON -- ARE SECRETLY HERE TO BETRAY THE PRAETORIANS.
AMONG THE CROWDS, NOT EVERYBODY IS HAPPY WITH THE NEW-FORMED ALLIANCE.
PRINCE JASON OF SPARTAX, HEIR TO THE THRONE, IS NO LONGER SURE THIS ALLIANCE WILL PROVIDE THE STABILITY HIS PEOPLE NEED.
HE FEARS THE SPARTOI HAVE SACRIFICED THEIR MOST IMPORTANT VALUES FOR THE SAKE OF THE SECURITY THE SHI'AR MAY OFFER.
HE STRONGLY BELIEVES THAT EVEN A SYMBOLIC MARRIAGE MUST HAVE NO VICTIMS...
...AND AMONG THE SUBMISSIVE KREE HERDED HERE, THERE ARE MANY.
LITTLE DOES JASON KNOW THAT THE THREE ALIEN BEINGS HE HAS BEFRIENDED IN RECENT DAYS ARE NOT REALLY KREE REFUGEES, BUT COMMANDOS WITH A DEADLY PURPOSE.
MEDUSA, BLACK BOLT, AND GORGON OF THE INHUMANS ARE HERE TO FULFILL A MISSION --
-- TO ASSASSINATE LILANDRA!

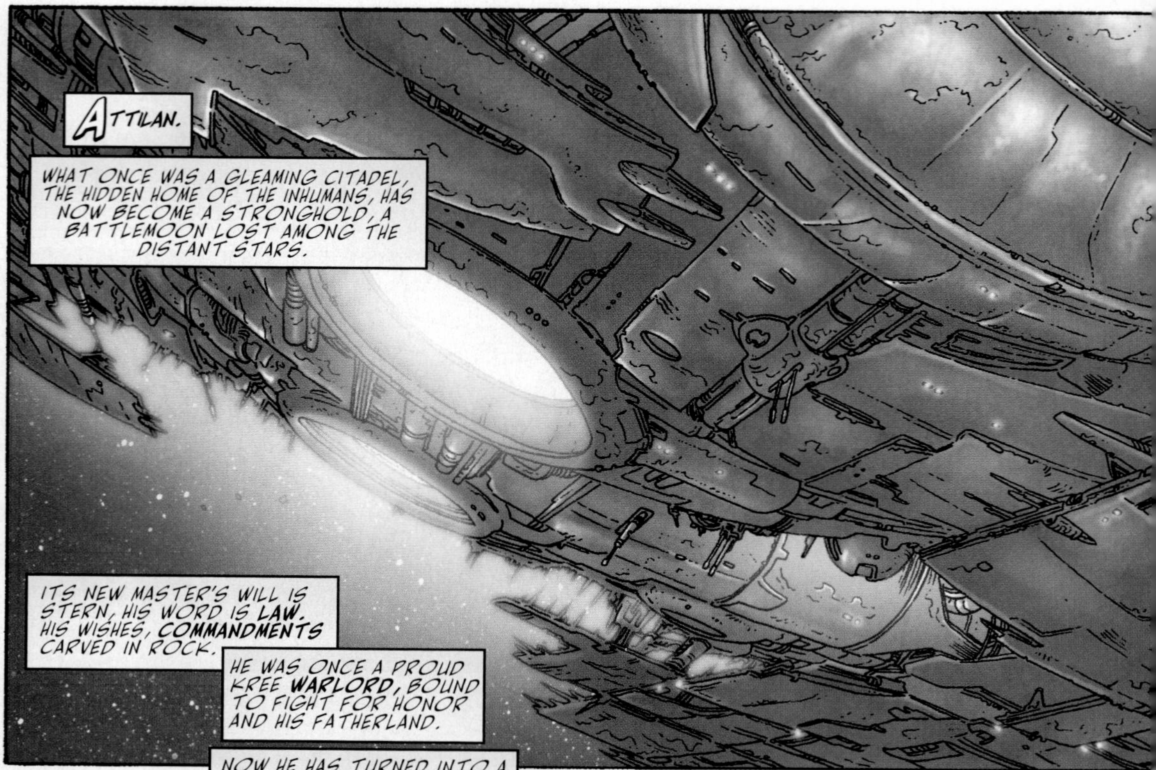
ATTILAN.
WHAT ONCE WAS A GLEAMING CITADEL, THE HIDDEN HOME OF THE INHUMANS, HAS NOW BECOME A STRONGHOLD, A BATTLEMOON LOST AMONG THE DISTANT STARS.
ITS NEW MASTER'S WILL IS STERN, HIS WORD IS LAW. HIS WISHES, COMMANDMENTS CARVED IN ROCK.
HE WAS ONCE A PROUD KREE WARLORD, BOUND TO FIGHT FOR HONOR AND HIS FATHERLAND.
NOW HE HAS TURNED INTO A PIRATE KING, THE MASTER OF A BROOD HE DESPISES.

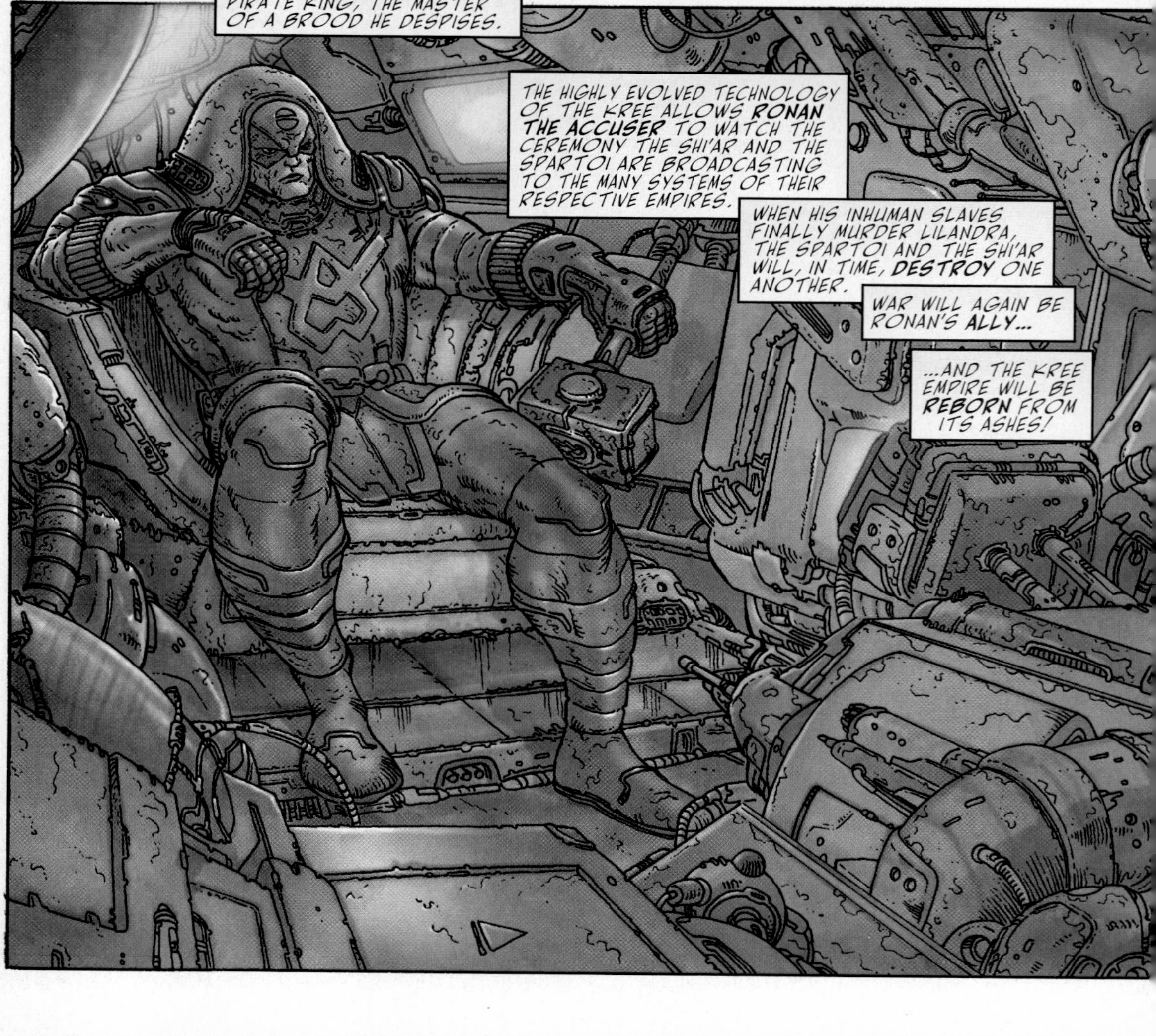
THE HIGHLY EVOLVED TECHNOLOGY OF THE KREE ALLOWS RONAN THE ACCUSER TO WATCH THE CEREMONY THE SHI'AR AND THE SPARTOI ARE BROADCASTING TO THE MANY SYSTEMS OF THEIR RESPECTIVE EMPIRES.
WHEN HIS INHUMAN SLAVES FINALLY MURDER LILANDRA, THE SPARTOI AND THE SHI'AR WILL, IN TIME, DESTROY ONE ANOTHER.
WAR WILL AGAIN BE RONAN'S ALLY...
...AND THE KREE EMPIRE WILL BE REBORN FROM ITS ASHES!

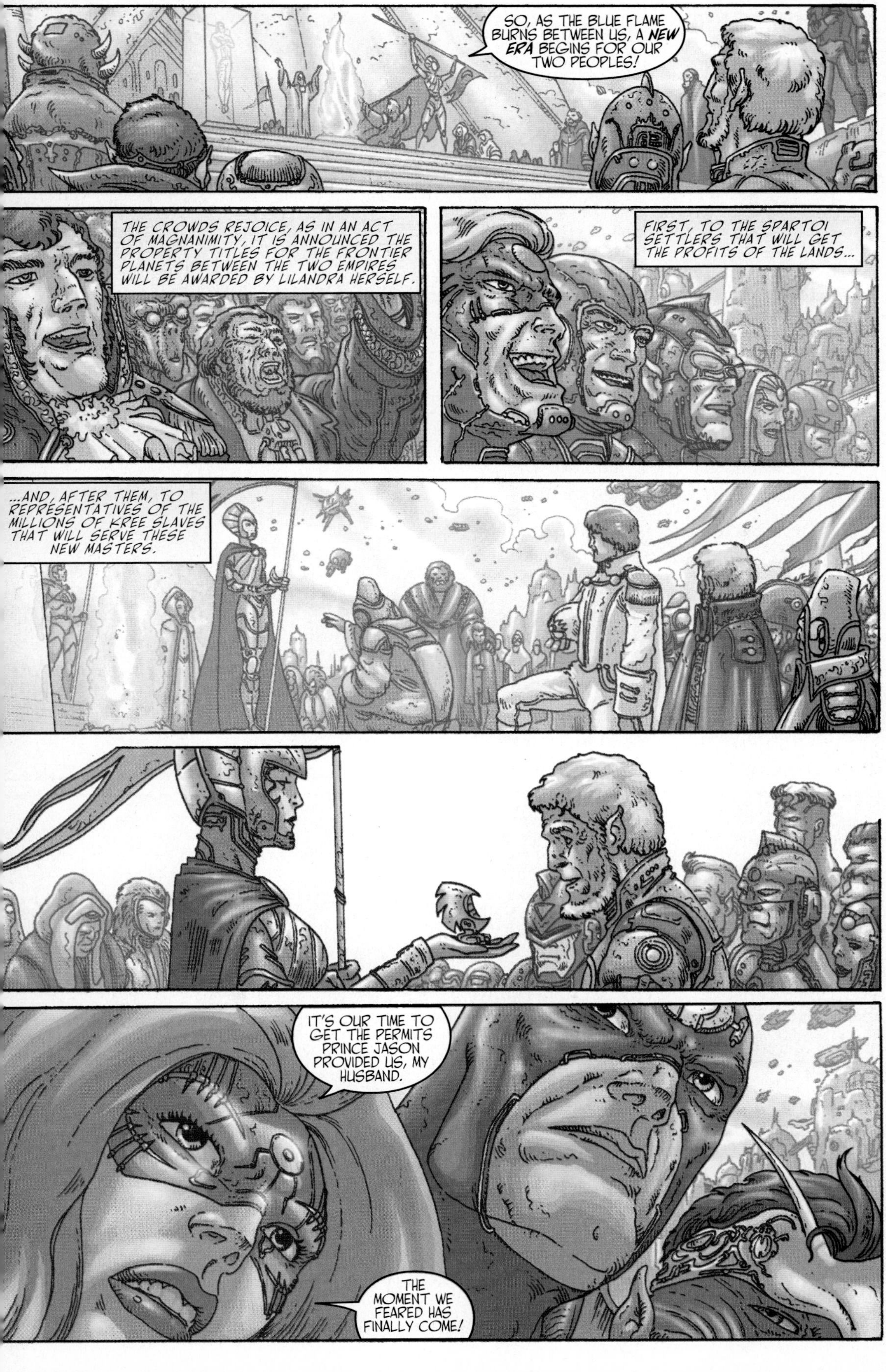

SO, AS THE BLUE FLAME BURNS BETWEEN US, A NEW ERA BEGINS FOR OUR TWO PEOPLES!
THE CROWDS REJOICE, AS IN AN ACT OF MAGNANIMITY, IT IS ANNOUNCED THE PROPERTY TITLES FOR THE FRONTIER PLANETS BETWEEN THE TWO EMPIRES WILL BE AWARDED BY LILANDRA HERSELF.
FIRST, TO THE SPARTOI SETTLERS THAT WILL GET THE PROFITS OF THE LANDS...
...AND, AFTER THEM, TO REPRESENTATIVES OF THE MILLIONS OF KREE SLAVES THAT WILL SERVE THESE NEW MASTERS.
IT'S OUR TIME TO GET THE PERMITS PRINCE JASON PROVIDED US, MY HUSBAND.
THE MOMENT WE FEARED HAS FINALLY COME!

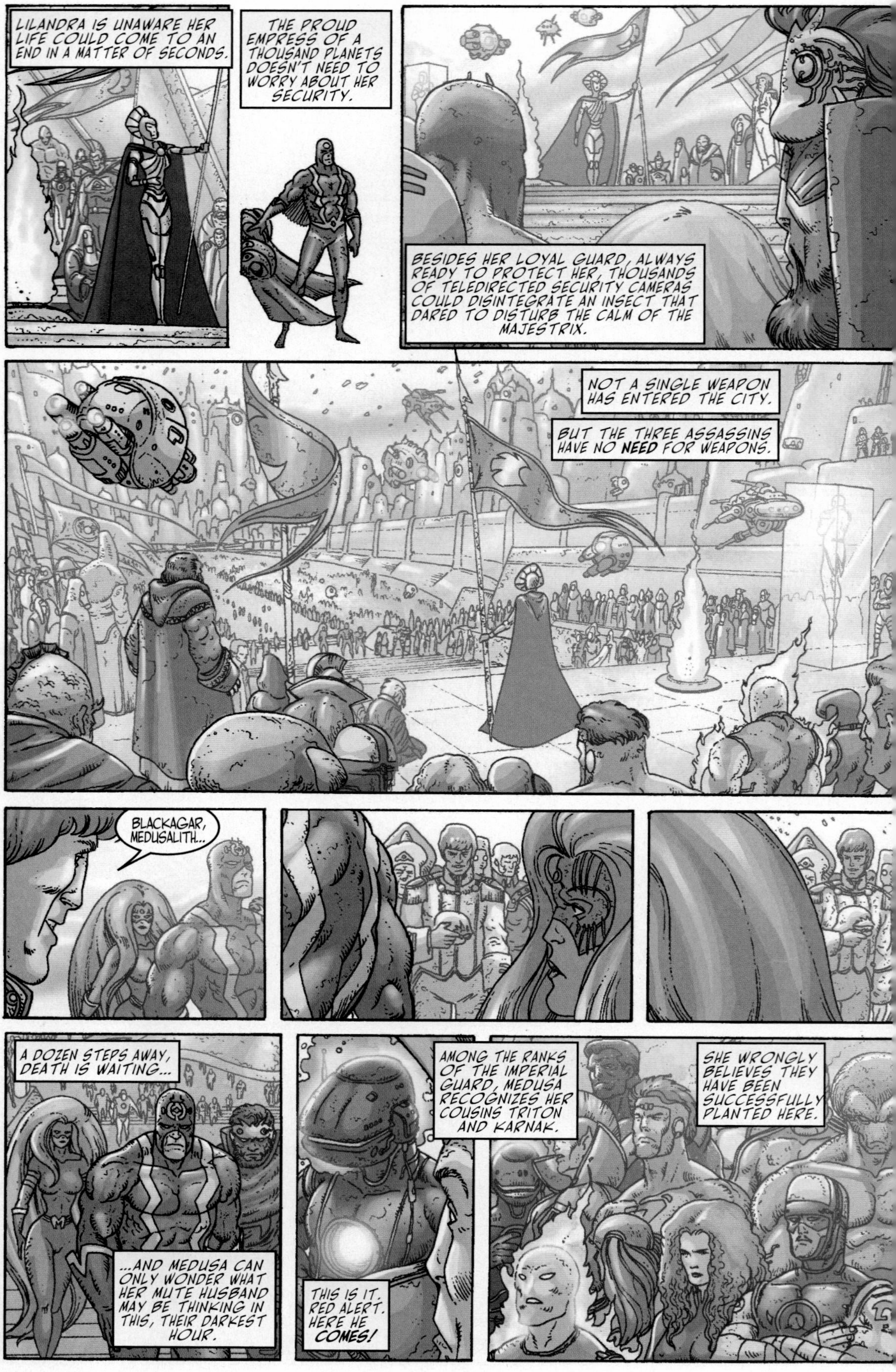
LILANDRA IS UNAWARE HER LIFE COULD COME TO AN END IN A MATTER OF SECONDS.
THE PROUD EMPRESS OF A THOUSAND PLANETS DOESN'T NEED TO WORRY ABOUT HER SECURITY.
BESIDES HER LOYAL GUARD, ALWAYS READY TO PROTECT HER, THOUSANDS OF TELEDIRECTED SECURITY CAMERAS COULD DISINTEGRATE AN INSECT THAT DARED TO DISTURB THE CALM OF THE MAJESTRIX.
NOT A SINGLE WEAPON HAS ENTERED THE CITY.
BUT THE THREE ASSASSINS HAVE NO NEED FOR WEAPONS.
BLACKAGAR, MEDUSALITH...
A DOZEN STEPS AWAY, DEATH IS WAITING...
...AND MEDUSA CAN ONLY WONDER WHAT HER MUTE HUSBAND MAY BE THINKING IN THIS, THEIR DARKEST HOUR.
THIS IS IT. RED ALERT. HERE HE COMES!
AMONG THE RANKS OF THE IMPERIAL GUARD, MEDUSA RECOGNIZES HER COUSINS TRITON AND KARNAK.
SHE WRONGLY BELIEVES THEY HAVE BEEN SUCCESSFULLY PLANTED HERE.

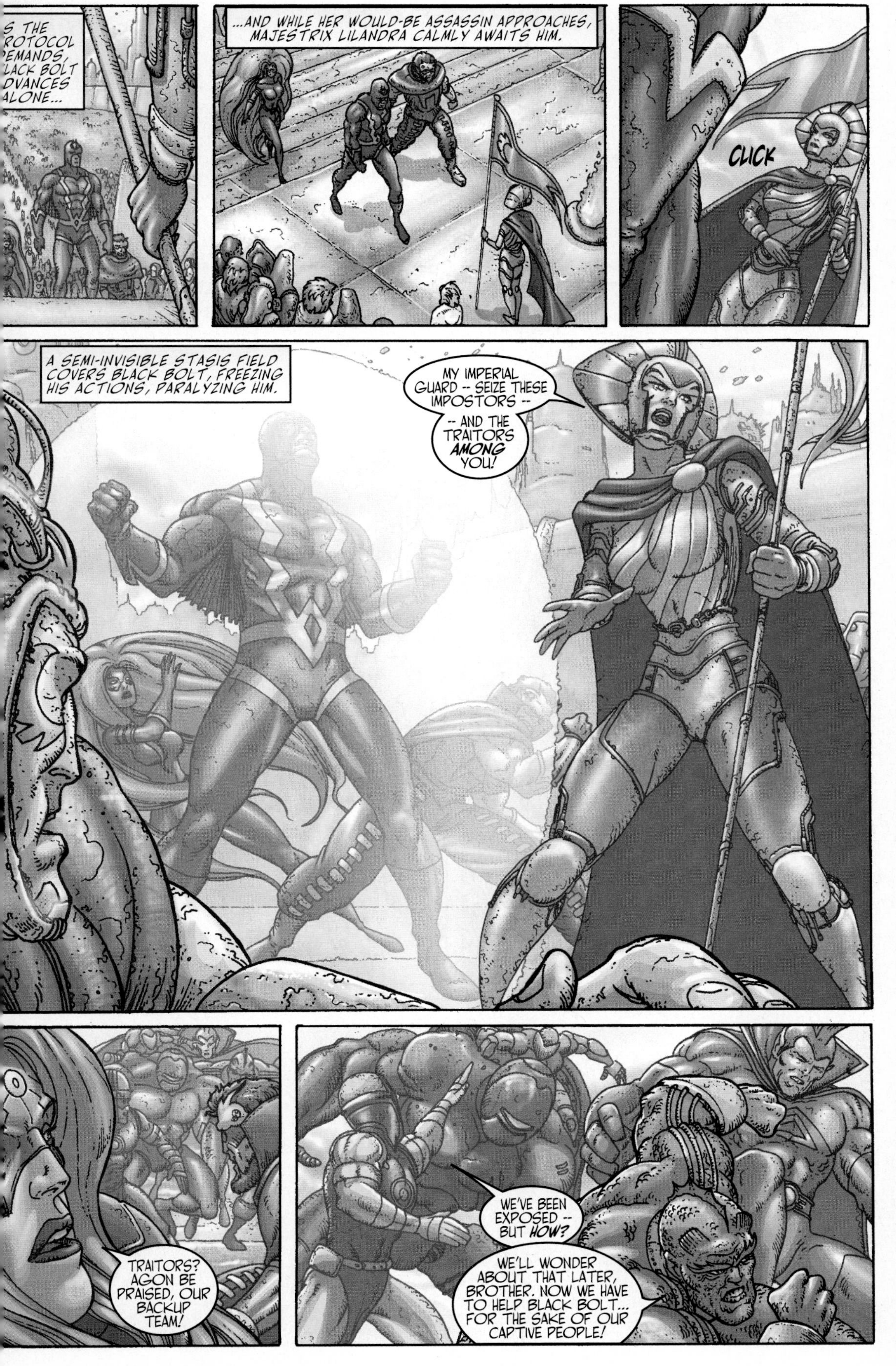
S THE
ROTOCOL
DEMANDS,
LACK BOLT
DVANCES
ALONE...
...AND WHILE HER WOULD-BE ASSASSIN APPROACHES, MAJESTRIX LILANDRA CALMLY AWAITS HIM.
CLICK
A SEMI-INVISIBLE STASIS FIELD COVERS BLACK BOLT, FREEZING HIS ACTIONS, PARALYZING HIM.
MY IMPERIAL GUARD -- SEIZE THESE IMPOSTORS --
-- AND THE TRAITORS AMONG YOU!
TRAITORS? AGON BE PRAISED, OUR BACKUP TEAM!
WE'VE BEEN EXPOSED -- BUT HOW?
WE'LL WONDER ABOUT THAT LATER, BROTHER. NOW WE HAVE TO HELP BLACK BOLT... FOR THE SAKE OF OUR CAPTIVE PEOPLE!

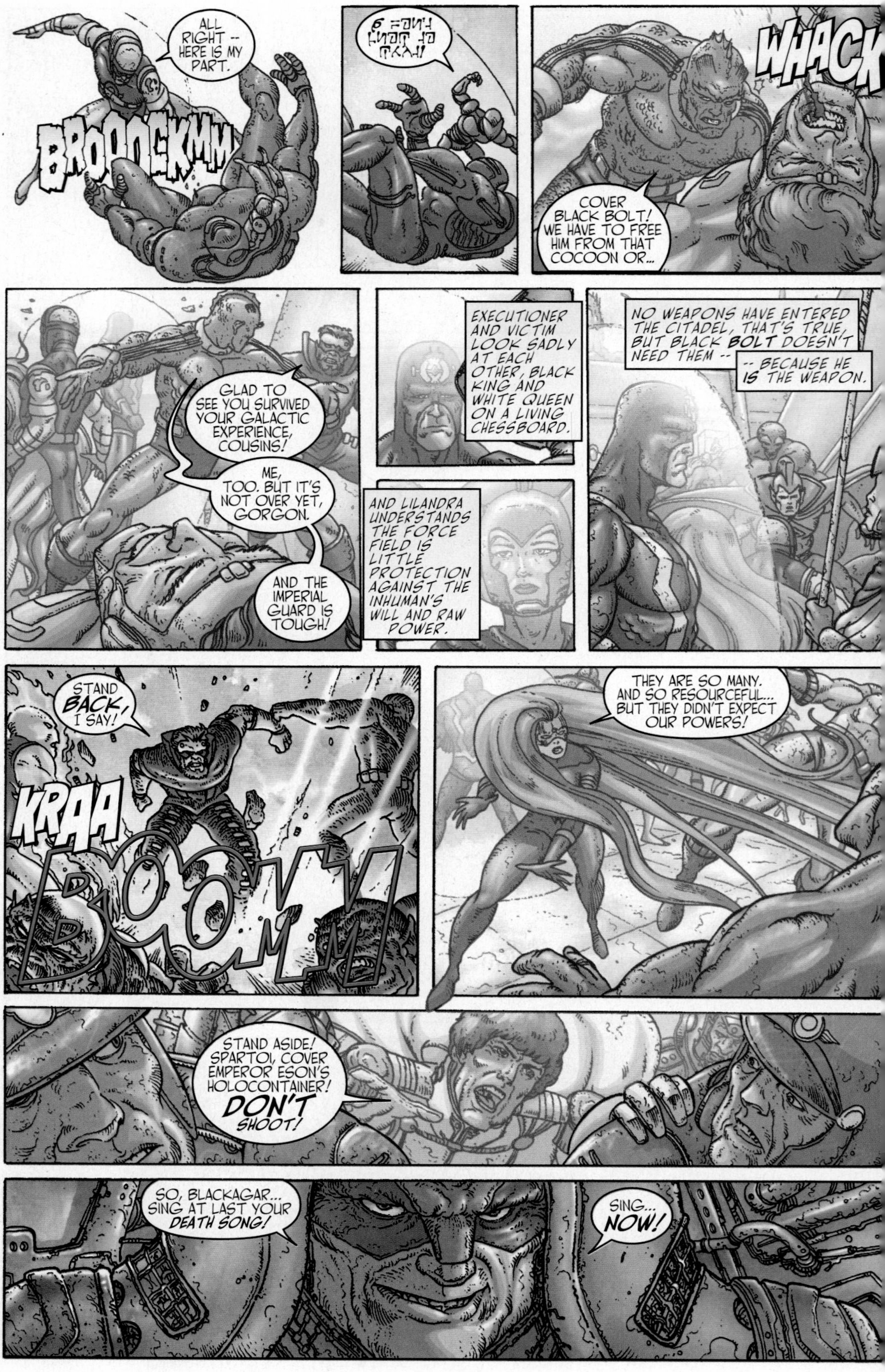
ALL RIGHT -- HERE IS MY PART.
BROOOCKMM
COVER BLACK BOLT! WE HAVE TO FREE HIM FROM THAT COCOON OR...
WHACK
GLAD TO SEE YOU SURVIVED YOUR GALACTIC EXPERIENCE, COUSINS!
ME, TOO. BUT IT'S NOT OVER YET, GORGON.
AND THE IMPERIAL GUARD IS TOUGH!
EXECUTIONER AND VICTIM LOOK SADLY AT EACH OTHER, BLACK KING AND WHITE QUEEN ON A LIVING CHESSBOARD.
AND LILANDRA UNDERSTANDS THE FORCE FIELD IS LITTLE PROTECTION AGAINST THE INHUMAN'S WILL AND RAW POWER.
NO WEAPONS HAVE ENTERED THE CITADEL, THAT'S TRUE, BUT BLACK BOLT DOESN'T NEED THEM --
-- BECAUSE HE IS THE WEAPON.
STAND BACK, I SAY!
KRAA
BOOMM
THEY ARE SO MANY. AND SO RESOURCEFUL... BUT THEY DIDN'T EXPECT OUR POWERS!
STAND ASIDE! SPARTOI, COVER EMPEROR ESON'S HOLOCONTAINER! DON'T SHOOT!
SO, BLACKAGAR... SING AT LAST YOUR DEATH SONG!
SING... NOW!

FROM DISTANT
ATTILAN, A DISCHARGE
OF ENERGY FLOWS
INTO BLACK BOLT'S
ANTENNA, THE DEVICE
HE USES TO CHANNEL
HIS POWER.

BLACK BOLT... WHY DOESN'T HE ACT?

THAT BUBBLE...
HE'LL BURST IF
HE USES HIS
POWER *INSIDE*
IT!

IT MUST HAVE
A WEAK POINT
SOMEWHERE...

KIIIA!

THE EFFECT OF KARNAK'S BLOW IS MINIMAL... BUT
IT IS MORE THAN ENOUGH TO ALLOW BLACK
BOLT TO DIRECT HIS POWER *OUTWARD*.

AT LONG
LAST, THE
INHUMANS'
SOVEREIGN
IS DETERMINED
TO *SPEAK*.

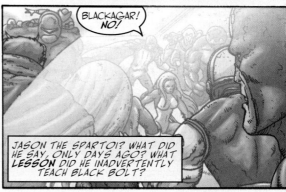
BLACKAGAR!
NO!

JASON THE SPARTOI? WHAT DID
HE SAY, ONLY DAYS AGO? WHAT
LESSON DID HE INADVERTENTLY
TEACH BLACK BOLT?

HE CAN'T BUILD THE UNCERTAIN
FUTURE OF HIS TRIBE ON THE BONES
OF OTHER PEOPLE.

LILANDRA'S DEATH WILL BRING *CHAOS*
TO THE GALAXY. WAR WILL IGNITE
PLANETS AND SUNS ALIKE.

AND BLACK BOLT, NOT RONAN, WILL BE
RESPONSIBLE FOR A *BILLION DEATHS*.

HOW CAN THIS BE?

NO MATTER
THE PRICE
HE PAYS, HE
MUST REMAIN --
SILENT!

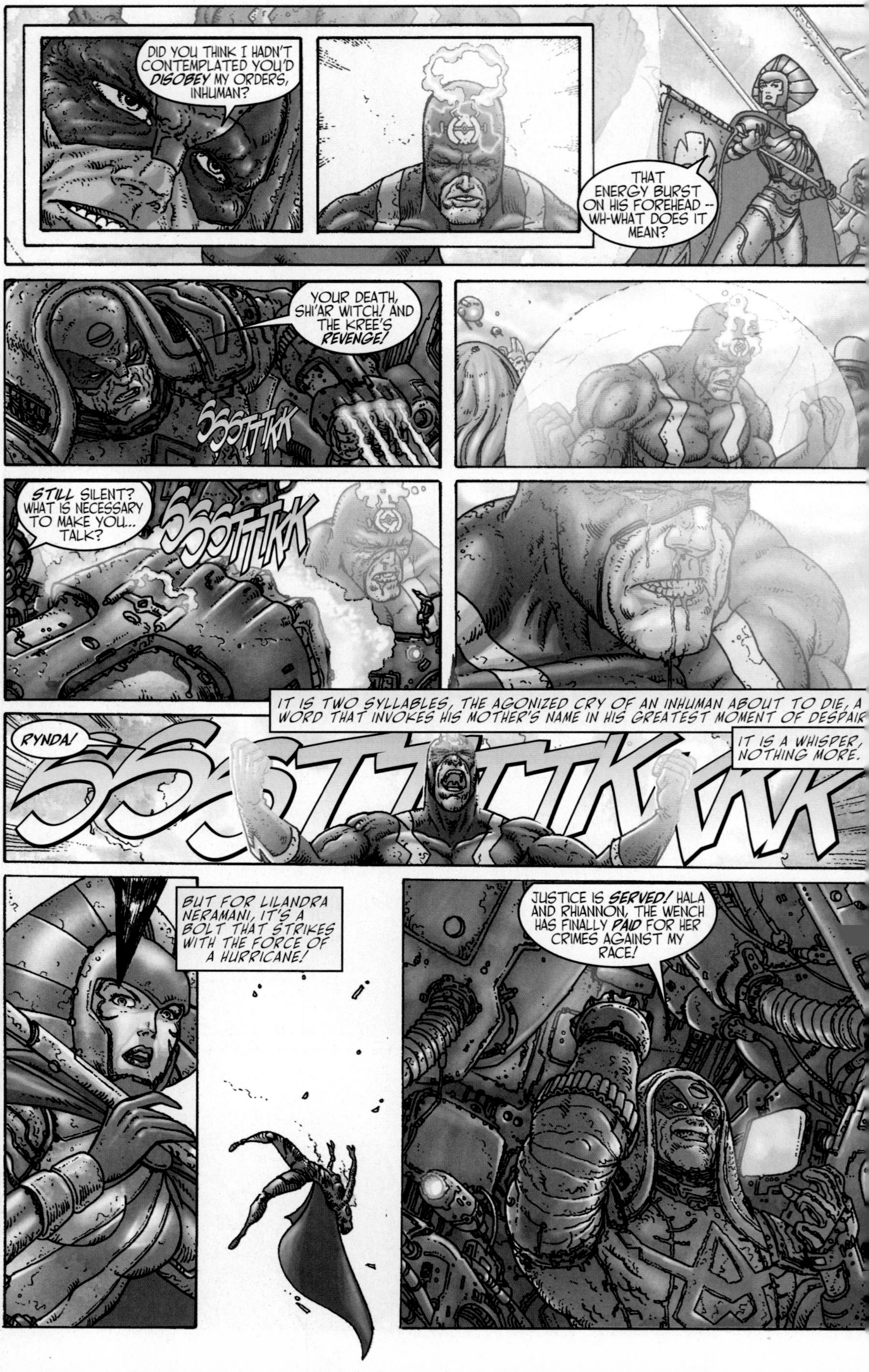
DID YOU THINK I HADN'T CONTEMPLATED YOU'D DISOBEY MY ORDERS, INHUMAN?
THAT ENERGY BURST ON HIS FOREHEAD -- WH-WHAT DOES IT MEAN?
YOUR DEATH, SHI'AR WITCH! AND THE KREE'S REVENGE!
SSSTTIKK
STILL SILENT? WHAT IS NECESSARY TO MAKE YOU... TALK?
SSSTTIKK
IT IS TWO SYLLABLES, THE AGONIZED CRY OF AN INHUMAN ABOUT TO DIE, A WORD THAT INVOKES HIS MOTHER'S NAME IN HIS GREATEST MOMENT OF DESPAIR
RYNDA!
IT IS A WHISPER, NOTHING MORE.
SSSTTTTIKKKK
BUT FOR LILANDRA NERAMANI, IT'S A BOLT THAT STRIKES WITH THE FORCE OF A HURRICANE!
JUSTICE IS SERVED! HALA AND RHIANNON, THE WENCH HAS FINALLY PAID FOR HER CRIMES AGAINST MY RACE!

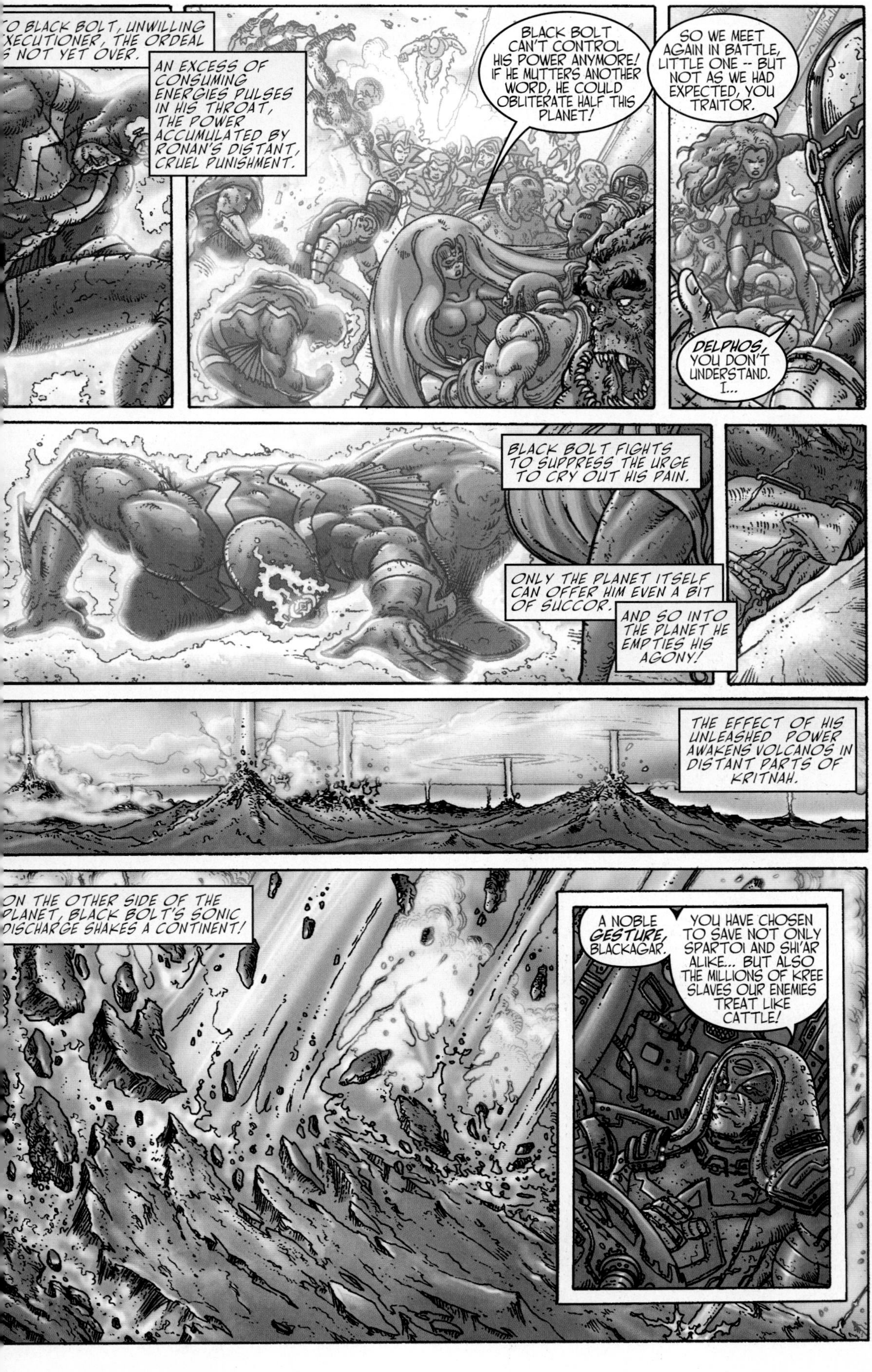

TO BLACK BOLT, UNWILLING EXECUTIONER, THE ORDEAL IS NOT YET OVER.
AN EXCESS OF CONSUMING ENERGIES PULSES IN HIS THROAT, THE POWER ACCUMULATED BY RONAN'S DISTANT, CRUEL PUNISHMENT.
BLACK BOLT CAN'T CONTROL HIS POWER ANYMORE! IF HE MUTTERS ANOTHER WORD, HE COULD OBLITERATE HALF THIS PLANET!
SO WE MEET AGAIN IN BATTLE, LITTLE ONE -- BUT NOT AS WE HAD EXPECTED, YOU TRAITOR.
DELPHOS, YOU DON'T UNDERSTAND. I...
BLACK BOLT FIGHTS TO SUPPRESS THE URGE TO CRY OUT HIS PAIN.
ONLY THE PLANET ITSELF CAN OFFER HIM EVEN A BIT OF SUCCOR.
AND SO INTO THE PLANET HE EMPTIES HIS AGONY!
THE EFFECT OF HIS UNLEASHED POWER AWAKENS VOLCANOS IN DISTANT PARTS OF KRITNAH.
ON THE OTHER SIDE OF THE PLANET, BLACK BOLT'S SONIC DISCHARGE SHAKES A CONTINENT!
A NOBLE GESTURE, BLACKAGAR.
YOU HAVE CHOSEN TO SAVE NOT ONLY SPARTOI AND SHI'AR ALIKE... BUT ALSO THE MILLIONS OF KREE SLAVES OUR ENEMIES TREAT LIKE CATTLE!

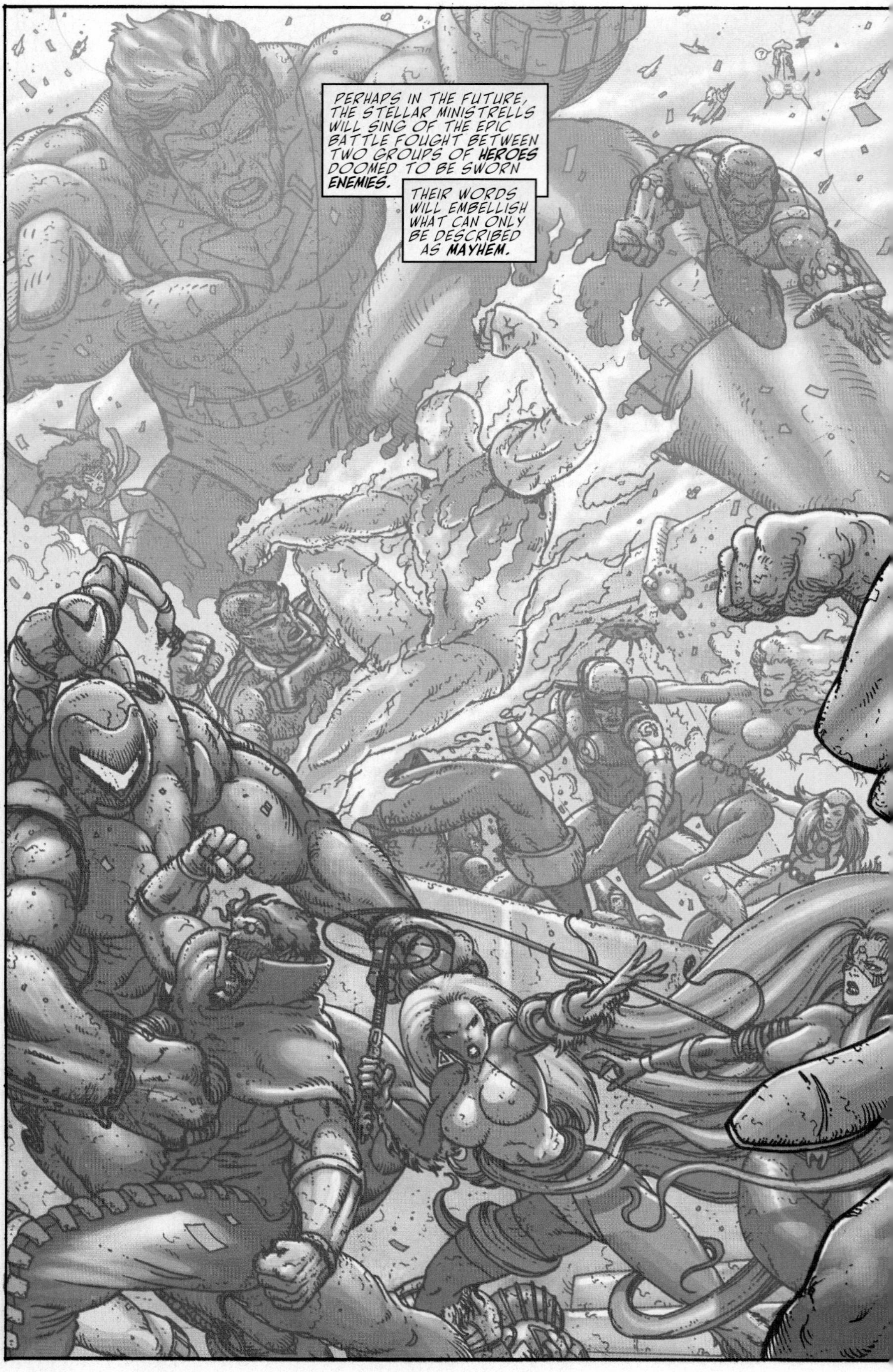
PERHAPS IN THE FUTURE, THE STELLAR MINISTRELLS WILL SING OF THE EPIC BATTLE FOUGHT BETWEEN TWO GROUPS OF HEROES DOOMED TO BE SWORN ENEMIES.
THEIR WORDS WILL EMBELLISH WHAT CAN ONLY BE DESCRIBED AS MAYHEM.

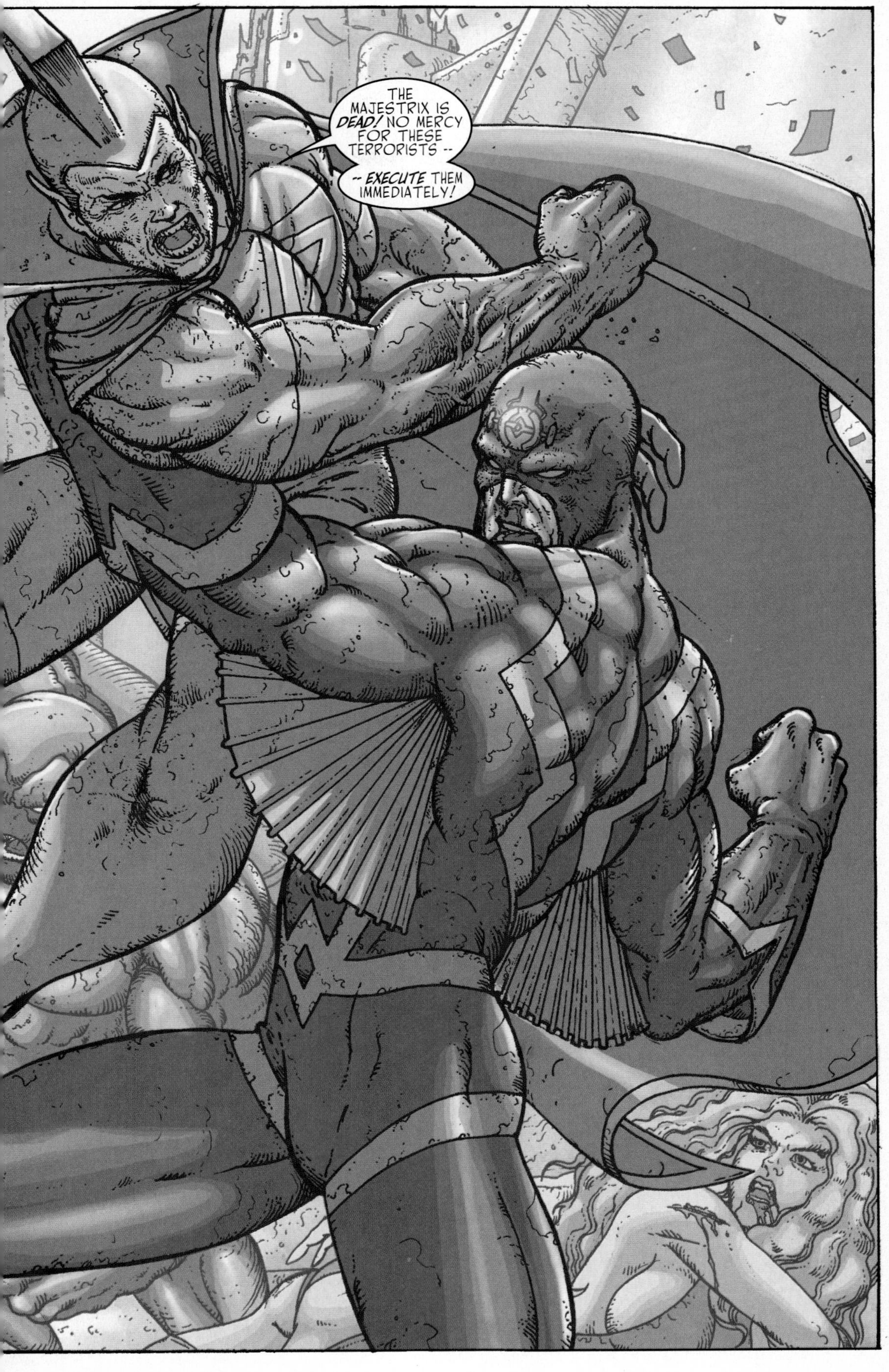
THE MAJESTRIX IS DEAD! NO MERCY FOR THESE TERRORISTS --
-- EXECUTE THEM IMMEDIATELY!

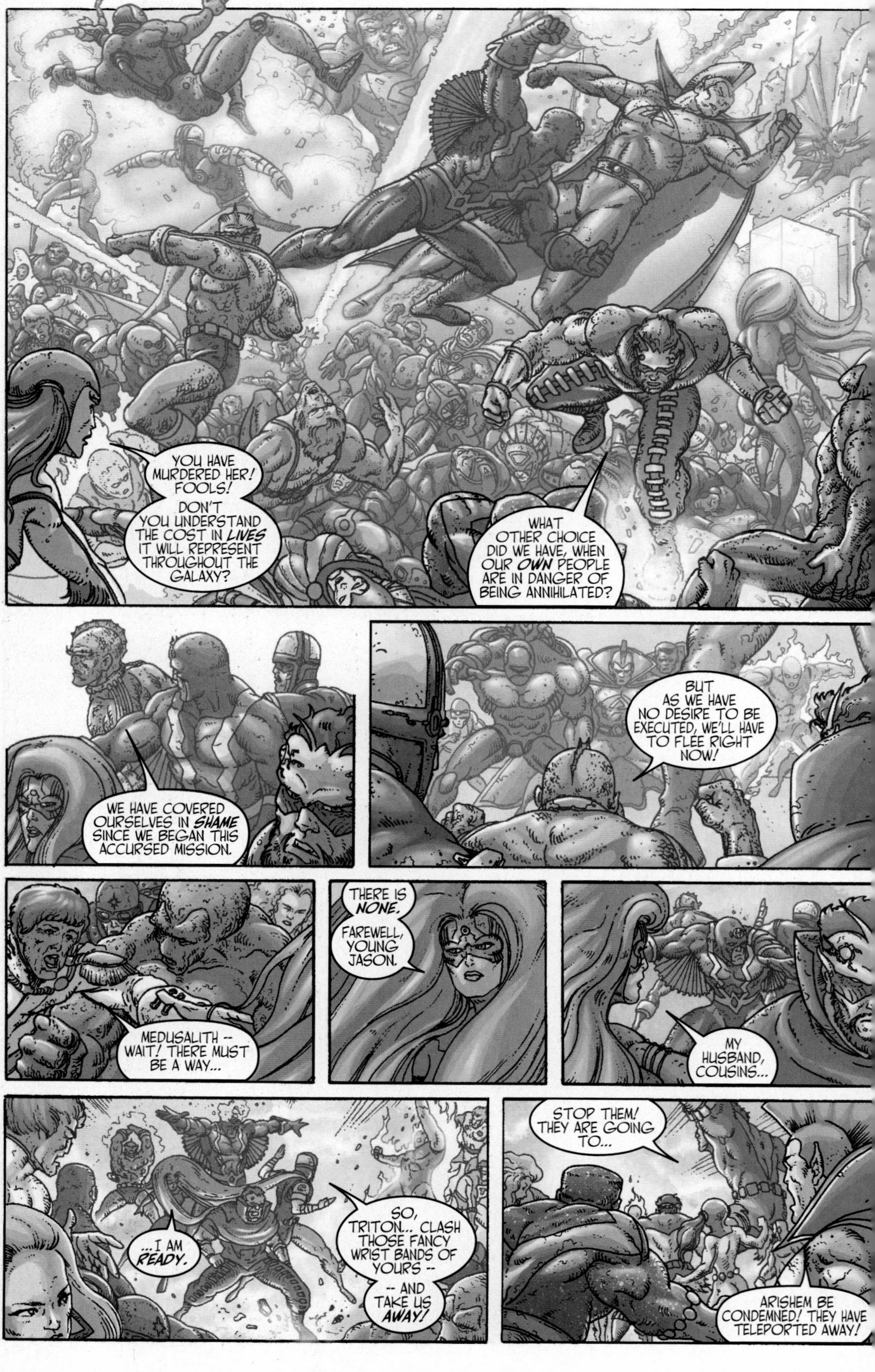
YOU HAVE MURDERED HER! FOOLS!
DON'T YOU UNDERSTAND THE COST IN *LIVES* IT WILL REPRESENT THROUGHOUT THE GALAXY?
WHAT OTHER CHOICE DID WE HAVE, WHEN OUR *OWN* PEOPLE ARE IN DANGER OF BEING ANNIHILATED?
WE HAVE COVERED OURSELVES IN *SHAME* SINCE WE BEGAN THIS ACCURSED MISSION.
BUT AS WE HAVE NO DESIRE TO BE EXECUTED, WE'LL HAVE TO FLEE RIGHT NOW!
MEDUSALITH -- WAIT! THERE MUST BE A WAY...
THERE IS *NONE.*
FAREWELL, YOUNG JASON.
MY HUSBAND, COUSINS...
...I AM *READY.*
SO, TRITON... CLASH THOSE FANCY WRIST BANDS OF YOURS --
-- AND TAKE US *AWAY!*
STOP THEM! THEY ARE GOING TO...
ARISHEM BE CONDEMNED! THEY HAVE TELEPORTED AWAY!

A LETHAL CALM SPREADS THROUGH THE DELEGATIONS OF SHI'AR AND SPARTOI.

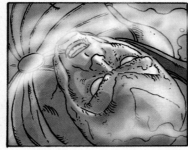

HOBGOBLIN. THE SHAPE-SHIFTER?!

SO... YOU *KNEW?*

WE *SUSPECTED.*

MAJESTRIX, YOU CAN ACTIVATE THE *HOLOGRAM* NOW.

WE COULD TAKE NO RISK, JASON OF SPARTAX. BUT WE WERE NOT CLEVER ENOUGH TO AVOID THIS COUP WITHOUT SACRIFICE.

WHAT BETTER WAY IS THERE FOR A ROYAL BODYGUARD TO DIE THAN TO GIVE HIS OR HER LIFE FOR THE *MAJESTRIX* WE LOVE?

B-BUT... HOW COULD YOU *KNOW* WHAT WAS GOING TO HAPPEN?

BECAUSE DELPHOS'S POWERS OF PRESCIENCE MANIFESTED RECENTLY, MERE DAYS AGO.

SHE GLIMPSED THE FUTURE, *THIS* VERY SCENE, AND ALERTED US.

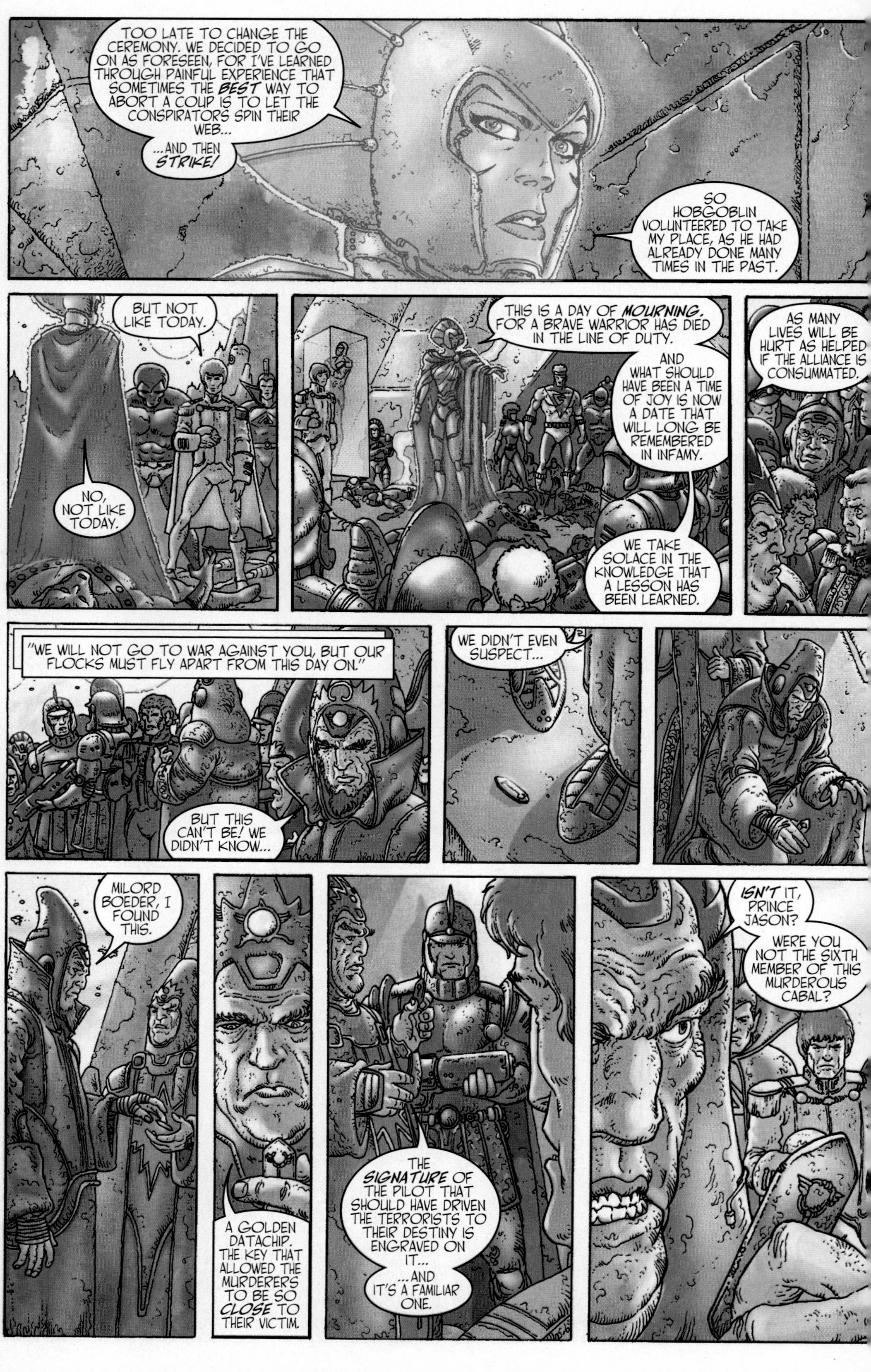
TOO LATE TO CHANGE THE CEREMONY. WE DECIDED TO GO ON AS FORESEEN, FOR I'VE LEARNED THROUGH PAINFUL EXPERIENCE THAT SOMETIMES THE BEST WAY TO ABORT A COUP IS TO LET THE CONSPIRATORS SPIN THEIR WEB...
...AND THEN STRIKE!
SO HOBGOBLIN VOLUNTEERED TO TAKE MY PLACE, AS HE HAD ALREADY DONE MANY TIMES IN THE PAST.
BUT NOT LIKE TODAY.
NO, NOT LIKE TODAY.
THIS IS A DAY OF MOURNING, FOR A BRAVE WARRIOR HAS DIED IN THE LINE OF DUTY.
AND WHAT SHOULD HAVE BEEN A TIME OF JOY IS NOW A DATE THAT WILL LONG BE REMEMBERED IN INFAMY.
WE TAKE SOLACE IN THE KNOWLEDGE THAT A LESSON HAS BEEN LEARNED.
AS MANY LIVES WILL BE HURT AS HELPED IF THE ALLIANCE IS CONSUMMATED.
"WE WILL NOT GO TO WAR AGAINST YOU, BUT OUR FLOCKS MUST FLY APART FROM THIS DAY ON."
BUT THIS CAN'T BE! WE DIDN'T KNOW...
WE DIDN'T EVEN SUSPECT...
MILORD BOEDER, I FOUND THIS.
A GOLDEN DATACHIP. THE KEY THAT ALLOWED THE MURDERERS TO BE SO CLOSE TO THEIR VICTIM.
THE SIGNATURE OF THE PILOT THAT SHOULD HAVE DRIVEN THE TERRORISTS TO THEIR DESTINY IS ENGRAVED ON IT...
...AND IT'S A FAMILIAR ONE.
ISN'T IT, PRINCE JASON?
WERE YOU NOT THE SIXTH MEMBER OF THIS MURDEROUS CABAL?

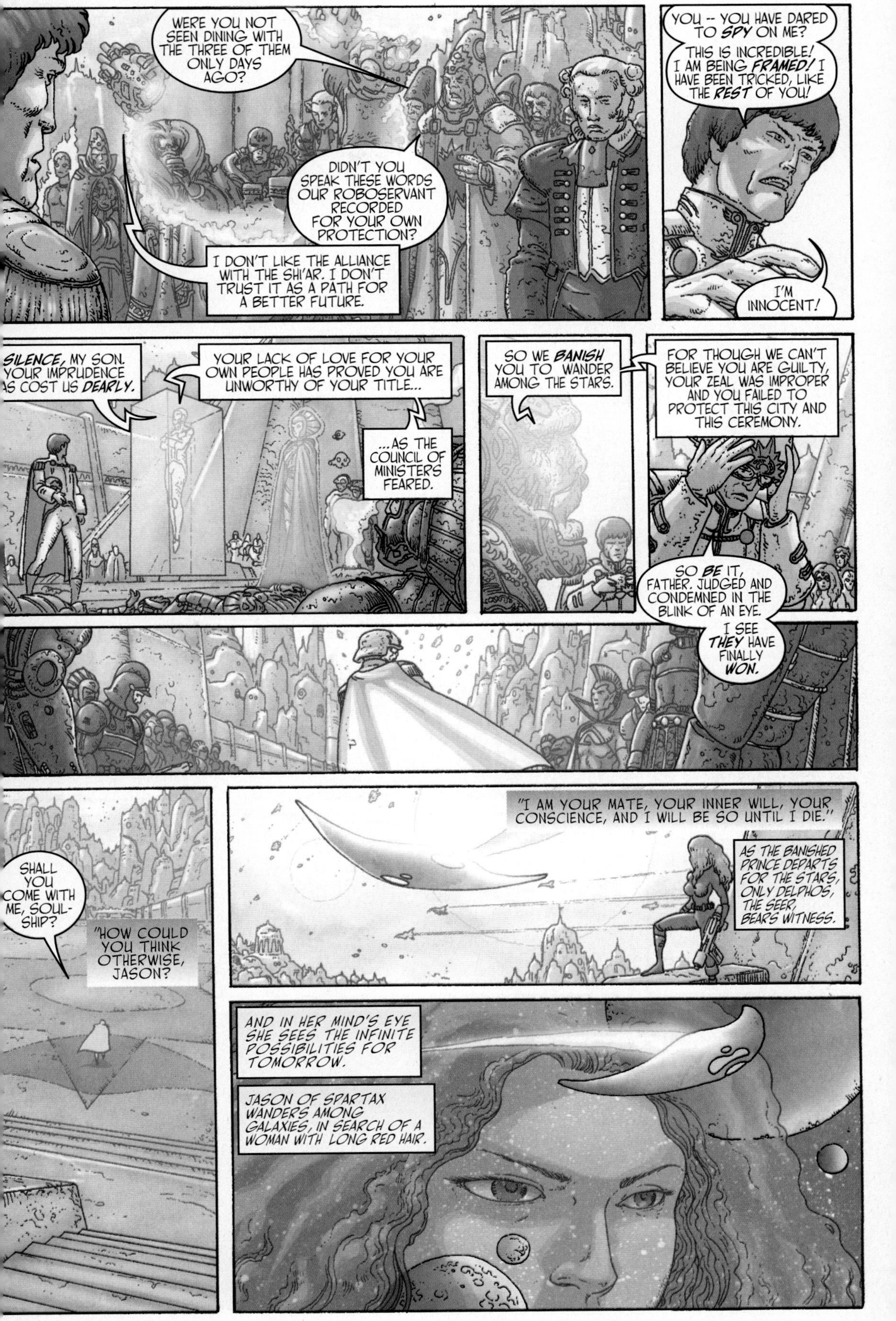
WERE YOU NOT SEEN DINING WITH THE THREE OF THEM ONLY DAYS AGO?
DIDN'T YOU SPEAK THESE WORDS OUR ROBOSERVANT RECORDED FOR YOUR OWN PROTECTION?
I DON'T LIKE THE ALLIANCE WITH THE SHI'AR. I DON'T TRUST IT AS A PATH FOR A BETTER FUTURE.
YOU -- YOU HAVE DARED TO SPY ON ME?
THIS IS INCREDIBLE! I AM BEING FRAMED! I HAVE BEEN TRICKED, LIKE THE REST OF YOU!
I'M INNOCENT!
SILENCE, MY SON. YOUR IMPRUDENCE AS COST US DEARLY.
YOUR LACK OF LOVE FOR YOUR OWN PEOPLE HAS PROVED YOU ARE UNWORTHY OF YOUR TITLE...
...AS THE COUNCIL OF MINISTERS FEARED.
SO WE BANISH YOU TO WANDER AMONG THE STARS.
FOR THOUGH WE CAN'T BELIEVE YOU ARE GUILTY, YOUR ZEAL WAS IMPROPER AND YOU FAILED TO PROTECT THIS CITY AND THIS CEREMONY.
SO BE IT, FATHER. JUDGED AND CONDEMNED IN THE BLINK OF AN EYE.
I SEE THEY HAVE FINALLY WON.
SHALL YOU COME WITH ME, SOUL-SHIP?
"HOW COULD YOU THINK OTHERWISE, JASON?
"I AM YOUR MATE, YOUR INNER WILL, YOUR CONSCIENCE, AND I WILL BE SO UNTIL I DIE."
AS THE BANISHED PRINCE DEPARTS FOR THE STARS, ONLY DELPHOS, THE SEER, BEARS WITNESS.
AND IN HER MIND'S EYE SHE SEES THE INFINITE POSSIBILITIES FOR TOMORROW.
JASON OF SPARTAX WANDERS AMONG GALAXIES, IN SEARCH OF A WOMAN WITH LONG RED HAIR.

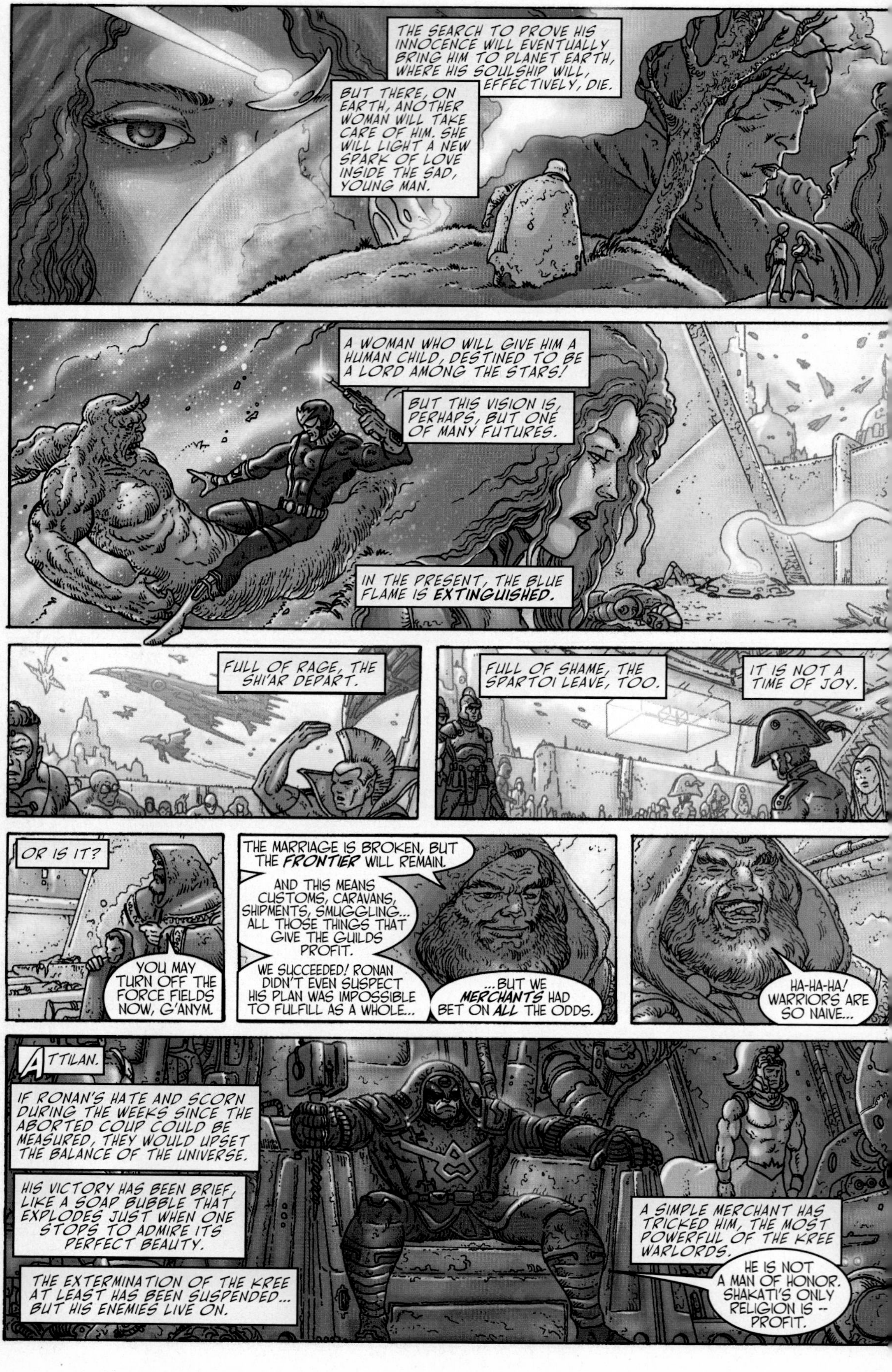

THE SEARCH TO PROVE HIS INNOCENCE WILL EVENTUALLY BRING HIM TO PLANET EARTH, WHERE HIS SOULSHIP WILL, EFFECTIVELY, DIE.
BUT THERE, ON EARTH, ANOTHER WOMAN WILL TAKE CARE OF HIM. SHE WILL LIGHT A NEW SPARK OF LOVE INSIDE THE SAD, YOUNG MAN.
A WOMAN WHO WILL GIVE HIM A HUMAN CHILD, DESTINED TO BE A LORD AMONG THE STARS!
BUT THIS VISION IS, PERHAPS, BUT ONE OF MANY FUTURES.
IN THE PRESENT, THE BLUE FLAME IS **EXTINGUISHED.**
FULL OF RAGE, THE SHI'AR DEPART.
FULL OF SHAME, THE SPARTOI LEAVE, TOO.
IT IS NOT A TIME OF JOY.
OR IS IT?
YOU MAY TURN OFF THE FORCE FIELDS NOW, G'ANYM.
THE MARRIAGE IS BROKEN, BUT THE *FRONTIER* WILL REMAIN.
AND THIS MEANS CUSTOMS, CARAVANS, SHIPMENTS, SMUGGLING... ALL THOSE THINGS THAT GIVE THE GUILDS PROFIT.
WE SUCCEEDED! RONAN DIDN'T EVEN SUSPECT HIS PLAN WAS IMPOSSIBLE TO FULFILL AS A WHOLE...
...BUT WE *MERCHANTS* HAD BET ON *ALL* THE ODDS.
HA-HA-HA! WARRIORS ARE SO NAIVE...
ATTILAN.
IF RONAN'S HATE AND SCORN DURING THE WEEKS SINCE THE ABORTED COUP COULD BE MEASURED, THEY WOULD UPSET THE BALANCE OF THE UNIVERSE.
HIS VICTORY HAS BEEN BRIEF, LIKE A SOAP BUBBLE THAT EXPLODES JUST WHEN ONE STOPS TO ADMIRE ITS PERFECT BEAUTY.
THE EXTERMINATION OF THE KREE AT LEAST HAS BEEN SUSPENDED... BUT HIS ENEMIES LIVE ON.
A SIMPLE MERCHANT HAS TRICKED HIM, THE MOST POWERFUL OF THE KREE WARLORDS.
HE IS NOT A MAN OF HONOR. SHAKATI'S ONLY RELIGION IS -- PROFIT.

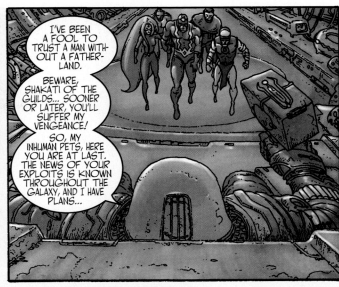

I SEE IT NOW. NO MATTER THE OUTCOME, HE'D ALWAYS HAVE HAD THE WINNING HAND. THE WAR OR A BROKEN ALLIANCE WOULD SUIT HIS INTERESTS *EQUALLY.*

AND EVEN THE MARRIAGE OF SHI'AR AND SPARTAX WOULD HAVE ONLY TAKEN OFF SOME DECIMALS FROM HIS PERCENTAGE.

I'VE BEEN A FOOL TO TRUST A MAN WITHOUT A FATHER-LAND.

BEWARE, SHAKATI OF THE GUILDS... SOONER OR LATER, YOU'LL SUFFER MY VENGEANCE!

SO, MY INHUMAN PETS, HERE YOU ARE AT LAST. THE NEWS OF YOUR EXPLOITS IS KNOWN THROUGHOUT THE GALAXY, AND I HAVE PLANS...

RONAN OF THE KREE, HEED THE WORDS MY HUSBAND PLACES ON MY LIPS!

OF KREE LINEAGE WE ALL ARE, *EQUAL* IN THE EYES OF HALA. AS SONS OF THE KREE, WE *CHALLENGE* YOU!

THE SYMBOL OF THE ROYAL FAMILY?

DO YOU THINK I'LL BE SO LOW AS TO ACCEPT THE CHALLENGE OF SUCH AN INFERIOR BEING AS AN -- INHUMAN?

FORCED TO ACT FOLLOWING YOUR ORDERS, BLACK BOLT HAS LOST HIS HONOR -- AS WE ALL HAVE.

FOR THE SAKE OF OUR PEOPLE, NOW IT'S TIME TO TAKE HIS -- OUR -- HONOR *BACK.*

BLACK BOLT HAS SPILLED HIS BLOOD, AND THE BLOOD OF THE KREE'S ENEMIES.

THAT MAKES HIM YOUR EQUAL, RONAN. HIS KREE LEGACY CHALLENGE YOU -- AND HE DEMANDS HIS RIGHT TO TAKE HIS HONOR BACK, TO BE YOUR SLAVE NO MORE.

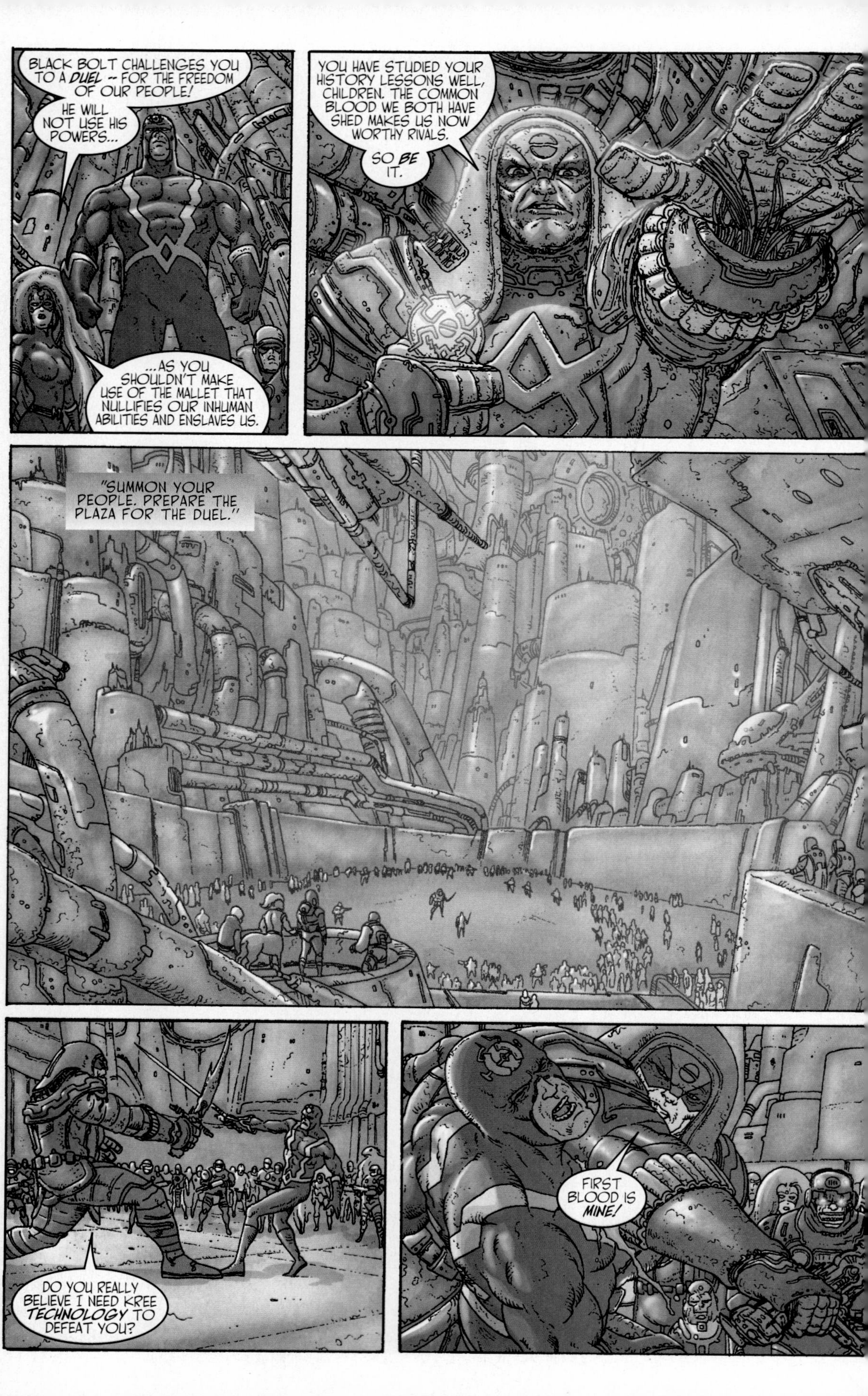
BLACK BOLT CHALLENGES YOU TO A DUEL -- FOR THE FREEDOM OF OUR PEOPLE!
HE WILL NOT USE HIS POWERS...
...AS YOU SHOULDN'T MAKE USE OF THE MALLET THAT NULLIFIES OUR INHUMAN ABILITIES AND ENSLAVES US.
YOU HAVE STUDIED YOUR HISTORY LESSONS WELL, CHILDREN. THE COMMON BLOOD WE BOTH HAVE SHED MAKES US NOW WORTHY RIVALS.
SO BE IT.
"SUMMON YOUR PEOPLE. PREPARE THE PLAZA FOR THE DUEL."
DO YOU REALLY BELIEVE I NEED KREE TECHNOLOGY TO DEFEAT YOU?
FIRST BLOOD IS MINE!

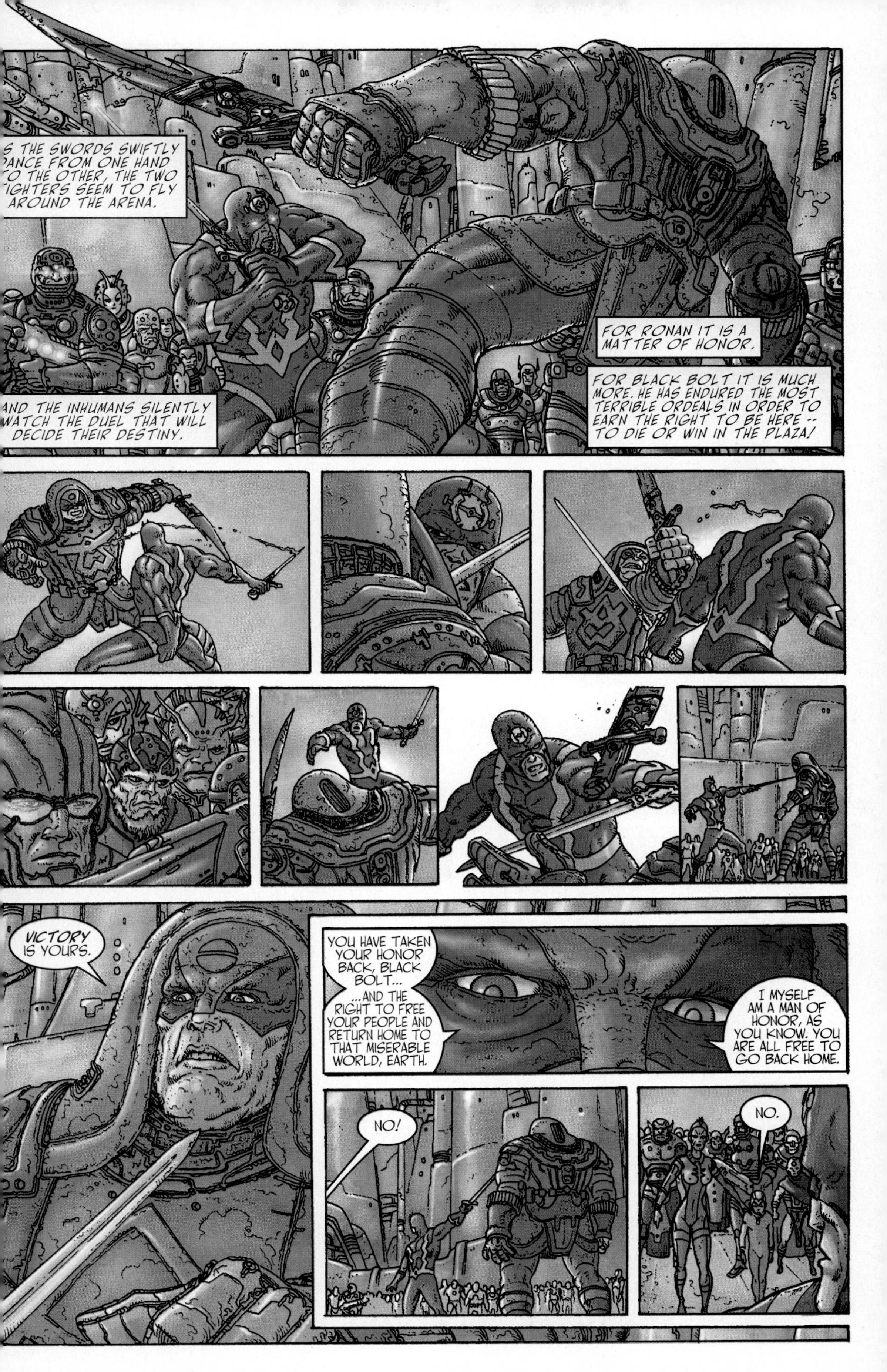

S THE SWORDS SWIFTLY DANCE FROM ONE HAND TO THE OTHER, THE TWO FIGHTERS SEEM TO FLY AROUND THE ARENA.
AND THE INHUMANS SILENTLY WATCH THE DUEL THAT WILL DECIDE THEIR DESTINY.
FOR RONAN IT IS A MATTER OF HONOR.
FOR BLACK BOLT IT IS MUCH MORE. HE HAS ENDURED THE MOST TERRIBLE ORDEALS IN ORDER TO EARN THE RIGHT TO BE HERE -- TO DIE OR WIN IN THE PLAZA!
VICTORY IS YOURS.
YOU HAVE TAKEN YOUR HONOR BACK, BLACK BOLT...
...AND THE RIGHT TO FREE YOUR PEOPLE AND RETURN HOME TO THAT MISERABLE WORLD, EARTH.
I MYSELF AM A MAN OF HONOR, AS YOU KNOW. YOU ARE ALL FREE TO GO BACK HOME.
NO!
NO.

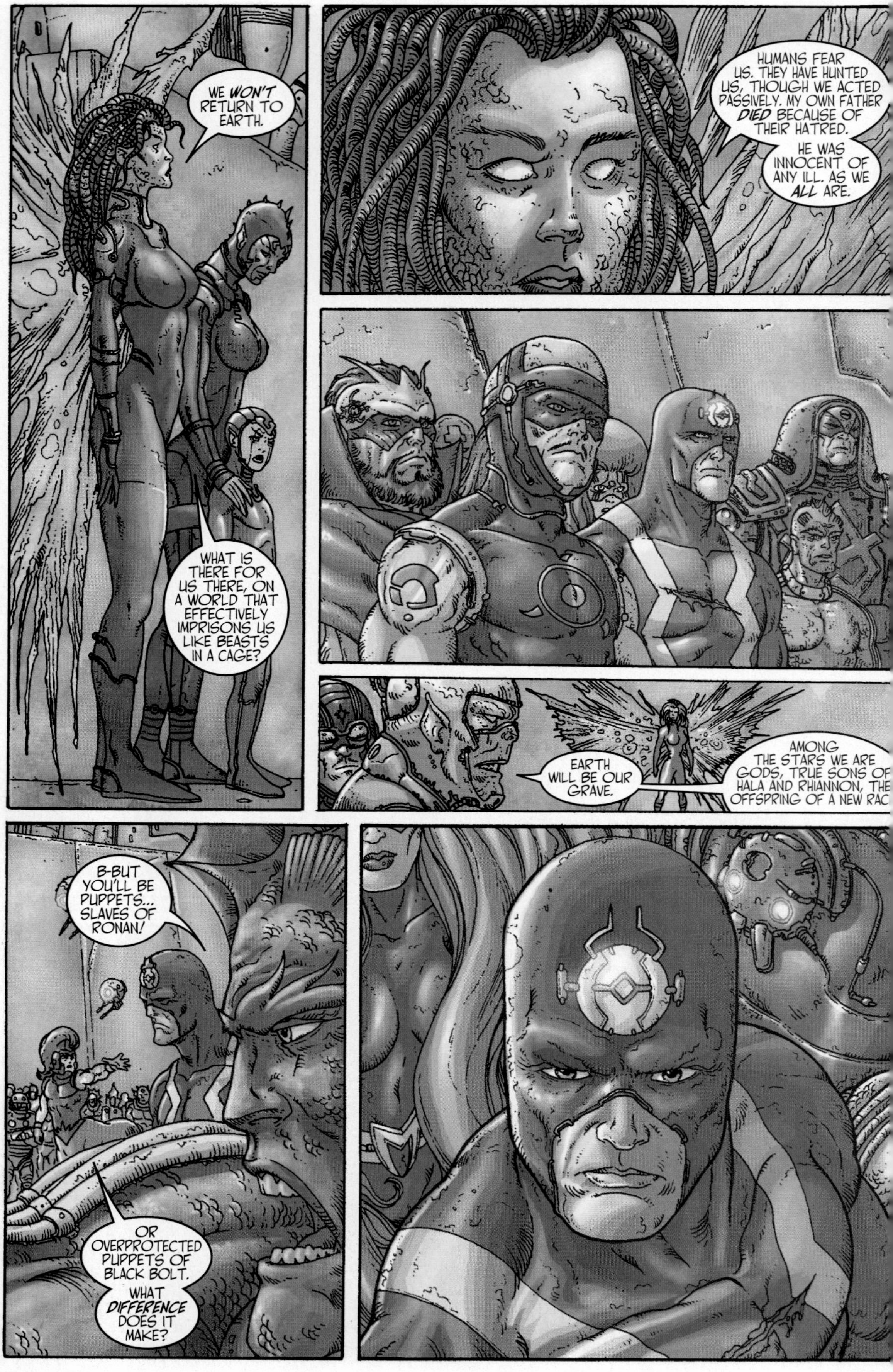
WE WON'T RETURN TO EARTH.
WHAT IS THERE FOR US THERE, ON A WORLD THAT EFFECTIVELY IMPRISONS US LIKE BEASTS IN A CAGE?
HUMANS FEAR US. THEY HAVE HUNTED US, THOUGH WE ACTED PASSIVELY. MY OWN FATHER DIED BECAUSE OF THEIR HATRED.
HE WAS INNOCENT OF ANY ILL, AS WE ALL ARE.
EARTH WILL BE OUR GRAVE.
AMONG THE STARS WE ARE GODS, TRUE SONS OF HALA AND RHIANNON, THE OFFSPRING OF A NEW RAC
B-BUT YOU'LL BE PUPPETS... SLAVES OF RONAN!
OR OVERPROTECTED PUPPETS OF BLACK BOLT.
WHAT DIFFERENCE DOES IT MAKE?

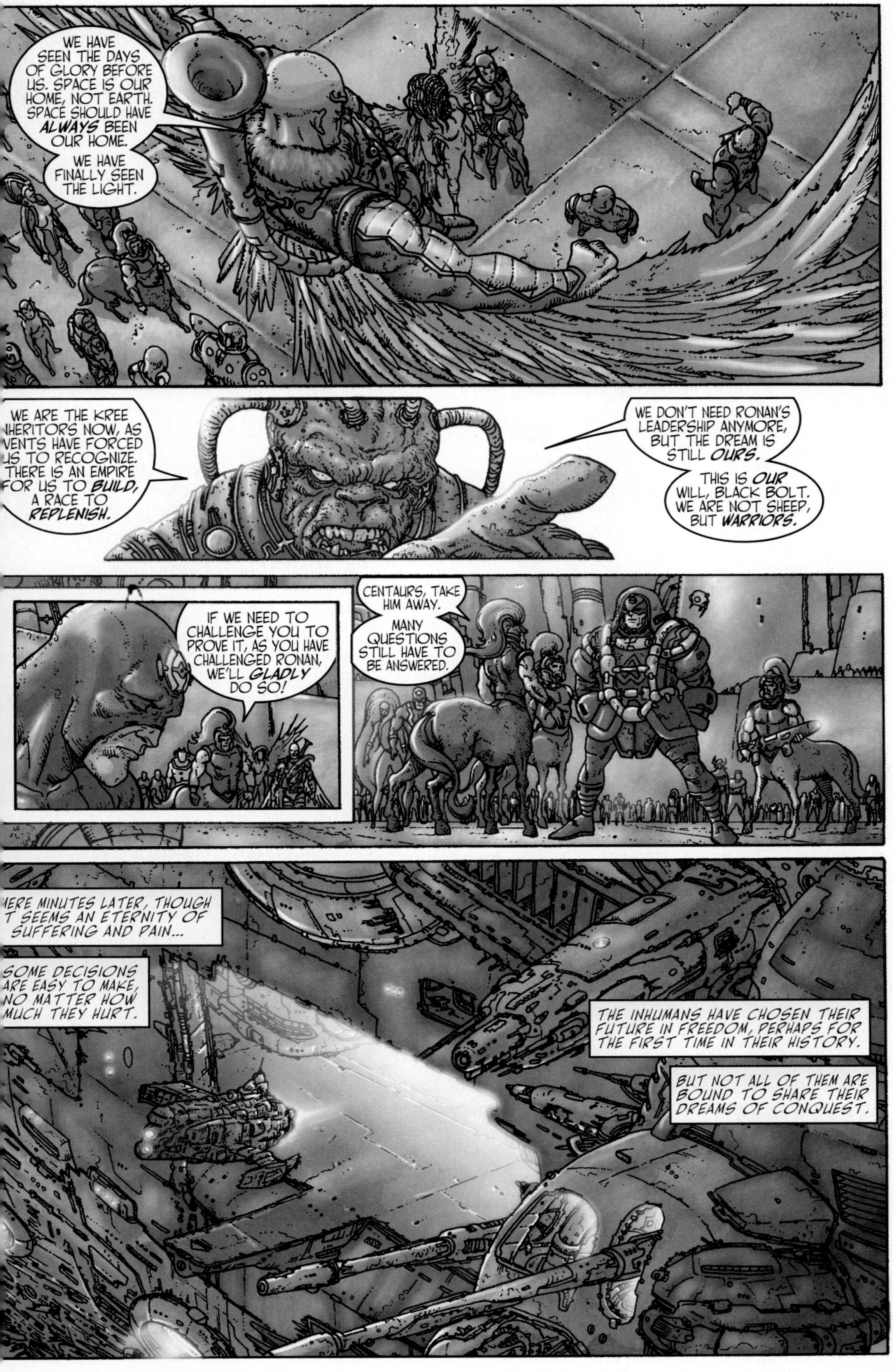

WE HAVE SEEN THE DAYS OF GLORY BEFORE US. SPACE IS OUR HOME, NOT EARTH. SPACE SHOULD HAVE ALWAYS BEEN OUR HOME.
WE HAVE FINALLY SEEN THE LIGHT.
WE ARE THE KREE INHERITORS NOW, AS EVENTS HAVE FORCED US TO RECOGNIZE. THERE IS AN EMPIRE FOR US TO BUILD, A RACE TO REPLENISH.
WE DON'T NEED RONAN'S LEADERSHIP ANYMORE, BUT THE DREAM IS STILL OURS.
THIS IS OUR WILL, BLACK BOLT. WE ARE NOT SHEEP, BUT WARRIORS.
IF WE NEED TO CHALLENGE YOU TO PROVE IT, AS YOU HAVE CHALLENGED RONAN, WE'LL GLADLY DO SO!
CENTAURS, TAKE HIM AWAY.
MANY QUESTIONS STILL HAVE TO BE ANSWERED.
MERE MINUTES LATER, THOUGH IT SEEMS AN ETERNITY OF SUFFERING AND PAIN...
SOME DECISIONS ARE EASY TO MAKE, NO MATTER HOW MUCH THEY HURT.
THE INHUMANS HAVE CHOSEN THEIR FUTURE IN FREEDOM, PERHAPS FOR THE FIRST TIME IN THEIR HISTORY.
BUT NOT ALL OF THEM ARE BOUND TO SHARE THEIR DREAMS OF CONQUEST.

NOBODY COMES TO SAY FAREWELL.

...AND A FUTURE IN WHICH THEIR FORMER SOVEREIGN AND THE ROYAL FAMILY WON'T SHARE.

THE INHUMANS ARE BUSY PREPARING THEMSELVES FOR WAR. BLACK BOLT'S ULTIMATE SACRIFICE HAS WON THEM THEIR FREEDOM...

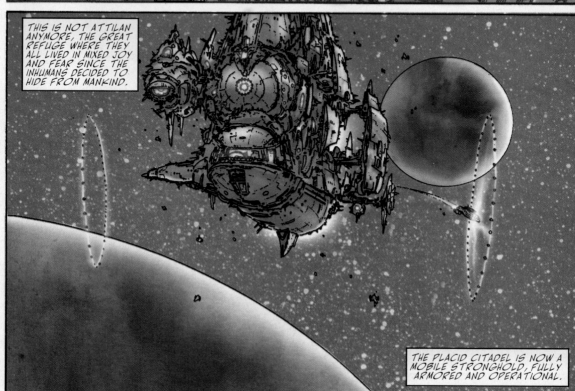

THIS IS NOT ATTILAN ANYMORE, THE GREAT REFUGE WHERE THEY ALL LIVED IN MIXED JOY AND FEAR SINCE THE INHUMANS DECIDED TO HIDE FROM MANKIND.

THE PLACID CITADEL IS NOW A MOBILE STRONGHOLD, FULLY ARMORED AND OPERATIONAL.

IT JUMPS TO HYPERSPACE...

...BOUND TO BECOME A HORNET INSIDE THE SHI'AR NESTS.

AND THE ROYAL FAMILY SUDDENLY FEEL THE WEIGHT OF THEIR SOLITUDE.

BLACK BOLT ACCEPTS THIS NEW TURN IN HIS LIFE. PERHAPS THIS IS THE PUNISHMENT HE DESERVES FOR HIS ACT OF TREASON...

...NOT ONLY AGAINST THE SHI'AR OR THE SPARTOI... BUT AGAINST HIS OWN BELIEFS.

HE REMEMBERS JASON'S WORDS: "WHAT MAKES A GOOD, WORTHY KING?

"ALL FOR MY PEOPLE. LIFE AND DEATH. FOR MY PEOPLE ONLY.

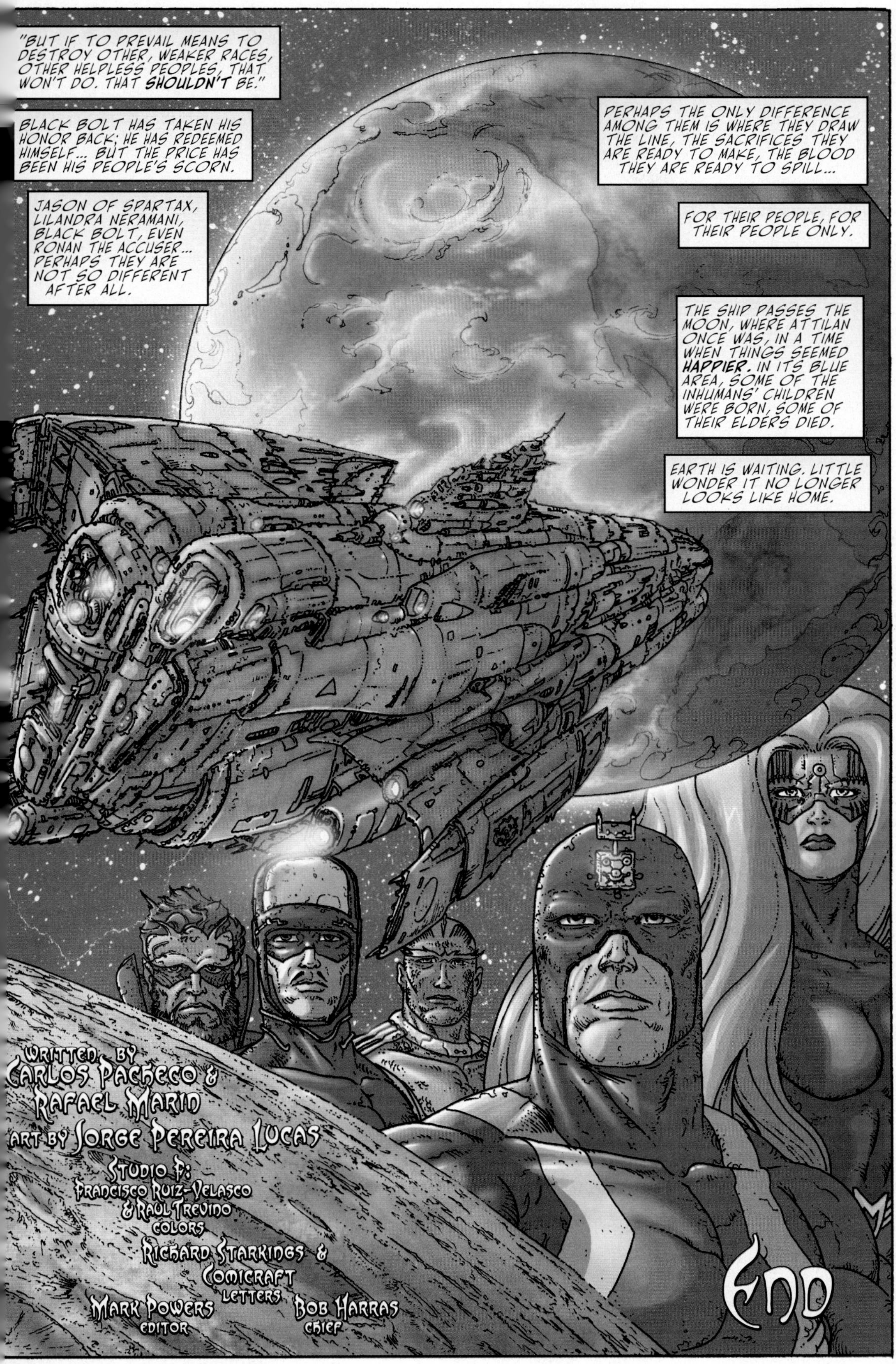
"BUT IF TO PREVAIL MEANS TO DESTROY OTHER, WEAKER RACES, OTHER HELPLESS PEOPLES, THAT WON'T DO. THAT **SHOULDN'T** BE."
BLACK BOLT HAS TAKEN HIS HONOR BACK; HE HAS REDEEMED HIMSELF... BUT THE PRICE HAS BEEN HIS PEOPLE'S SCORN.
JASON OF SPARTAX, LILANDRA NERAMANI, BLACK BOLT, EVEN RONAN THE ACCUSER... PERHAPS THEY ARE NOT SO DIFFERENT AFTER ALL.
PERHAPS THE ONLY DIFFERENCE AMONG THEM IS WHERE THEY DRAW THE LINE, THE SACRIFICES THEY ARE READY TO MAKE, THE BLOOD THEY ARE READY TO SPILL...
FOR THEIR PEOPLE, FOR THEIR PEOPLE ONLY.
THE SHIP PASSES THE MOON, WHERE ATTILAN ONCE WAS, IN A TIME WHEN THINGS SEEMED **HAPPIER.** IN ITS BLUE AREA, SOME OF THE INHUMANS' CHILDREN WERE BORN, SOME OF THEIR ELDERS DIED.
EARTH IS WAITING. LITTLE WONDER IT NO LONGER LOOKS LIKE HOME.
WRITTEN BY CARLOS PACHECO & RAFAEL MARIN
ART BY JORGE PEREIRA LUCAS
STUDIO F: FRANCISCO RUIZ-VELASCO & RAUL TREVINO COLORS
RICHARD STARKINGS & COMICRAFT LETTERS
MARK POWERS EDITOR
BOB HARRAS CHIEF
END

As Black Bolt guided his family back to Earth, events were already transpiring on the Inhumans' home world that would soon engulf them.

The Inhumans' longtime friends in the Fantastic Four had encountered a mysterious and beautiful woman known as Senso. Senso guided the Grey Gargoyle into a confrontation with the Thing that left the hero petrified into stone by the villain's touch. When the Thing was cured of the Gargoyle's power, he found he had gained the ability to transform back into Ben Grimm. Senso evaded the Fantastic Four, and her true purpose remained a mystery.

During an exploration of the Negative Zone, the Fantastic Four came across Maximus, still trapped there in exile. However, Maximus had been joined by his ever-faithful Alpha Primitives, similarly exiled by Ronan. Discovering the equipment of the Four Freedoms Plaza building that Nathaniel Richards had sent to the Negative Zone for protection years earlier, Maximus had begun to amass a new power base and came to the Fantastic Four's aid against Annihilus. Maximus remained in the Negative Zone to continue ruling over his new empire.

The Human Torch had set his sights on Hollywood, intent at achieving his dream of film stardom. Little did Johnny Storm suspect that his co-worker Lon Zelig was in reality his old foe, the Super-Skrull, gone undercover.

In other developments, the Invisible Woman and Mr. Fantastic were expecting their second child, and the infant's birth was imminent. They were also reunited with their son Franklin, recently returned from an off-planet excursion they had subjected him to for his own protection.

Cast out by a people who no longer wanted them, Black Bolt, Gorgon, Karnak, Medusa and Triton were about to find themselves reunited with a world even less hospitable to them than when they had left it.

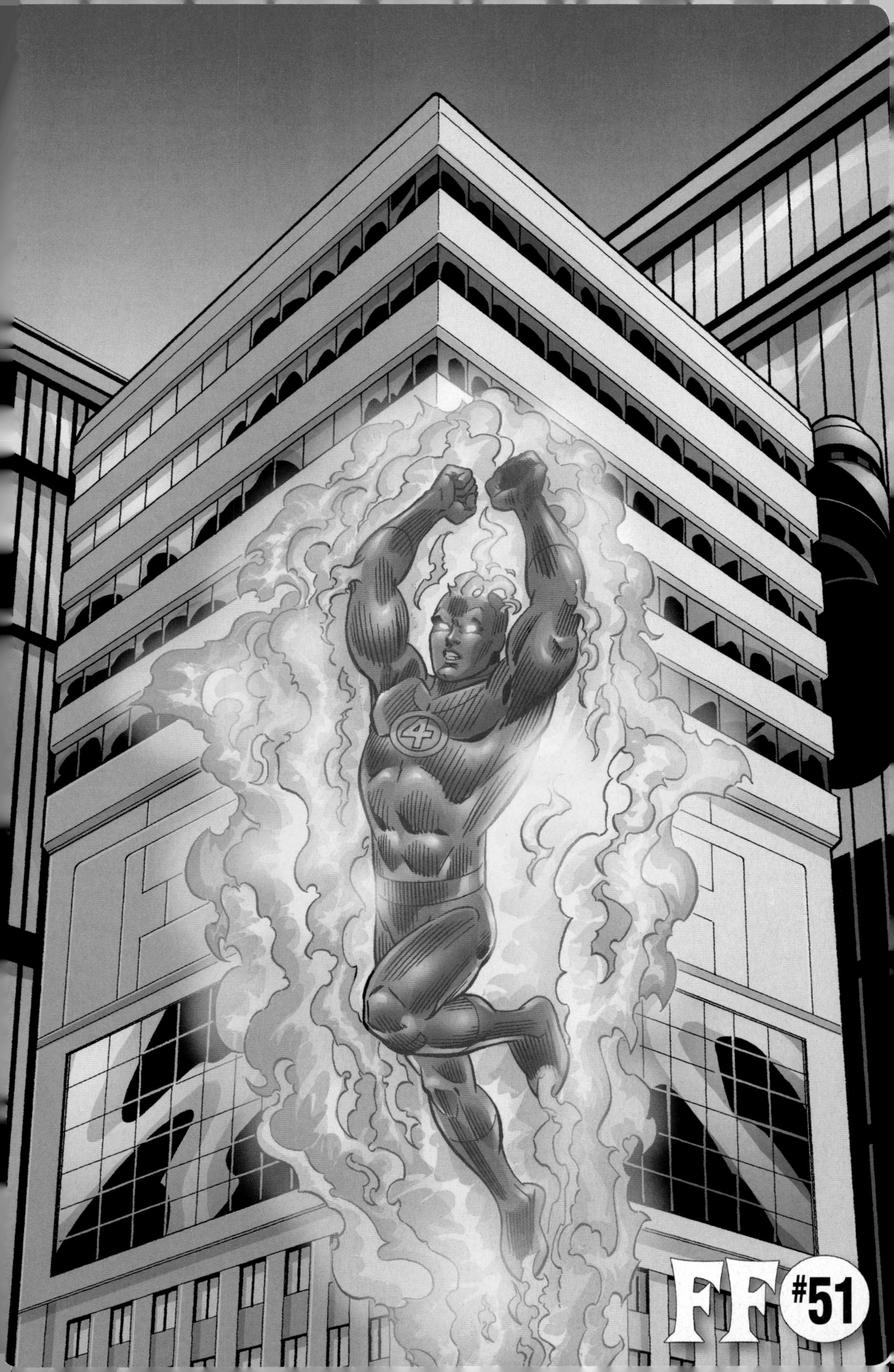
FF #51

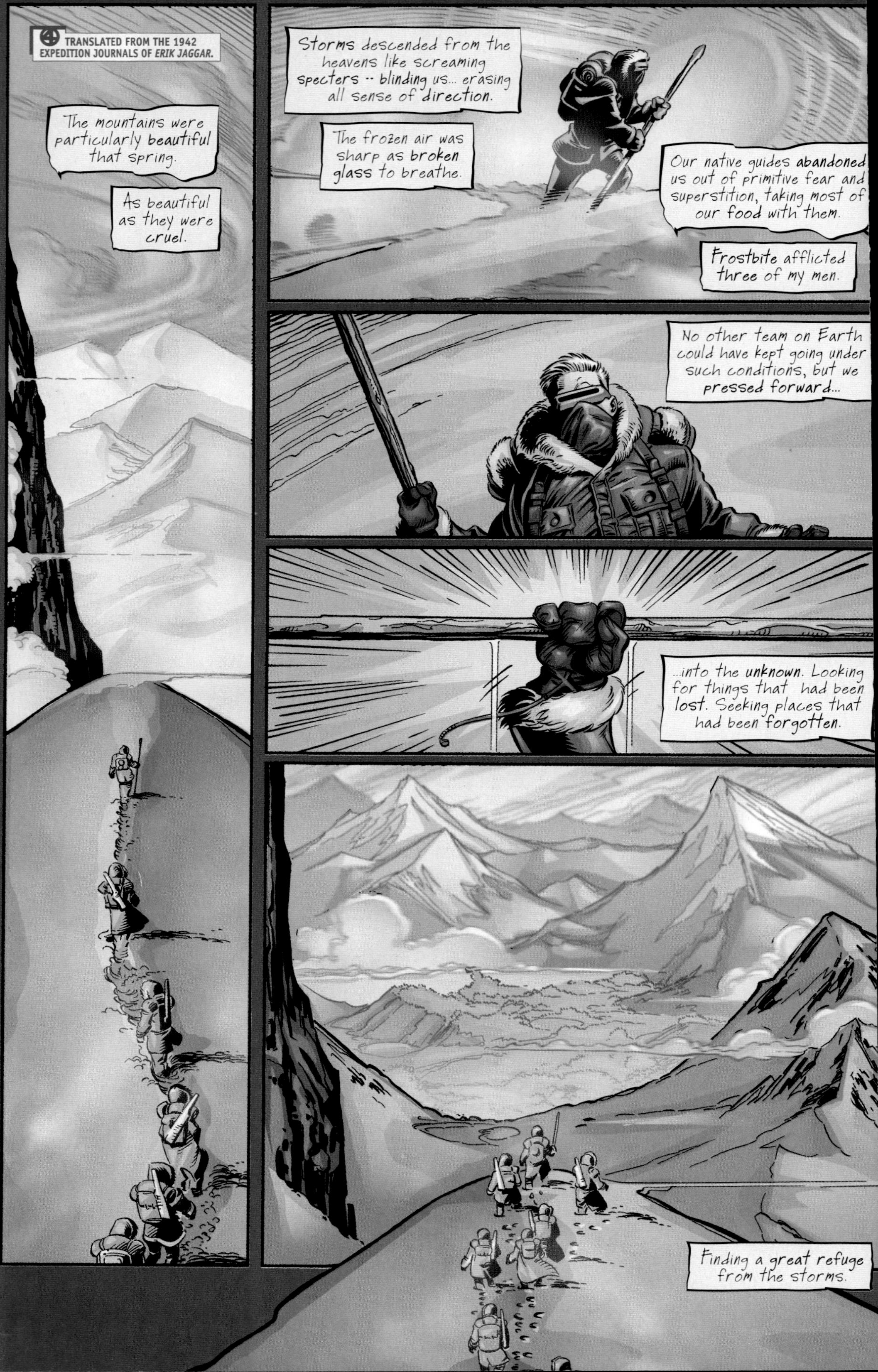
TRANSLATED FROM THE 1942 EXPEDITION JOURNALS OF ERIK JAGGAR.
The mountains were particularly beautiful that spring.
As beautiful as they were cruel.
Storms descended from the heavens like screaming specters -- blinding us... erasing all sense of direction.
The frozen air was sharp as broken glass to breathe.
Our native guides abandoned us out of primitive fear and superstition, taking most of our food with them.
Frostbite afflicted three of my men.
No other team on Earth could have kept going under such conditions, but we pressed forward...
...into the unknown. Looking for things that had been lost. Seeking places that had been forgotten.
Finding a great refuge from the storms.

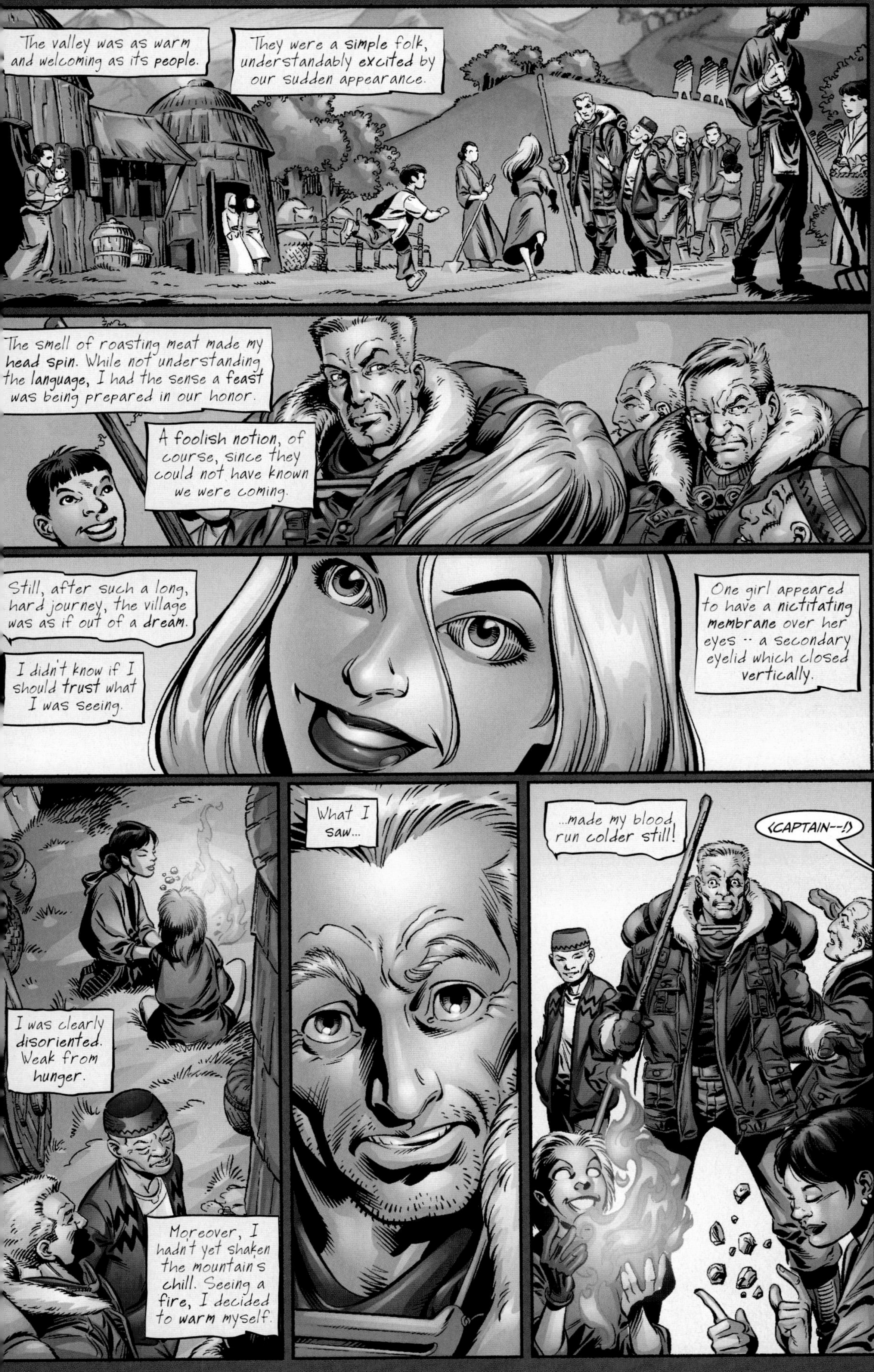
The valley was as warm and welcoming as its people.
They were a simple folk, understandably excited by our sudden appearance.
The smell of roasting meat made my head spin. While not understanding the language, I had the sense a feast was being prepared in our honor.
A foolish notion, of course, since they could not have known we were coming.
Still, after such a long, hard journey, the village was as if out of a dream.
I didn't know if I should trust what I was seeing.
One girl appeared to have a nictitating membrane over her eyes -- a secondary eyelid which closed vertically.
I was clearly disoriented. Weak from hunger.
Moreover, I hadn't yet shaken the mountain's chill. Seeing a fire, I decided to warm myself.
What I saw...
...made my blood run colder still!
‹CAPTAIN--!›

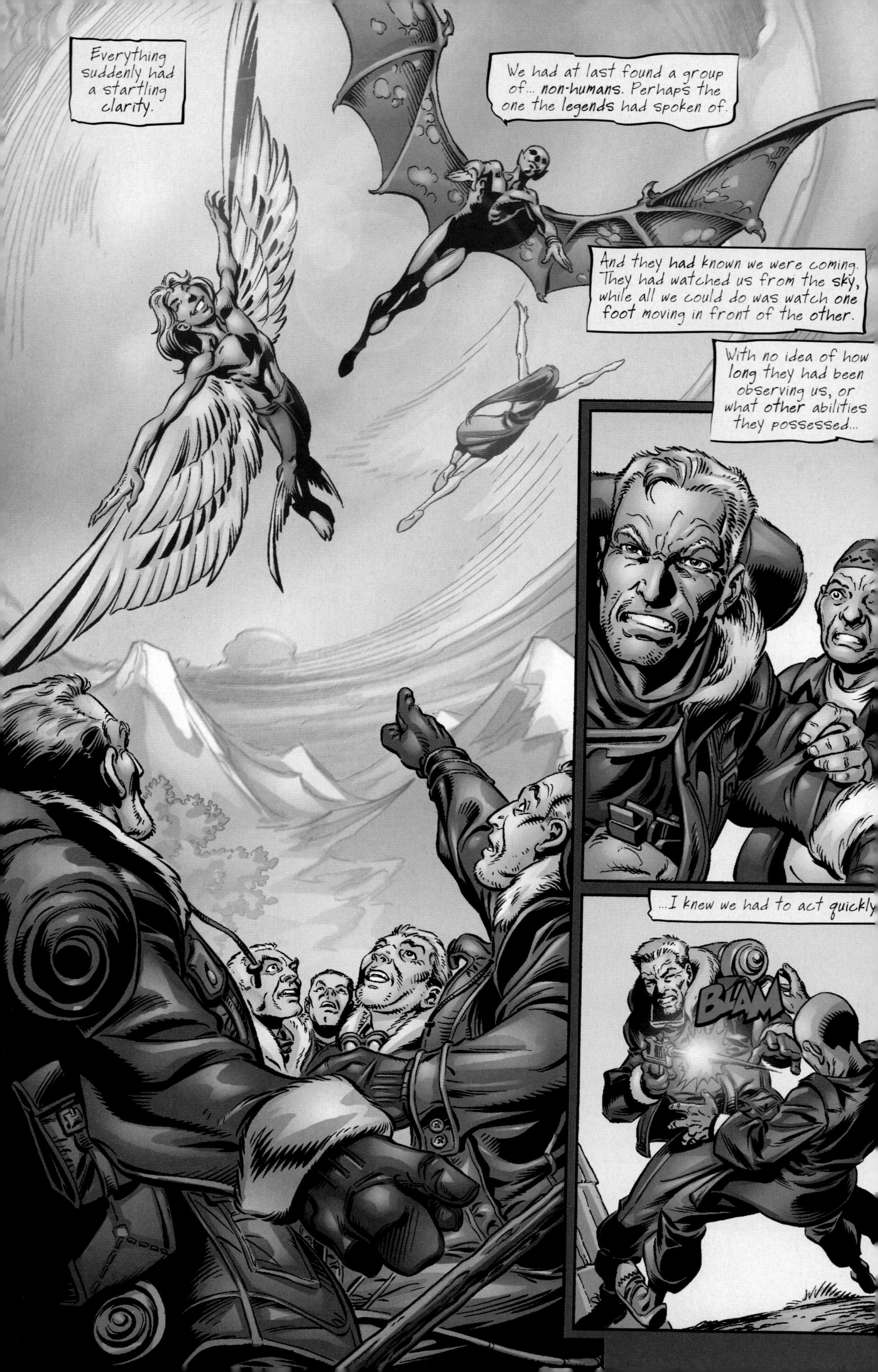
Everything suddenly had a startling clarity.
We had at last found a group of... non-humans. Perhaps the one the legends had spoken of.
And they had known we were coming. They had watched us from the sky, while all we could do was watch one foot moving in front of the other.
With no idea of how long they had been observing us, or what other abilities they possessed...
...I knew we had to act quickly.
BLAM

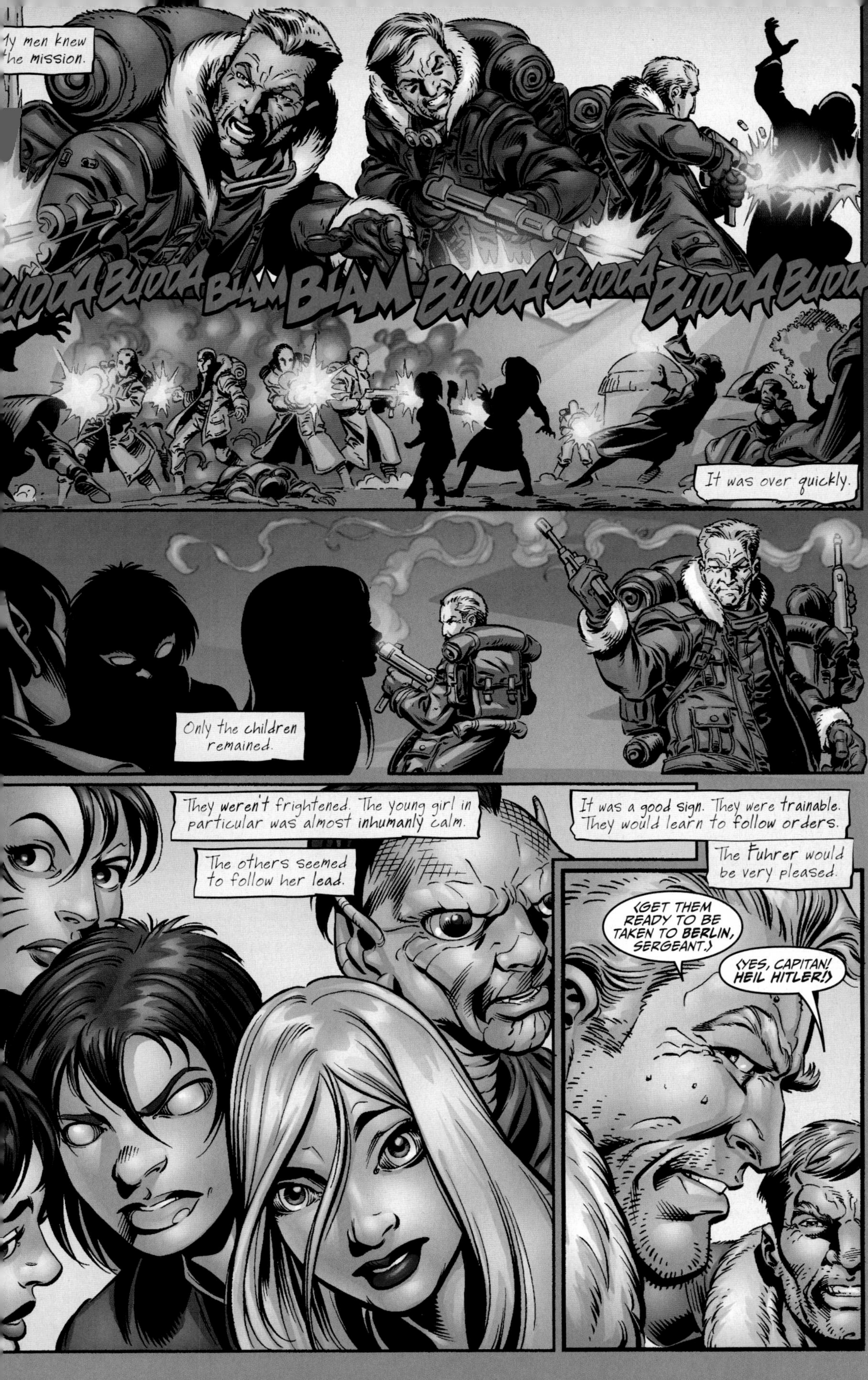

My men knew the mission.
BUDDA BUDDA BLAM BLAM BUDDA BUDDA BUDDA BUDDA
It was over quickly.
Only the children remained.
They weren't frightened. The young girl in particular was almost inhumanly calm.
The others seemed to follow her lead.
It was a good sign. They were trainable. They would learn to follow orders.
The Fuhrer would be very pleased.
‹GET THEM READY TO BE TAKEN TO BERLIN, SERGEANT.›
‹YES, CAPITAN! HEIL HITLER!›

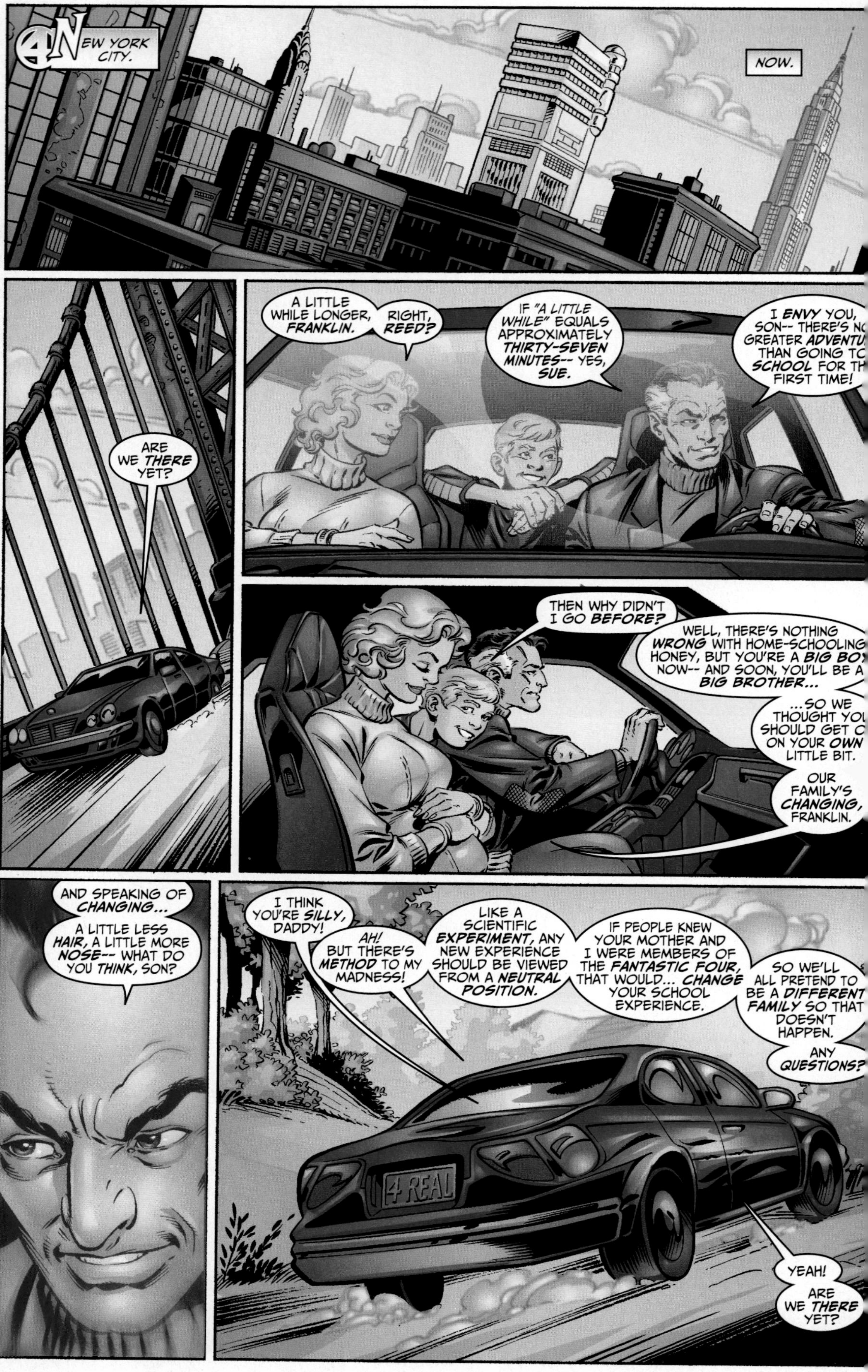

NEW YORK CITY.
NOW.
ARE WE THERE YET?
A LITTLE WHILE LONGER, FRANKLIN.
RIGHT, REED?
IF "A LITTLE WHILE" EQUALS APPROXIMATELY THIRTY-SEVEN MINUTES-- YES, SUE.
I ENVY YOU, SON-- THERE'S NO GREATER ADVENTU THAN GOING TO SCHOOL FOR TH FIRST TIME!
THEN WHY DIDN'T I GO BEFORE?
WELL, THERE'S NOTHING WRONG WITH HOME-SCHOOLING HONEY, BUT YOU'RE A BIG BO NOW-- AND SOON, YOU'LL BE A BIG BROTHER...
...SO WE THOUGHT YO SHOULD GET O ON YOUR OWN LITTLE BIT.
OUR FAMILY'S CHANGING, FRANKLIN.
AND SPEAKING OF CHANGING...
A LITTLE LESS HAIR, A LITTLE MORE NOSE-- WHAT DO YOU THINK, SON?
I THINK YOU'RE SILLY, DADDY!
AH! BUT THERE'S METHOD TO MY MADNESS!
LIKE A SCIENTIFIC EXPERIMENT, ANY NEW EXPERIENCE SHOULD BE VIEWED FROM A NEUTRAL POSITION.
IF PEOPLE KNEW YOUR MOTHER AND I WERE MEMBERS OF THE FANTASTIC FOUR, THAT WOULD... CHANGE YOUR SCHOOL EXPERIENCE.
SO WE'LL ALL PRETEND TO BE A DIFFERENT FAMILY SO THAT DOESN'T HAPPEN.
ANY QUESTIONS?
4 REAL
YEAH!
ARE WE THERE YET?

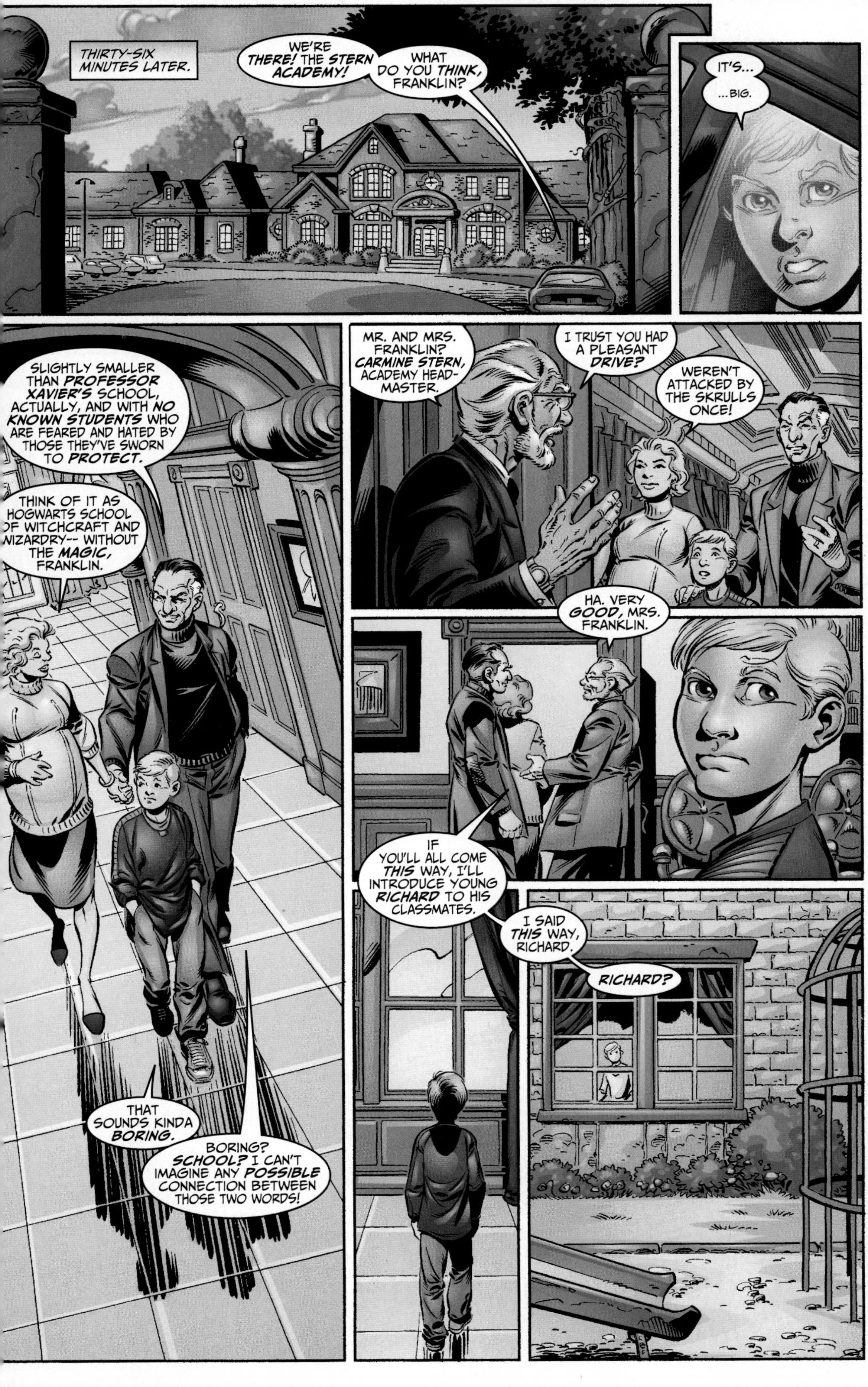
THIRTY-SIX MINUTES LATER.
WE'RE THERE! THE STERN ACADEMY!
WHAT DO YOU THINK, FRANKLIN?
IT'S...
...BIG.
SLIGHTLY SMALLER THAN PROFESSOR XAVIER'S SCHOOL, ACTUALLY, AND WITH NO KNOWN STUDENTS WHO ARE FEARED AND HATED BY THOSE THEY'VE SWORN TO PROTECT.
THINK OF IT AS HOGWARTS SCHOOL OF WITCHCRAFT AND WIZARDRY-- WITHOUT THE MAGIC, FRANKLIN.
THAT SOUNDS KINDA BORING.
BORING? SCHOOL? I CAN'T IMAGINE ANY POSSIBLE CONNECTION BETWEEN THOSE TWO WORDS!
MR. AND MRS. FRANKLIN? CARMINE STERN, ACADEMY HEAD-MASTER.
I TRUST YOU HAD A PLEASANT DRIVE?
WEREN'T ATTACKED BY THE SKRULLS ONCE!
HA. VERY GOOD, MRS. FRANKLIN.
IF YOU'LL ALL COME THIS WAY, I'LL INTRODUCE YOUNG RICHARD TO HIS CLASSMATES.
I SAID THIS WAY, RICHARD.
RICHARD?

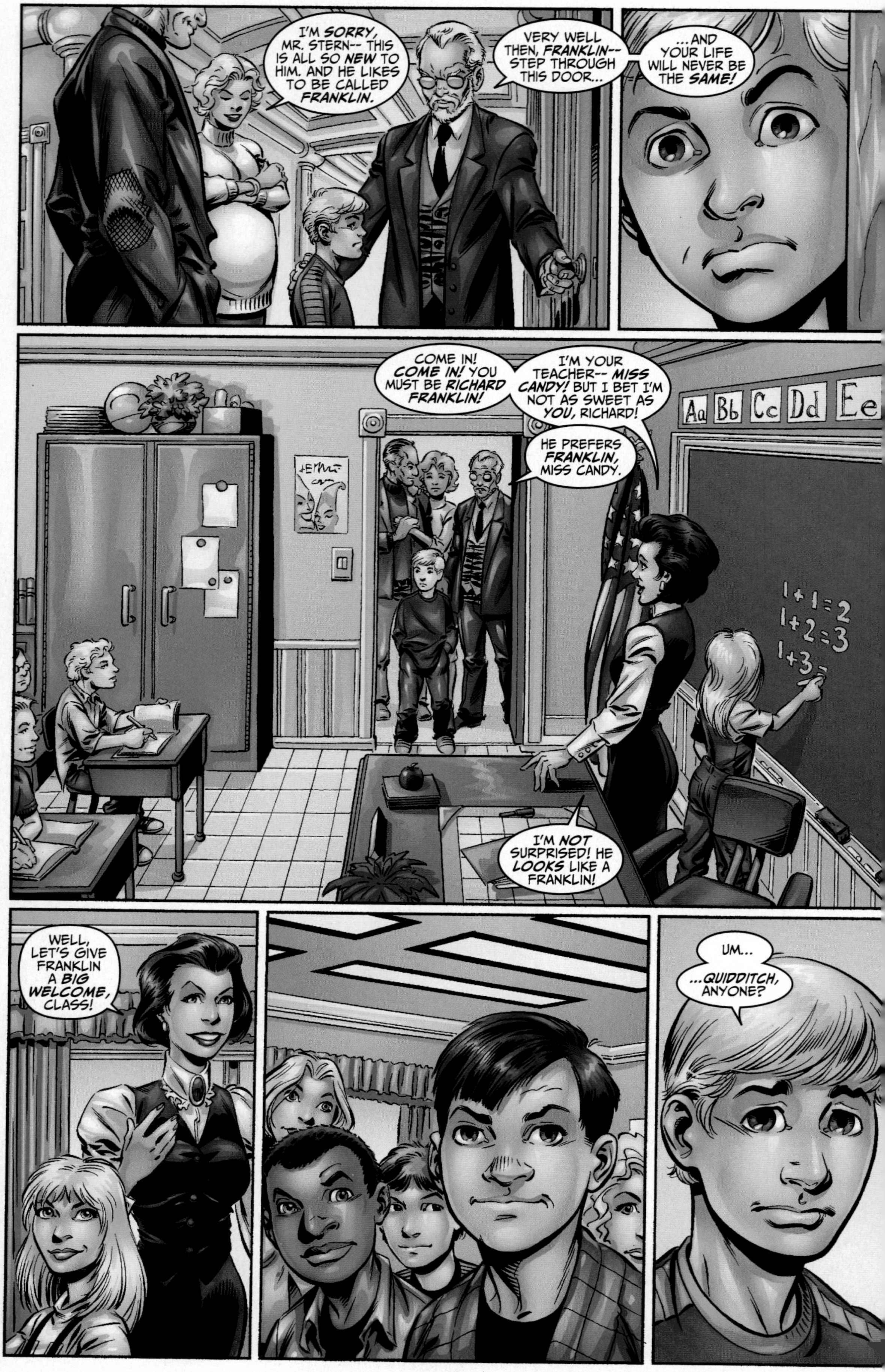
I'M SORRY, MR. STERN-- THIS IS ALL SO NEW TO HIM. AND HE LIKES TO BE CALLED FRANKLIN.
VERY WELL THEN, FRANKLIN-- STEP THROUGH THIS DOOR...
...AND YOUR LIFE WILL NEVER BE THE SAME!
COME IN! COME IN! YOU MUST BE RICHARD FRANKLIN!
I'M YOUR TEACHER-- MISS CANDY! BUT I BET I'M NOT AS SWEET AS YOU, RICHARD!
HE PREFERS FRANKLIN, MISS CANDY.
Aa Bb Cc Dd Ee
1+1=2
1+2=3
1+3=
I'M NOT SURPRISED! HE LOOKS LIKE A FRANKLIN!
WELL, LET'S GIVE FRANKLIN A BIG WELCOME, CLASS!
UM...
...QUIDDITCH, ANYONE?

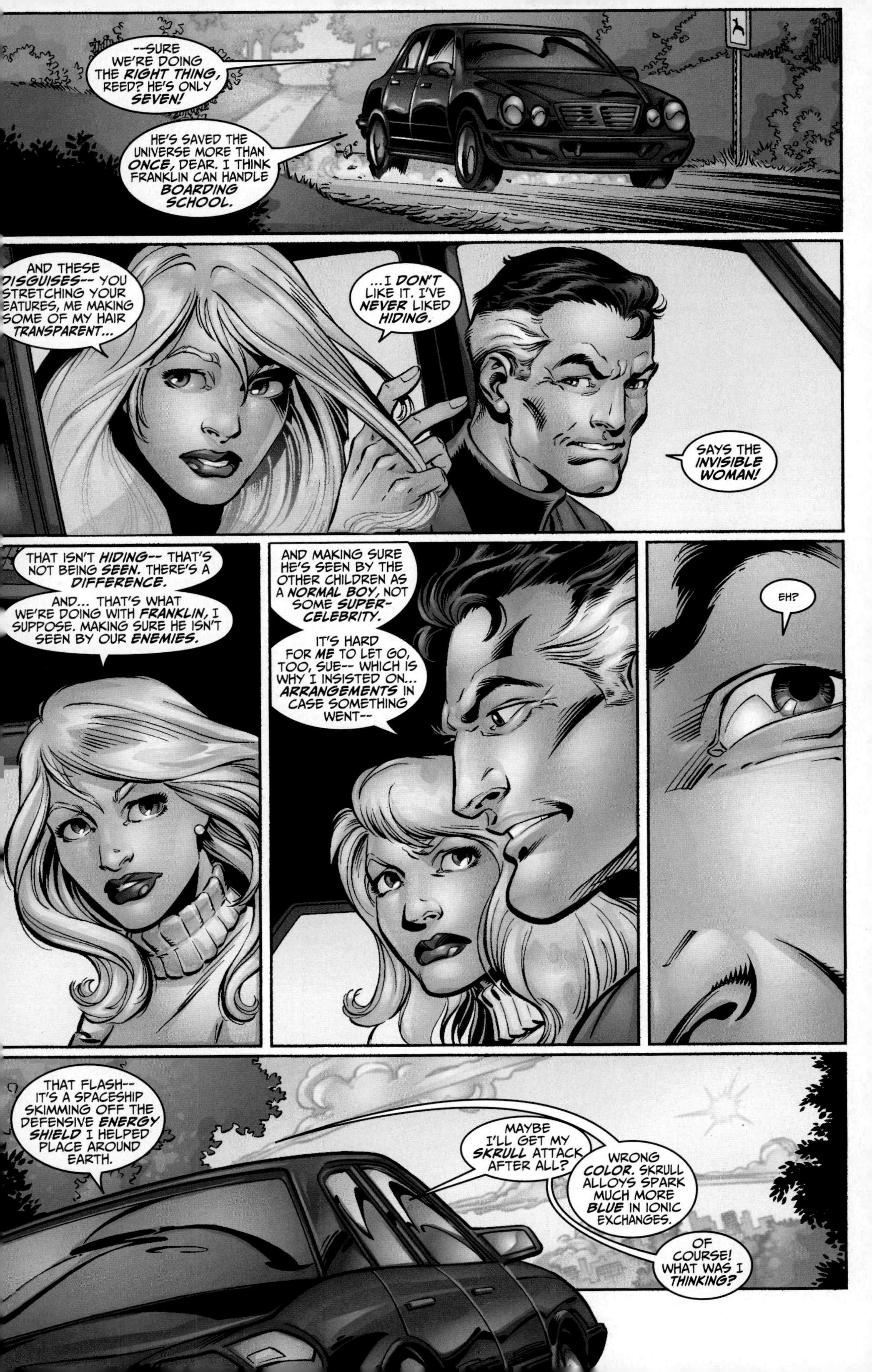
--SURE WE'RE DOING THE RIGHT THING, REED? HE'S ONLY SEVEN!
HE'S SAVED THE UNIVERSE MORE THAN ONCE, DEAR. I THINK FRANKLIN CAN HANDLE BOARDING SCHOOL.
AND THESE DISGUISES-- YOU STRETCHING YOUR FEATURES, ME MAKING SOME OF MY HAIR TRANSPARENT...
...I DON'T LIKE IT. I'VE NEVER LIKED HIDING.
SAYS THE INVISIBLE WOMAN!
THAT ISN'T HIDING-- THAT'S NOT BEING SEEN. THERE'S A DIFFERENCE.
AND... THAT'S WHAT WE'RE DOING WITH FRANKLIN, I SUPPOSE. MAKING SURE HE ISN'T SEEN BY OUR ENEMIES.
AND MAKING SURE HE'S SEEN BY THE OTHER CHILDREN AS A NORMAL BOY, NOT SOME SUPER-CELEBRITY.
IT'S HARD FOR ME TO LET GO, TOO, SUE-- WHICH IS WHY I INSISTED ON... ARRANGEMENTS IN CASE SOMETHING WENT--
EH?
THAT FLASH-- IT'S A SPACESHIP SKIMMING OFF THE DEFENSIVE ENERGY SHIELD I HELPED PLACE AROUND EARTH.
MAYBE I'LL GET MY SKRULL ATTACK AFTER ALL?
WRONG COLOR. SKRULL ALLOYS SPARK MUCH MORE BLUE IN IONIC EXCHANGES.
OF COURSE! WHAT WAS I THINKING?

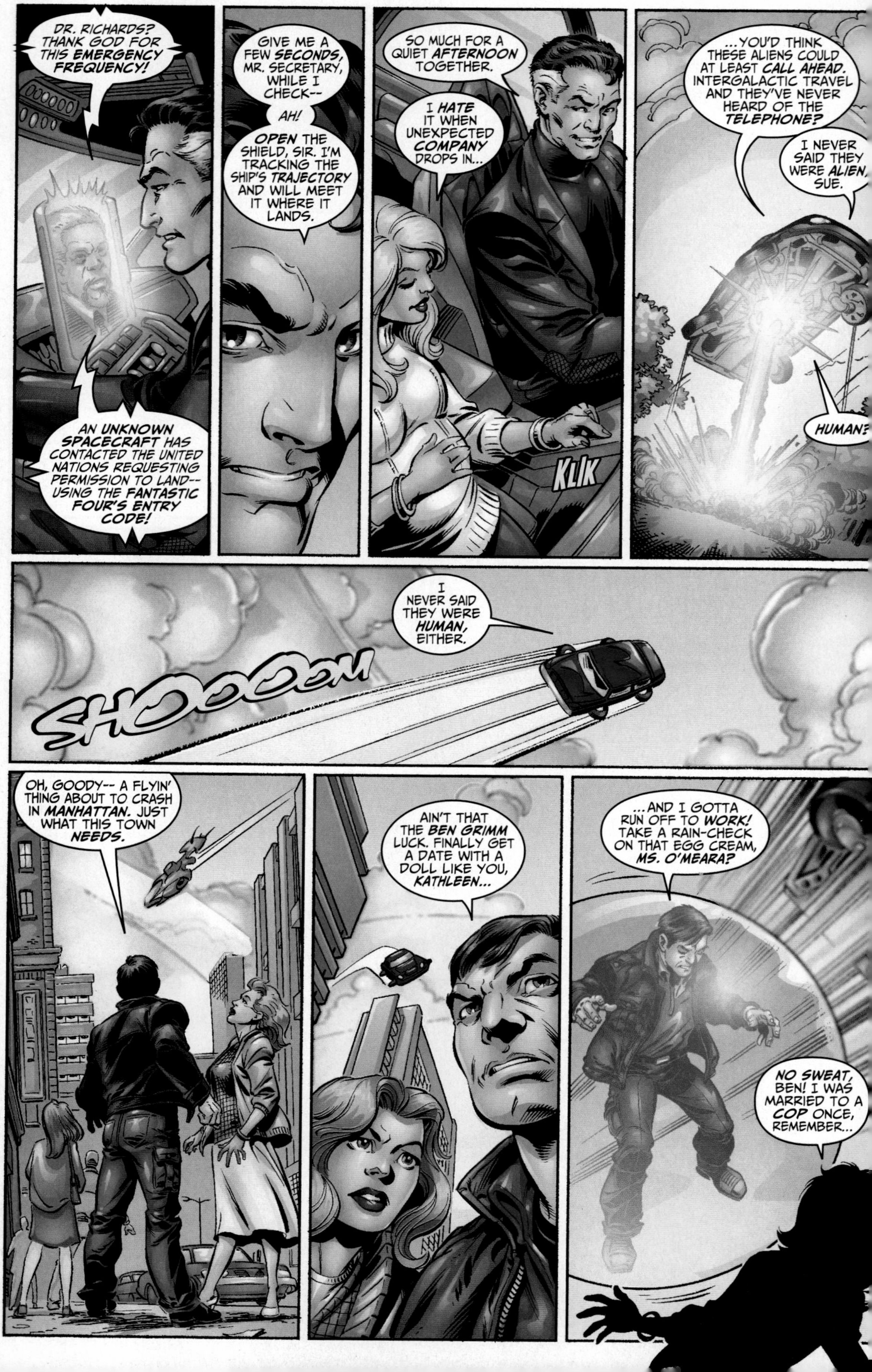
DR. RICHARDS? THANK GOD FOR THIS EMERGENCY FREQUENCY!
AN UNKNOWN SPACECRAFT HAS CONTACTED THE UNITED NATIONS REQUESTING PERMISSION TO LAND--USING THE FANTASTIC FOUR'S ENTRY CODE!
GIVE ME A FEW SECONDS, MR. SECRETARY, WHILE I CHECK--
AH!
OPEN THE SHIELD, SIR. I'M TRACKING THE SHIP'S TRAJECTORY AND WILL MEET IT WHERE IT LANDS.
SO MUCH FOR A QUIET AFTERNOON TOGETHER.
I HATE IT WHEN UNEXPECTED COMPANY DROPS IN...
KLIK
...YOU'D THINK THESE ALIENS COULD AT LEAST CALL AHEAD. INTERGALACTIC TRAVEL AND THEY'VE NEVER HEARD OF THE TELEPHONE?
I NEVER SAID THEY WERE ALIEN, SUE.
HUMAN?
I NEVER SAID THEY WERE HUMAN, EITHER.
SHOOOOOM
OH, GOODY-- A FLYIN' THING ABOUT TO CRASH IN MANHATTAN. JUST WHAT THIS TOWN NEEDS.
AIN'T THAT THE BEN GRIMM LUCK. FINALLY GET A DATE WITH A DOLL LIKE YOU, KATHLEEN...
...AND I GOTTA RUN OFF TO WORK! TAKE A RAIN-CHECK ON THAT EGG CREAM, MS. O'MEARA?
NO SWEAT, BEN! I WAS MARRIED TO A COP ONCE, REMEMBER...

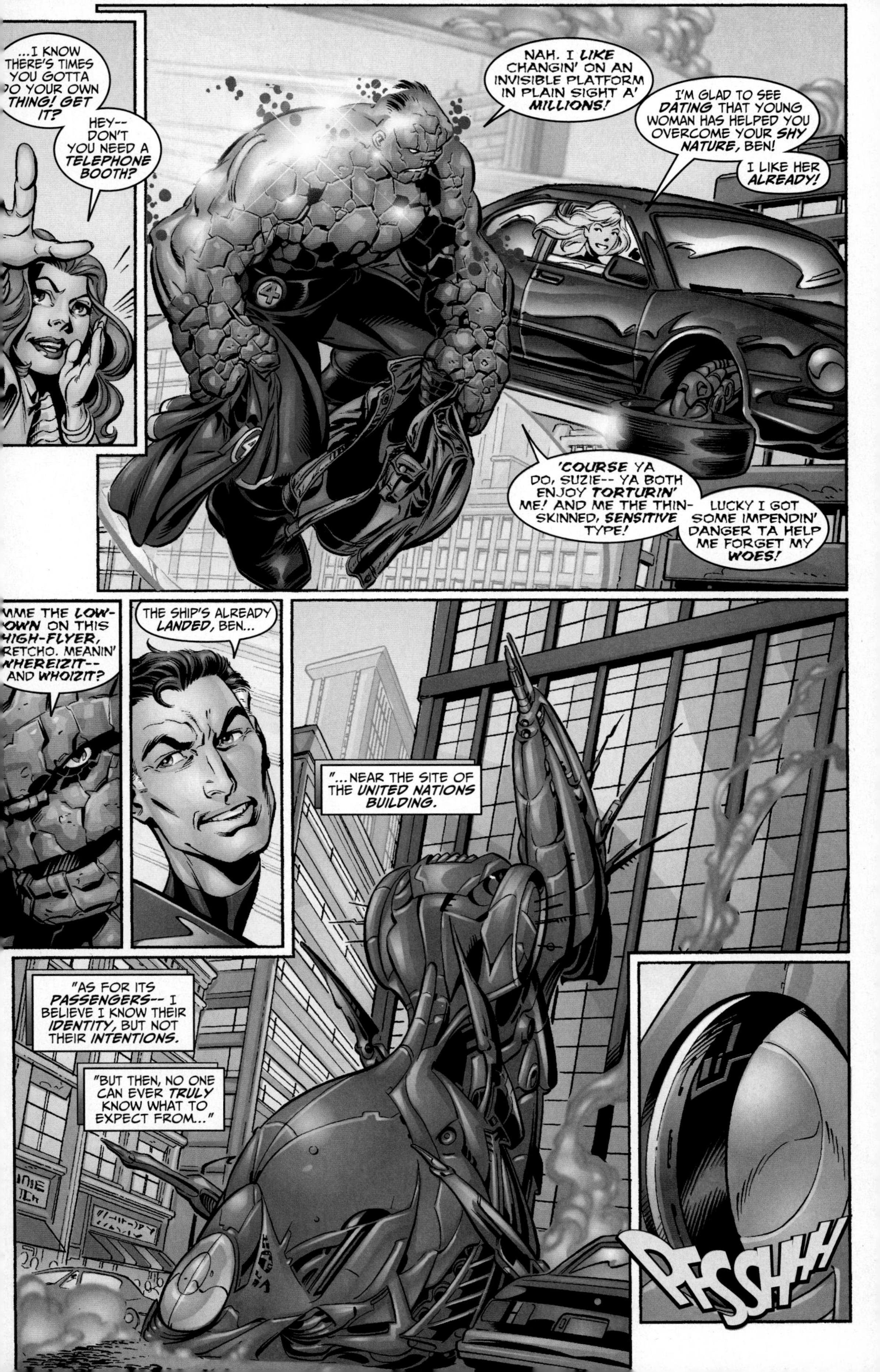

...I KNOW THERE'S TIMES YOU GOTTA DO YOUR OWN THING! GET IT?
HEY-- DON'T YOU NEED A TELEPHONE BOOTH?
NAH. I LIKE CHANGIN' ON AN INVISIBLE PLATFORM IN PLAIN SIGHT A' MILLIONS!
I'M GLAD TO SEE DATING THAT YOUNG WOMAN HAS HELPED YOU OVERCOME YOUR SHY NATURE, BEN!
I LIKE HER ALREADY!
'COURSE YA DO, SUZIE-- YA BOTH ENJOY TORTURIN' ME! AND ME THE THIN-SKINNED, SENSITIVE TYPE!
LUCKY I GOT SOME IMPENDIN' DANGER TA HELP ME FORGET MY WOES!
MME THE LOW-DOWN ON THIS HIGH-FLYER, RETCHO. MEANIN' WHEREIZIT-- AND WHOIZIT?
THE SHIP'S ALREADY LANDED, BEN...
"...NEAR THE SITE OF THE UNITED NATIONS BUILDING.
"AS FOR ITS PASSENGERS-- I BELIEVE I KNOW THEIR IDENTITY, BUT NOT THEIR INTENTIONS.
"BUT THEN, NO ONE CAN EVER TRULY KNOW WHAT TO EXPECT FROM..."
PFSSHH

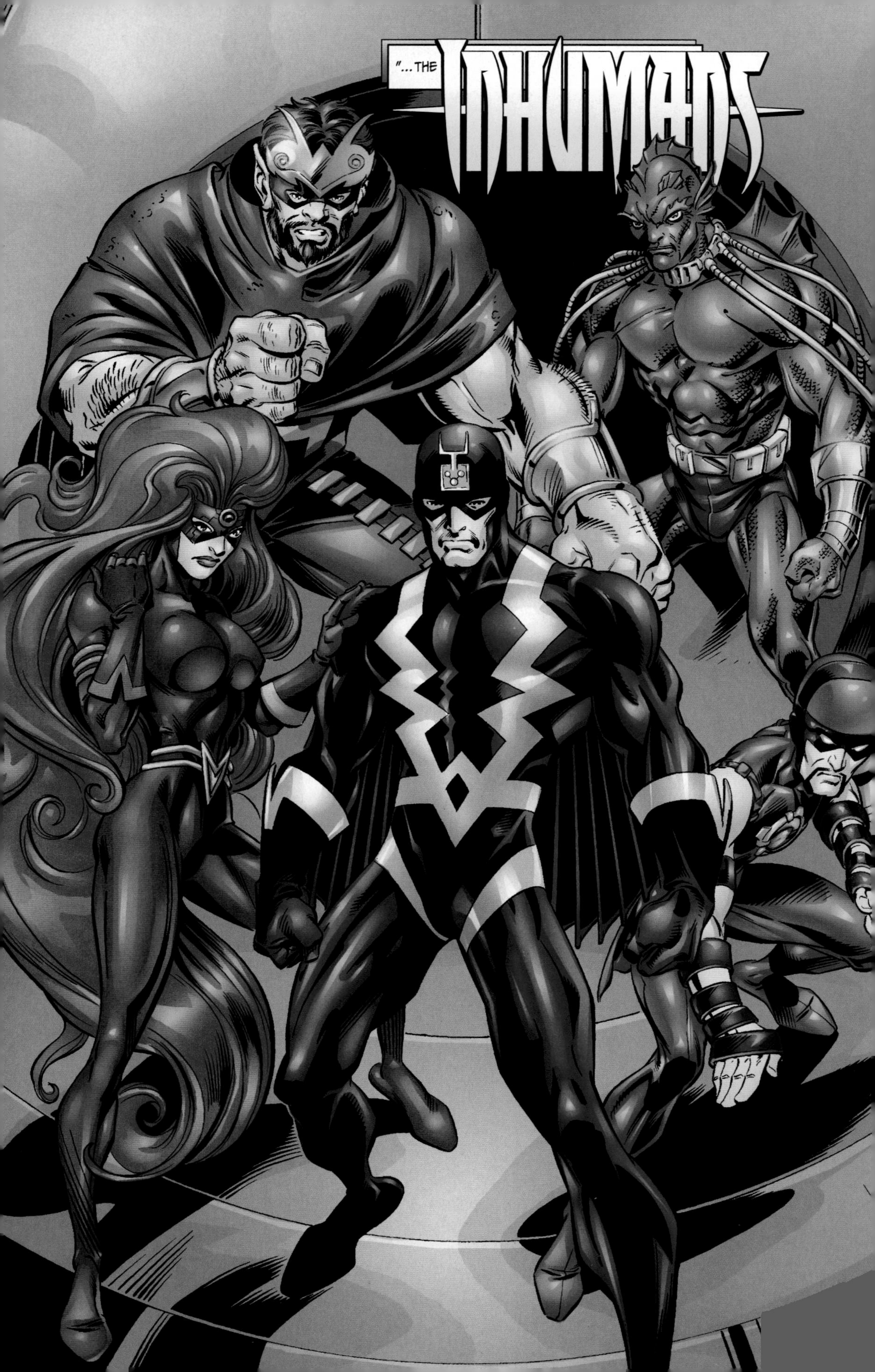
"...THE
INHUMANS

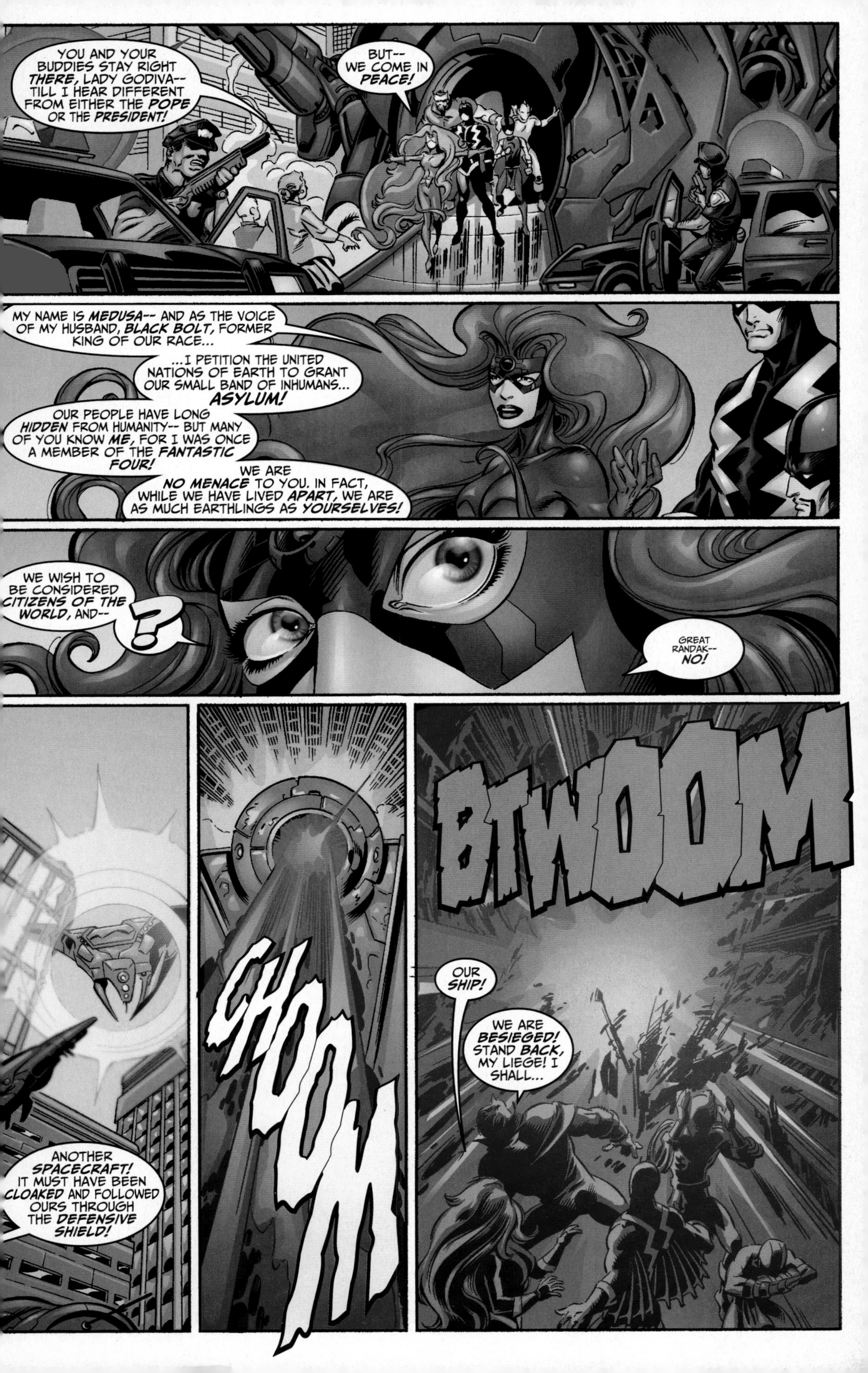

YOU AND YOUR BUDDIES STAY RIGHT THERE, LADY GODIVA-- TILL I HEAR DIFFERENT FROM EITHER THE POPE OR THE PRESIDENT!
BUT-- WE COME IN PEACE!
MY NAME IS MEDUSA-- AND AS THE VOICE OF MY HUSBAND, BLACK BOLT, FORMER KING OF OUR RACE...
...I PETITION THE UNITED NATIONS OF EARTH TO GRANT OUR SMALL BAND OF INHUMANS... ASYLUM!
OUR PEOPLE HAVE LONG HIDDEN FROM HUMANITY-- BUT MANY OF YOU KNOW ME, FOR I WAS ONCE A MEMBER OF THE FANTASTIC FOUR!
WE ARE NO MENACE TO YOU. IN FACT, WHILE WE HAVE LIVED APART, WE ARE AS MUCH EARTHLINGS AS YOURSELVES!
WE WISH TO BE CONSIDERED CITIZENS OF THE WORLD, AND--
?
GREAT RANDAK-- NO!
ANOTHER SPACECRAFT! IT MUST HAVE BEEN CLOAKED AND FOLLOWED OURS THROUGH THE DEFENSIVE SHIELD!
CHOOM
BTWOOM
OUR SHIP!
WE ARE BESIEGED! STAND BACK, MY LIEGE! I SHALL...

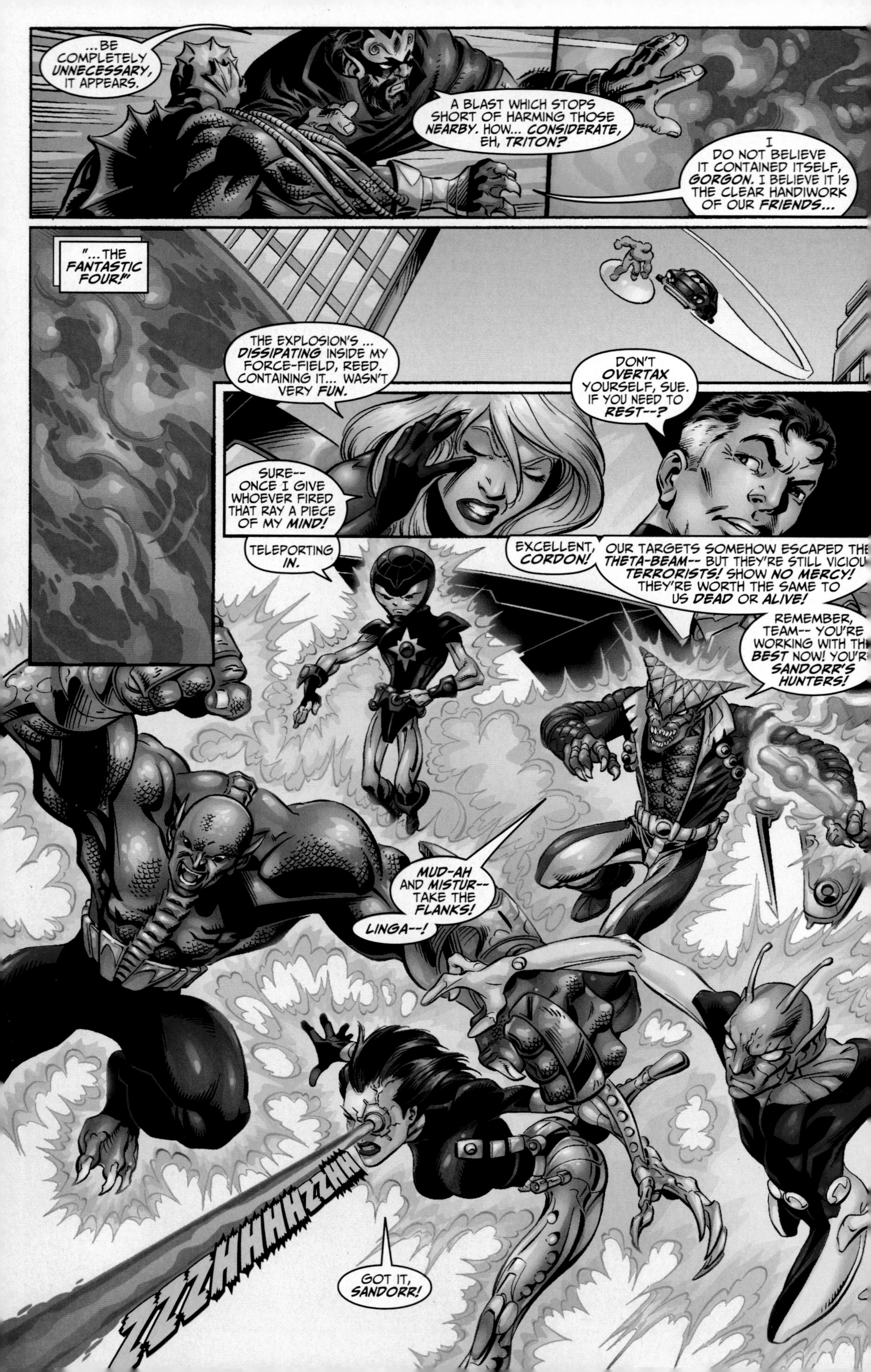
...BE COMPLETELY UNNECESSARY, IT APPEARS.
A BLAST WHICH STOPS SHORT OF HARMING THOSE NEARBY. HOW... CONSIDERATE, EH, TRITON?
I DO NOT BELIEVE IT CONTAINED ITSELF, GORGON. I BELIEVE IT IS THE CLEAR HANDIWORK OF OUR FRIENDS...
"...THE FANTASTIC FOUR!"
THE EXPLOSION'S ... DISSIPATING INSIDE MY FORCE-FIELD, REED. CONTAINING IT... WASN'T VERY FUN.
DON'T OVERTAX YOURSELF, SUE. IF YOU NEED TO REST--?
SURE-- ONCE I GIVE WHOEVER FIRED THAT RAY A PIECE OF MY MIND!
TELEPORTING IN.
EXCELLENT, CORDON!
OUR TARGETS SOMEHOW ESCAPED THE THETA-BEAM-- BUT THEY'RE STILL VICIOU TERRORISTS! SHOW NO MERCY! THEY'RE WORTH THE SAME TO US DEAD OR ALIVE!
REMEMBER, TEAM-- YOU'RE WORKING WITH TH BEST NOW! YOU'R SANDORR'S HUNTERS!
MUD-AH AND MISTUR-- TAKE THE FLANKS!
LINGA--!
ZZZHHHHHZZHH
GOT IT, SANDORR!

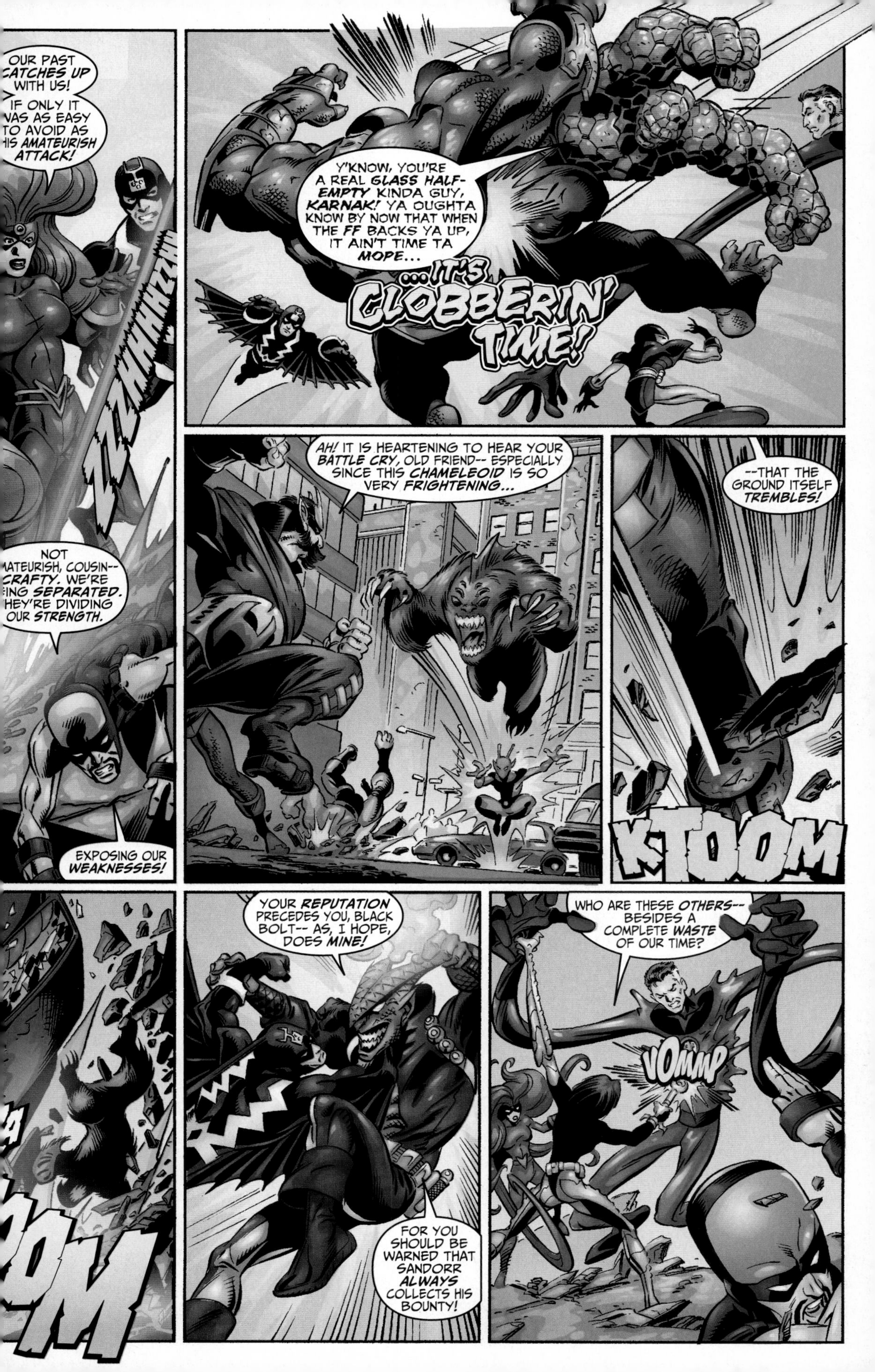

OUR PAST CATCHES UP WITH US!
IF ONLY IT WAS AS EASY TO AVOID AS THIS AMATEURISH ATTACK!
ZZZHHHHZZH
Y'KNOW, YOU'RE A REAL GLASS HALF-EMPTY KINDA GUY, KARNAK! YA OUGHTA KNOW BY NOW THAT WHEN THE FF BACKS YA UP, IT AIN'T TIME TA MOPE...
...IT'S CLOBBERIN' TIME!
NOT AMATEURISH, COUSIN-- CRAFTY. WE'RE BEING SEPARATED. THEY'RE DIVIDING OUR STRENGTH.
EXPOSING OUR WEAKNESSES!
AH! IT IS HEARTENING TO HEAR YOUR BATTLE CRY, OLD FRIEND-- ESPECIALLY SINCE THIS CHAMELEOID IS SO VERY FRIGHTENING...
--THAT THE GROUND ITSELF TREMBLES!
KTOOM
YOUR REPUTATION PRECEDES YOU, BLACK BOLT-- AS, I HOPE, DOES MINE!
FOR YOU SHOULD BE WARNED THAT SANDORR ALWAYS COLLECTS HIS BOUNTY!
WHO ARE THESE OTHERS-- BESIDES A COMPLETE WASTE OF OUR TIME?
VOMMP

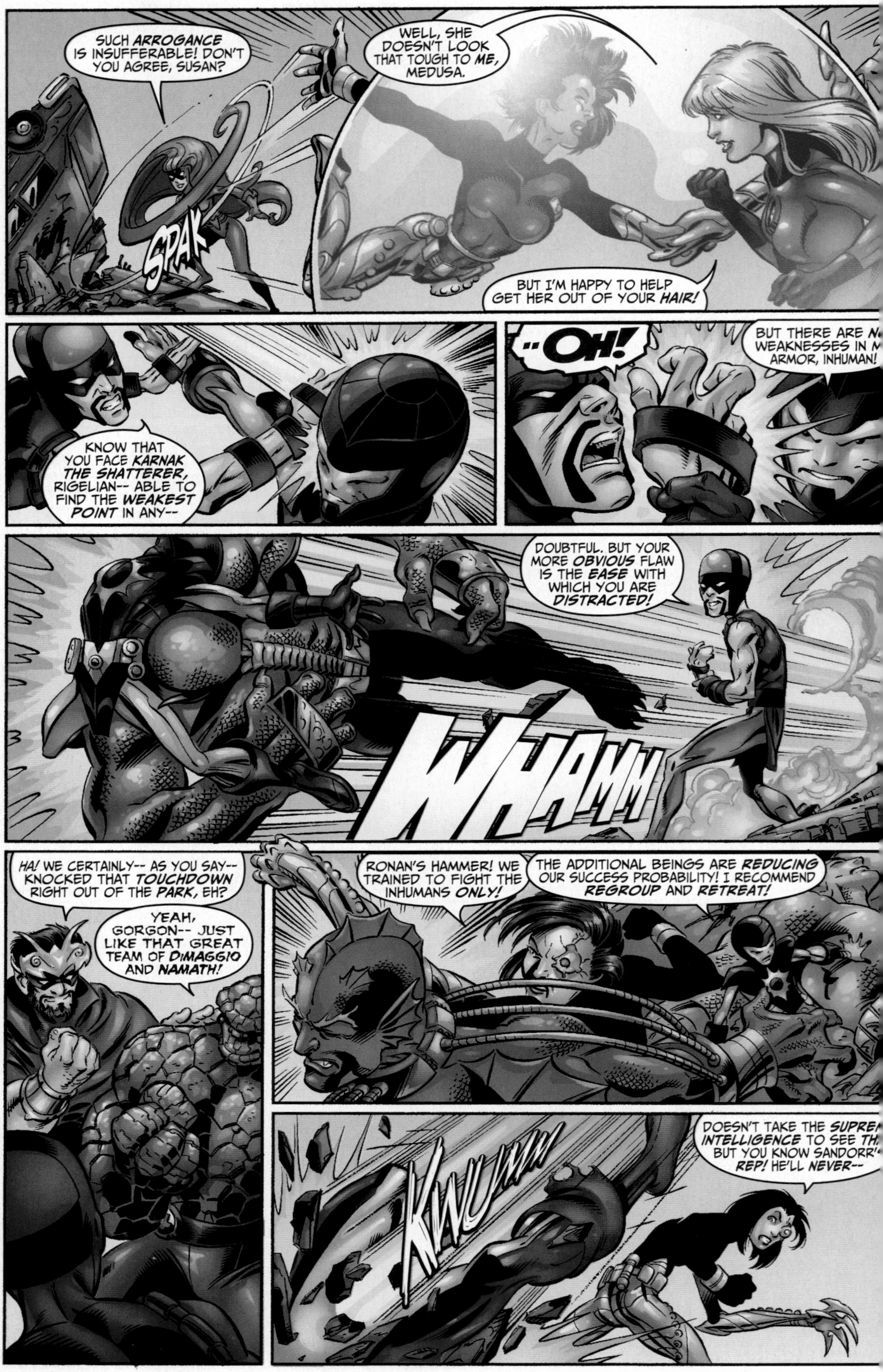

SUCH ARROGANCE IS INSUFFERABLE! DON'T YOU AGREE, SUSAN?
WELL, SHE DOESN'T LOOK THAT TOUGH TO ME, MEDUSA.
SPAK
BUT I'M HAPPY TO HELP GET HER OUT OF YOUR HAIR!
KNOW THAT YOU FACE KARNAK THE SHATTERER, RIGELIAN-- ABLE TO FIND THE WEAKEST POINT IN ANY--
--OH!
BUT THERE ARE NO WEAKNESSES IN MY ARMOR, INHUMAN!
DOUBTFUL. BUT YOUR MORE OBVIOUS FLAW IS THE EASE WITH WHICH YOU ARE DISTRACTED!
WHAMM
HA! WE CERTAINLY-- AS YOU SAY-- KNOCKED THAT TOUCHDOWN RIGHT OUT OF THE PARK, EH?
YEAH, GORGON-- JUST LIKE THAT GREAT TEAM OF DIMAGGIO AND NAMATH!
RONAN'S HAMMER! WE TRAINED TO FIGHT THE INHUMANS ONLY!
THE ADDITIONAL BEINGS ARE REDUCING OUR SUCCESS PROBABILITY! I RECOMMEND REGROUP AND RETREAT!
KWUMM
DOESN'T TAKE THE SUPREME INTELLIGENCE TO SEE THAT. BUT YOU KNOW SANDORR'S REP! HE'LL NEVER--

EVACUATE! TELEPORT US OUT OF HERE, CORDON!

BUT... MISTUR IS OUT OF RANGE!

NO-- HE'S OUT OF LUCK!

DO IT, RIGELIAN-- NOW!

AS YOU WISH-- "FEARLESS" LEADER.

TOK

WE RETURN TO THE SHIP...

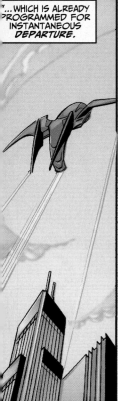

"...WHICH IS ALREADY PROGRAMMED FOR INSTANTANEOUS DEPARTURE.

"PEOPLE WHISPER OF YOU LEAVING DEATH AND DESTRUCTION IN YOUR WAKE, SANDORR.

"HOW OFTEN HAVE YOU LEFT OTHERS BEHIND, TOO?"

LISTEN, CORDON-- EVERYONE-- I KNOW WHAT I'M DOING!

RULE NUMBER ONE-- LIVE TO FIGHT ANOTHER DAY!

ALIEN CRAFT SIGHTED.

SCANNING.

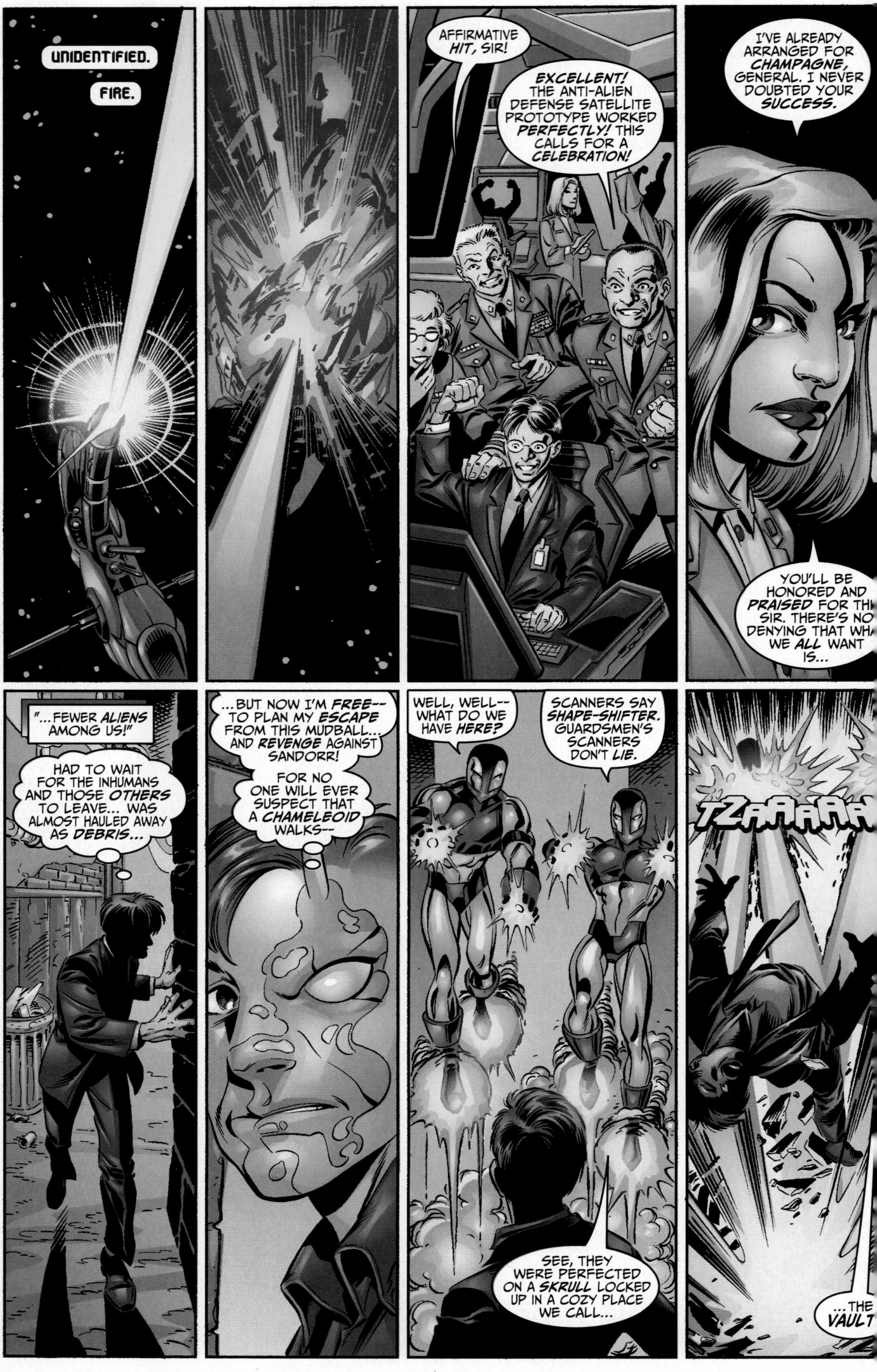
UNIDENTIFIED.
FIRE.
AFFIRMATIVE HIT, SIR!
EXCELLENT! THE ANTI-ALIEN DEFENSE SATELLITE PROTOTYPE WORKED PERFECTLY! THIS CALLS FOR A CELEBRATION!
I'VE ALREADY ARRANGED FOR CHAMPAGNE, GENERAL. I NEVER DOUBTED YOUR SUCCESS.
YOU'LL BE HONORED AND PRAISED FOR TH SIR. THERE'S NO DENYING THAT WH WE ALL WANT IS...
"...FEWER ALIENS AMONG US!"
HAD TO WAIT FOR THE INHUMANS AND THOSE OTHERS TO LEAVE... WAS ALMOST HAULED AWAY AS DEBRIS...
...BUT NOW I'M FREE-- TO PLAN MY ESCAPE FROM THIS MUDBALL... AND REVENGE AGAINST SANDORR!
FOR NO ONE WILL EVER SUSPECT THAT A CHAMELEOID WALKS--
WELL, WELL-- WHAT DO WE HAVE HERE?
SCANNERS SAY SHAPE-SHIFTER. GUARDSMEN'S SCANNERS DON'T LIE.
SEE, THEY WERE PERFECTED ON A SKRULL LOCKED UP IN A COZY PLACE WE CALL...
TZAAAAA
...THE VAULT

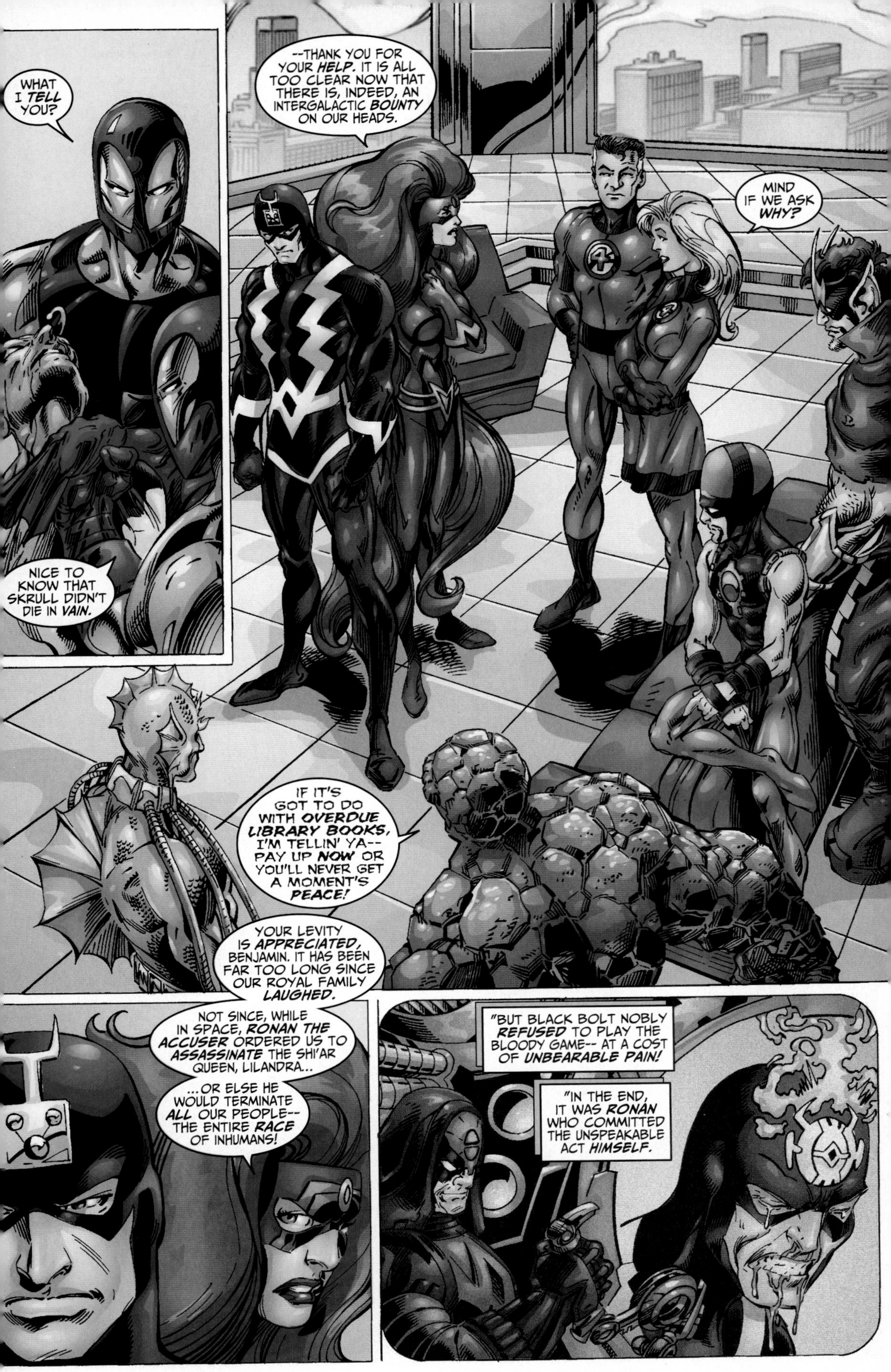
WHAT I TELL YOU?
--THANK YOU FOR YOUR HELP. IT IS ALL TOO CLEAR NOW THAT THERE IS, INDEED, AN INTERGALACTIC BOUNTY ON OUR HEADS.
MIND IF WE ASK WHY?
NICE TO KNOW THAT SKRULL DIDN'T DIE IN VAIN.
IF IT'S GOT TO DO WITH OVERDUE LIBRARY BOOKS, I'M TELLIN' YA-- PAY UP NOW OR YOU'LL NEVER GET A MOMENT'S PEACE!
YOUR LEVITY IS APPRECIATED, BENJAMIN. IT HAS BEEN FAR TOO LONG SINCE OUR ROYAL FAMILY LAUGHED.
NOT SINCE, WHILE IN SPACE, RONAN THE ACCUSER ORDERED US TO ASSASSINATE THE SHI'AR QUEEN, LILANDRA...
...OR ELSE HE WOULD TERMINATE ALL OUR PEOPLE-- THE ENTIRE RACE OF INHUMANS!
"BUT BLACK BOLT NOBLY REFUSED TO PLAY THE BLOODY GAME-- AT A COST OF UNBEARABLE PAIN!
"IN THE END, IT WAS RONAN WHO COMMITTED THE UNSPEAKABLE ACT HIMSELF.

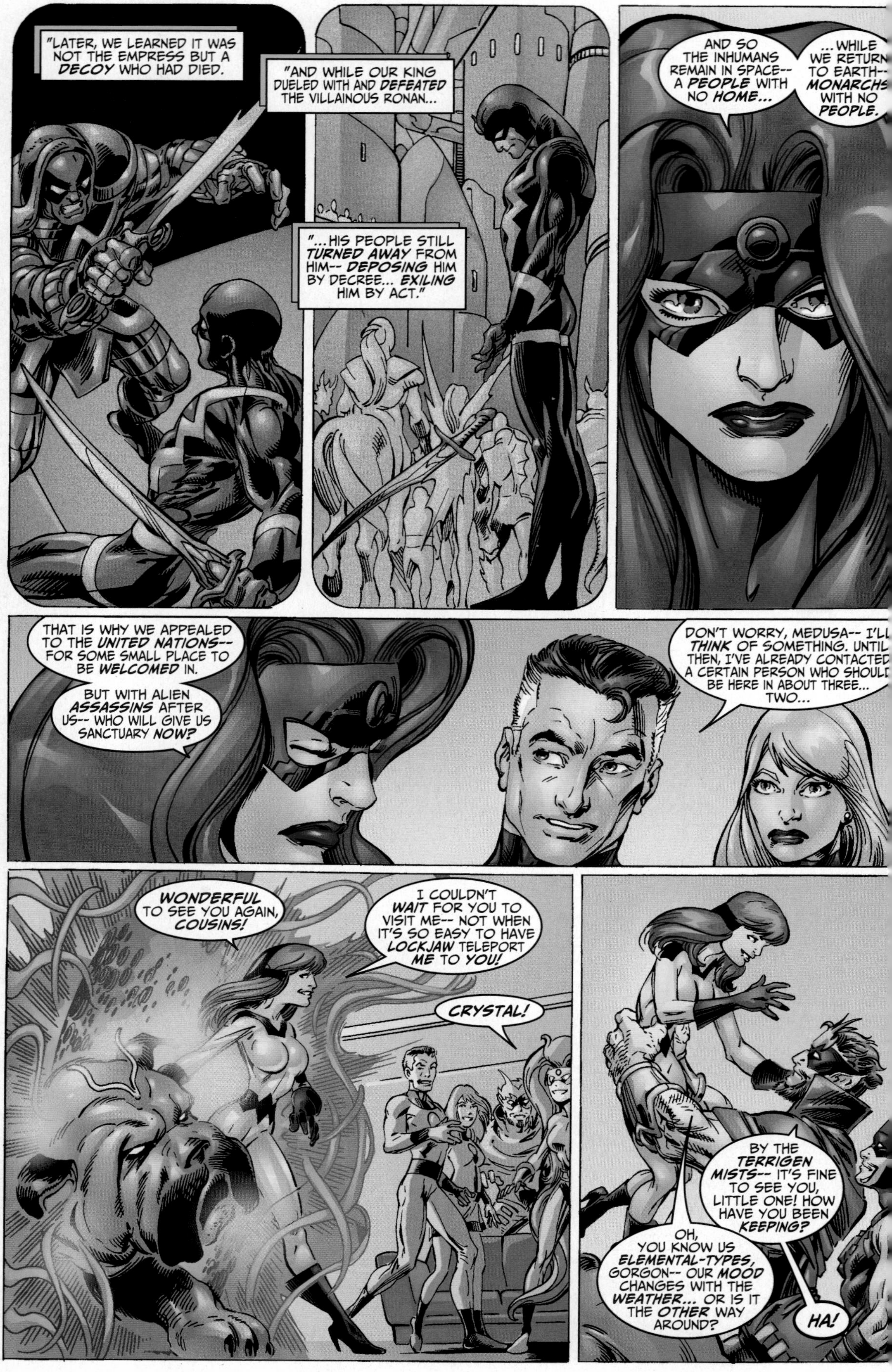
"LATER, WE LEARNED IT WAS NOT THE EMPRESS BUT A DECOY WHO HAD DIED.
"AND WHILE OUR KING DUELED WITH AND DEFEATED THE VILLAINOUS RONAN...
"...HIS PEOPLE STILL TURNED AWAY FROM HIM-- DEPOSING HIM BY DECREE... EXILING HIM BY ACT."
AND SO THE INHUMANS REMAIN IN SPACE-- A PEOPLE WITH NO HOME...
...WHILE WE RETURN TO EARTH-- MONARCHS WITH NO PEOPLE.
THAT IS WHY WE APPEALED TO THE UNITED NATIONS-- FOR SOME SMALL PLACE TO BE WELCOMED IN.
BUT WITH ALIEN ASSASSINS AFTER US-- WHO WILL GIVE US SANCTUARY NOW?
DON'T WORRY, MEDUSA-- I'LL THINK OF SOMETHING. UNTIL THEN, I'VE ALREADY CONTACTED A CERTAIN PERSON WHO SHOULD BE HERE IN ABOUT THREE... TWO...
WONDERFUL TO SEE YOU AGAIN, COUSINS!
I COULDN'T WAIT FOR YOU TO VISIT ME-- NOT WHEN IT'S SO EASY TO HAVE LOCKJAW TELEPORT ME TO YOU!
CRYSTAL!
BY THE TERRIGEN MISTS-- IT'S FINE TO SEE YOU, LITTLE ONE! HOW HAVE YOU BEEN KEEPING?
OH, YOU KNOW US ELEMENTAL-TYPES, GORGON-- OUR MOOD CHANGES WITH THE WEATHER... OR IS IT THE OTHER WAY AROUND?
HA!

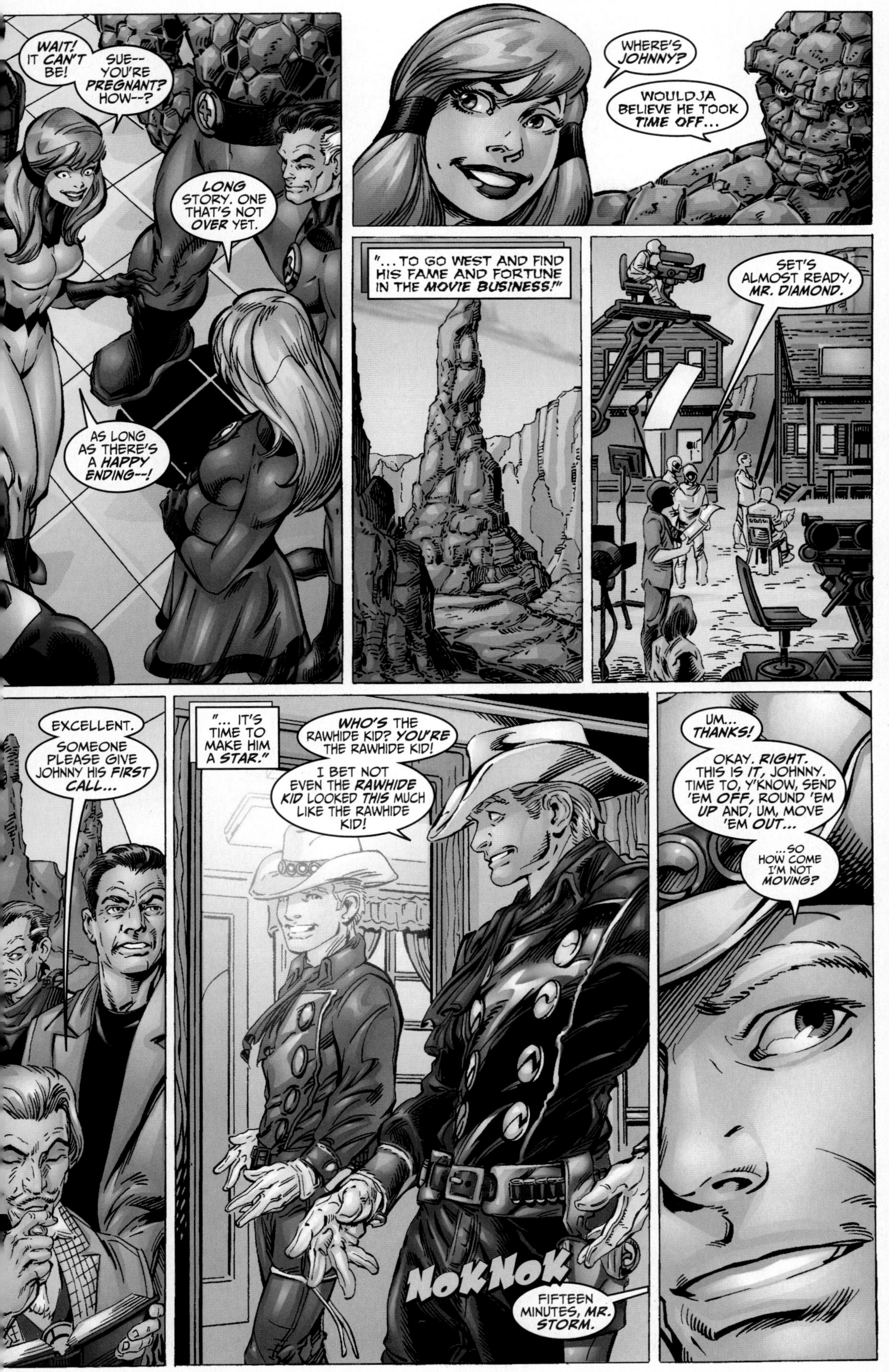
WAIT! IT CAN'T BE!
SUE-- YOU'RE PREGNANT? HOW--?
LONG STORY. ONE THAT'S NOT OVER YET.
AS LONG AS THERE'S A HAPPY ENDING--!
WHERE'S JOHNNY?
WOULDJA BELIEVE HE TOOK TIME OFF...
"...TO GO WEST AND FIND HIS FAME AND FORTUNE IN THE MOVIE BUSINESS!"
SET'S ALMOST READY, MR. DIAMOND.
EXCELLENT. SOMEONE PLEASE GIVE JOHNNY HIS FIRST CALL...
"... IT'S TIME TO MAKE HIM A STAR."
WHO'S THE RAWHIDE KID? YOU'RE THE RAWHIDE KID!
I BET NOT EVEN THE RAWHIDE KID LOOKED THIS MUCH LIKE THE RAWHIDE KID!
NOK NOK
FIFTEEN MINUTES, MR. STORM.
UM... THANKS!
OKAY. RIGHT. THIS IS IT, JOHNNY. TIME TO, Y'KNOW, SEND 'EM OFF, ROUND 'EM UP AND, UM, MOVE 'EM OUT...
...SO HOW COME I'M NOT MOVING?

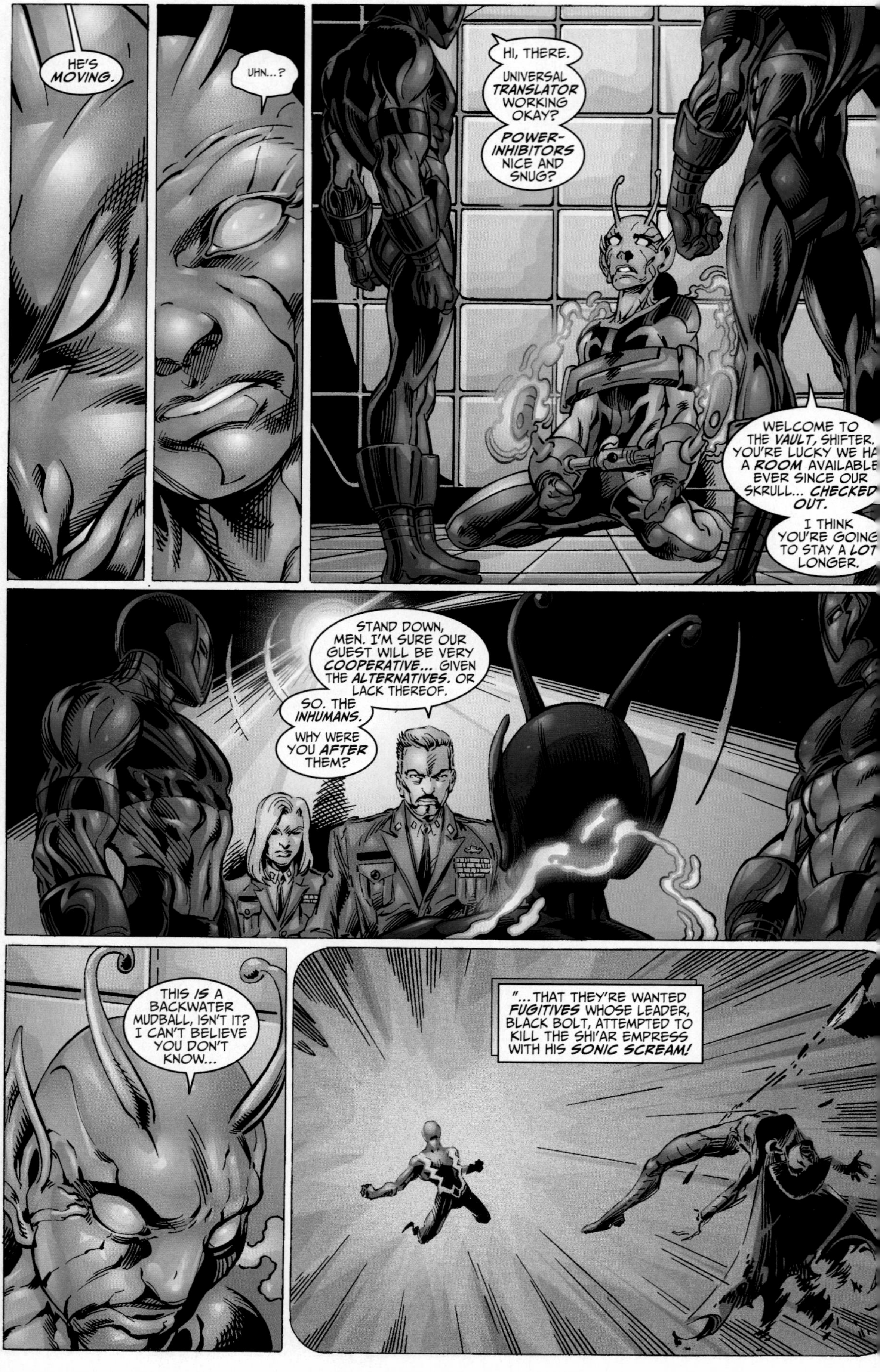
HE'S MOVING.
UHN...?
HI, THERE.
UNIVERSAL TRANSLATOR WORKING OKAY?
POWER-INHIBITORS NICE AND SNUG?
WELCOME TO THE VAULT, SHIFTER. YOU'RE LUCKY WE HA A ROOM AVAILABLE EVER SINCE OUR SKRULL... CHECKED OUT.
I THINK YOU'RE GOING TO STAY A LOT LONGER.
STAND DOWN, MEN. I'M SURE OUR GUEST WILL BE VERY COOPERATIVE... GIVEN THE ALTERNATIVES. OR LACK THEREOF.
SO. THE INHUMANS.
WHY WERE YOU AFTER THEM?
THIS IS A BACKWATER MUDBALL, ISN'T IT? I CAN'T BELIEVE YOU DON'T KNOW...
"...THAT THEY'RE WANTED FUGITIVES WHOSE LEADER, BLACK BOLT, ATTEMPTED TO KILL THE SHI'AR EMPRESS WITH HIS SONIC SCREAM!

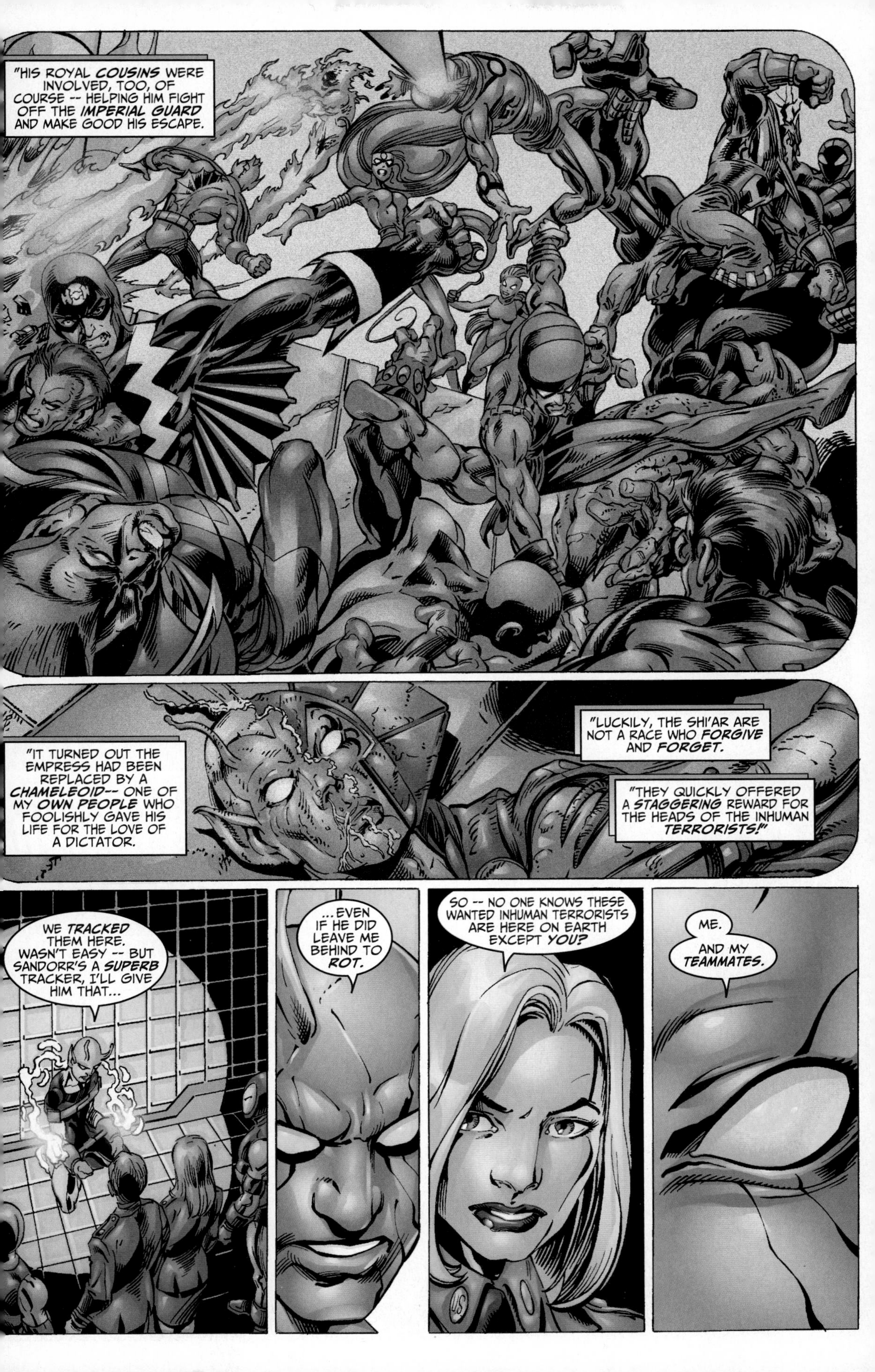
"HIS ROYAL COUSINS WERE INVOLVED, TOO, OF COURSE -- HELPING HIM FIGHT OFF THE IMPERIAL GUARD AND MAKE GOOD HIS ESCAPE.
"IT TURNED OUT THE EMPRESS HAD BEEN REPLACED BY A CHAMELEOID-- ONE OF MY OWN PEOPLE WHO FOOLISHLY GAVE HIS LIFE FOR THE LOVE OF A DICTATOR.
"LUCKILY, THE SHI'AR ARE NOT A RACE WHO FORGIVE AND FORGET.
"THEY QUICKLY OFFERED A STAGGERING REWARD FOR THE HEADS OF THE INHUMAN TERRORISTS!"
WE TRACKED THEM HERE. WASN'T EASY -- BUT SANDORR'S A SUPERB TRACKER, I'LL GIVE HIM THAT...
...EVEN IF HE DID LEAVE ME BEHIND TO ROT.
SO -- NO ONE KNOWS THESE WANTED INHUMAN TERRORISTS ARE HERE ON EARTH EXCEPT YOU?
ME.
AND MY TEAMMATES.

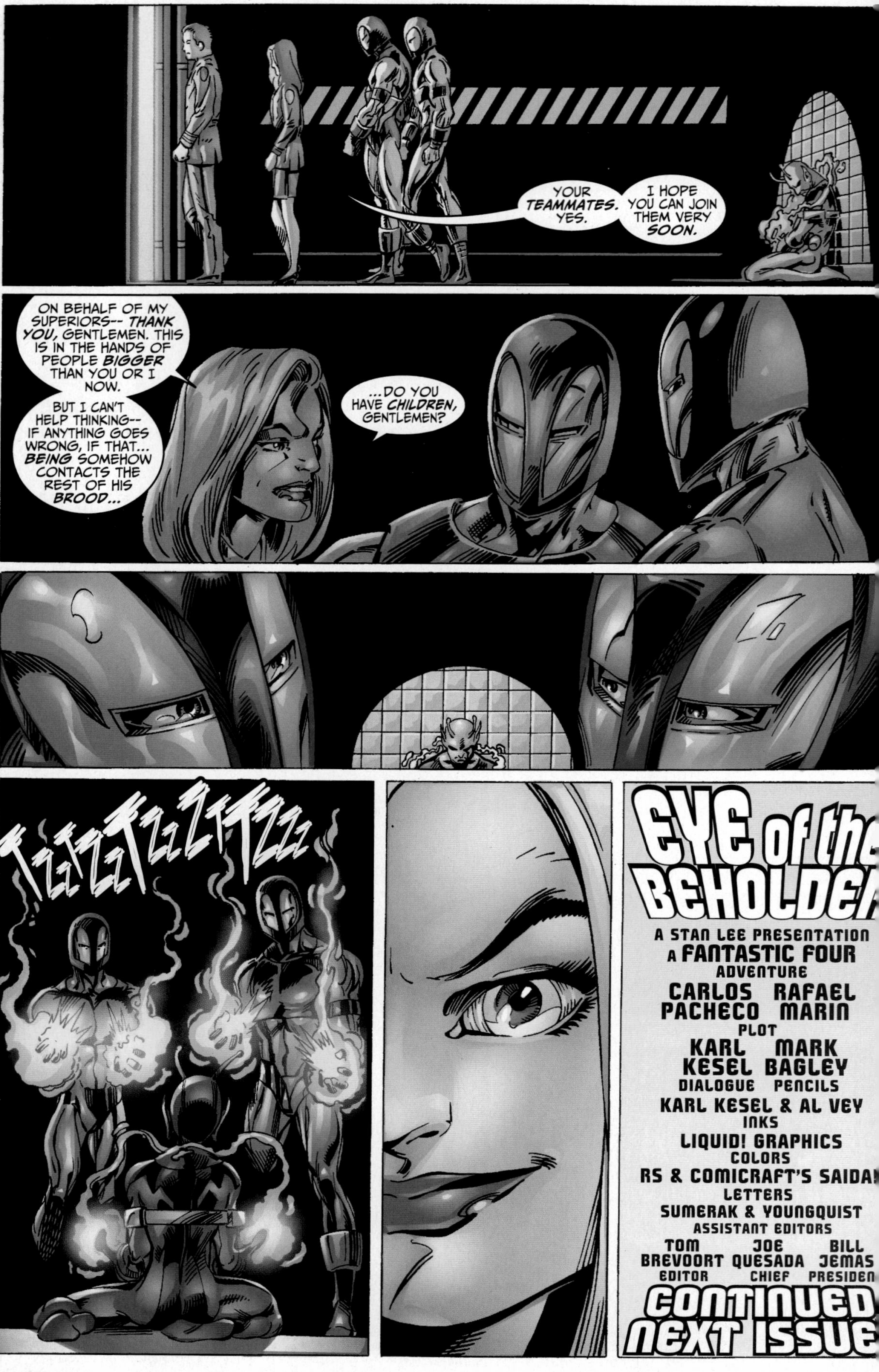
YOUR TEAMMATES. YES.
I HOPE YOU CAN JOIN THEM VERY SOON.
ON BEHALF OF MY SUPERIORS-- THANK YOU, GENTLEMEN. THIS IS IN THE HANDS OF PEOPLE BIGGER THAN YOU OR I NOW.
BUT I CAN'T HELP THINKING-- IF ANYTHING GOES WRONG, IF THAT... BEING SOMEHOW CONTACTS THE REST OF HIS BROOD...
...DO YOU HAVE CHILDREN, GENTLEMEN?
TZZZTZZZTZZZTZZZ
EYE of the
BEHOLDE
A STAN LEE PRESENTATION
A FANTASTIC FOUR ADVENTURE
CARLOS PACHECO RAFAEL MARIN
PLOT
KARL KESEL DIALOGUE
MARK BAGLEY PENCILS
KARL KESEL & AL VEY
INKS
LIQUID! GRAPHICS
COLORS
RS & COMICRAFT'S SAIDA
LETTERS
SUMERAK & YOUNGQUIST
ASSISTANT EDITORS
TOM BREVOORT EDITOR
JOE QUESADA CHIEF
BILL JEMAS PRESIDEN
CONTINUED NEXT ISSUE

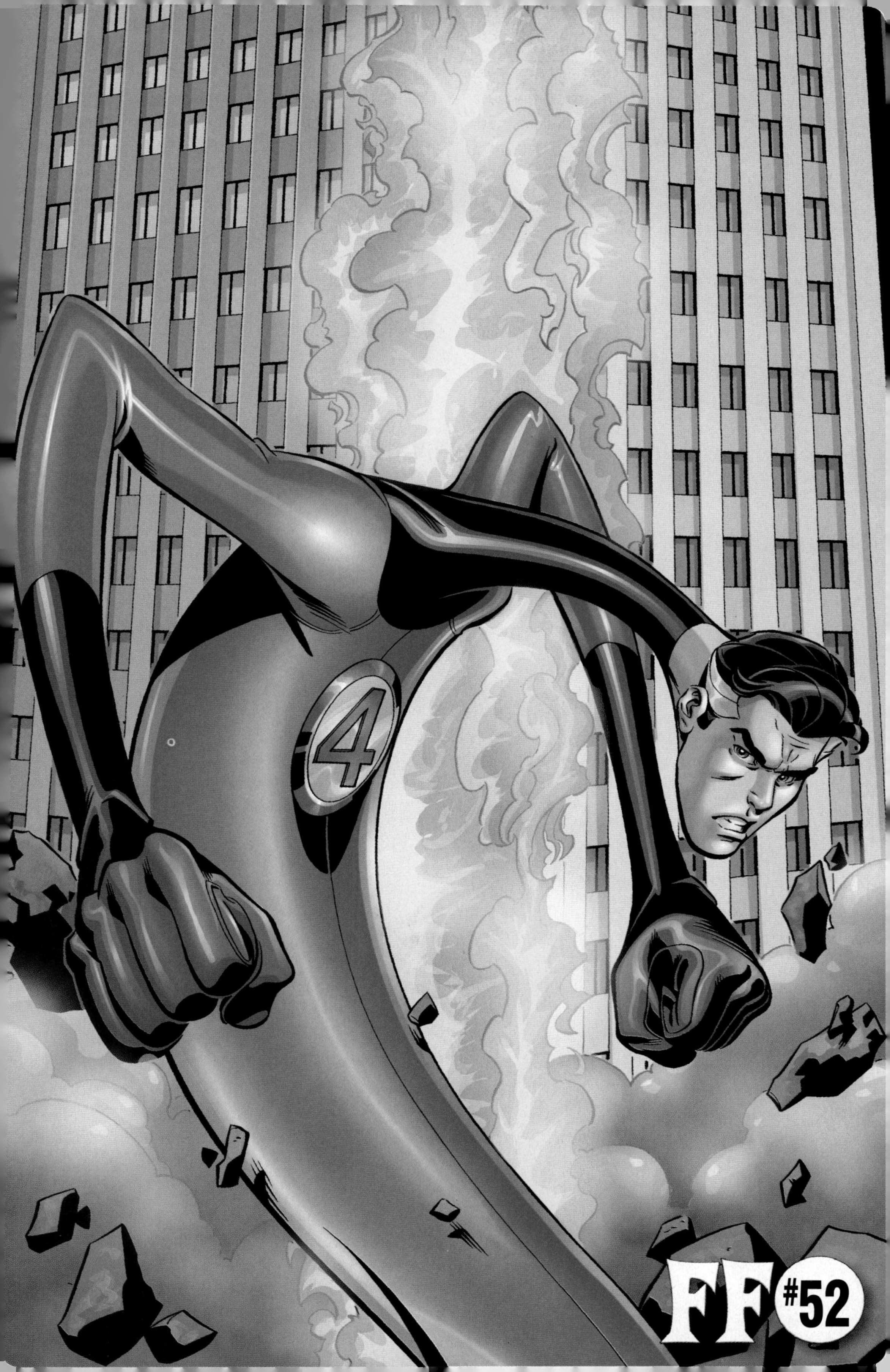
FF #52

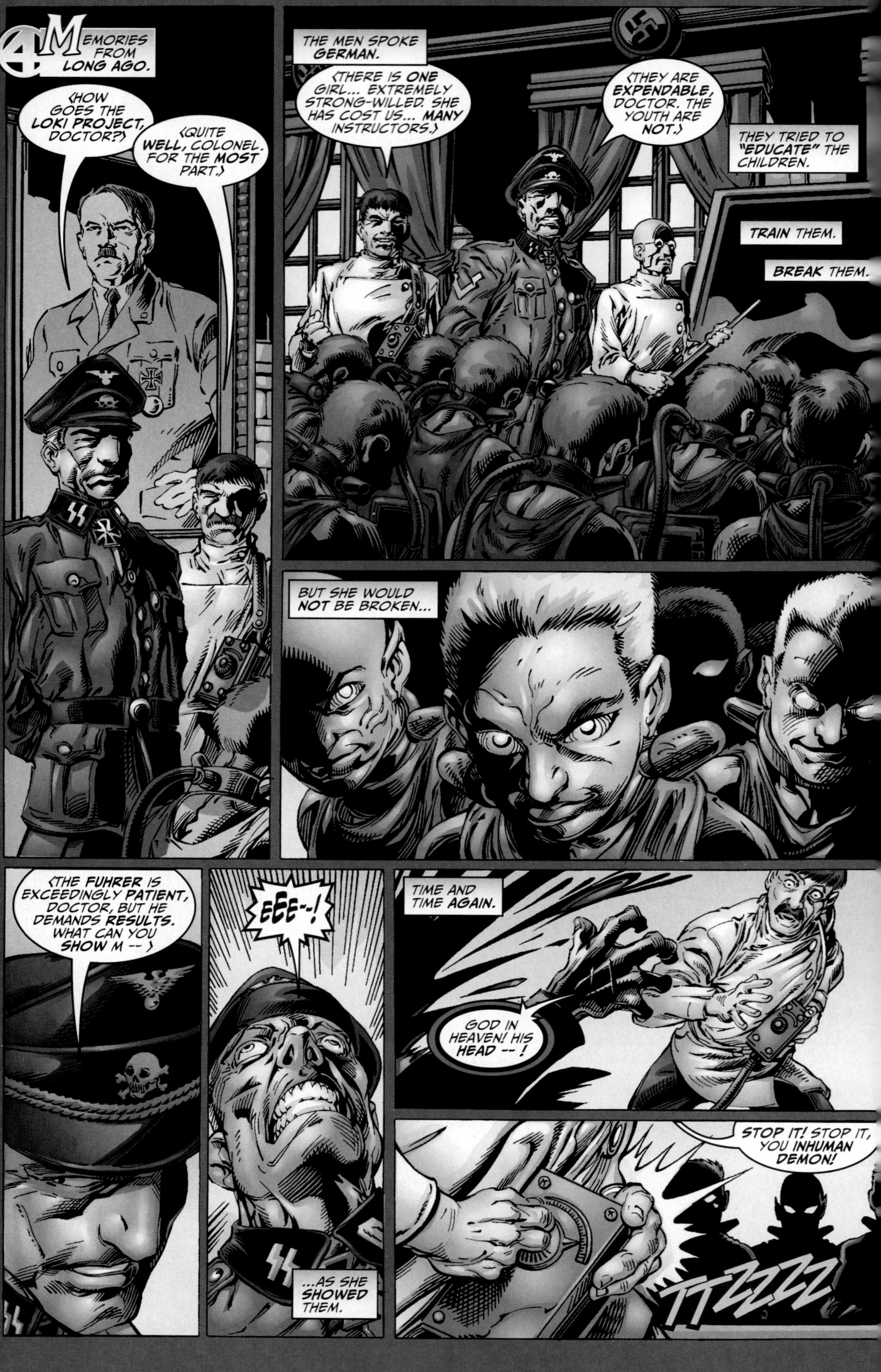
MEMORIES FROM LONG AGO.
‹HOW GOES THE LOKI PROJECT, DOCTOR?›
‹QUITE WELL, COLONEL. FOR THE MOST PART.›
THE MEN SPOKE GERMAN.
‹THERE IS ONE GIRL... EXTREMELY STRONG-WILLED. SHE HAS COST US... MANY INSTRUCTORS.›
‹THEY ARE EXPENDABLE, DOCTOR. THE YOUTH ARE NOT.›
THEY TRIED TO "EDUCATE" THE CHILDREN.
TRAIN THEM.
BREAK THEM.
BUT SHE WOULD NOT BE BROKEN...
‹THE FUHRER IS EXCEEDINGLY PATIENT, DOCTOR, BUT HE DEMANDS RESULTS. WHAT CAN YOU SHOW M -- ›
EEE--!
...AS SHE SHOWED THEM.
TIME AND TIME AGAIN.
GOD IN HEAVEN! HIS HEAD -- !
STOP IT! STOP IT, YOU INHUMAN DEMON!
TTZZZZZ

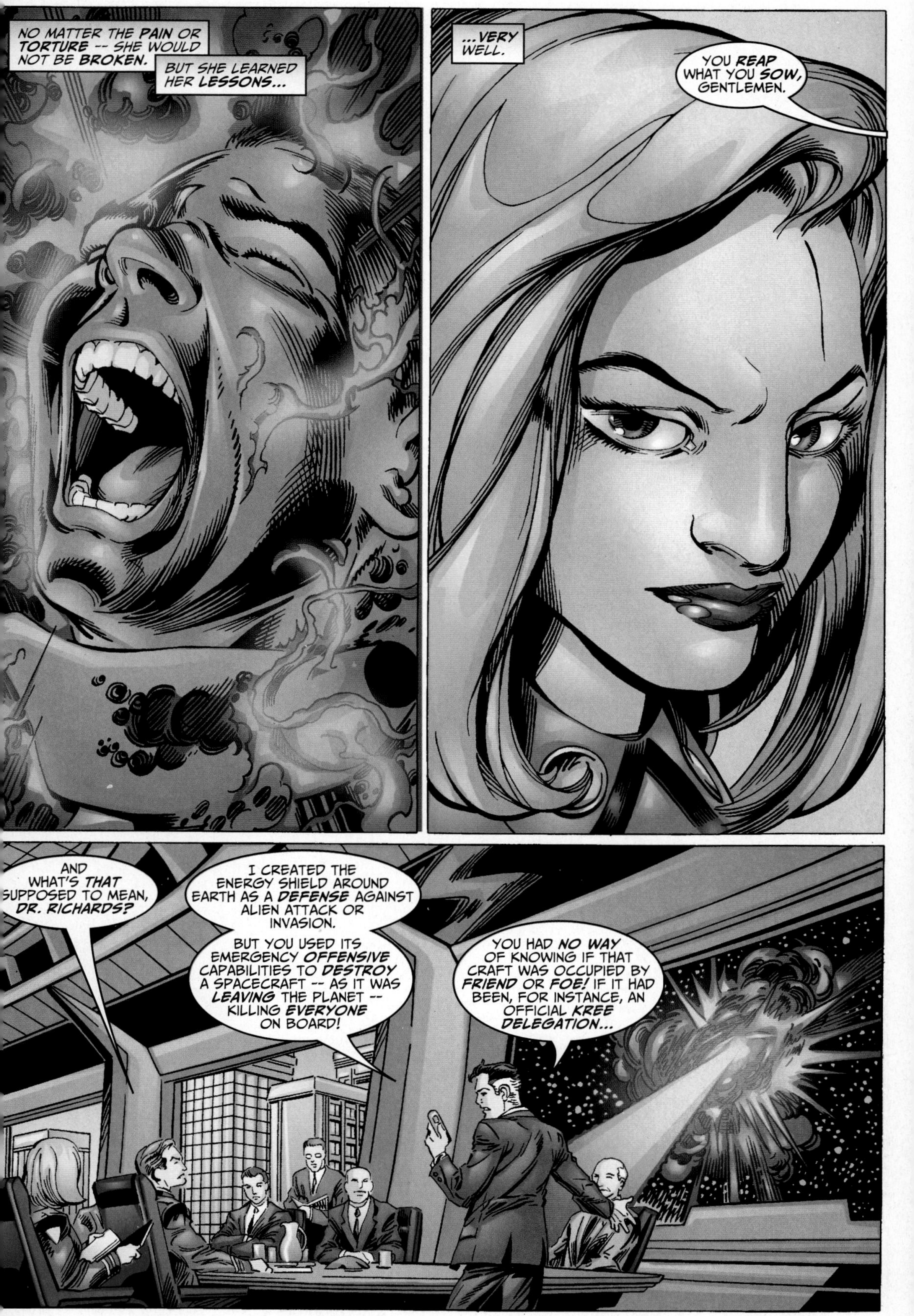
NO MATTER THE PAIN OR TORTURE -- SHE WOULD NOT BE BROKEN.
BUT SHE LEARNED HER LESSONS...
...VERY WELL.
YOU REAP WHAT YOU SOW, GENTLEMEN.
AND WHAT'S THAT SUPPOSED TO MEAN, DR. RICHARDS?
I CREATED THE ENERGY SHIELD AROUND EARTH AS A DEFENSE AGAINST ALIEN ATTACK OR INVASION.
BUT YOU USED ITS EMERGENCY OFFENSIVE CAPABILITIES TO DESTROY A SPACECRAFT -- AS IT WAS LEAVING THE PLANET -- KILLING EVERYONE ON BOARD!
YOU HAD NO WAY OF KNOWING IF THAT CRAFT WAS OCCUPIED BY FRIEND OR FOE! IF IT HAD BEEN, FOR INSTANCE, AN OFFICIAL KREE DELEGATION...

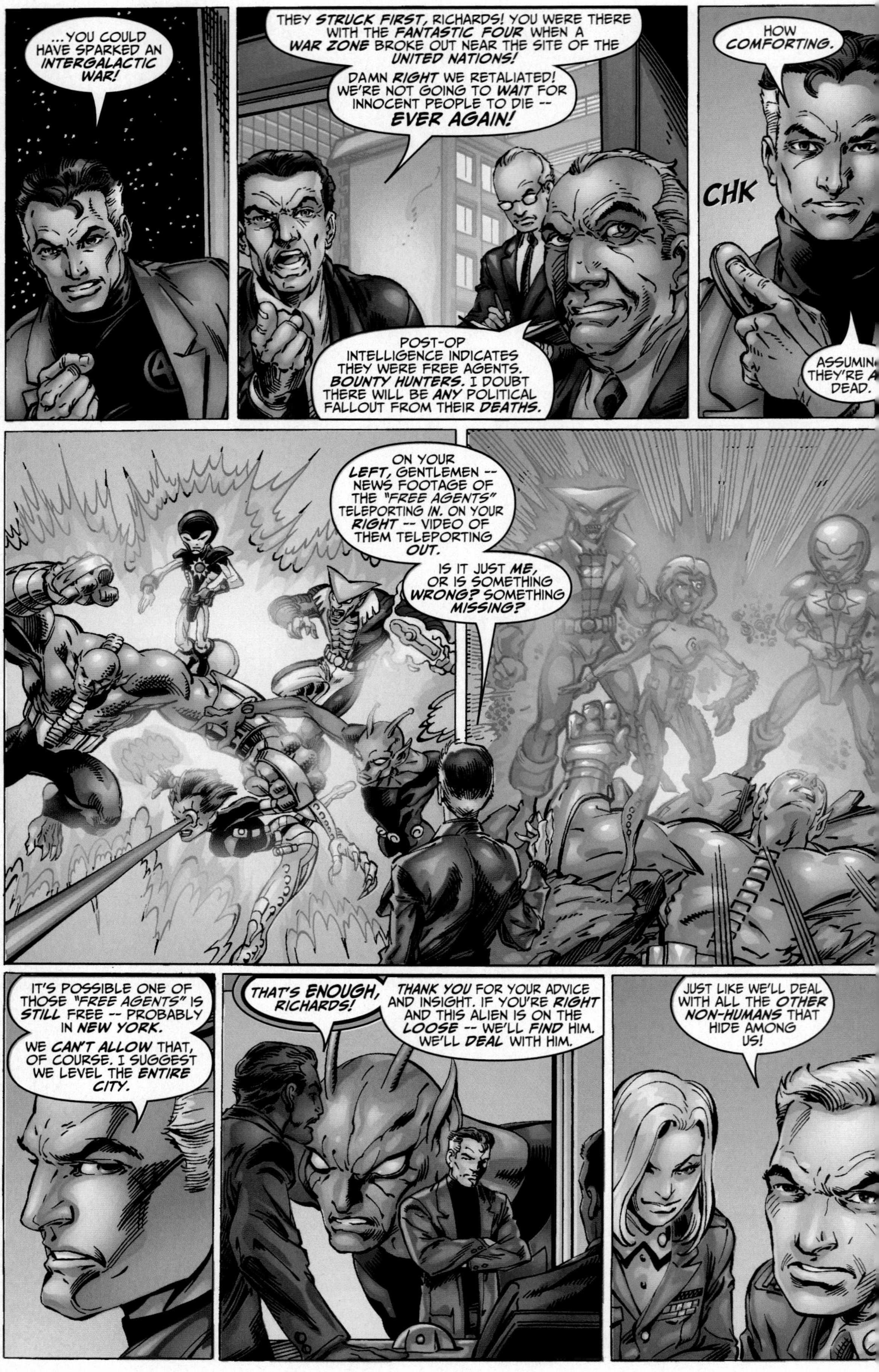
...YOU COULD HAVE SPARKED AN INTERGALACTIC WAR!
THEY STRUCK FIRST, RICHARDS! YOU WERE THERE WITH THE FANTASTIC FOUR WHEN A WAR ZONE BROKE OUT NEAR THE SITE OF THE UNITED NATIONS!
DAMN RIGHT WE RETALIATED! WE'RE NOT GOING TO WAIT FOR INNOCENT PEOPLE TO DIE -- EVER AGAIN!
POST-OP INTELLIGENCE INDICATES THEY WERE FREE AGENTS. BOUNTY HUNTERS. I DOUBT THERE WILL BE ANY POLITICAL FALLOUT FROM THEIR DEATHS.
HOW COMFORTING.
CHK
ASSUMIN THEY'RE A DEAD.
ON YOUR LEFT, GENTLEMEN -- NEWS FOOTAGE OF THE "FREE AGENTS" TELEPORTING IN. ON YOUR RIGHT -- VIDEO OF THEM TELEPORTING OUT.
IS IT JUST ME, OR IS SOMETHING WRONG? SOMETHING MISSING?
IT'S POSSIBLE ONE OF THOSE "FREE AGENTS" IS STILL FREE -- PROBABLY IN NEW YORK.
WE CAN'T ALLOW THAT, OF COURSE. I SUGGEST WE LEVEL THE ENTIRE CITY.
THAT'S ENOUGH, RICHARDS!
THANK YOU FOR YOUR ADVICE AND INSIGHT. IF YOU'RE RIGHT AND THIS ALIEN IS ON THE LOOSE -- WE'LL FIND HIM. WE'LL DEAL WITH HIM.
JUST LIKE WE'LL DEAL WITH ALL THE OTHER NON-HUMANS THAT HIDE AMONG US!

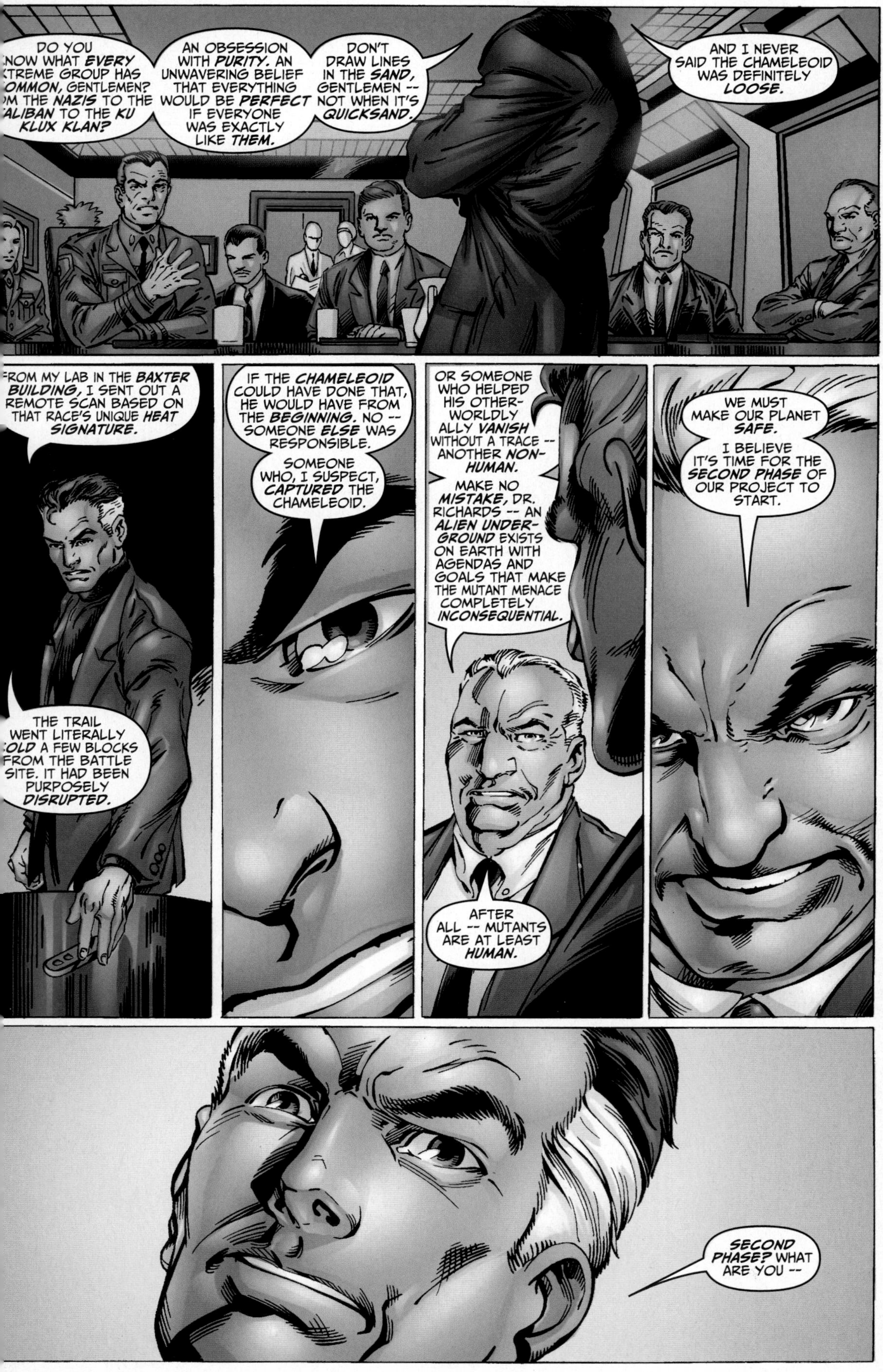
DO YOU KNOW WHAT EVERY EXTREME GROUP HAS IN COMMON, GENTLEMEN? FROM THE NAZIS TO THE TALIBAN TO THE KU KLUX KLAN?
AN OBSESSION WITH PURITY. AN UNWAVERING BELIEF THAT EVERYTHING WOULD BE PERFECT IF EVERYONE WAS EXACTLY LIKE THEM.
DON'T DRAW LINES IN THE SAND, GENTLEMEN -- NOT WHEN IT'S QUICKSAND.
AND I NEVER SAID THE CHAMELEOID WAS DEFINITELY LOOSE.
FROM MY LAB IN THE BAXTER BUILDING, I SENT OUT A REMOTE SCAN BASED ON THAT RACE'S UNIQUE HEAT SIGNATURE.
THE TRAIL WENT LITERALLY COLD A FEW BLOCKS FROM THE BATTLE SITE. IT HAD BEEN PURPOSELY DISRUPTED.
IF THE CHAMELEOID COULD HAVE DONE THAT, HE WOULD HAVE FROM THE BEGINNING. NO -- SOMEONE ELSE WAS RESPONSIBLE.
SOMEONE WHO, I SUSPECT, CAPTURED THE CHAMELEOID.
OR SOMEONE WHO HELPED HIS OTHER-WORLDLY ALLY VANISH WITHOUT A TRACE -- ANOTHER NON-HUMAN.
MAKE NO MISTAKE, DR. RICHARDS -- AN ALIEN UNDERGROUND EXISTS ON EARTH WITH AGENDAS AND GOALS THAT MAKE THE MUTANT MENACE COMPLETELY INCONSEQUENTIAL.
AFTER ALL -- MUTANTS ARE AT LEAST HUMAN.
WE MUST MAKE OUR PLANET SAFE.
I BELIEVE IT'S TIME FOR THE SECOND PHASE OF OUR PROJECT TO START.
SECOND PHASE? WHAT ARE YOU --

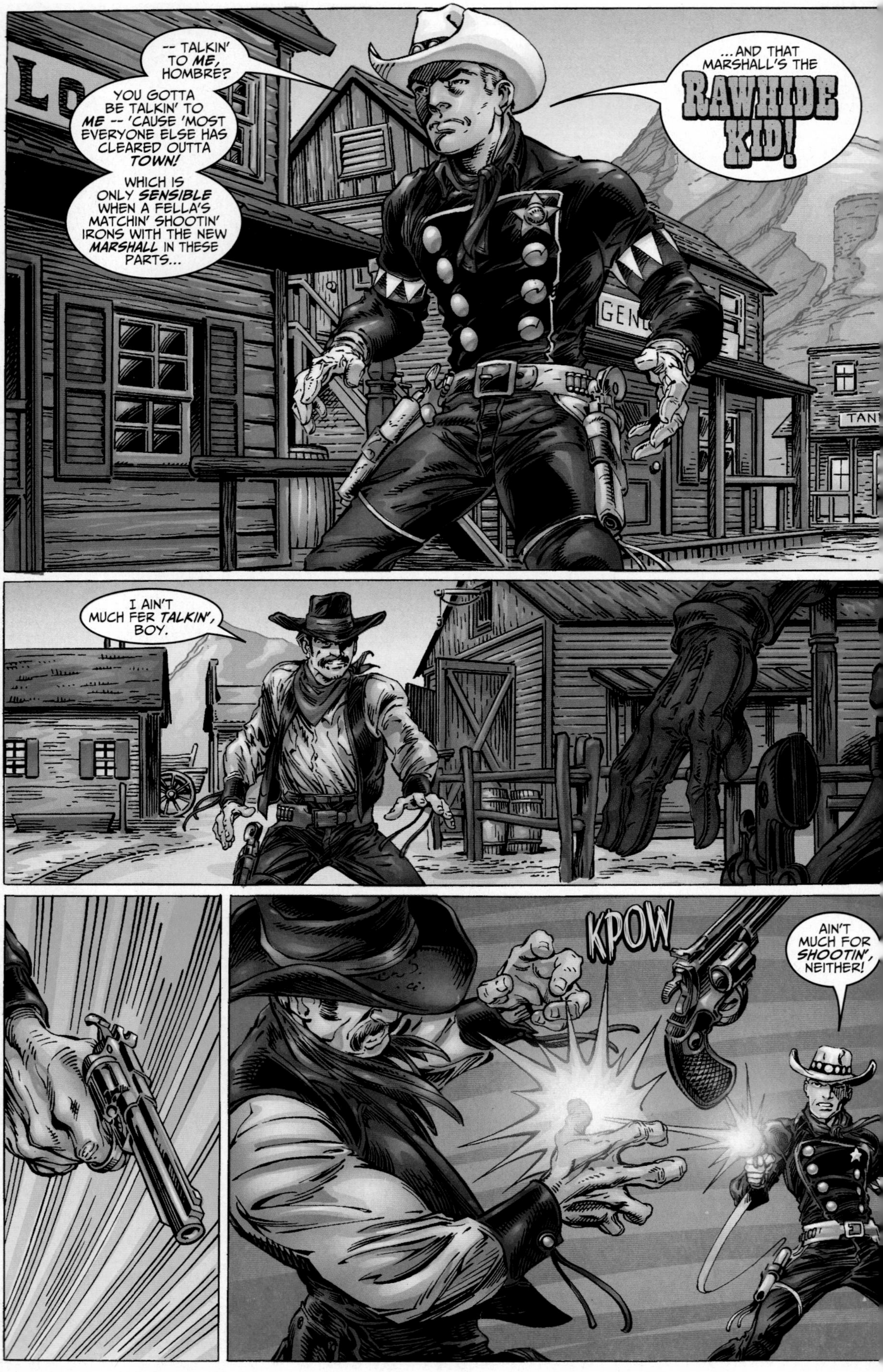
-- TALKIN' TO ME, HOMBRE?
YOU GOTTA BE TALKIN' TO ME -- 'CAUSE 'MOST EVERYONE ELSE HAS CLEARED OUTTA TOWN!
WHICH IS ONLY SENSIBLE WHEN A FELLA'S MATCHIN' SHOOTIN' IRONS WITH THE NEW MARSHALL IN THESE PARTS...
...AND THAT MARSHALL'S THE RAWHIDE KID!
I AIN'T MUCH FER TALKIN', BOY.
KPOW
AIN'T MUCH FOR SHOOTIN', NEITHER!

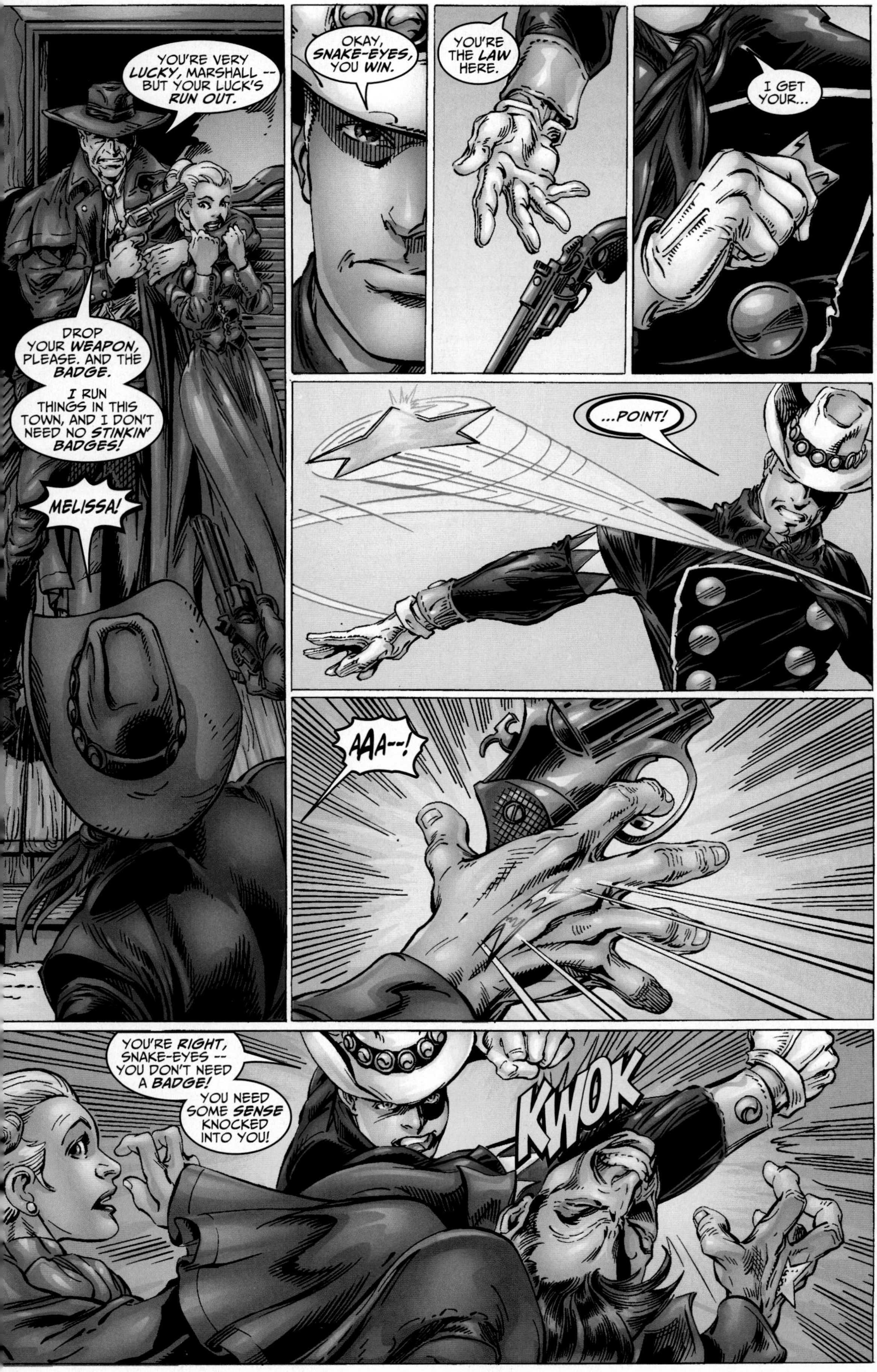
YOU'RE VERY LUCKY, MARSHALL -- BUT YOUR LUCK'S RUN OUT.
DROP YOUR WEAPON, PLEASE. AND THE BADGE.
I RUN THINGS IN THIS TOWN, AND I DON'T NEED NO STINKIN' BADGES!
MELISSA!
OKAY, SNAKE-EYES, YOU WIN.
YOU'RE THE LAW HERE.
I GET YOUR...
...POINT!
AAA--!
YOU'RE RIGHT, SNAKE-EYES -- YOU DON'T NEED A BADGE!
YOU NEED SOME SENSE KNOCKED INTO YOU!
KWOK

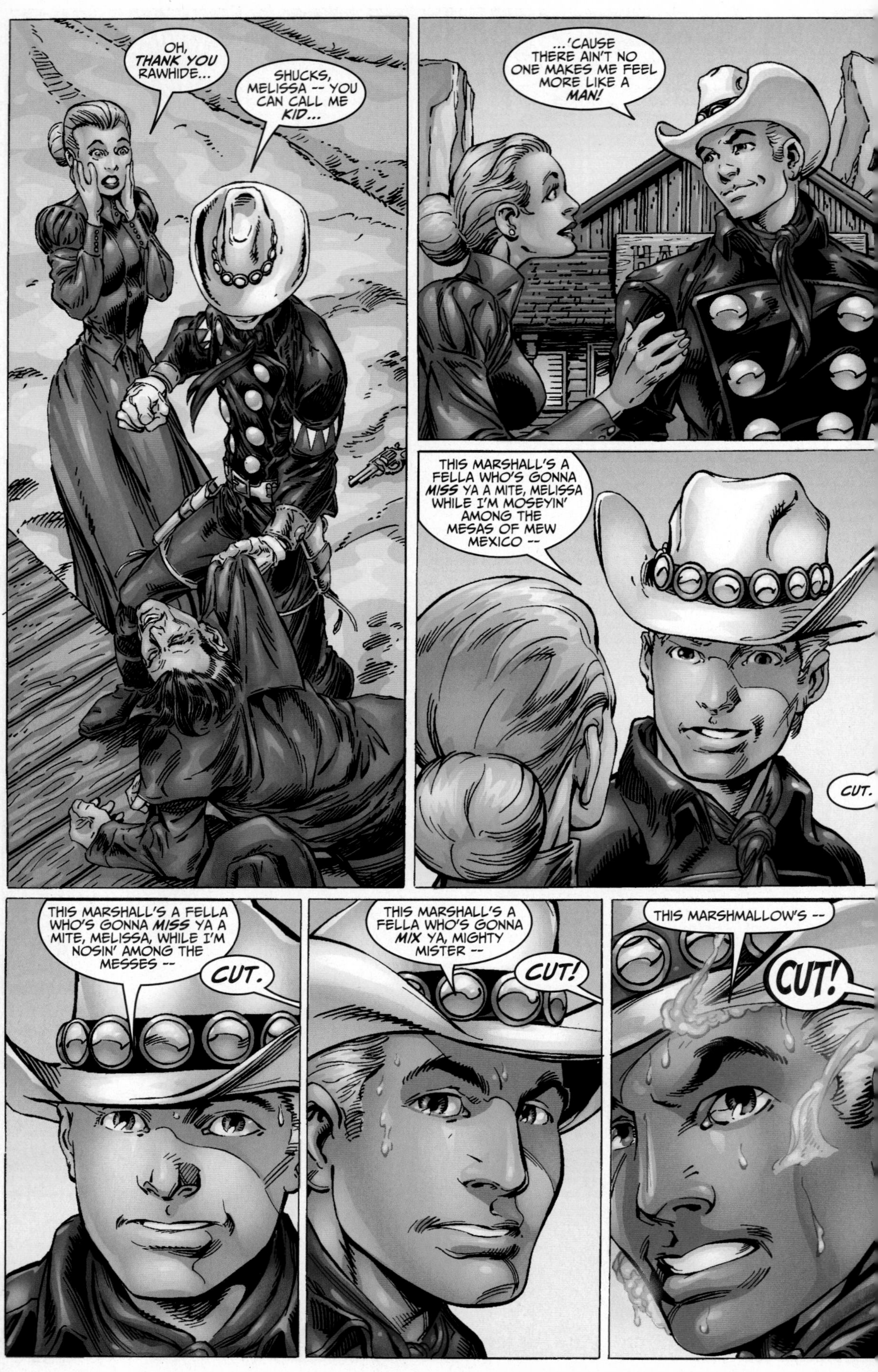
OH, *THANK YOU* RAWHIDE...
SHUCKS, MELISSA -- YOU CAN CALL ME *KID...*
...'CAUSE THERE AIN'T NO ONE MAKES ME FEEL MORE LIKE A *MAN!*
THIS MARSHALL'S A FELLA WHO'S GONNA *MISS* YA A MITE, MELISSA WHILE I'M MOSEYIN' AMONG THE MESAS OF MEW MEXICO --
CUT.
THIS MARSHALL'S A FELLA WHO'S GONNA *MISS* YA A MITE, MELISSA, WHILE I'M NOSIN' AMONG THE MESSES --
CUT.
THIS MARSHALL'S A FELLA WHO'S GONNA *MIX* YA, MIGHTY MISTER --
CUT!
THIS MARSHMALLOW'S --
CUT!

HEAVEN'S TE! WHAT'S RONG?!

YOU'RE THE *RAWHIDE KID* -- THE ORIGINAL *TOP GUN!* YOU'RE *JOHNNY STORM* -- THIS *MOVIE'S STAR!*

CAN'T YOU TALK TO ONE *GIRL* WITHOUT TRIPPING OVER YOUR OWN *TONGUE?!*

EASY, BOB...

SORRY, *MR. DIAMOND.* THIS... IT'S ALL SO *NEW* TO ME. I... I THINK I JUST NEED TO...

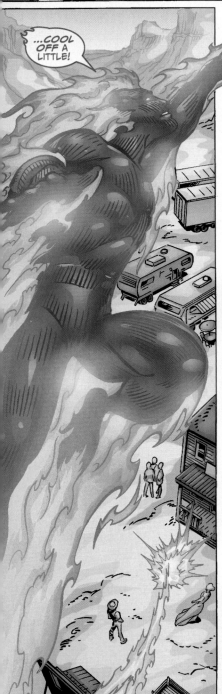

...COOL OFF A LITTLE!

THERE GOES *ANOTHER* COSTUME UP IN FLAMES!

WE *ANTICIPATED* THIS, BOB. IT'S IN THE *BUDGET.*

THE KID'S *GOOD* -- IN HIS *ACTION* SCENES, AT LEAST. AND HE'S GOT *PRESENCE* -- HE *LIGHTS UP* THE SCREEN!

TOO BAD HE *CAN'T ACT.*

SHOULD I GO SEE IF HE CAN MEMORIZE *TOMORROW'S* LINES?

LIKE A GOOD PRODUCER'S ASSISTANT *SHOULD,* ROBERTA.

I'M SORRY, *HAWK.* I KNOW WHAT THIS FILM *MEANS* TO YOU... TO THE MEMORY OF YOUR *FATHER.*

I'M DOING WHAT I *CAN* -- BUT A *DIRECTOR* CAN ONLY DO *SO MUCH.*

DON'T WORRY, BOB -- I KNOW YOU'RE GIVING IT YOUR *BEST.*

IT'S *NOT OVER* YET.

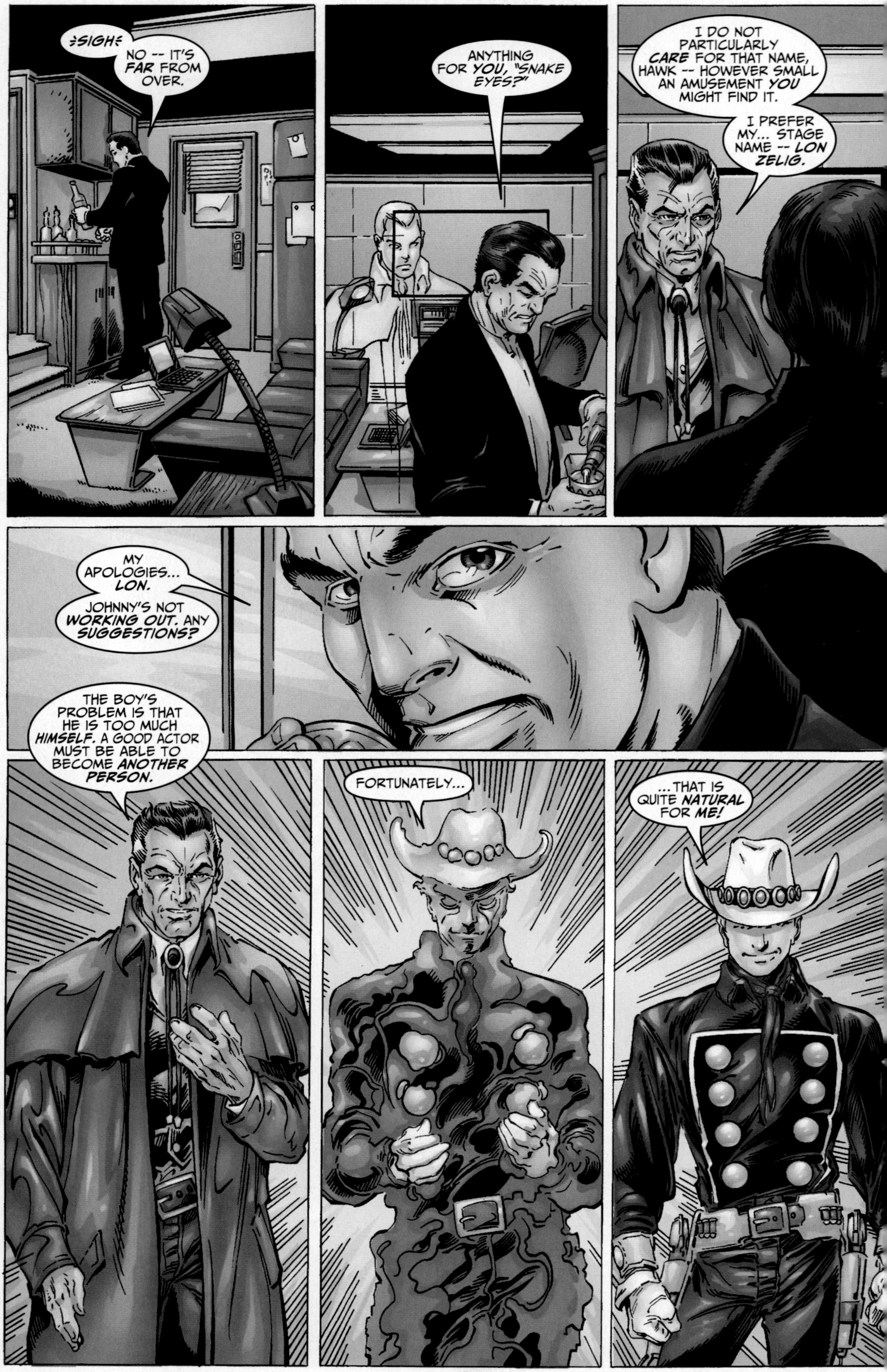
SIGH
NO -- IT'S FAR FROM OVER.
ANYTHING FOR YOU, "SNAKE EYES?"
I DO NOT PARTICULARLY CARE FOR THAT NAME, HAWK -- HOWEVER SMALL AN AMUSEMENT YOU MIGHT FIND IT.
I PREFER MY... STAGE NAME -- LON ZELIG.
MY APOLOGIES... LON.
JOHNNY'S NOT WORKING OUT. ANY SUGGESTIONS?
THE BOY'S PROBLEM IS THAT HE IS TOO MUCH HIMSELF. A GOOD ACTOR MUST BE ABLE TO BECOME ANOTHER PERSON.
FORTUNATELY...
...THAT IS QUITE NATURAL FOR ME!

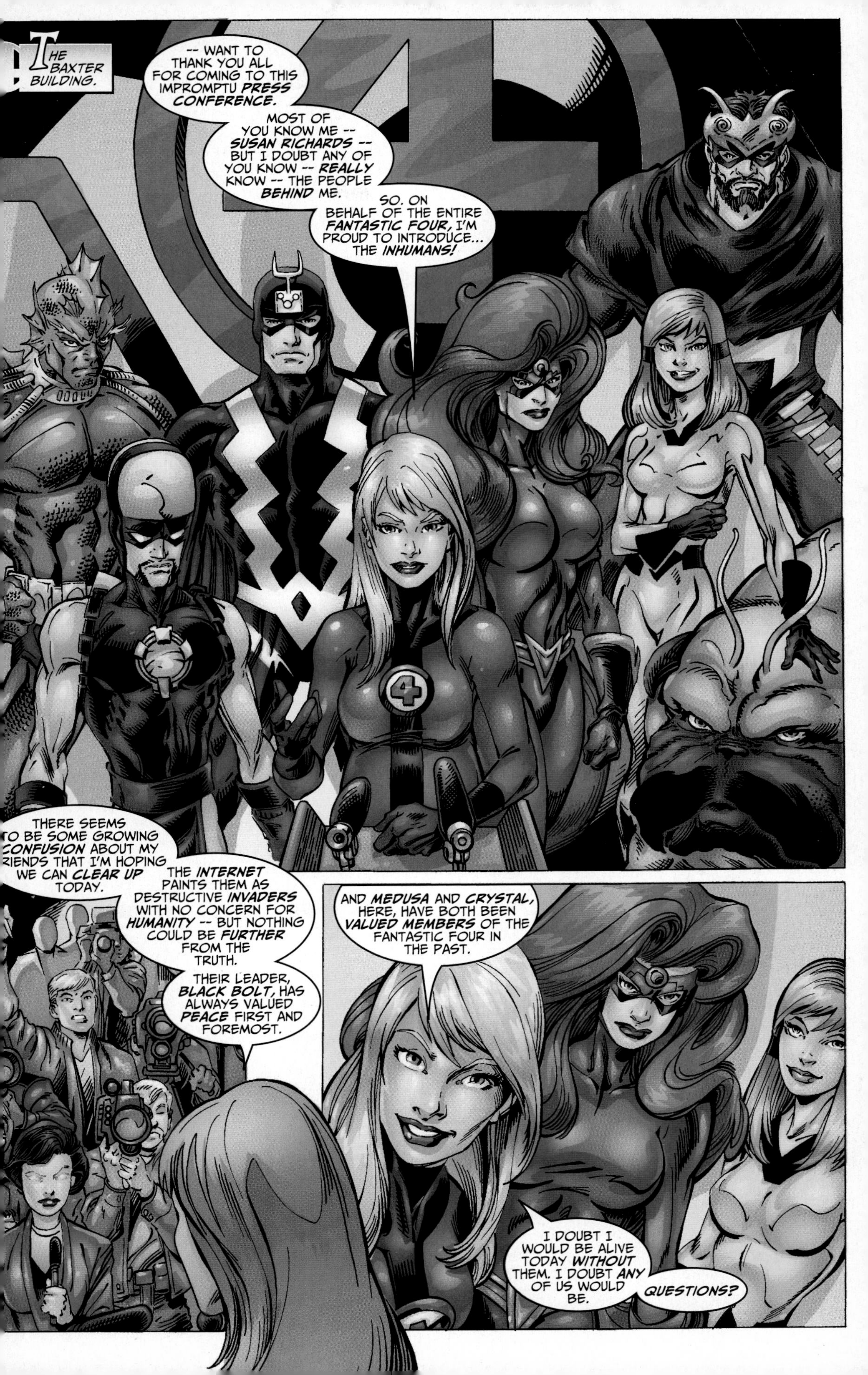
THE BAXTER BUILDING.
-- WANT TO THANK YOU ALL FOR COMING TO THIS IMPROMPTU PRESS CONFERENCE.
MOST OF YOU KNOW ME -- SUSAN RICHARDS -- BUT I DOUBT ANY OF YOU KNOW -- REALLY KNOW -- THE PEOPLE BEHIND ME.
SO. ON BEHALF OF THE ENTIRE FANTASTIC FOUR, I'M PROUD TO INTRODUCE... THE INHUMANS!
THERE SEEMS TO BE SOME GROWING CONFUSION ABOUT MY RIENDS THAT I'M HOPING WE CAN CLEAR UP TODAY.
THE INTERNET PAINTS THEM AS DESTRUCTIVE INVADERS WITH NO CONCERN FOR HUMANITY -- BUT NOTHING COULD BE FURTHER FROM THE TRUTH.
THEIR LEADER, BLACK BOLT, HAS ALWAYS VALUED PEACE FIRST AND FOREMOST.
AND MEDUSA AND CRYSTAL, HERE, HAVE BOTH BEEN VALUED MEMBERS OF THE FANTASTIC FOUR IN THE PAST.
I DOUBT I WOULD BE ALIVE TODAY WITHOUT THEM. I DOUBT ANY OF US WOULD BE.
QUESTIONS?

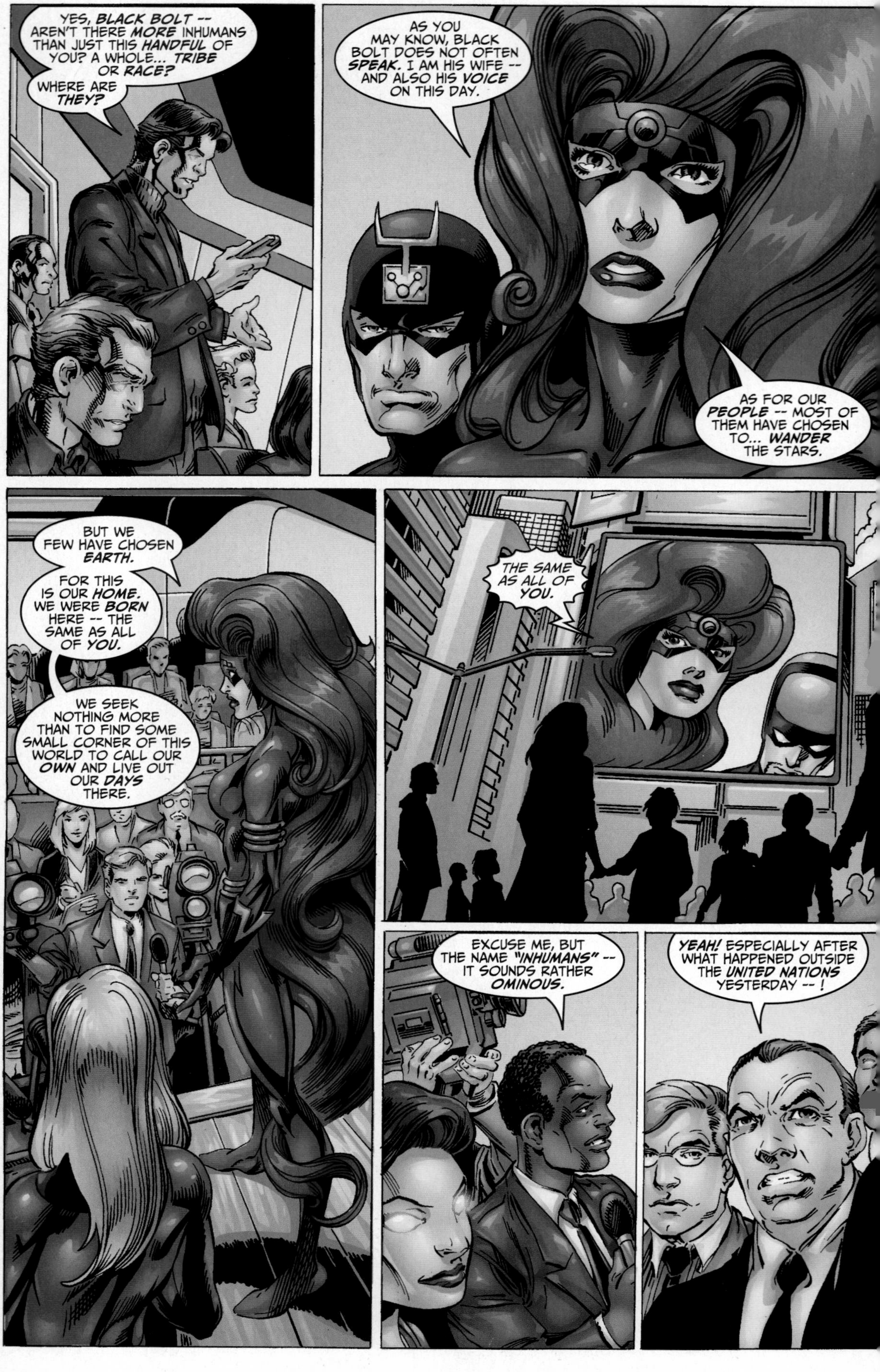
YES, BLACK BOLT -- AREN'T THERE MORE INHUMANS THAN JUST THIS HANDFUL OF YOU? A WHOLE... TRIBE OR RACE?
WHERE ARE THEY?
AS YOU MAY KNOW, BLACK BOLT DOES NOT OFTEN SPEAK. I AM HIS WIFE -- AND ALSO HIS VOICE ON THIS DAY.
AS FOR OUR PEOPLE -- MOST OF THEM HAVE CHOSEN TO... WANDER THE STARS.
BUT WE FEW HAVE CHOSEN EARTH.
FOR THIS IS OUR HOME. WE WERE BORN HERE -- THE SAME AS ALL OF YOU.
WE SEEK NOTHING MORE THAN TO FIND SOME SMALL CORNER OF THIS WORLD TO CALL OUR OWN AND LIVE OUT OUR DAYS THERE.
THE SAME AS ALL OF YOU.
EXCUSE ME, BUT THE NAME "INHUMANS" -- IT SOUNDS RATHER OMINOUS.
YEAH! ESPECIALLY AFTER WHAT HAPPENED OUTSIDE THE UNITED NATIONS YESTERDAY -- !

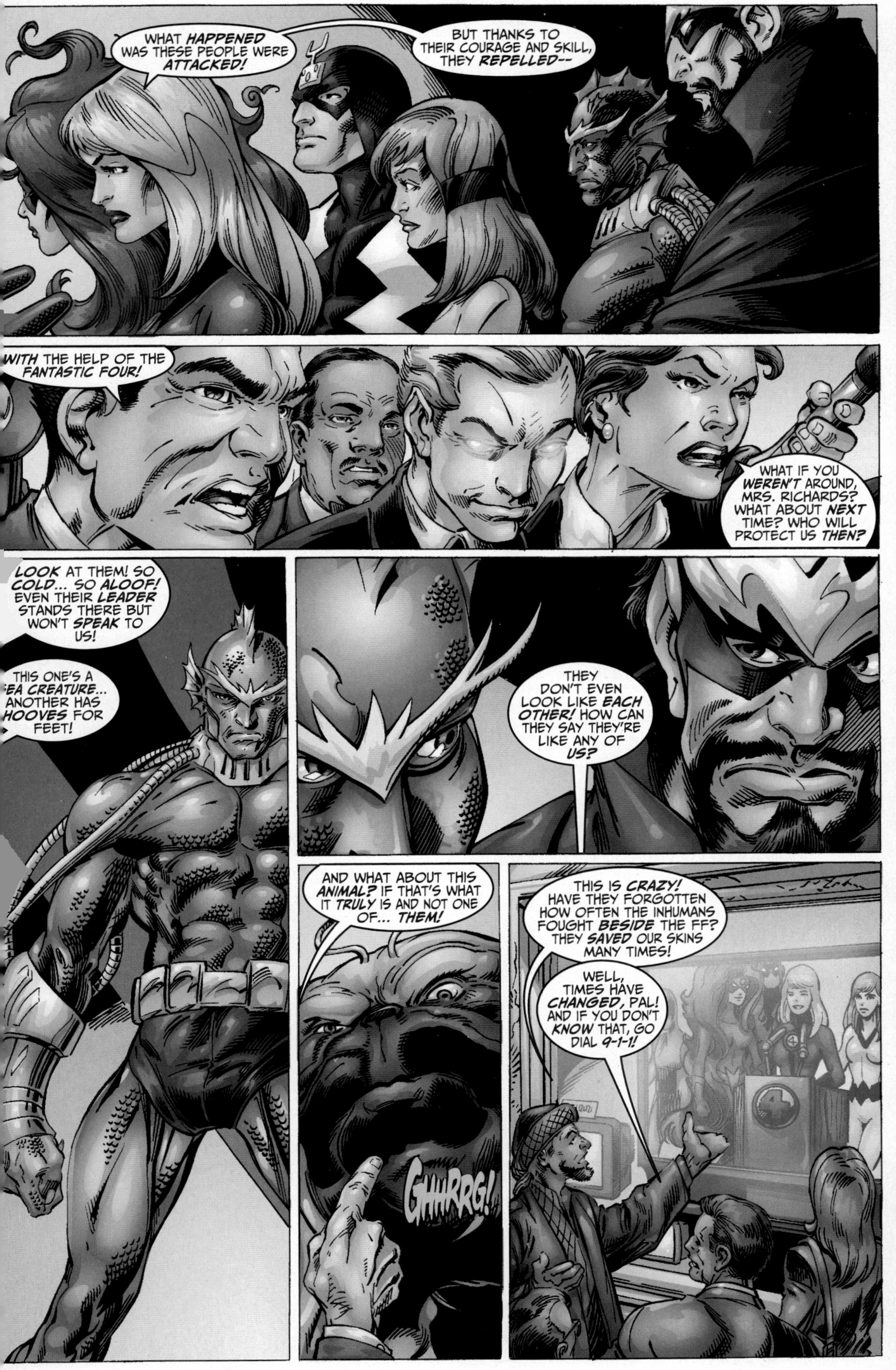
WHAT HAPPENED WAS THESE PEOPLE WERE ATTACKED!
BUT THANKS TO THEIR COURAGE AND SKILL, THEY REPELLED--
WITH THE HELP OF THE FANTASTIC FOUR!
WHAT IF YOU WEREN'T AROUND, MRS. RICHARDS? WHAT ABOUT NEXT TIME? WHO WILL PROTECT US THEN?
LOOK AT THEM! SO COLD... SO ALOOF! EVEN THEIR LEADER STANDS THERE BUT WON'T SPEAK TO US!
THIS ONE'S A SEA CREATURE... ANOTHER HAS HOOVES FOR FEET!
THEY DON'T EVEN LOOK LIKE EACH OTHER! HOW CAN THEY SAY THEY'RE LIKE ANY OF US?
AND WHAT ABOUT THIS ANIMAL? IF THAT'S WHAT IT TRULY IS AND NOT ONE OF... THEM!
GHHRRG!
THIS IS CRAZY! HAVE THEY FORGOTTEN HOW OFTEN THE INHUMANS FOUGHT BESIDE THE FF? THEY SAVED OUR SKINS MANY TIMES!
WELL, TIMES HAVE CHANGED, PAL! AND IF YOU DON'T KNOW THAT, GO DIAL 9-1-1!

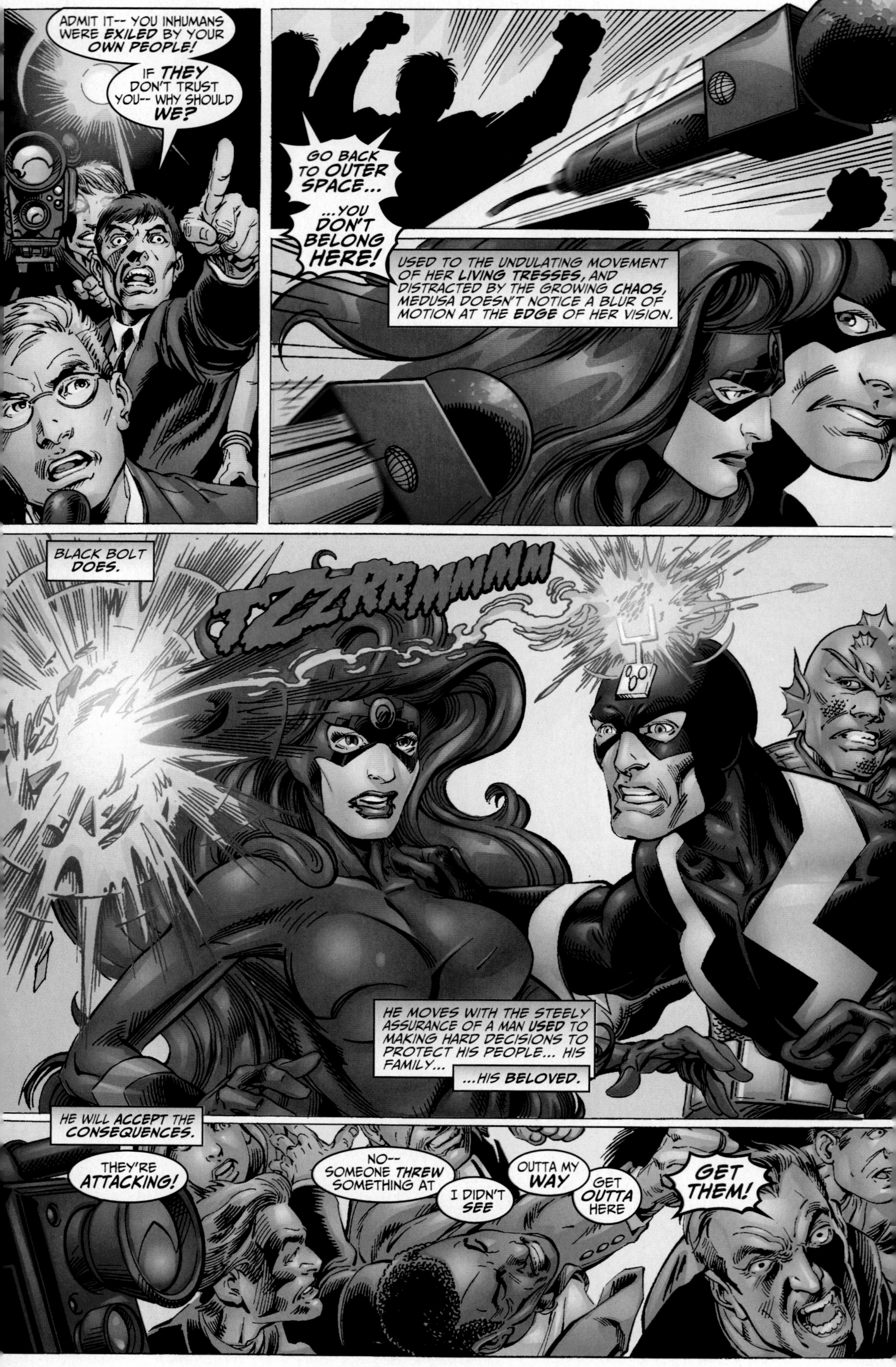
ADMIT IT-- YOU INHUMANS WERE EXILED BY YOUR OWN PEOPLE!
IF THEY DON'T TRUST YOU-- WHY SHOULD WE?
GO BACK TO OUTER SPACE...
...YOU DON'T BELONG HERE!
USED TO THE UNDULATING MOVEMENT OF HER LIVING TRESSES, AND DISTRACTED BY THE GROWING CHAOS, MEDUSA DOESN'T NOTICE A BLUR OF MOTION AT THE EDGE OF HER VISION.
BLACK BOLT DOES.
TZZRRRMMMMM
HE MOVES WITH THE STEELY ASSURANCE OF A MAN USED TO MAKING HARD DECISIONS TO PROTECT HIS PEOPLE... HIS FAMILY...
...HIS BELOVED.
HE WILL ACCEPT THE CONSEQUENCES.
THEY'RE ATTACKING!
NO-- SOMEONE THREW SOMETHING AT
I DIDN'T SEE
OUTTA MY WAY
GET OUTTA HERE
GET THEM!

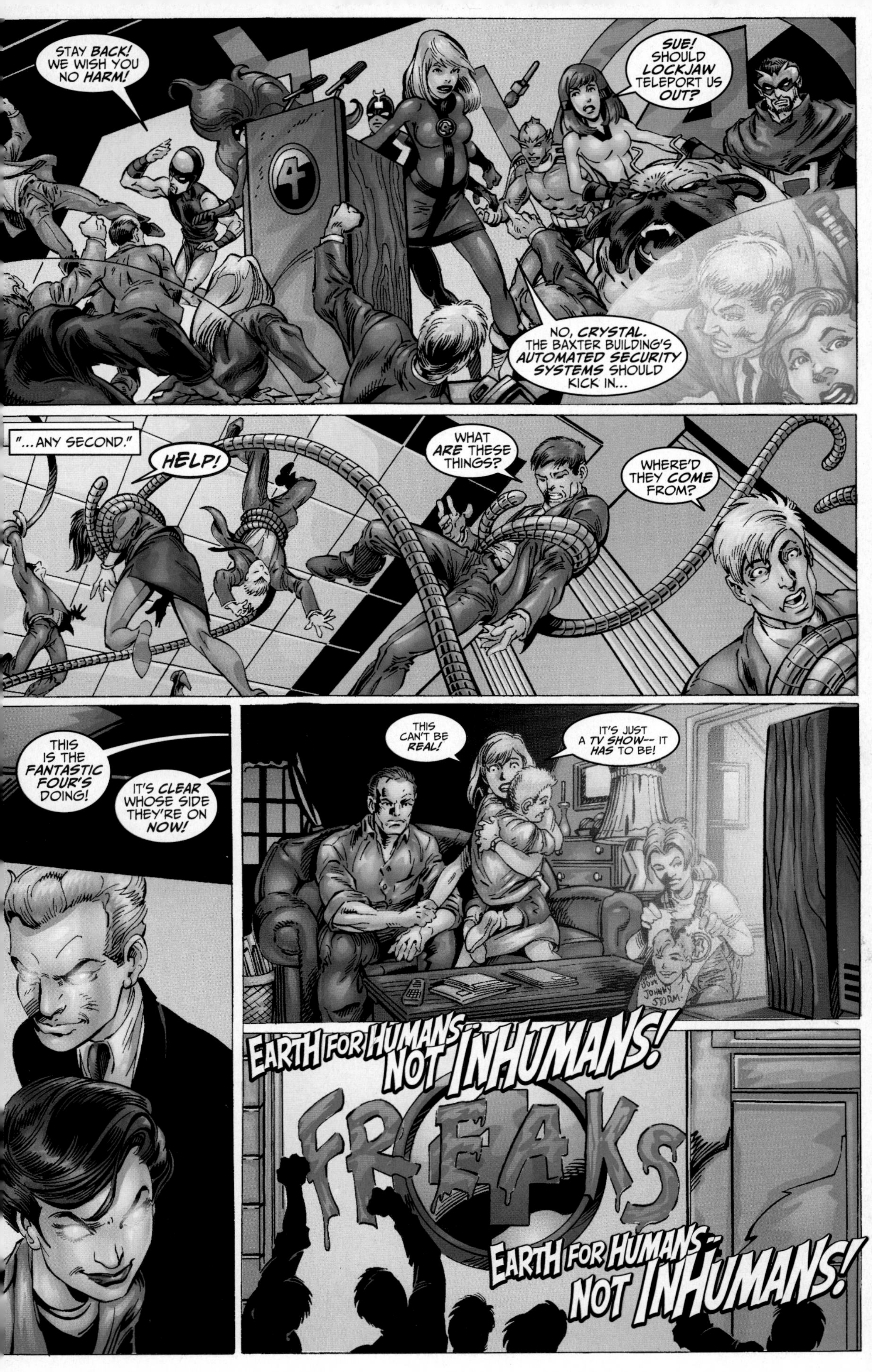
STAY BACK! WE WISH YOU NO HARM!
SUE! SHOULD LOCKJAW TELEPORT US OUT?
NO, CRYSTAL. THE BAXTER BUILDING'S AUTOMATED SECURITY SYSTEMS SHOULD KICK IN...
"...ANY SECOND."
HELP!
WHAT ARE THESE THINGS?
WHERE'D THEY COME FROM?
THIS IS THE FANTASTIC FOUR'S DOING!
IT'S CLEAR WHOSE SIDE THEY'RE ON NOW!
THIS CAN'T BE REAL!
IT'S JUST A TV SHOW-- IT HAS TO BE!
EARTH FOR HUMANS-- NOT INHUMANS!
FREAKS
EARTH FOR HUMANS-- NOT INHUMANS!

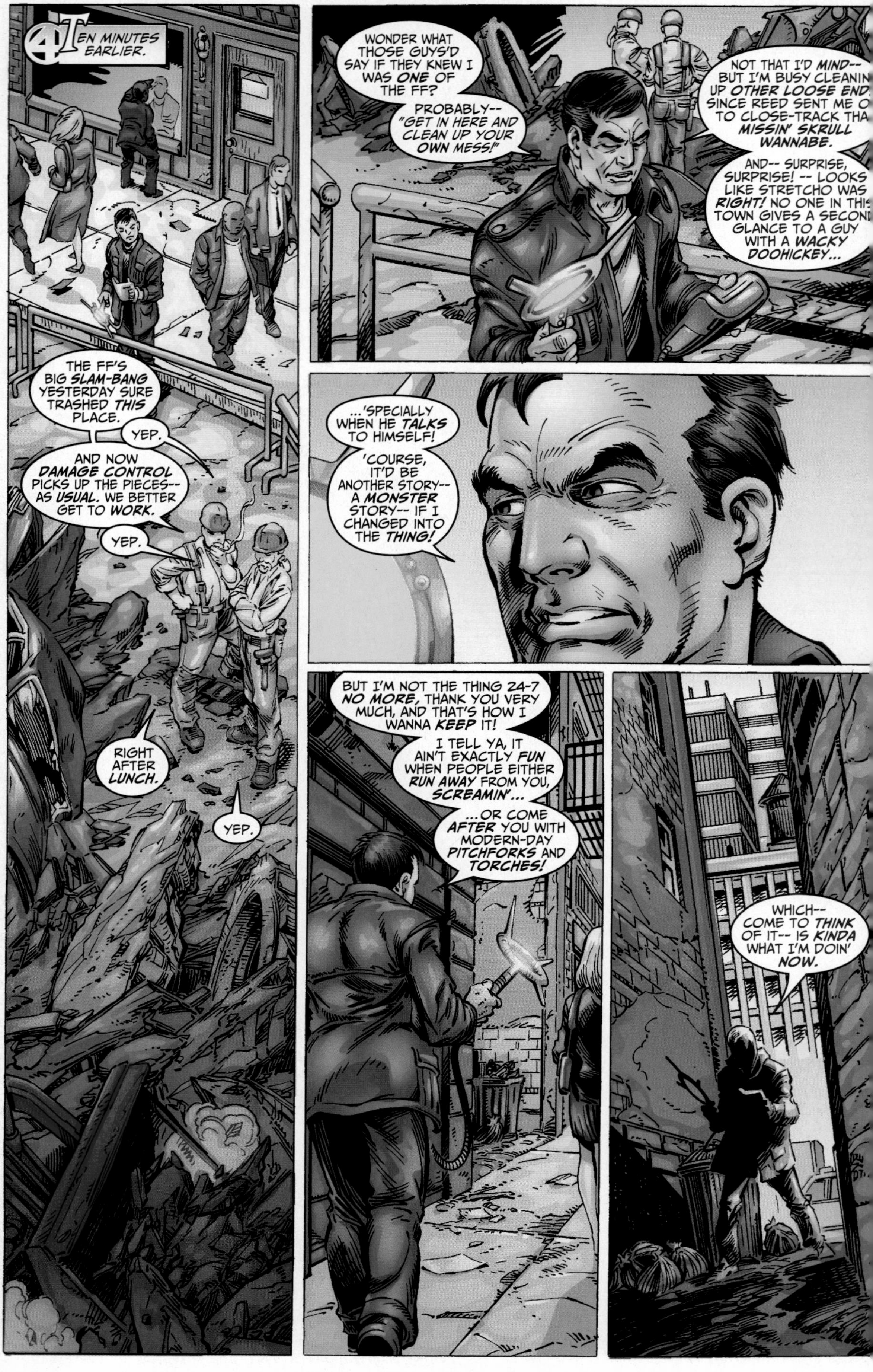
TEN MINUTES EARLIER.
THE FF'S BIG SLAM-BANG YESTERDAY SURE TRASHED THIS PLACE.
YEP.
AND NOW DAMAGE CONTROL PICKS UP THE PIECES-- AS USUAL. WE BETTER GET TO WORK.
YEP.
RIGHT AFTER LUNCH.
YEP.
WONDER WHAT THOSE GUYS'D SAY IF THEY KNEW I WAS ONE OF THE FF?
PROBABLY-- "GET IN HERE AND CLEAN UP YOUR OWN MESS!"
NOT THAT I'D MIND-- BUT I'M BUSY CLEANIN' UP OTHER LOOSE END SINCE REED SENT ME O TO CLOSE-TRACK THA MISSIN' SKRULL WANNABE.
AND-- SURPRISE, SURPRISE! -- LOOKS LIKE STRETCHO WAS RIGHT! NO ONE IN THIS TOWN GIVES A SECOND GLANCE TO A GUY WITH A WACKY DOOHICKEY...
...'SPECIALLY WHEN HE TALKS TO HIMSELF!
'COURSE, IT'D BE ANOTHER STORY-- A MONSTER STORY-- IF I CHANGED INTO THE THING!
BUT I'M NOT THE THING 24-7 NO MORE, THANK YOU VERY MUCH, AND THAT'S HOW I WANNA KEEP IT!
I TELL YA, IT AIN'T EXACTLY FUN WHEN PEOPLE EITHER RUN AWAY FROM YOU, SCREAMIN'...
...OR COME AFTER YOU WITH MODERN-DAY PITCHFORKS AND TORCHES!
WHICH-- COME TO THINK OF IT-- IS KINDA WHAT I'M DOIN' NOW.

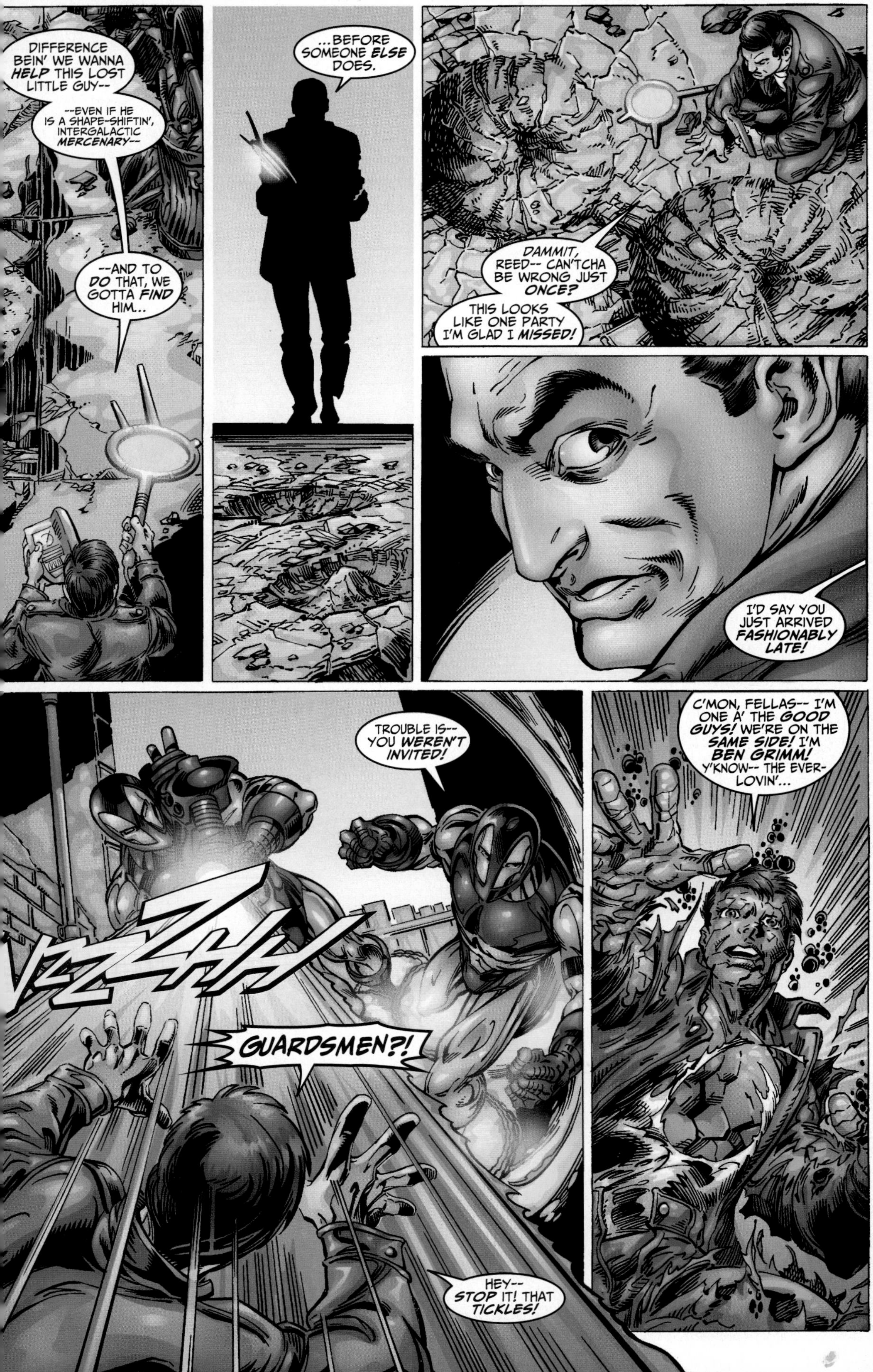

DIFFERENCE BEIN' WE WANNA HELP THIS LOST LITTLE GUY--
--EVEN IF HE IS A SHAPE-SHIFTIN', INTERGALACTIC MERCENARY--
--AND TO DO THAT, WE GOTTA FIND HIM...
...BEFORE SOMEONE ELSE DOES.
DAMMIT, REED-- CAN'TCHA BE WRONG JUST ONCE?
THIS LOOKS LIKE ONE PARTY I'M GLAD I MISSED!
I'D SAY YOU JUST ARRIVED FASHIONABLY LATE!
TROUBLE IS-- YOU WEREN'T INVITED!
VZZHH
GUARDSMEN?!
HEY-- STOP IT! THAT TICKLES!
C'MON, FELLAS-- I'M ONE A' THE GOOD GUYS! WE'RE ON THE SAME SIDE! I'M BEN GRIMM! Y'KNOW-- THE EVER-LOVIN'...

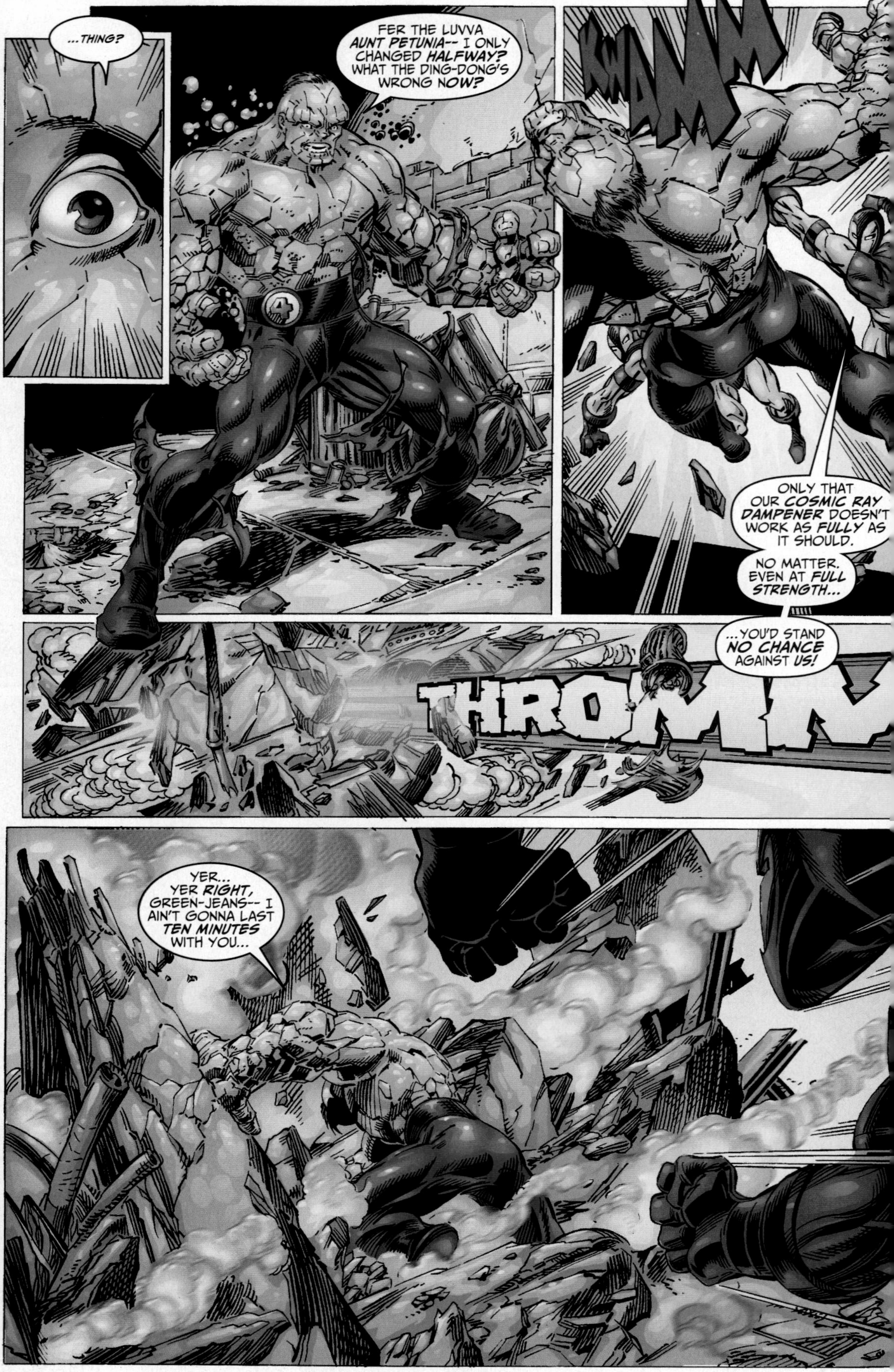
...THING?
FER THE LUVVA AUNT PETUNIA-- I ONLY CHANGED HALFWAY? WHAT THE DING-DONG'S WRONG NOW?
KWAMM
ONLY THAT OUR COSMIC RAY DAMPENER DOESN'T WORK AS FULLY AS IT SHOULD.
NO MATTER. EVEN AT FULL STRENGTH...
...YOU'D STAND NO CHANCE AGAINST US!
THROMM
YER... YER RIGHT, GREEN-JEANS-- I AIN'T GONNA LAST TEN MINUTES WITH YOU...

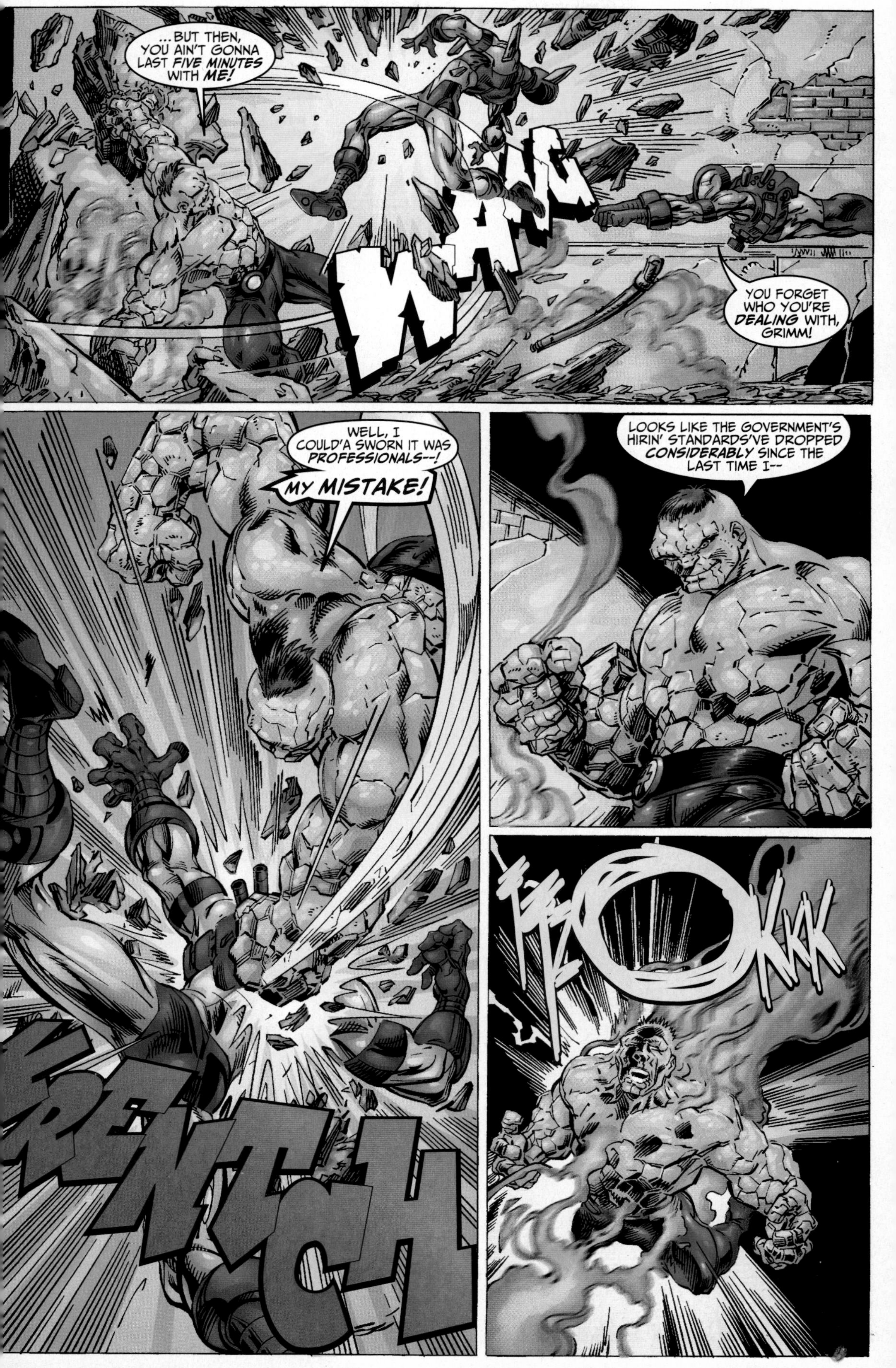

...BUT THEN, YOU AIN'T GONNA LAST *FIVE MINUTES* WITH *ME!*
WANG
YOU FORGET WHO YOU'RE *DEALING* WITH, GRIMM!
WELL, I COULD'A SWORN IT WAS *PROFESSIONALS*--!
MY *MISTAKE!*
LOOKS LIKE THE GOVERNMENT'S HIRIN' STANDARDS'VE DROPPED *CONSIDERABLY* SINCE THE LAST TIME I--

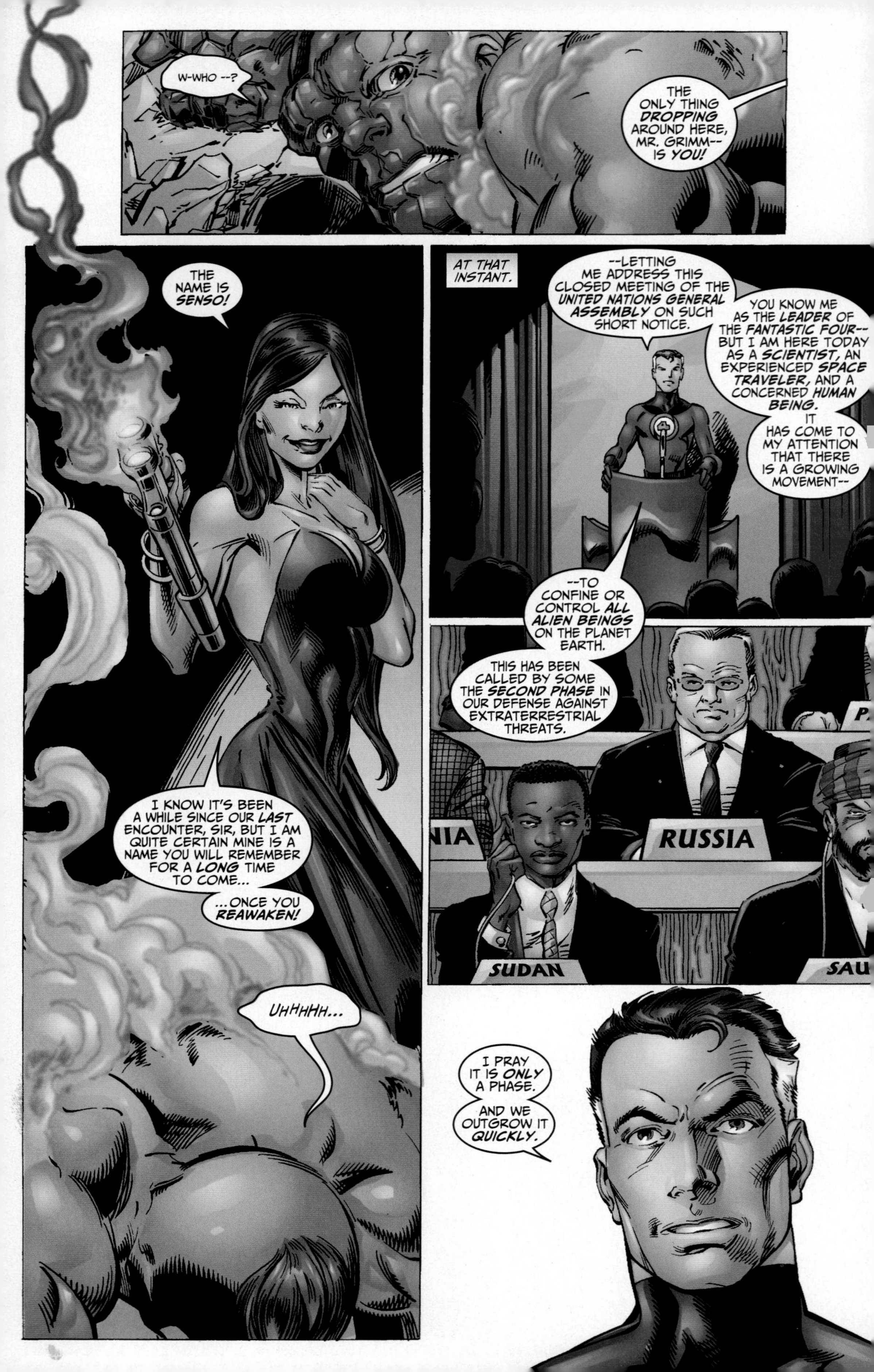
W-WHO --?
THE ONLY THING DROPPING AROUND HERE, MR. GRIMM-- IS YOU!
THE NAME IS SENSO!
I KNOW IT'S BEEN A WHILE SINCE OUR LAST ENCOUNTER, SIR, BUT I AM QUITE CERTAIN MINE IS A NAME YOU WILL REMEMBER FOR A LONG TIME TO COME...
...ONCE YOU REAWAKEN!
UHHHHH...
AT THAT INSTANT.
--LETTING ME ADDRESS THIS CLOSED MEETING OF THE UNITED NATIONS GENERAL ASSEMBLY ON SUCH SHORT NOTICE.
YOU KNOW ME AS THE LEADER OF THE FANTASTIC FOUR-- BUT I AM HERE TODAY AS A SCIENTIST, AN EXPERIENCED SPACE TRAVELER, AND A CONCERNED HUMAN BEING.
IT HAS COME TO MY ATTENTION THAT THERE IS A GROWING MOVEMENT--
--TO CONFINE OR CONTROL ALL ALIEN BEINGS ON THE PLANET EARTH.
THIS HAS BEEN CALLED BY SOME THE SECOND PHASE IN OUR DEFENSE AGAINST EXTRATERRESTRIAL THREATS.
NIA
RUSSIA
SUDAN
SAU
I PRAY IT IS ONLY A PHASE.
AND WE OUTGROW IT QUICKLY.

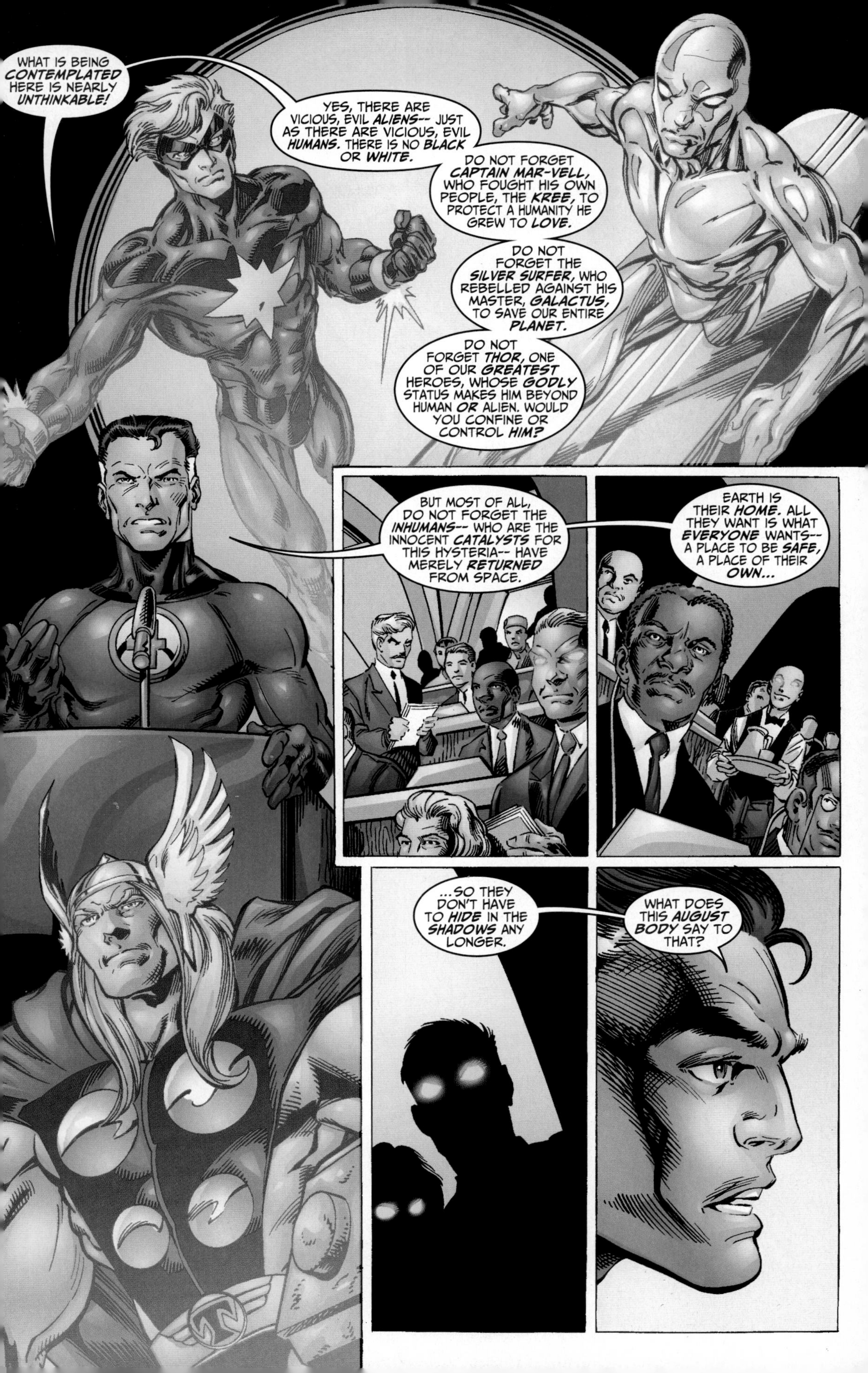

WHAT IS BEING CONTEMPLATED HERE IS NEARLY UNTHINKABLE!
YES, THERE ARE VICIOUS, EVIL ALIENS-- JUST AS THERE ARE VICIOUS, EVIL HUMANS. THERE IS NO BLACK OR WHITE.
DO NOT FORGET CAPTAIN MAR-VELL, WHO FOUGHT HIS OWN PEOPLE, THE KREE, TO PROTECT A HUMANITY HE GREW TO LOVE.
DO NOT FORGET THE SILVER SURFER, WHO REBELLED AGAINST HIS MASTER, GALACTUS, TO SAVE OUR ENTIRE PLANET.
DO NOT FORGET THOR, ONE OF OUR GREATEST HEROES, WHOSE GODLY STATUS MAKES HIM BEYOND HUMAN OR ALIEN. WOULD YOU CONFINE OR CONTROL HIM?
BUT MOST OF ALL, DO NOT FORGET THE INHUMANS-- WHO ARE THE INNOCENT CATALYSTS FOR THIS HYSTERIA-- HAVE MERELY RETURNED FROM SPACE.
EARTH IS THEIR HOME. ALL THEY WANT IS WHAT EVERYONE WANTS-- A PLACE TO BE SAFE, A PLACE OF THEIR OWN...
...SO THEY DON'T HAVE TO HIDE IN THE SHADOWS ANY LONGER.
WHAT DOES THIS AUGUST BODY SAY TO THAT?

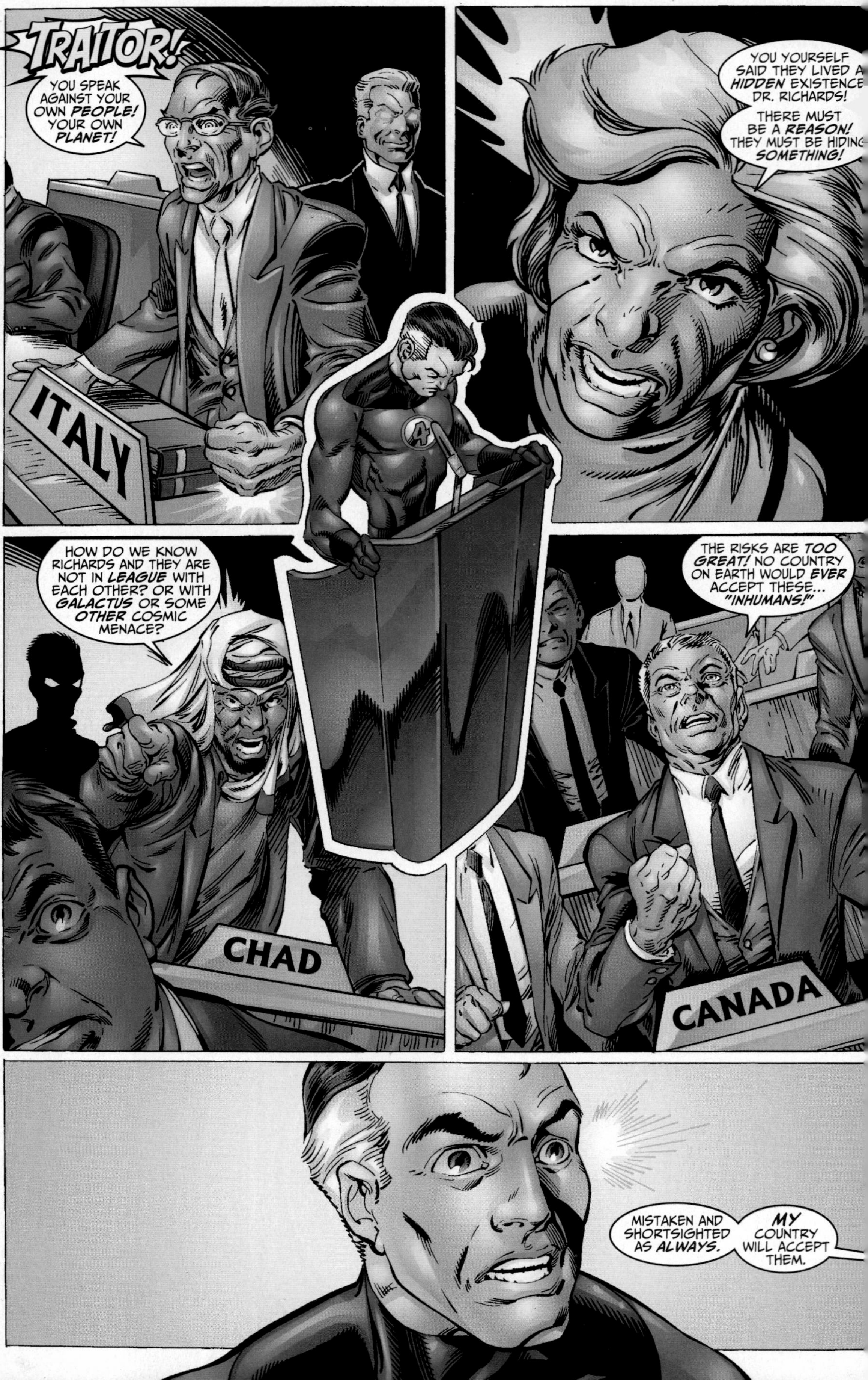
TRAITOR!
YOU SPEAK AGAINST YOUR OWN PEOPLE! YOUR OWN PLANET!
ITALY
YOU YOURSELF SAID THEY LIVED A HIDDEN EXISTENCE DR. RICHARDS!
THERE MUST BE A REASON! THEY MUST BE HIDING SOMETHING!
HOW DO WE KNOW RICHARDS AND THEY ARE NOT IN LEAGUE WITH EACH OTHER? OR WITH GALACTUS OR SOME OTHER COSMIC MENACE?
CHAD
THE RISKS ARE TOO GREAT! NO COUNTRY ON EARTH WOULD EVER ACCEPT THESE... "INHUMANS!"
CANADA
MISTAKEN AND SHORTSIGHTED AS ALWAYS.
MY COUNTRY WILL ACCEPT THEM.

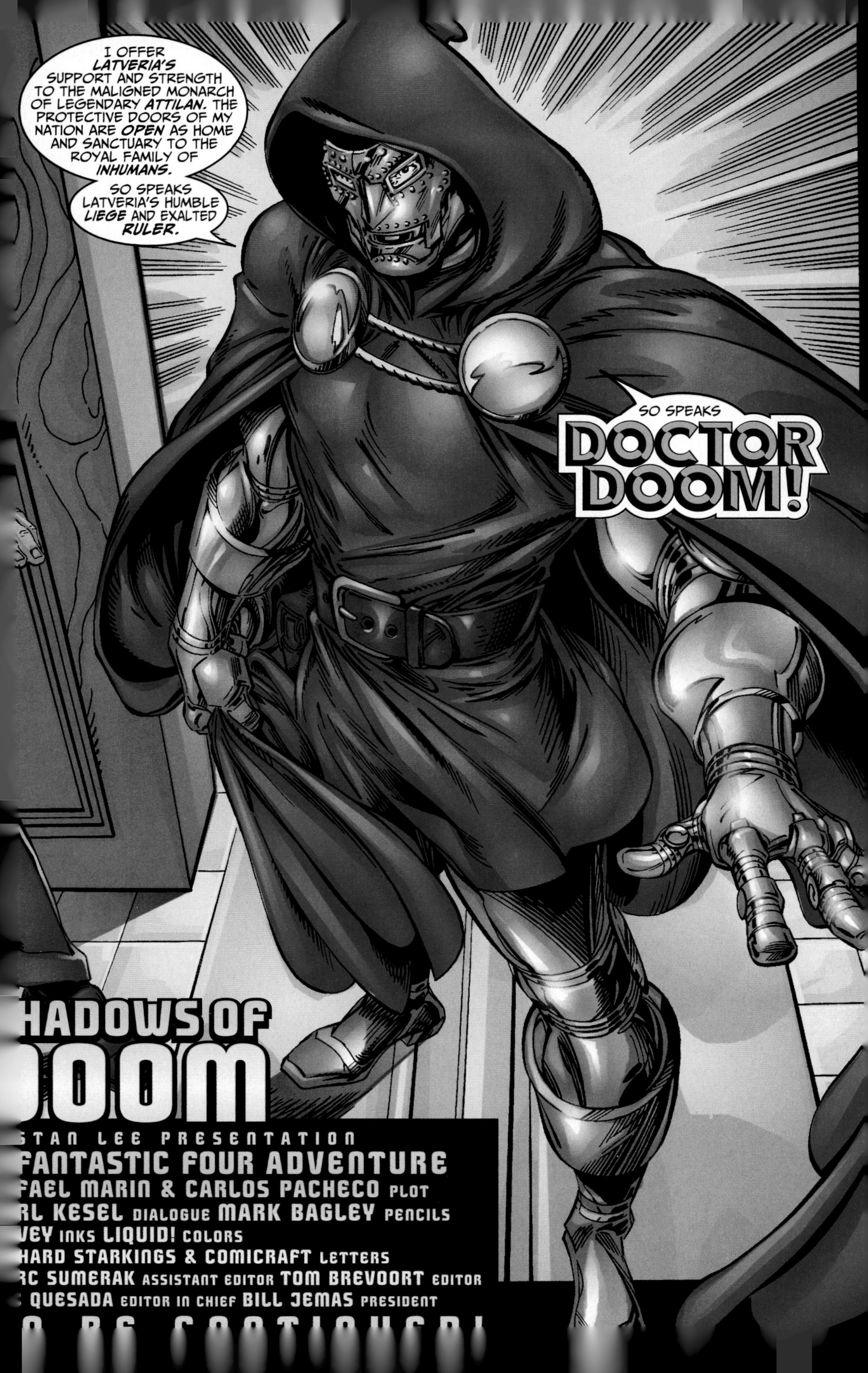

I OFFER LATVERIA'S SUPPORT AND STRENGTH TO THE MALIGNED MONARCH OF LEGENDARY ATTILAN. THE PROTECTIVE DOORS OF MY NATION ARE OPEN AS HOME AND SANCTUARY TO THE ROYAL FAMILY OF INHUMANS.
SO SPEAKS LATVERIA'S HUMBLE LIEGE AND EXALTED RULER.
SO SPEAKS DOCTOR DOOM!
HADOWS OF
OOM
STAN LEE PRESENTATION
FANTASTIC FOUR ADVENTURE
FAEL MARIN & CARLOS PACHECO PLOT
RL KESEL DIALOGUE MARK BAGLEY PENCILS
VEY INKS LIQUID! COLORS
HARD STARKINGS & COMICRAFT LETTERS
RC SUMERAK ASSISTANT EDITOR TOM BREVOORT EDITOR
QUESADA EDITOR IN CHIEF BILL JEMAS PRESIDENT

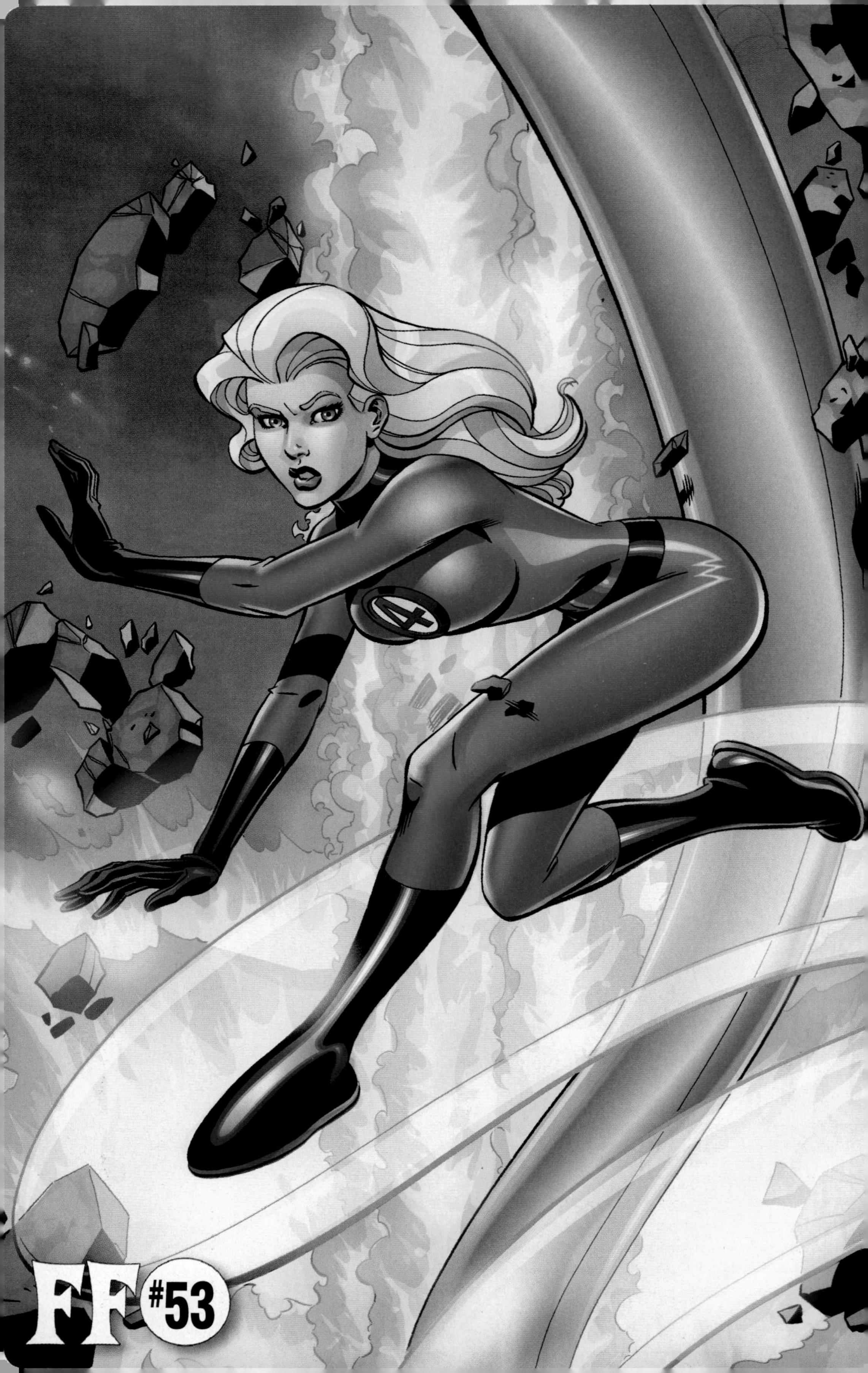
FF #53
4

STAN LEE PRESENTS: THE FABULOUS FANTASTIC FOUR FACING...

THE FIRE THIS TIME!

THE HUMAN TORCH -- THE ORIGINAL, ANDROID HUMAN TORCH -- REDUCES THE CORPSE OF GERMANY'S FÜHRER TO ASHES, ENDING THE THIRD REICH'S LONG NIGHT OF BARBARISM WITH ONE HOT, BLINDING BURST.

BERLIN, 1945.

THE TORCH'S PARTNER *TORO* IS THE ONLY WITNESS TO THE EVENT.

OR SO IT'S ALWAYS BEEN BELIEVED.

CARLOS PACHECO & RAFAEL MARIN plot • KARL KESEL dialogue
MARK BAGLEY pencils • AL VEY inks • LIQUID! GRAPHICS colors
RS & COMICRAFT'S ALBERT DESCHESNE letters • MARC SUMERAK assistant editor
TOM BREVOORT editor • JOE QUESADA editor in chief • BILL JEMAS president

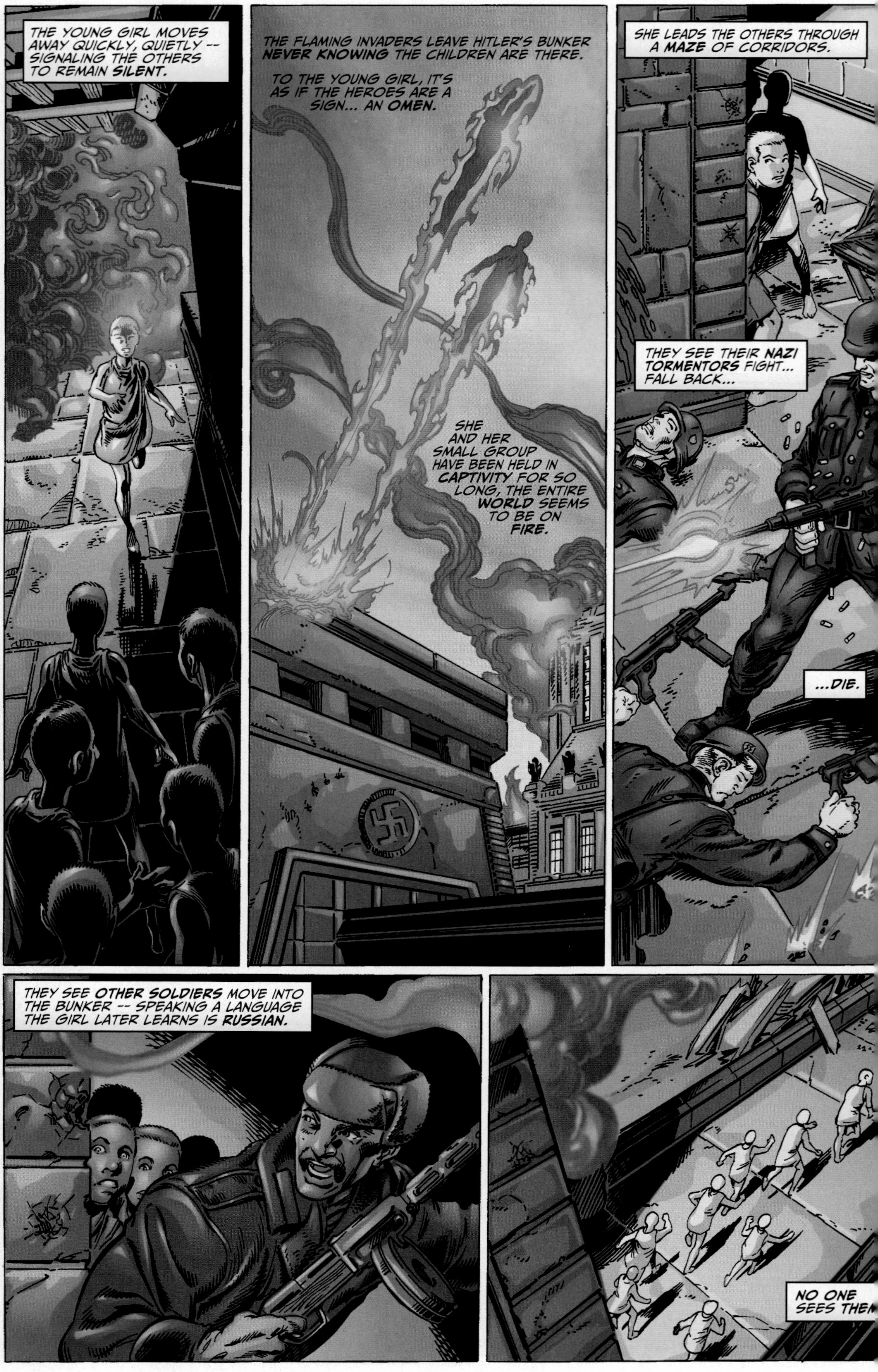
THE YOUNG GIRL MOVES AWAY QUICKLY, QUIETLY -- SIGNALING THE OTHERS TO REMAIN SILENT.
THE FLAMING INVADERS LEAVE HITLER'S BUNKER NEVER KNOWING THE CHILDREN ARE THERE.
TO THE YOUNG GIRL, IT'S AS IF THE HEROES ARE A SIGN... AN OMEN.
SHE AND HER SMALL GROUP HAVE BEEN HELD IN CAPTIVITY FOR SO LONG, THE ENTIRE WORLD SEEMS TO BE ON FIRE.
SHE LEADS THE OTHERS THROUGH A MAZE OF CORRIDORS.
THEY SEE THEIR NAZI TORMENTORS FIGHT... FALL BACK...
...DIE.
THEY SEE OTHER SOLDIERS MOVE INTO THE BUNKER -- SPEAKING A LANGUAGE THE GIRL LATER LEARNS IS RUSSIAN.
NO ONE SEES THEM

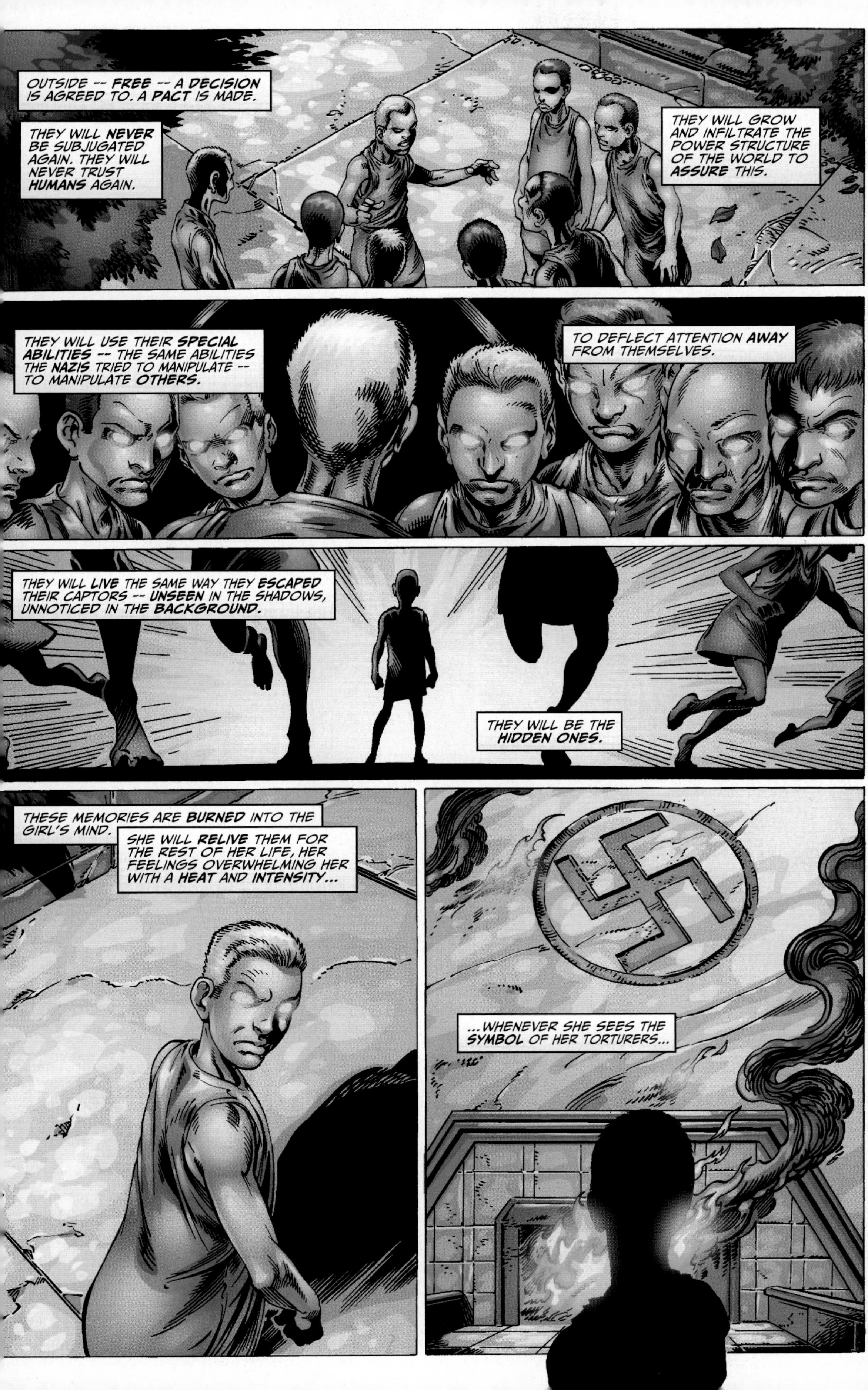
OUTSIDE -- FREE -- A DECISION IS AGREED TO. A PACT IS MADE.
THEY WILL NEVER BE SUBJUGATED AGAIN. THEY WILL NEVER TRUST HUMANS AGAIN.
THEY WILL GROW AND INFILTRATE THE POWER STRUCTURE OF THE WORLD TO ASSURE THIS.
THEY WILL USE THEIR SPECIAL ABILITIES -- THE SAME ABILITIES THE NAZIS TRIED TO MANIPULATE -- TO MANIPULATE OTHERS.
TO DEFLECT ATTENTION AWAY FROM THEMSELVES.
THEY WILL LIVE THE SAME WAY THEY ESCAPED THEIR CAPTORS -- UNSEEN IN THE SHADOWS, UNNOTICED IN THE BACKGROUND.
THEY WILL BE THE HIDDEN ONES.
THESE MEMORIES ARE BURNED INTO THE GIRL'S MIND.
SHE WILL RELIVE THEM FOR THE REST OF HER LIFE, HER FEELINGS OVERWHELMING HER WITH A HEAT AND INTENSITY...
...WHENEVER SHE SEES THE SYMBOL OF HER TORTURERS...

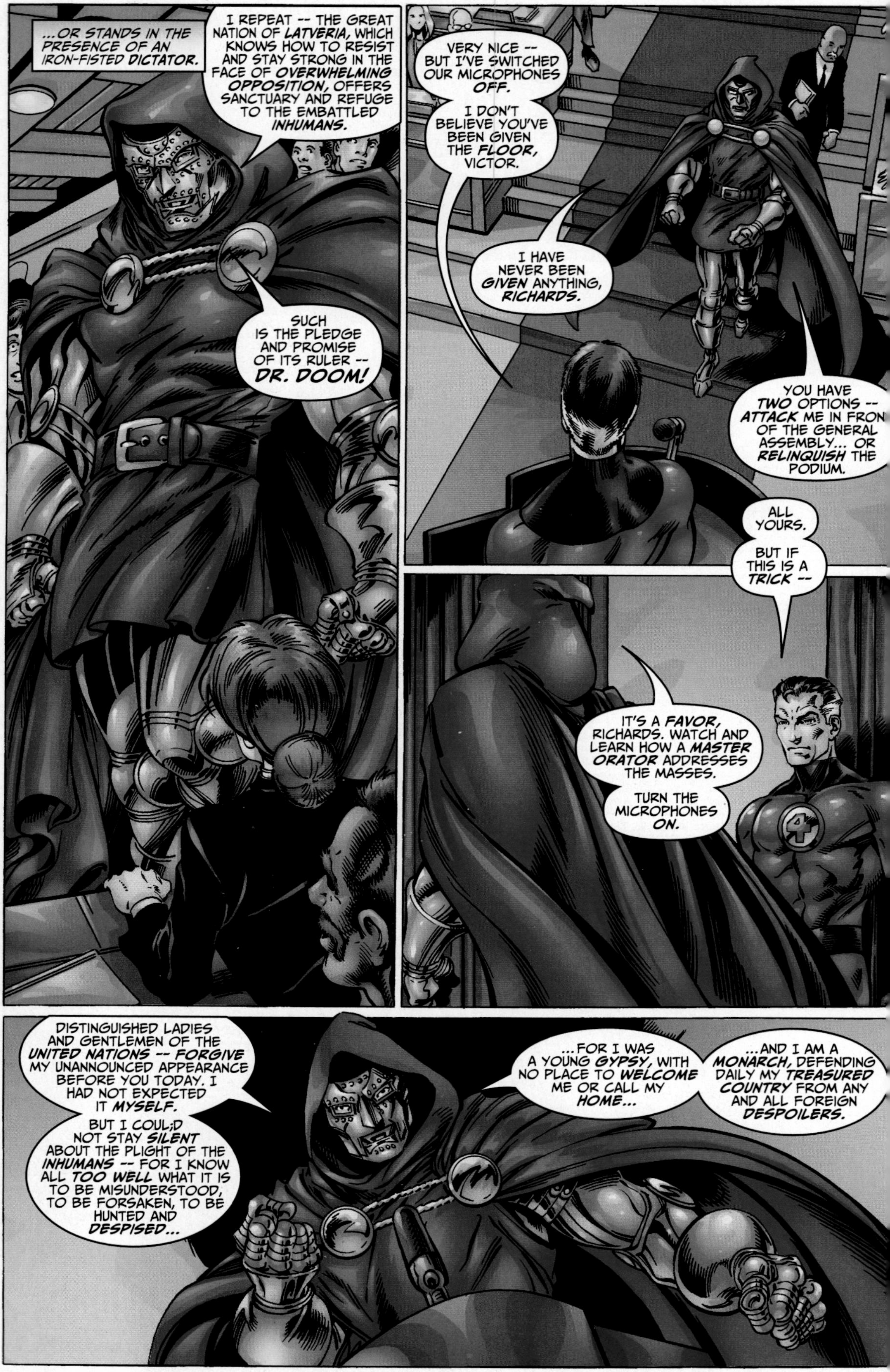

...OR STANDS IN THE PRESENCE OF AN IRON-FISTED DICTATOR.
I REPEAT -- THE GREAT NATION OF LATVERIA, WHICH KNOWS HOW TO RESIST AND STAY STRONG IN THE FACE OF OVERWHELMING OPPOSITION, OFFERS SANCTUARY AND REFUGE TO THE EMBATTLED INHUMANS.
SUCH IS THE PLEDGE AND PROMISE OF ITS RULER -- DR. DOOM!
VERY NICE -- BUT I'VE SWITCHED OUR MICROPHONES OFF.
I DON'T BELIEVE YOU'VE BEEN GIVEN THE FLOOR, VICTOR.
I HAVE NEVER BEEN GIVEN ANYTHING, RICHARDS.
YOU HAVE TWO OPTIONS -- ATTACK ME IN FRON OF THE GENERAL ASSEMBLY... OR RELINQUISH THE PODIUM.
ALL YOURS.
BUT IF THIS IS A TRICK --
IT'S A FAVOR, RICHARDS. WATCH AND LEARN HOW A MASTER ORATOR ADDRESSES THE MASSES.
TURN THE MICROPHONES ON.
DISTINGUISHED LADIES AND GENTLEMEN OF THE UNITED NATIONS -- FORGIVE MY UNANNOUNCED APPEARANCE BEFORE YOU TODAY. I HAD NOT EXPECTED IT MYSELF.
BUT I COUL;D NOT STAY SILENT ABOUT THE PLIGHT OF THE INHUMANS -- FOR I KNOW ALL TOO WELL WHAT IT IS TO BE MISUNDERSTOOD, TO BE FORSAKEN, TO BE HUNTED AND DESPISED...
...FOR I WAS A YOUNG GYPSY, WITH NO PLACE TO WELCOME ME OR CALL MY HOME...
...AND I AM A MONARCH, DEFENDING DAILY MY TREASURED COUNTRY FROM ANY AND ALL FOREIGN DESPOILERS.

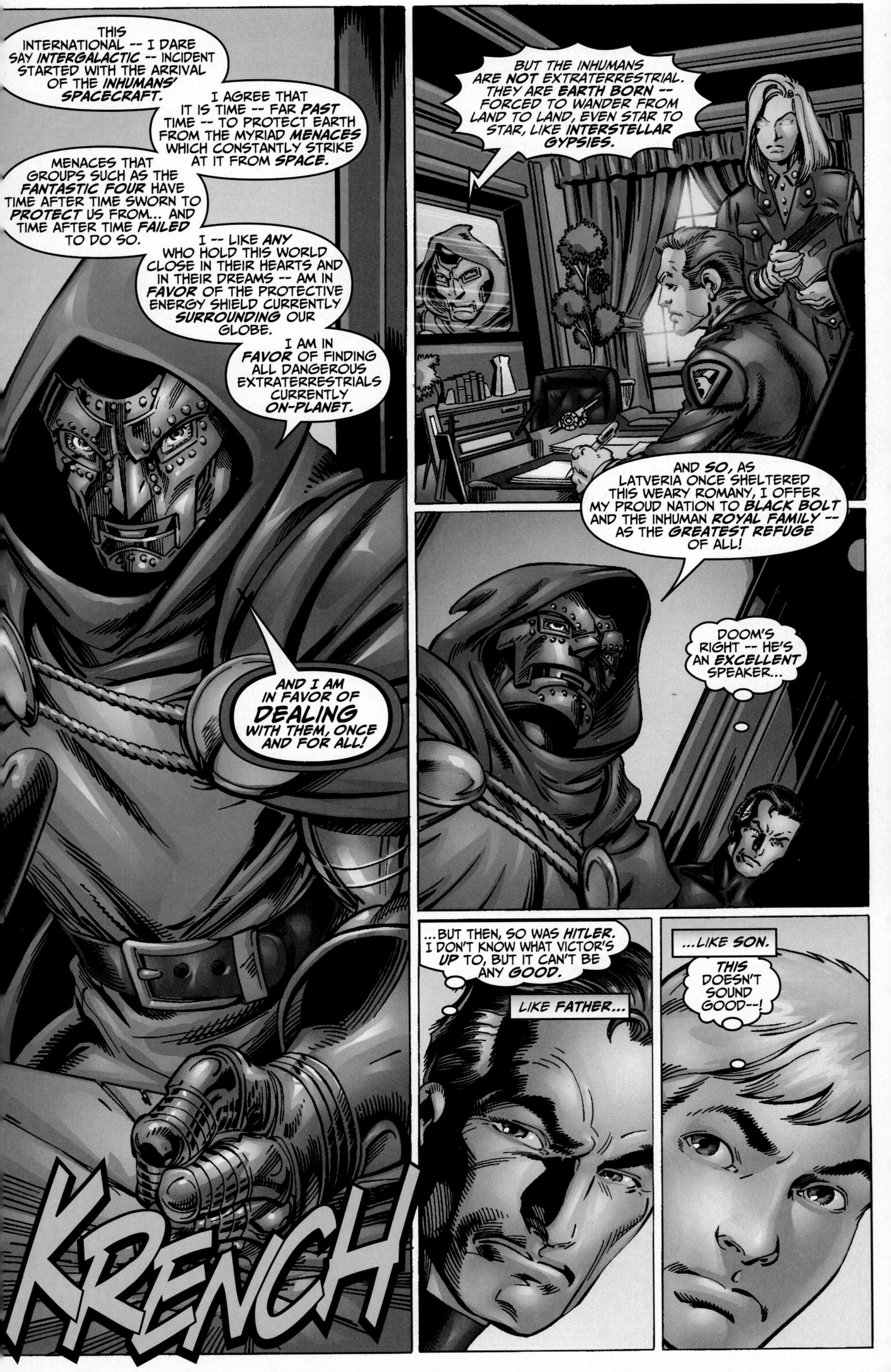
THIS INTERNATIONAL -- I DARE SAY INTERGALACTIC -- INCIDENT STARTED WITH THE ARRIVAL OF THE INHUMANS' SPACECRAFT.
I AGREE THAT IT IS TIME -- FAR PAST TIME -- TO PROTECT EARTH FROM THE MYRIAD MENACES WHICH CONSTANTLY STRIKE AT IT FROM SPACE.
MENACES THAT GROUPS SUCH AS THE FANTASTIC FOUR HAVE TIME AFTER TIME SWORN TO PROTECT US FROM... AND TIME AFTER TIME FAILED TO DO SO.
I -- LIKE ANY WHO HOLD THIS WORLD CLOSE IN THEIR HEARTS AND IN THEIR DREAMS -- AM IN FAVOR OF THE PROTECTIVE ENERGY SHIELD CURRENTLY SURROUNDING OUR GLOBE.
I AM IN FAVOR OF FINDING ALL DANGEROUS EXTRATERRESTRIALS CURRENTLY ON-PLANET.
AND I AM IN FAVOR OF DEALING WITH THEM, ONCE AND FOR ALL!
KRENCH
BUT THE INHUMANS ARE NOT EXTRATERRESTRIAL. THEY ARE EARTH BORN -- FORCED TO WANDER FROM LAND TO LAND, EVEN STAR TO STAR, LIKE INTERSTELLAR GYPSIES.
AND SO, AS LATVERIA ONCE SHELTERED THIS WEARY ROMANY, I OFFER MY PROUD NATION TO BLACK BOLT AND THE INHUMAN ROYAL FAMILY -- AS THE GREATEST REFUGE OF ALL!
DOOM'S RIGHT -- HE'S AN EXCELLENT SPEAKER...
...BUT THEN, SO WAS HITLER. I DON'T KNOW WHAT VICTOR'S UP TO, BUT IT CAN'T BE ANY GOOD.
LIKE FATHER...
...LIKE SON.
THIS DOESN'T SOUND GOOD--!

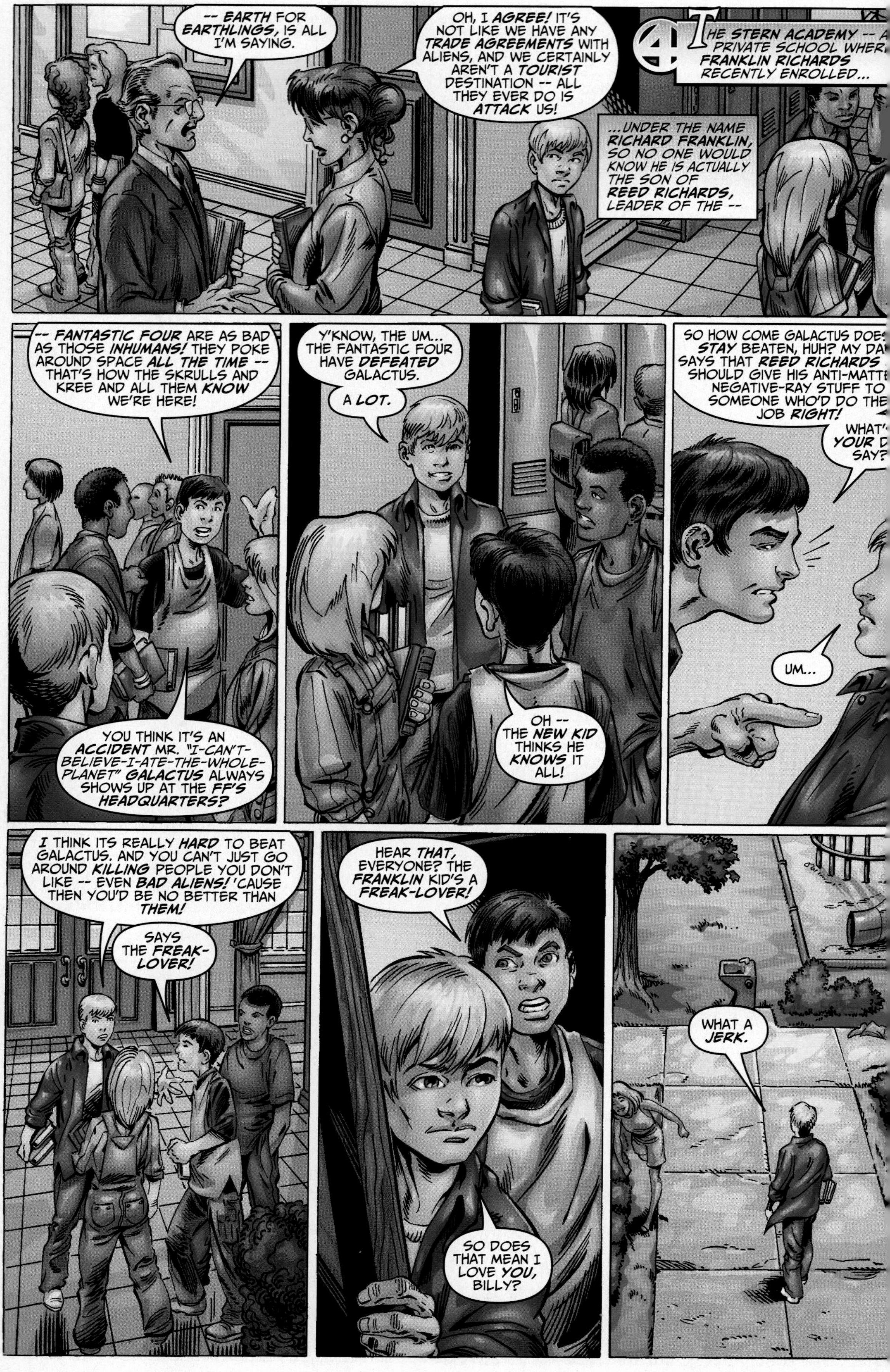
-- EARTH FOR EARTHLINGS, IS ALL I'M SAYING.
OH, I AGREE! IT'S NOT LIKE WE HAVE ANY TRADE AGREEMENTS WITH ALIENS, AND WE CERTAINLY AREN'T A TOURIST DESTINATION -- ALL THEY EVER DO IS ATTACK US!
THE STERN ACADEMY -- A PRIVATE SCHOOL WHERE FRANKLIN RICHARDS RECENTLY ENROLLED...
...UNDER THE NAME RICHARD FRANKLIN, SO NO ONE WOULD KNOW HE IS ACTUALLY THE SON OF REED RICHARDS, LEADER OF THE --
-- FANTASTIC FOUR ARE AS BAD AS THOSE INHUMANS! THEY POKE AROUND SPACE ALL THE TIME -- THAT'S HOW THE SKRULLS AND KREE AND ALL THEM KNOW WE'RE HERE!
YOU THINK IT'S AN ACCIDENT MR. "I-CAN'T-BELIEVE-I-ATE-THE-WHOLE-PLANET" GALACTUS ALWAYS SHOWS UP AT THE FF'S HEADQUARTERS?
Y'KNOW, THE UM... THE FANTASTIC FOUR HAVE DEFEATED GALACTUS.
A LOT.
OH -- THE NEW KID THINKS HE KNOWS IT ALL!
SO HOW COME GALACTUS DOES STAY BEATEN, HUH? MY DA SAYS THAT REED RICHARDS SHOULD GIVE HIS ANTI-MATTE NEGATIVE-RAY STUFF TO SOMEONE WHO'D DO THE JOB RIGHT!
WHAT' YOUR D SAY?
UM...
I THINK ITS REALLY HARD TO BEAT GALACTUS. AND YOU CAN'T JUST GO AROUND KILLING PEOPLE YOU DON'T LIKE -- EVEN BAD ALIENS! 'CAUSE THEN YOU'D BE NO BETTER THAN THEM!
SAYS THE FREAK-LOVER!
HEAR THAT, EVERYONE? THE FRANKLIN KID'S A FREAK-LOVER!
SO DOES THAT MEAN I LOVE YOU, BILLY?
WHAT A JERK.

HEY! YOU CAN'T SAY SOMETHING LIKE THAT AND *WALK AWAY!*

NO ONE *DISSES* BILLY MCGURK!

YOU CALLED ME A NAME *FIRST.* YOU *STARTED* IT.

AND I'M GONNA *END* IT RIGHT --

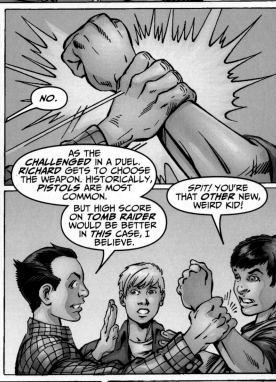

NO.

AS THE *CHALLENGED* IN A DUEL. *RICHARD* GETS TO CHOOSE THE WEAPON. HISTORICALLY, *PISTOLS* ARE MOST COMMON.

BUT HIGH SCORE ON *TOMB RAIDER* WOULD BE BETTER IN *THIS* CASE, I BELIEVE.

SPIT! YOU'RE THAT *OTHER* NEW, WEIRD KID!

YOU TWO *DESERVE* EACH OTHER!

HAVE *FUN,* GIRLS!

I HOPE WILLIAM LEARNS THE *DIFFERENCE* BETWEEN BOYS AND GIRLS BEFORE HE GETS MUCH *OLDER.*

HELLO. MY NAME IS *ROBERT HERBERT MARKS III.* MY FRIENDS CALL ME *ROBBIE.*

YOU CAN CALL ME ROBBIE, RICHARD.

AND YOU CAN CALL ME *FRANKLIN.*

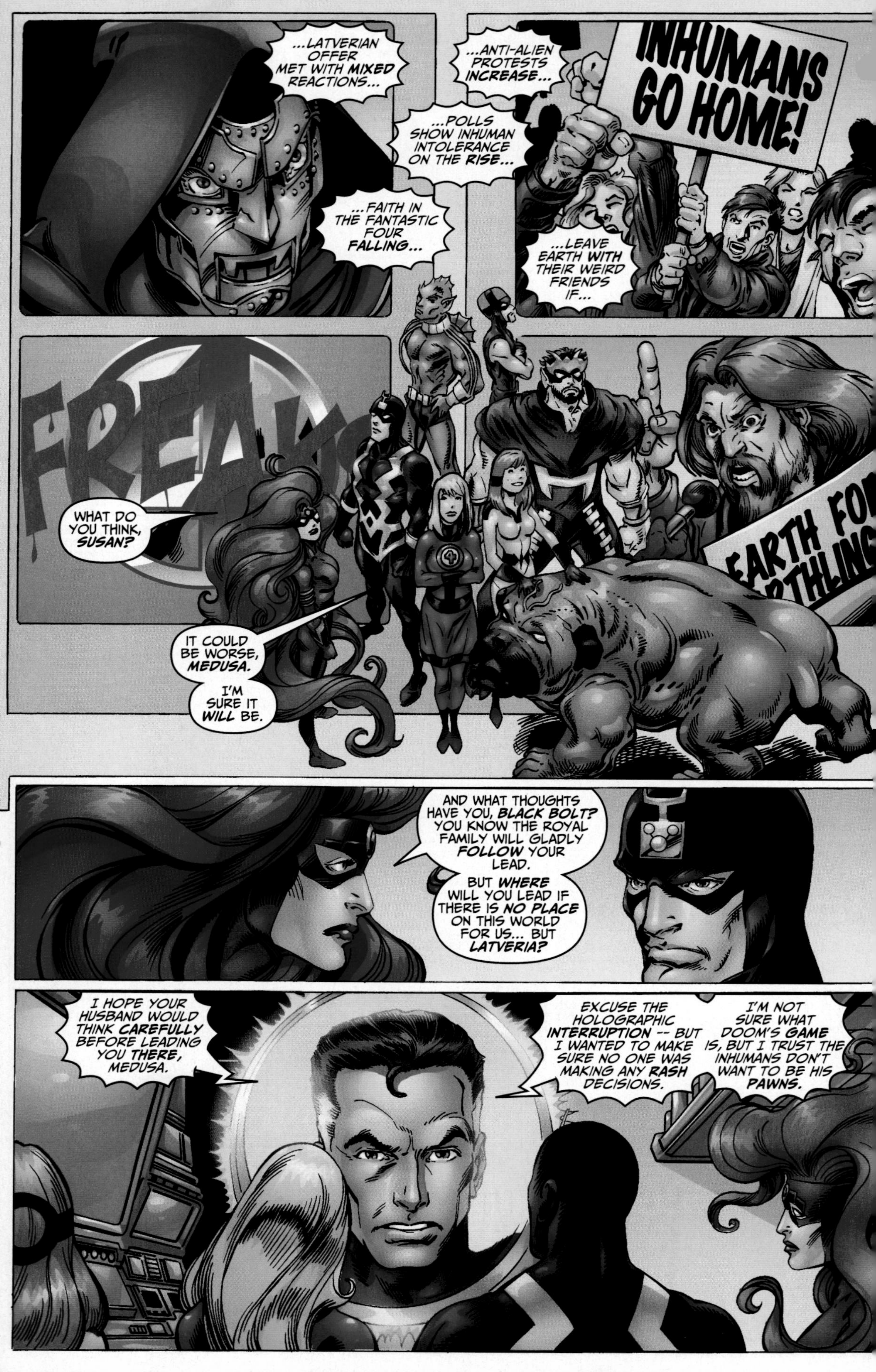

...LATVERIAN OFFER MET WITH MIXED REACTIONS...
...ANTI-ALIEN PROTESTS INCREASE...
INHUMANS GO HOME!
...POLLS SHOW INHUMAN INTOLERANCE ON THE RISE...
...FAITH IN THE FANTASTIC FOUR FALLING...
...LEAVE EARTH WITH THEIR WEIRD FRIENDS IF...
WHAT DO YOU THINK, SUSAN?
IT COULD BE WORSE, MEDUSA.
I'M SURE IT WILL BE.
AND WHAT THOUGHTS HAVE YOU, BLACK BOLT? YOU KNOW THE ROYAL FAMILY WILL GLADLY FOLLOW YOUR LEAD.
BUT WHERE WILL YOU LEAD IF THERE IS NO PLACE ON THIS WORLD FOR US... BUT LATVERIA?
I HOPE YOUR HUSBAND WOULD THINK CAREFULLY BEFORE LEADING YOU THERE, MEDUSA.
EXCUSE THE HOLOGRAPHIC INTERRUPTION -- BUT I WANTED TO MAKE SURE NO ONE WAS MAKING ANY RASH DECISIONS.
I'M NOT SURE WHAT DOOM'S GAME IS, BUT I TRUST THE INHUMANS DON'T WANT TO BE HIS PAWNS.

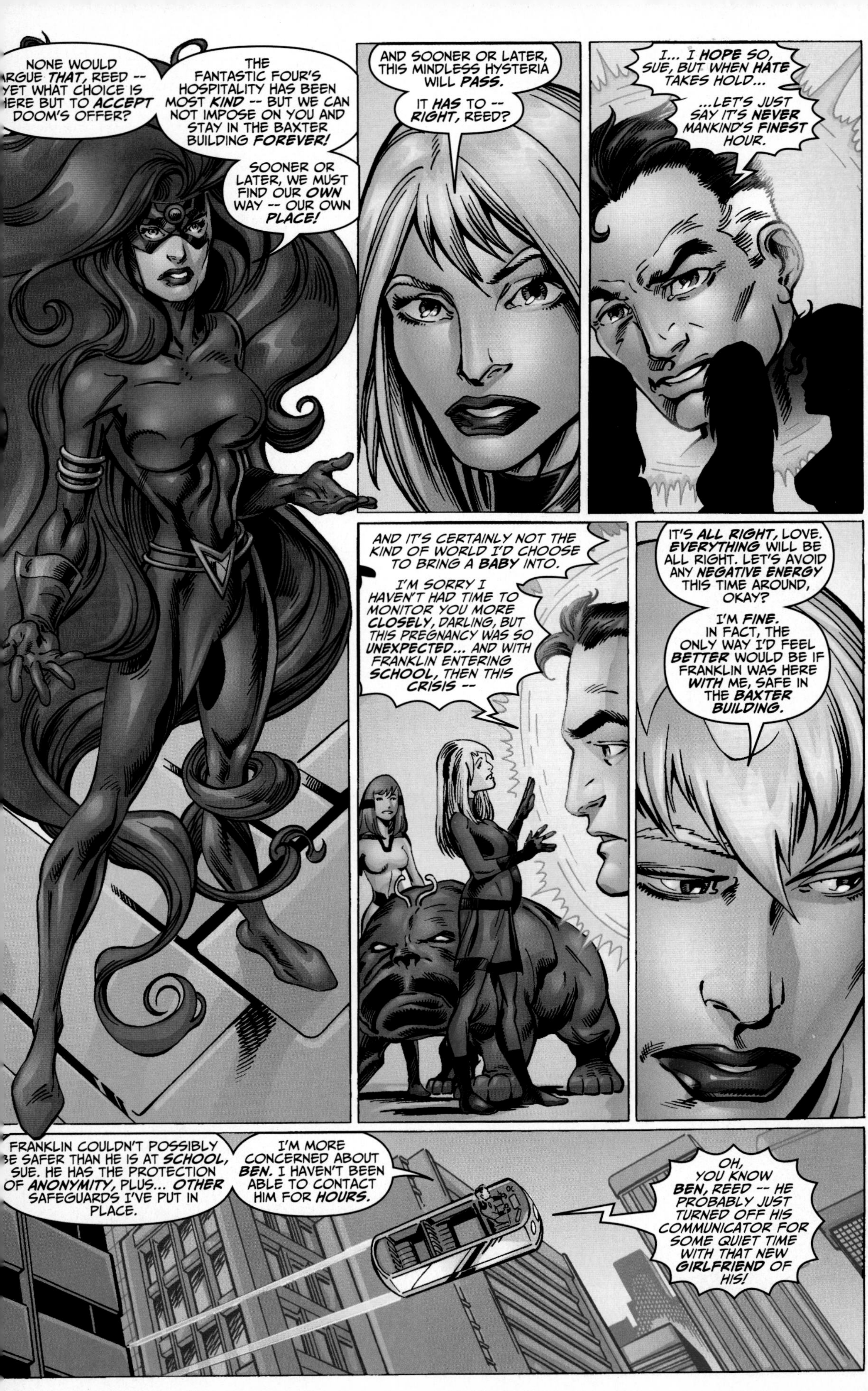

NONE WOULD ARGUE THAT, REED -- YET WHAT CHOICE IS THERE BUT TO ACCEPT DOOM'S OFFER?
THE FANTASTIC FOUR'S HOSPITALITY HAS BEEN MOST KIND -- BUT WE CAN NOT IMPOSE ON YOU AND STAY IN THE BAXTER BUILDING FOREVER!
SOONER OR LATER, WE MUST FIND OUR OWN WAY -- OUR OWN PLACE!
AND SOONER OR LATER, THIS MINDLESS HYSTERIA WILL PASS.
IT HAS TO -- RIGHT, REED?
I... I HOPE SO, SUE, BUT WHEN HATE TAKES HOLD...
...LET'S JUST SAY IT'S NEVER MANKIND'S FINEST HOUR.
AND IT'S CERTAINLY NOT THE KIND OF WORLD I'D CHOOSE TO BRING A BABY INTO.
I'M SORRY I HAVEN'T HAD TIME TO MONITOR YOU MORE CLOSELY, DARLING, BUT THIS PREGNANCY WAS SO UNEXPECTED... AND WITH FRANKLIN ENTERING SCHOOL, THEN THIS CRISIS --
IT'S ALL RIGHT, LOVE. EVERYTHING WILL BE ALL RIGHT. LET'S AVOID ANY NEGATIVE ENERGY THIS TIME AROUND, OKAY?
I'M FINE. IN FACT, THE ONLY WAY I'D FEEL BETTER WOULD BE IF FRANKLIN WAS HERE WITH ME, SAFE IN THE BAXTER BUILDING.
FRANKLIN COULDN'T POSSIBLY BE SAFER THAN HE IS AT SCHOOL, SUE. HE HAS THE PROTECTION OF ANONYMITY, PLUS... OTHER SAFEGUARDS I'VE PUT IN PLACE.
I'M MORE CONCERNED ABOUT BEN. I HAVEN'T BEEN ABLE TO CONTACT HIM FOR HOURS.
OH, YOU KNOW BEN, REED -- HE PROBABLY JUST TURNED OFF HIS COMMUNICATOR FOR SOME QUIET TIME WITH THAT NEW GIRLFRIEND OF HIS!

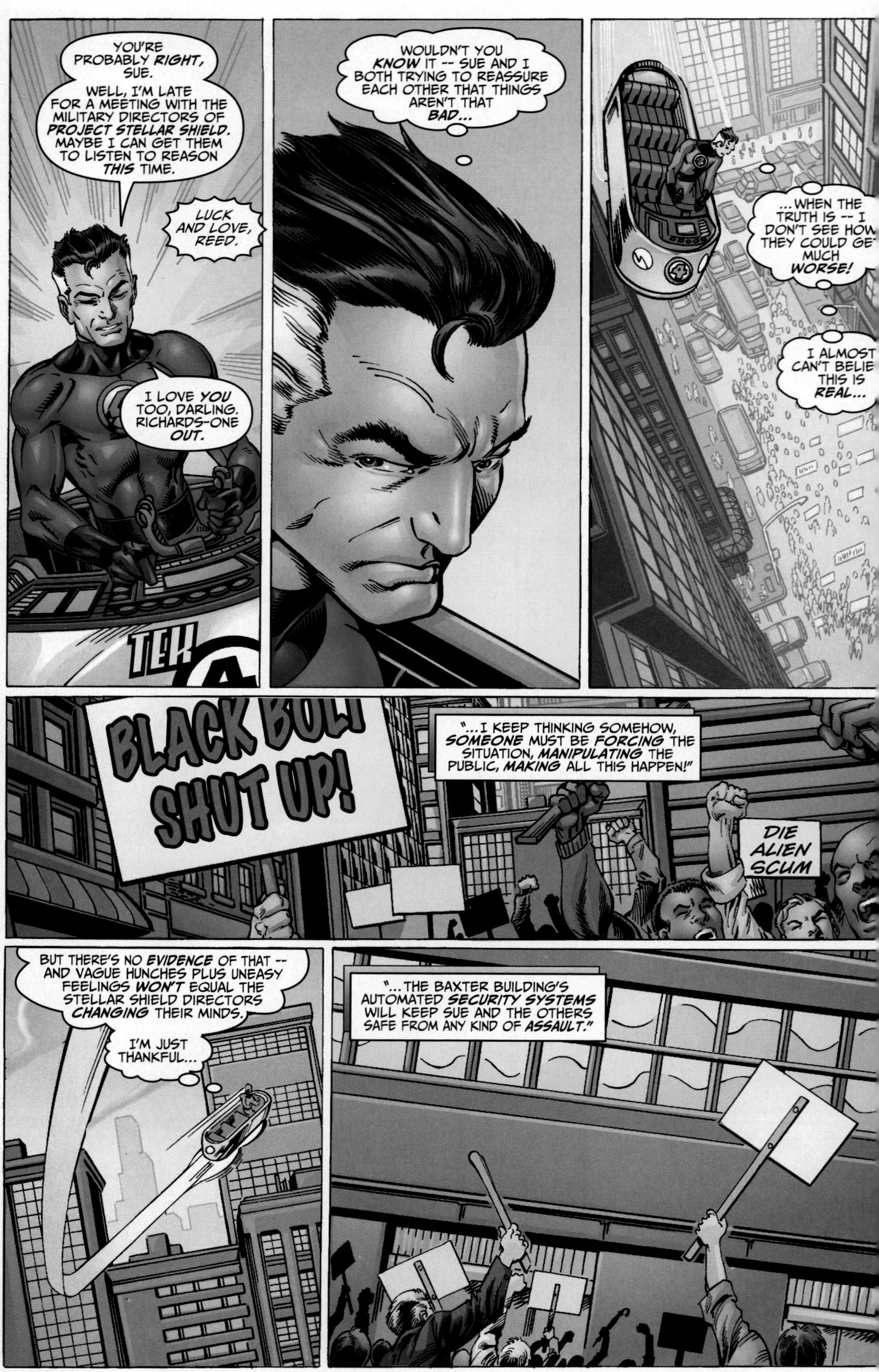
YOU'RE PROBABLY RIGHT, SUE.
WELL, I'M LATE FOR A MEETING WITH THE MILITARY DIRECTORS OF PROJECT STELLAR SHIELD. MAYBE I CAN GET THEM TO LISTEN TO REASON THIS TIME.
LUCK AND LOVE, REED.
I LOVE YOU TOO, DARLING. RICHARDS-ONE OUT.
TEK
WOULDN'T YOU KNOW IT -- SUE AND I BOTH TRYING TO REASSURE EACH OTHER THAT THINGS AREN'T THAT BAD...
...WHEN THE TRUTH IS -- I DON'T SEE HOW THEY COULD GET MUCH WORSE!
I ALMOST CAN'T BELIE THIS IS REAL...
BLACK BOLT SHUT UP!
"...I KEEP THINKING SOMEHOW, SOMEONE MUST BE FORCING THE SITUATION, MANIPULATING THE PUBLIC, MAKING ALL THIS HAPPEN!"
DIE ALIEN SCUM
BUT THERE'S NO EVIDENCE OF THAT -- AND VAGUE HUNCHES PLUS UNEASY FEELINGS WON'T EQUAL THE STELLAR SHIELD DIRECTORS CHANGING THEIR MINDS.
I'M JUST THANKFUL...
"...THE BAXTER BUILDING'S AUTOMATED SECURITY SYSTEMS WILL KEEP SUE AND THE OTHERS SAFE FROM ANY KIND OF ASSAULT."

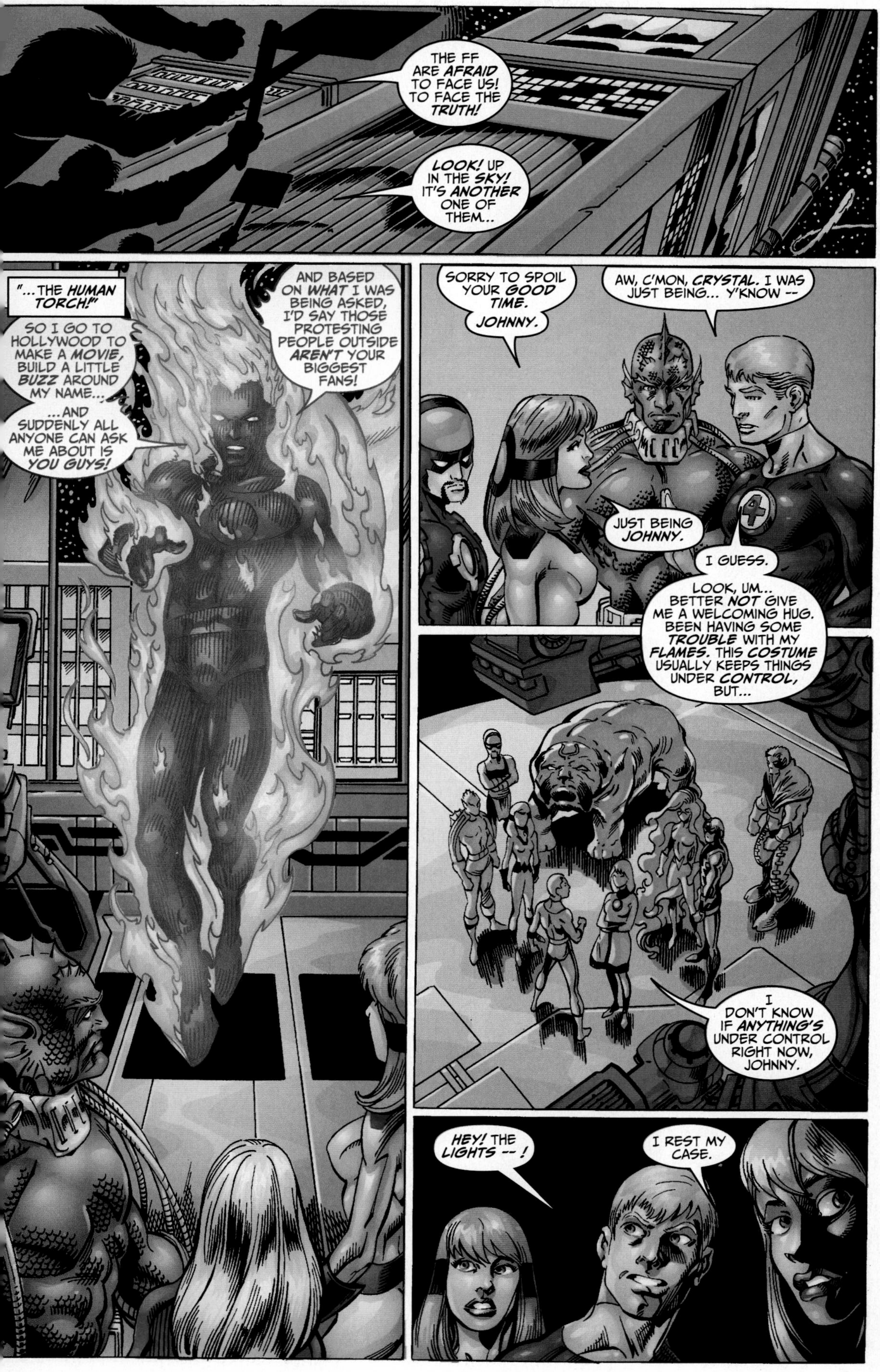
THE FF ARE AFRAID TO FACE US! TO FACE THE TRUTH!
LOOK! UP IN THE SKY! IT'S ANOTHER ONE OF THEM...
"...THE HUMAN TORCH!"
SO I GO TO HOLLYWOOD TO MAKE A MOVIE, BUILD A LITTLE BUZZ AROUND MY NAME...
...AND SUDDENLY ALL ANYONE CAN ASK ME ABOUT IS YOU GUYS!
AND BASED ON WHAT I WAS BEING ASKED, I'D SAY THOSE PROTESTING PEOPLE OUTSIDE AREN'T YOUR BIGGEST FANS!
SORRY TO SPOIL YOUR GOOD TIME. JOHNNY.
AW, C'MON, CRYSTAL. I WAS JUST BEING... Y'KNOW --
JUST BEING JOHNNY.
I GUESS.
LOOK, UM... BETTER NOT GIVE ME A WELCOMING HUG. BEEN HAVING SOME TROUBLE WITH MY FLAMES. THIS COSTUME USUALLY KEEPS THINGS UNDER CONTROL, BUT...
I DON'T KNOW IF ANYTHING'S UNDER CONTROL RIGHT NOW, JOHNNY.
HEY! THE LIGHTS -- !
I REST MY CASE.

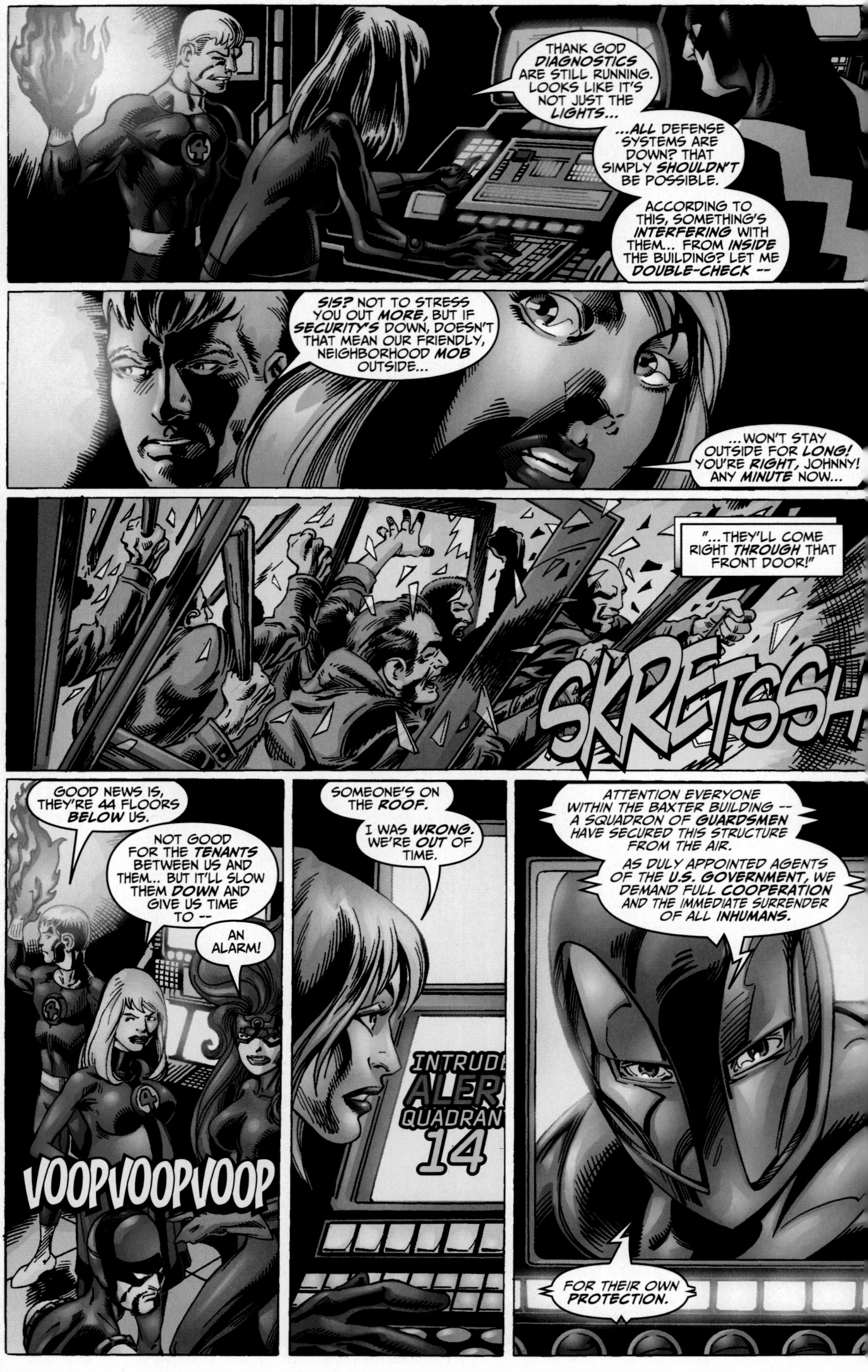
THANK GOD DIAGNOSTICS ARE STILL RUNNING. LOOKS LIKE IT'S NOT JUST THE LIGHTS...
...ALL DEFENSE SYSTEMS ARE DOWN? THAT SIMPLY SHOULDN'T BE POSSIBLE.
ACCORDING TO THIS, SOMETHING'S INTERFERING WITH THEM... FROM INSIDE THE BUILDING? LET ME DOUBLE-CHECK --
SIS? NOT TO STRESS YOU OUT MORE, BUT IF SECURITY'S DOWN, DOESN'T THAT MEAN OUR FRIENDLY, NEIGHBORHOOD MOB OUTSIDE...
...WON'T STAY OUTSIDE FOR LONG! YOU'RE RIGHT, JOHNNY! ANY MINUTE NOW...
"...THEY'LL COME RIGHT THROUGH THAT FRONT DOOR!"
SKRETSSH
GOOD NEWS IS, THEY'RE 44 FLOORS BELOW US.
NOT GOOD FOR THE TENANTS BETWEEN US AND THEM... BUT IT'LL SLOW THEM DOWN AND GIVE US TIME TO --
AN ALARM!
VOOPVOOPVOOP
SOMEONE'S ON THE ROOF.
I WAS WRONG. WE'RE OUT OF TIME.
INTRUDE ALER QUADRAN 14
ATTENTION EVERYONE WITHIN THE BAXTER BUILDING -- A SQUADRON OF GUARDSMEN HAVE SECURED THIS STRUCTURE FROM THE AIR.
AS DULY APPOINTED AGENTS OF THE U.S. GOVERNMENT, WE DEMAND FULL COOPERATION AND THE IMMEDIATE SURRENDER OF ALL INHUMANS.
FOR THEIR OWN PROTECTION.

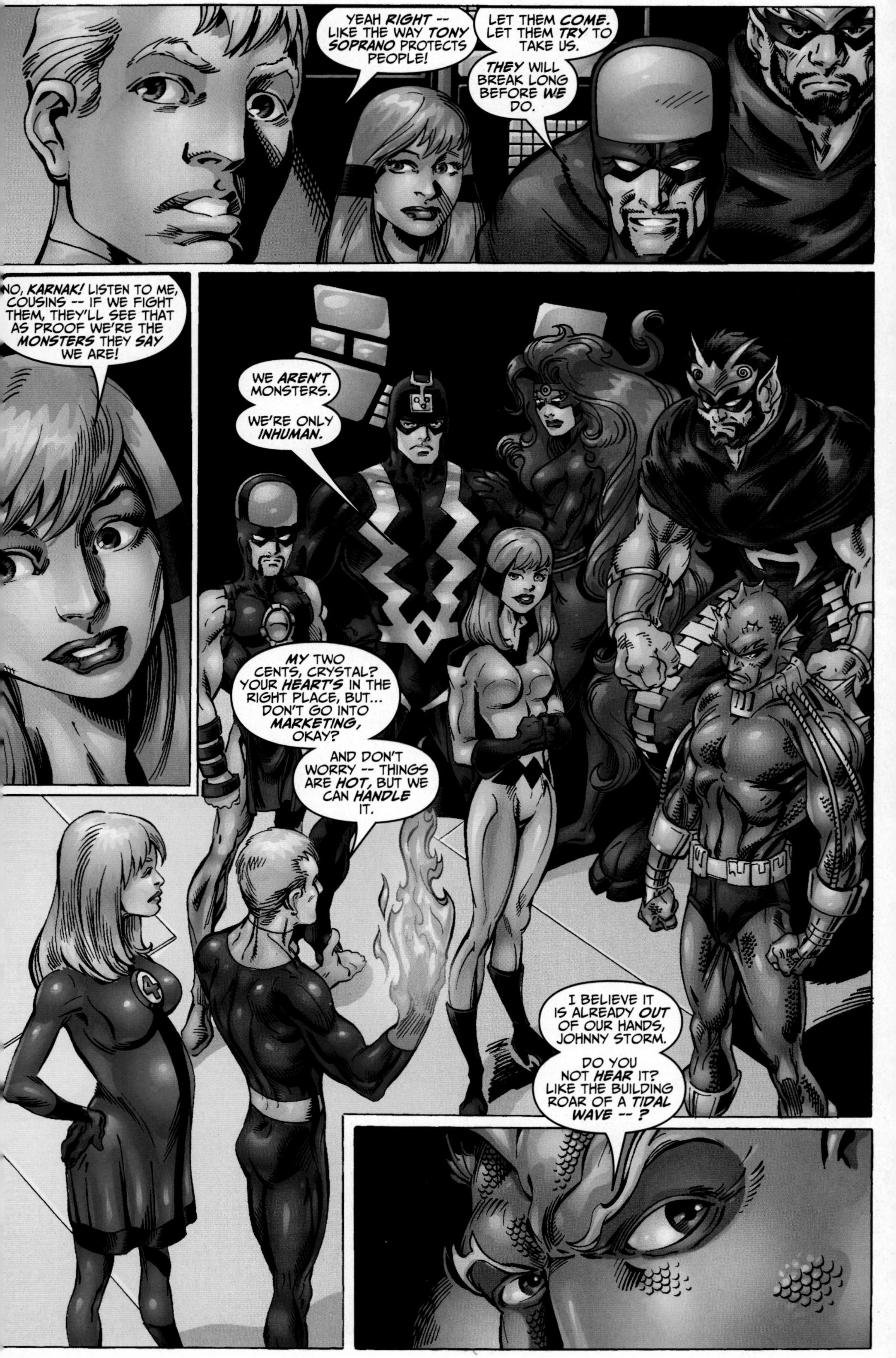
YEAH RIGHT -- LIKE THE WAY TONY SOPRANO PROTECTS PEOPLE!
LET THEM COME. LET THEM TRY TO TAKE US.
THEY WILL BREAK LONG BEFORE WE DO.
NO, KARNAK! LISTEN TO ME, COUSINS -- IF WE FIGHT THEM, THEY'LL SEE THAT AS PROOF WE'RE THE MONSTERS THEY SAY WE ARE!
WE AREN'T MONSTERS.
WE'RE ONLY INHUMAN.
MY TWO CENTS, CRYSTAL? YOUR HEART'S IN THE RIGHT PLACE, BUT... DON'T GO INTO MARKETING, OKAY?
AND DON'T WORRY -- THINGS ARE HOT, BUT WE CAN HANDLE IT.
I BELIEVE IT IS ALREADY OUT OF OUR HANDS, JOHNNY STORM.
DO YOU NOT HEAR IT? LIKE THE BUILDING ROAR OF A TIDAL WAVE -- ?

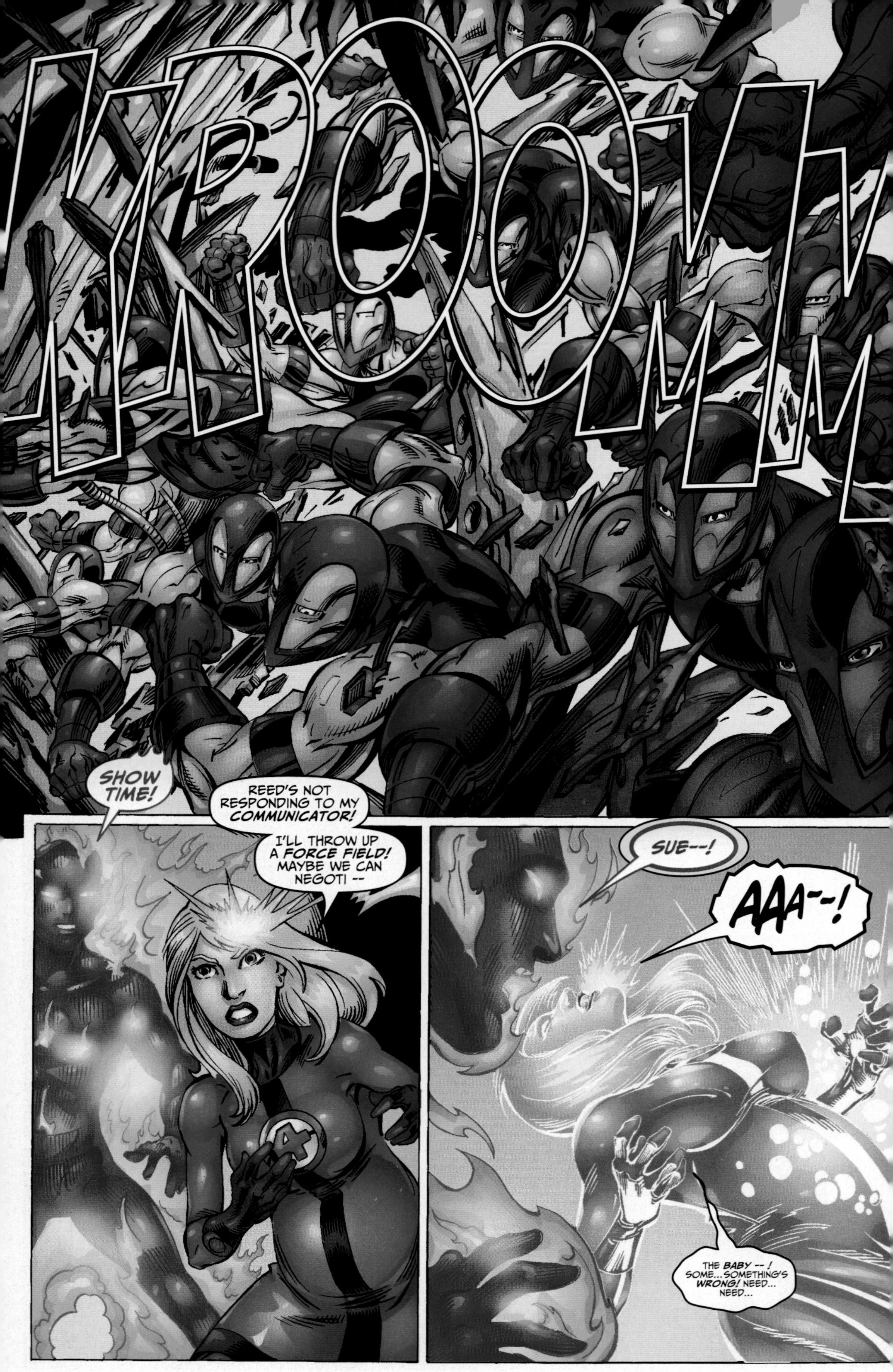
KRA-KROOOM
SHOW TIME!
REED'S NOT RESPONDING TO MY COMMUNICATOR!
I'LL THROW UP A FORCE FIELD! MAYBE WE CAN NEGOTI --
SUE--!
AAA--!
THE BABY -- ! SOME...SOMETHING'S WRONG! NEED... NEED...

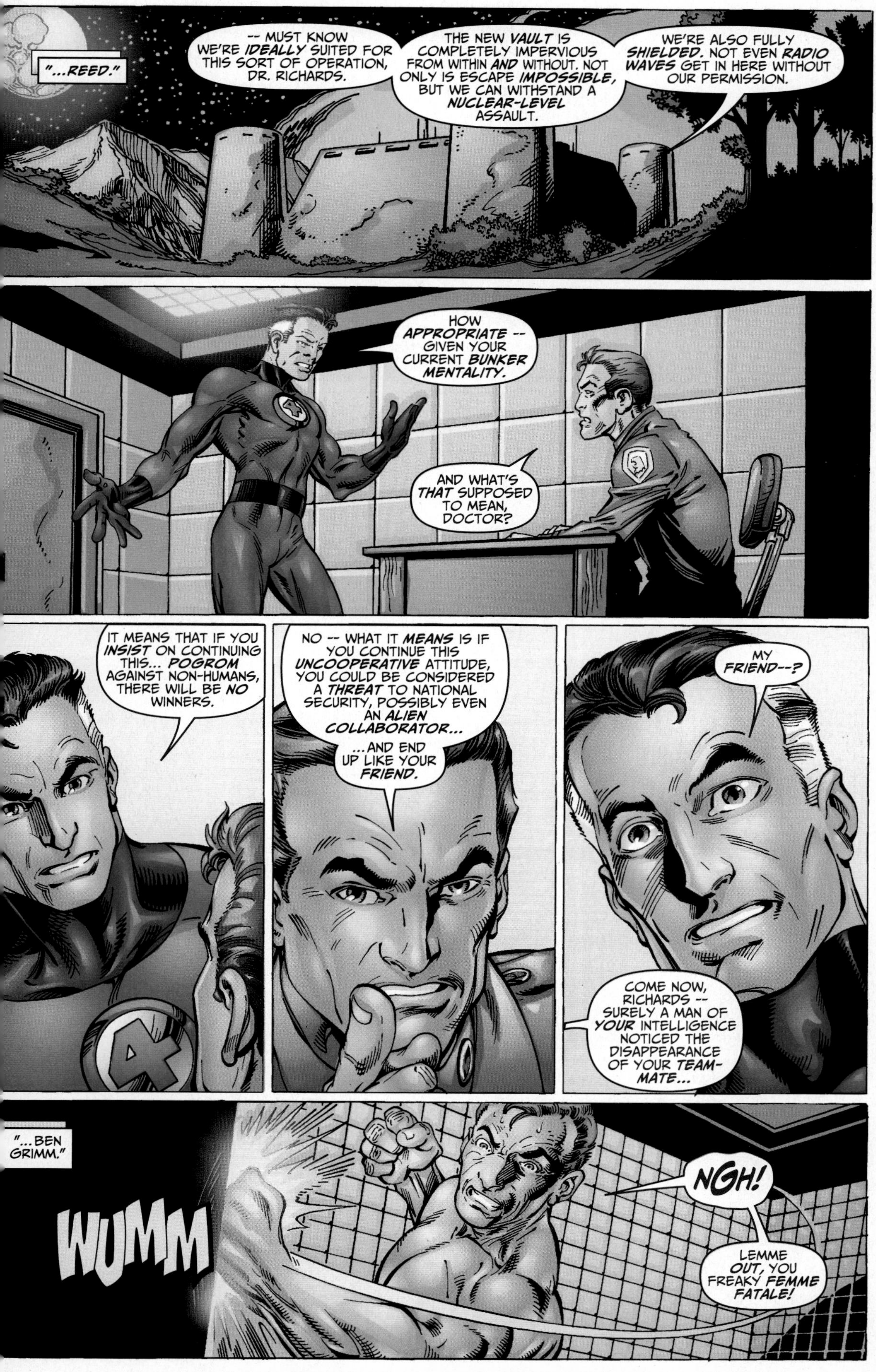
"...REED."
-- MUST KNOW WE'RE IDEALLY SUITED FOR THIS SORT OF OPERATION, DR. RICHARDS.
THE NEW VAULT IS COMPLETELY IMPERVIOUS FROM WITHIN AND WITHOUT. NOT ONLY IS ESCAPE IMPOSSIBLE, BUT WE CAN WITHSTAND A NUCLEAR-LEVEL ASSAULT.
WE'RE ALSO FULLY SHIELDED. NOT EVEN RADIO WAVES GET IN HERE WITHOUT OUR PERMISSION.
HOW APPROPRIATE -- GIVEN YOUR CURRENT BUNKER MENTALITY.
AND WHAT'S THAT SUPPOSED TO MEAN, DOCTOR?
IT MEANS THAT IF YOU INSIST ON CONTINUING THIS... POGROM AGAINST NON-HUMANS, THERE WILL BE NO WINNERS.
NO -- WHAT IT MEANS IS IF YOU CONTINUE THIS UNCOOPERATIVE ATTITUDE, YOU COULD BE CONSIDERED A THREAT TO NATIONAL SECURITY, POSSIBLY EVEN AN ALIEN COLLABORATOR...
...AND END UP LIKE YOUR FRIEND.
MY FRIEND--?
COME NOW, RICHARDS -- SURELY A MAN OF YOUR INTELLIGENCE NOTICED THE DISAPPEARANCE OF YOUR TEAM-MATE...
"...BEN GRIMM."
WUMM
NGH!
LEMME OUT, YOU FREAKY FEMME FATALE!

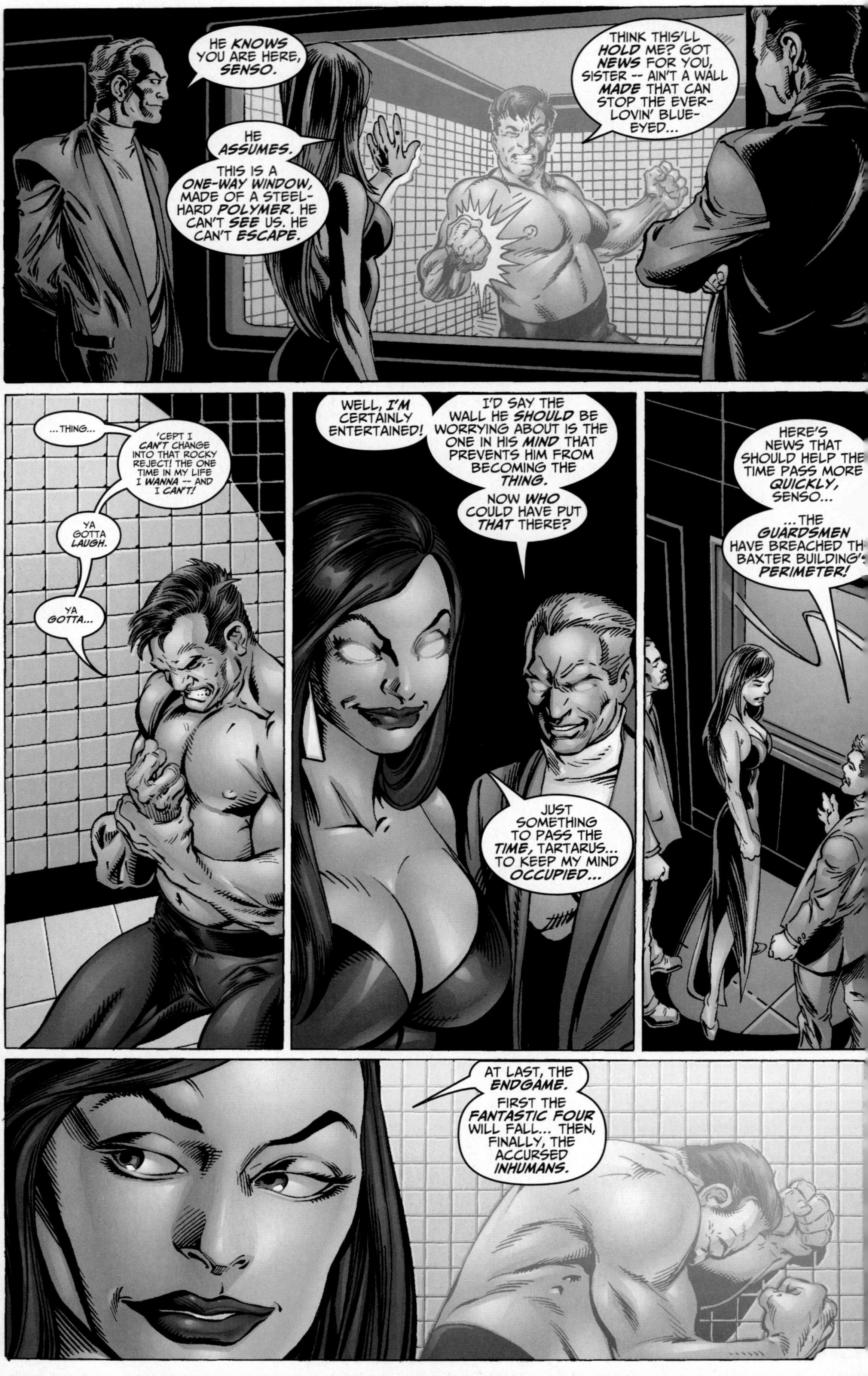

HE KNOWS YOU ARE HERE, SENSO.
HE ASSUMES.
THIS IS A ONE-WAY WINDOW, MADE OF A STEEL-HARD POLYMER. HE CAN'T SEE US. HE CAN'T ESCAPE.
THINK THIS'LL HOLD ME? GOT NEWS FOR YOU, SISTER -- AIN'T A WALL MADE THAT CAN STOP THE EVER-LOVIN' BLUE-EYED...
...THING...
'CEPT I CAN'T CHANGE INTO THAT ROCKY REJECT! THE ONE TIME IN MY LIFE I WANNA -- AND I CAN'T!
YA GOTTA LAUGH.
YA GOTTA...
WELL, I'M CERTAINLY ENTERTAINED!
I'D SAY THE WALL HE SHOULD BE WORRYING ABOUT IS THE ONE IN HIS MIND THAT PREVENTS HIM FROM BECOMING THE THING.
NOW WHO COULD HAVE PUT THAT THERE?
JUST SOMETHING TO PASS THE TIME, TARTARUS... TO KEEP MY MIND OCCUPIED...
HERE'S NEWS THAT SHOULD HELP THE TIME PASS MORE QUICKLY, SENSO...
...THE GUARDSMEN HAVE BREACHED THE BAXTER BUILDING'S PERIMETER!
AT LAST, THE ENDGAME.
FIRST THE FANTASTIC FOUR WILL FALL... THEN, FINALLY, THE ACCURSED INHUMANS.

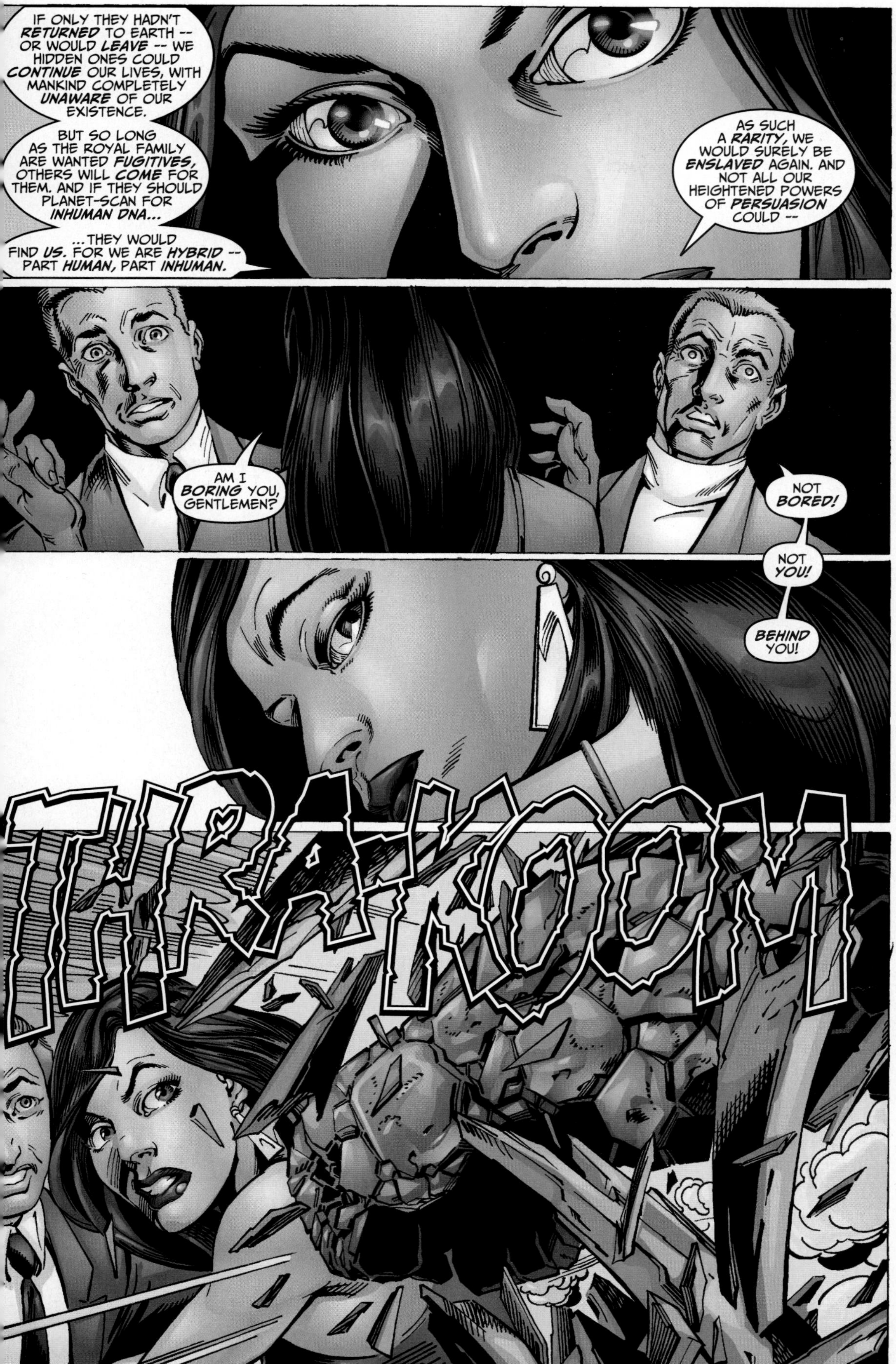
IF ONLY THEY HADN'T RETURNED TO EARTH -- OR WOULD LEAVE -- WE HIDDEN ONES COULD CONTINUE OUR LIVES, WITH MANKIND COMPLETELY UNAWARE OF OUR EXISTENCE.
BUT SO LONG AS THE ROYAL FAMILY ARE WANTED FUGITIVES, OTHERS WILL COME FOR THEM. AND IF THEY SHOULD PLANET-SCAN FOR INHUMAN DNA...
...THEY WOULD FIND US. FOR WE ARE HYBRID -- PART HUMAN, PART INHUMAN.
AS SUCH A RARITY, WE WOULD SURELY BE ENSLAVED AGAIN. AND NOT ALL OUR HEIGHTENED POWERS OF PERSUASION COULD --
AM I BORING YOU, GENTLEMEN?
NOT BORED!
NOT YOU!
BEHIND YOU!
THRAKOOM

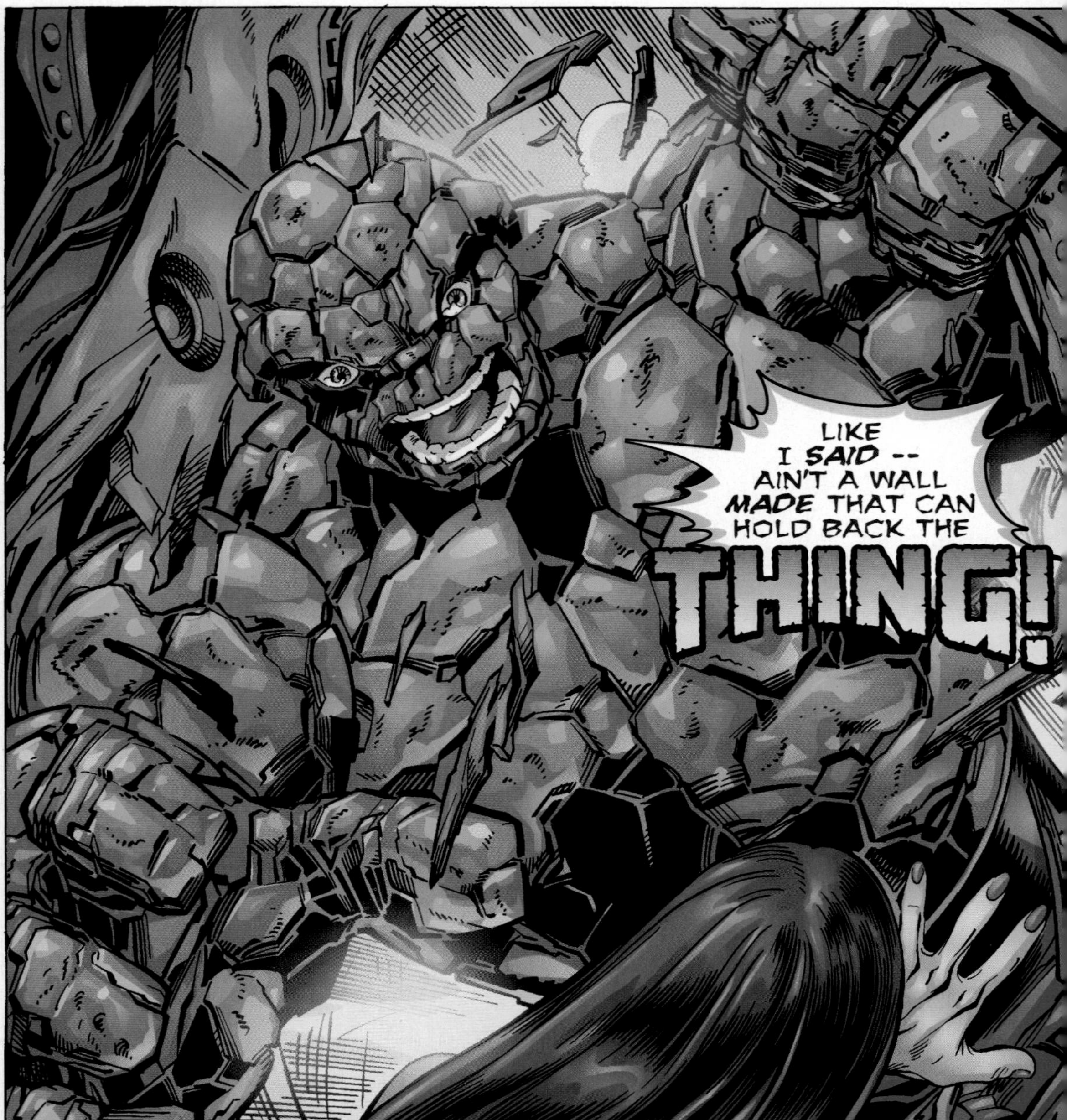
LIKE I SAID -- AIN'T A WALL MADE THAT CAN HOLD BACK THE
THING!

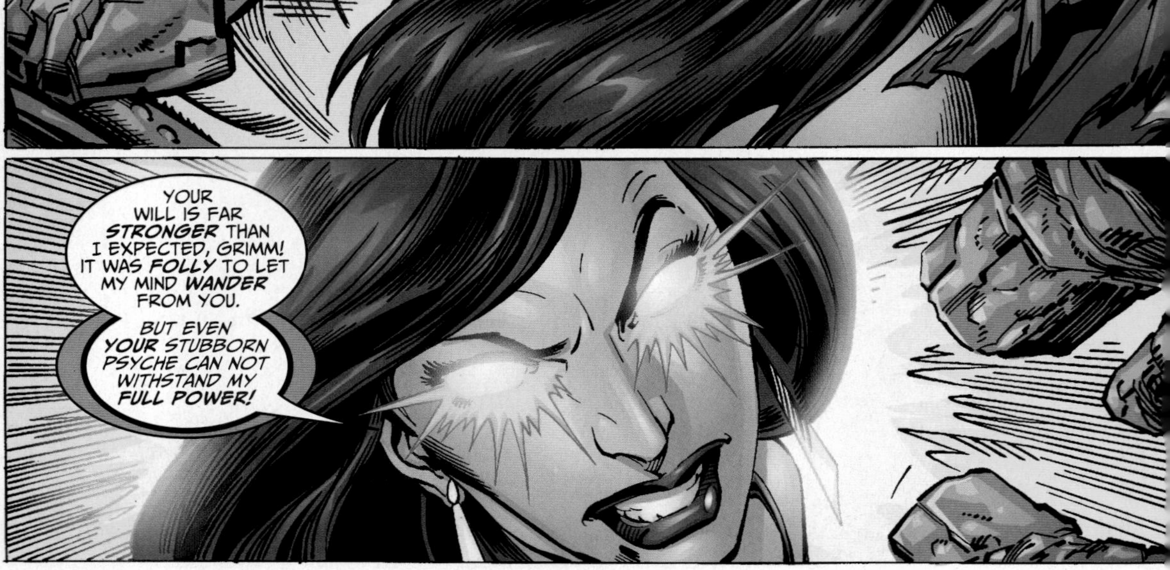
YOUR WILL IS FAR STRONGER THAN I EXPECTED, GRIMM! IT WAS FOLLY TO LET MY MIND WANDER FROM YOU.
BUT EVEN YOUR STUBBORN PSYCHE CAN NOT WITHSTAND MY FULL POWER!

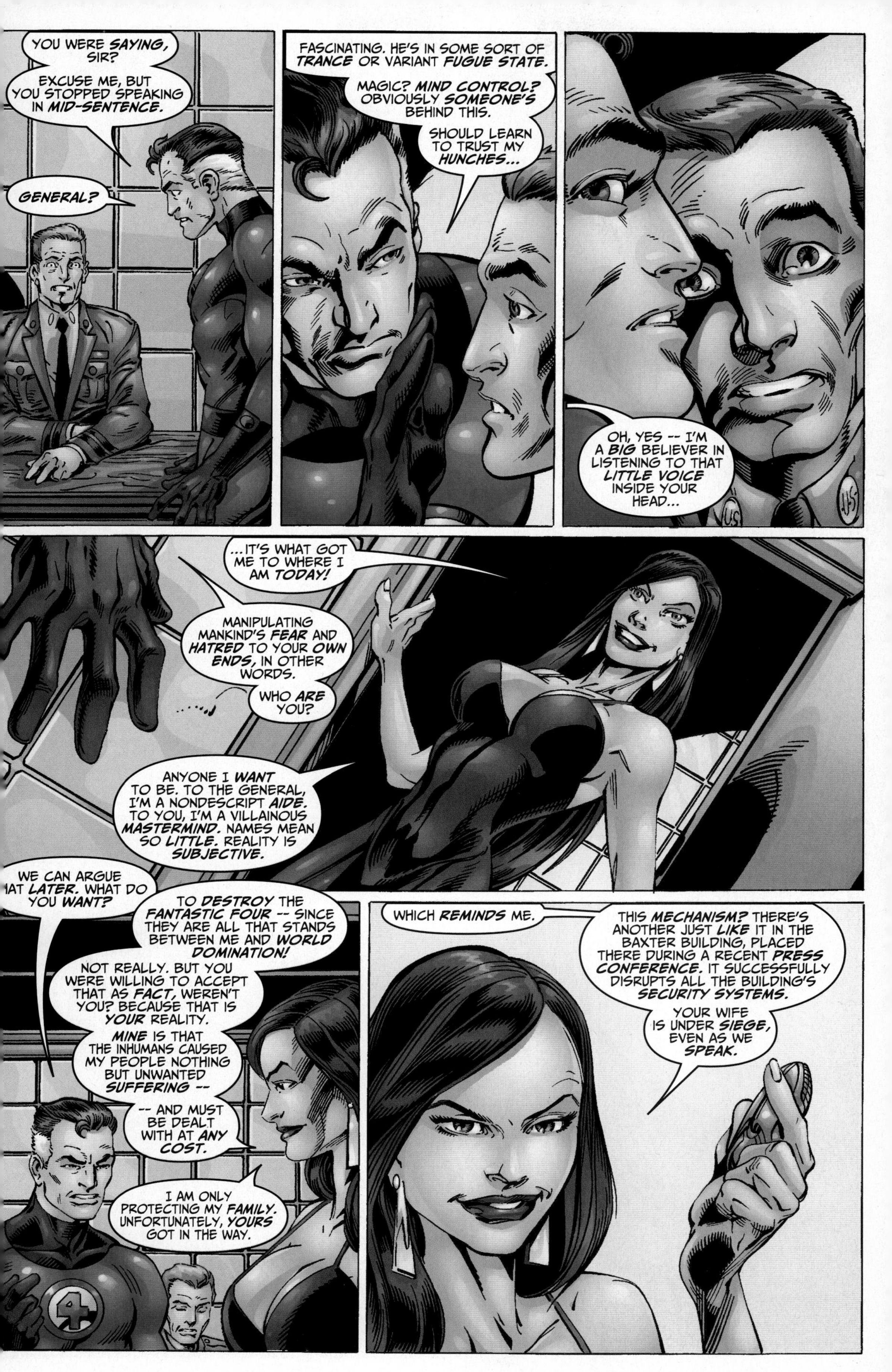
YOU WERE SAYING, SIR?
EXCUSE ME, BUT YOU STOPPED SPEAKING IN MID-SENTENCE.
GENERAL?
FASCINATING. HE'S IN SOME SORT OF TRANCE OR VARIANT FUGUE STATE.
MAGIC? MIND CONTROL? OBVIOUSLY SOMEONE'S BEHIND THIS.
SHOULD LEARN TO TRUST MY HUNCHES...
OH, YES -- I'M A BIG BELIEVER IN LISTENING TO THAT LITTLE VOICE INSIDE YOUR HEAD...
...IT'S WHAT GOT ME TO WHERE I AM TODAY!
MANIPULATING MANKIND'S FEAR AND HATRED TO YOUR OWN ENDS, IN OTHER WORDS.
WHO ARE YOU?
...
ANYONE I WANT TO BE. TO THE GENERAL, I'M A NONDESCRIPT AIDE. TO YOU, I'M A VILLAINOUS MASTERMIND. NAMES MEAN SO LITTLE. REALITY IS SUBJECTIVE.
WE CAN ARGUE THAT LATER. WHAT DO YOU WANT?
TO DESTROY THE FANTASTIC FOUR -- SINCE THEY ARE ALL THAT STANDS BETWEEN ME AND WORLD DOMINATION!
NOT REALLY. BUT YOU WERE WILLING TO ACCEPT THAT AS FACT, WEREN'T YOU? BECAUSE THAT IS YOUR REALITY.
MINE IS THAT THE INHUMANS CAUSED MY PEOPLE NOTHING BUT UNWANTED SUFFERING --
-- AND MUST BE DEALT WITH AT ANY COST.
I AM ONLY PROTECTING MY FAMILY. UNFORTUNATELY, YOURS GOT IN THE WAY.
WHICH REMINDS ME.
THIS MECHANISM? THERE'S ANOTHER JUST LIKE IT IN THE BAXTER BUILDING, PLACED THERE DURING A RECENT PRESS CONFERENCE. IT SUCCESSFULLY DISRUPTS ALL THE BUILDING'S SECURITY SYSTEMS.
YOUR WIFE IS UNDER SIEGE, EVEN AS WE SPEAK.

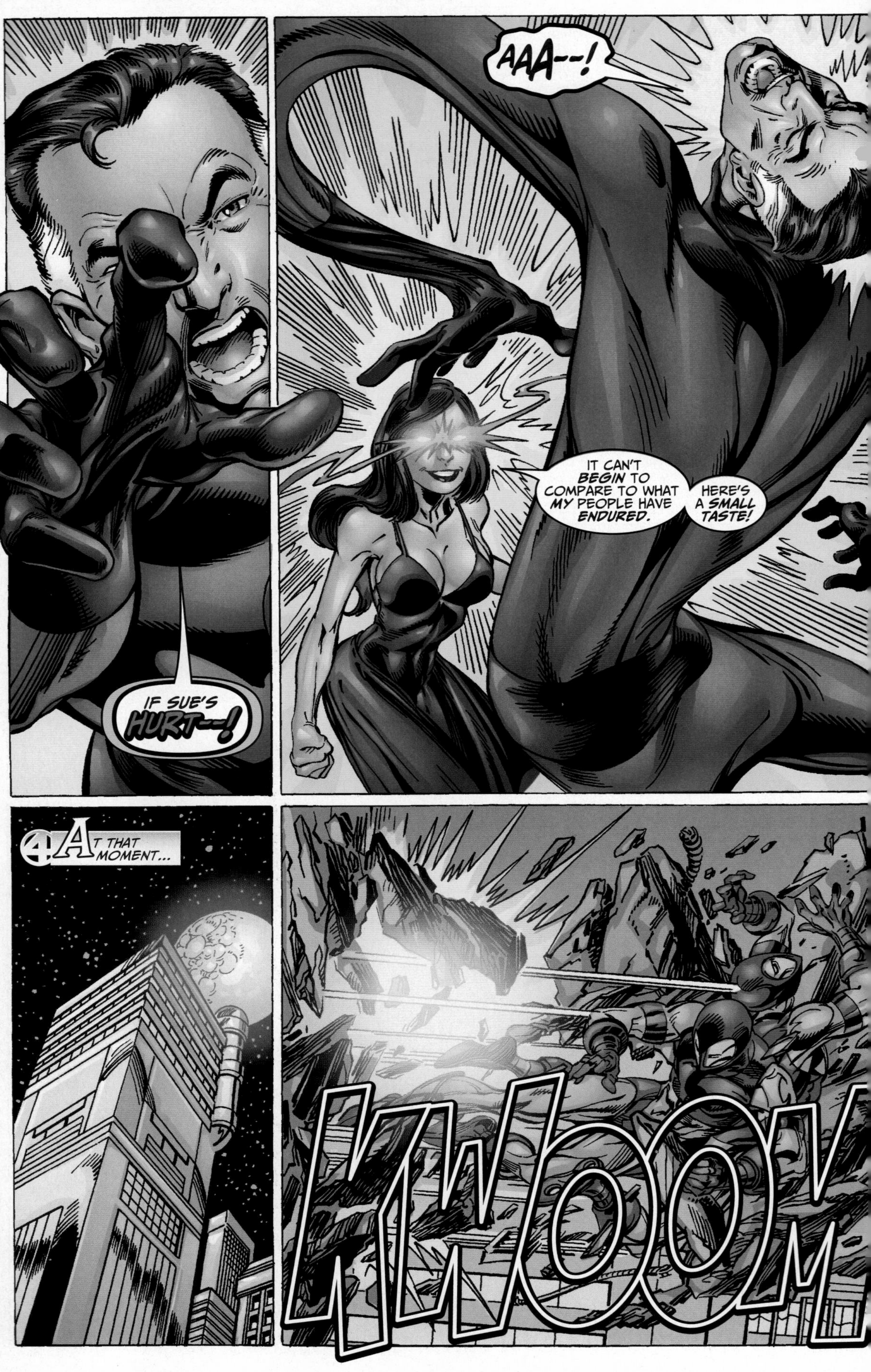
AAA--!
IF SUE'S HURT--!
IT CAN'T BEGIN TO COMPARE TO WHAT MY PEOPLE HAVE ENDURED.
HERE'S A SMALL TASTE!
AT THAT MOMENT...
KWOOM

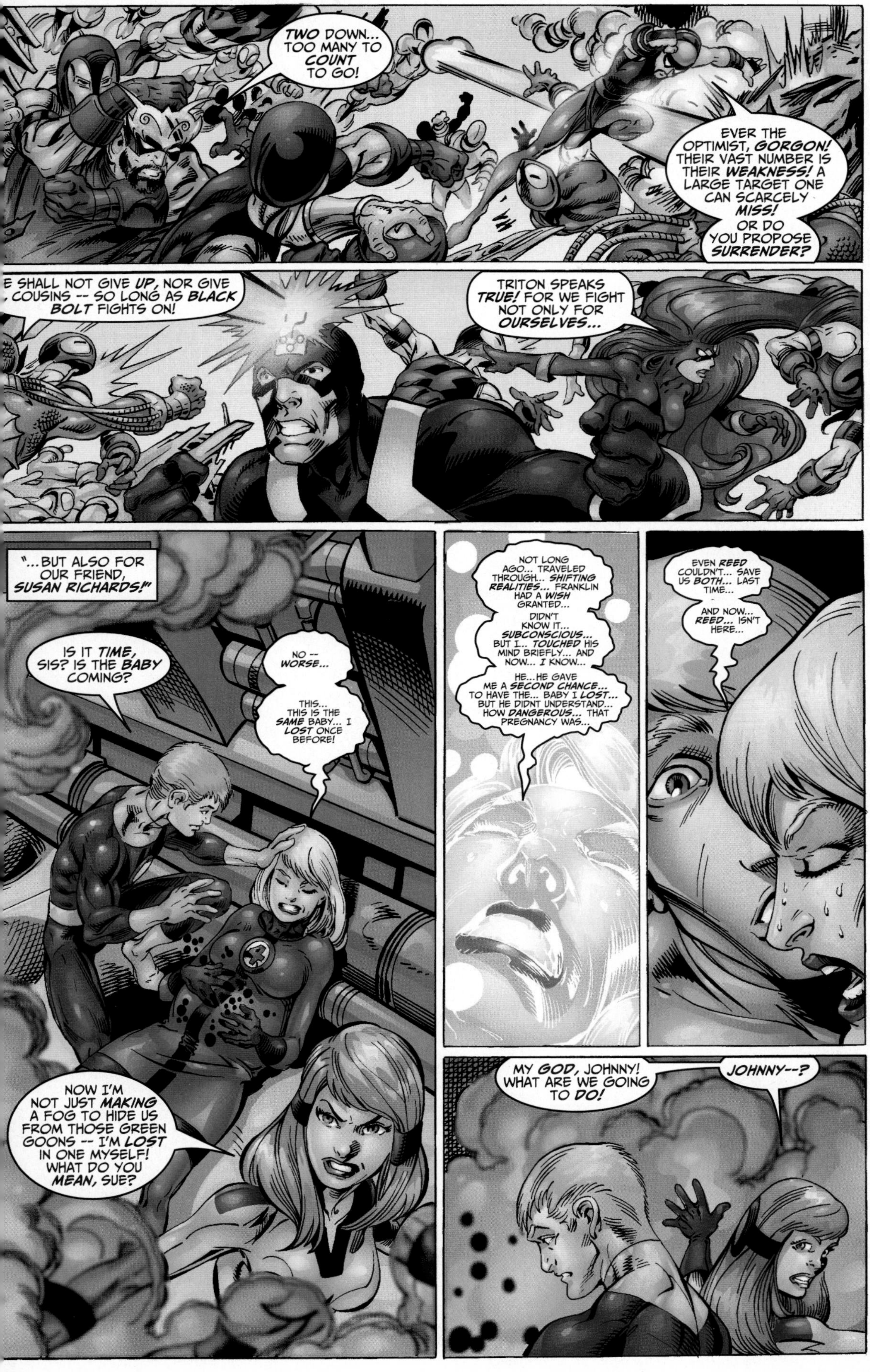

TWO DOWN... TOO MANY TO COUNT TO GO!
EVER THE OPTIMIST, GORGON! THEIR VAST NUMBER IS THEIR WEAKNESS! A LARGE TARGET ONE CAN SCARCELY MISS! OR DO YOU PROPOSE SURRENDER?
E SHALL NOT GIVE UP, NOR GIVE , COUSINS -- SO LONG AS BLACK BOLT FIGHTS ON!
TRITON SPEAKS TRUE! FOR WE FIGHT NOT ONLY FOR OURSELVES...
"...BUT ALSO FOR OUR FRIEND, SUSAN RICHARDS!"
IS IT TIME, SIS? IS THE BABY COMING?
NO -- WORSE...
THIS... THIS IS THE SAME BABY... I LOST ONCE BEFORE!
NOT LONG AGO... TRAVELED THROUGH... SHIFTING REALITIES... FRANKLIN HAD A WISH GRANTED...
DIDN'T KNOW IT... SUBCONSCIOUS... BUT I... TOUCHED HIS MIND BRIEFLY... AND NOW... I KNOW...
HE...HE GAVE ME A SECOND CHANCE... TO HAVE THE... BABY I LOST... BUT HE DIDNT UNDERSTAND... HOW DANGEROUS... THAT PREGNANCY WAS...
EVEN REED COULDN'T... SAVE US BOTH... LAST TIME...
AND NOW... REED... ISN'T HERE...
NOW I'M NOT JUST MAKING A FOG TO HIDE US FROM THOSE GREEN GOONS -- I'M LOST IN ONE MYSELF! WHAT DO YOU MEAN, SUE?
MY GOD, JOHNNY! WHAT ARE WE GOING TO DO!
JOHNNY--?

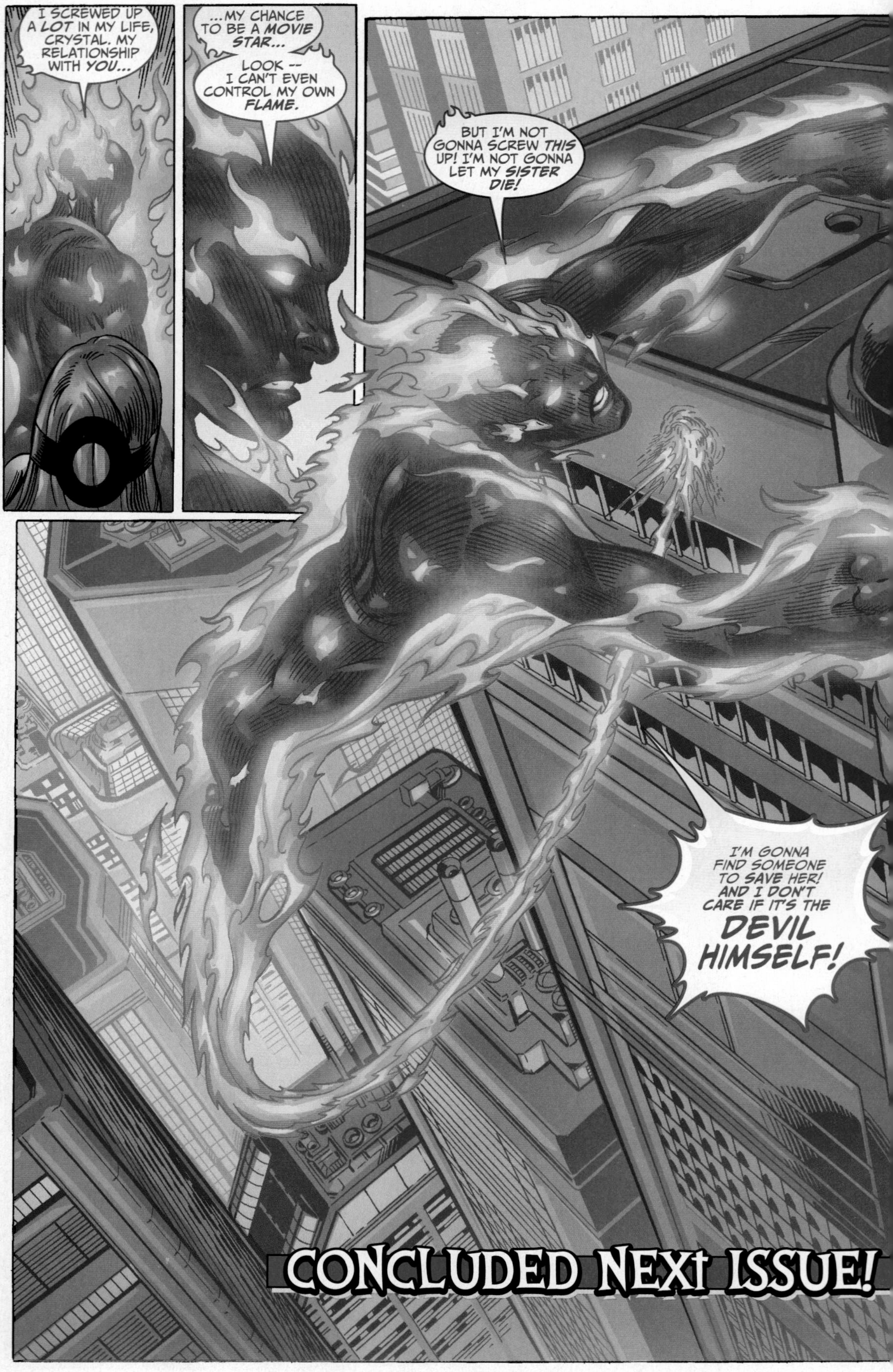
I SCREWED UP A LOT IN MY LIFE, CRYSTAL. MY RELATIONSHIP WITH YOU...
...MY CHANCE TO BE A MOVIE STAR...
LOOK -- I CAN'T EVEN CONTROL MY OWN FLAME.
BUT I'M NOT GONNA SCREW THIS UP! I'M NOT GONNA LET MY SISTER DIE!
I'M GONNA FIND SOMEONE TO SAVE HER! AND I DON'T CARE IF IT'S THE DEVIL HIMSELF!
CONCLUDED NEXt ISSUE!

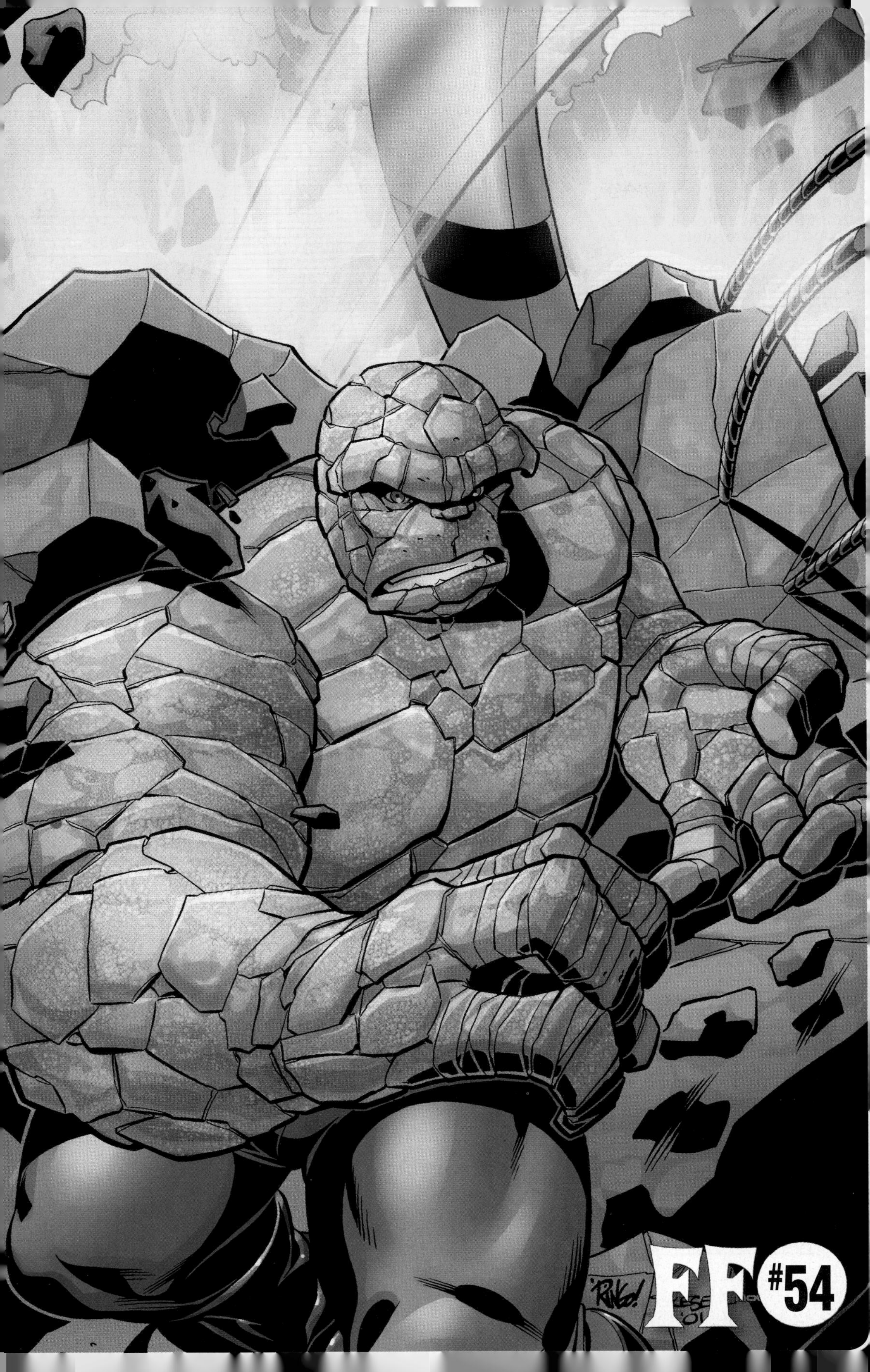
FF
#54
RINGO!

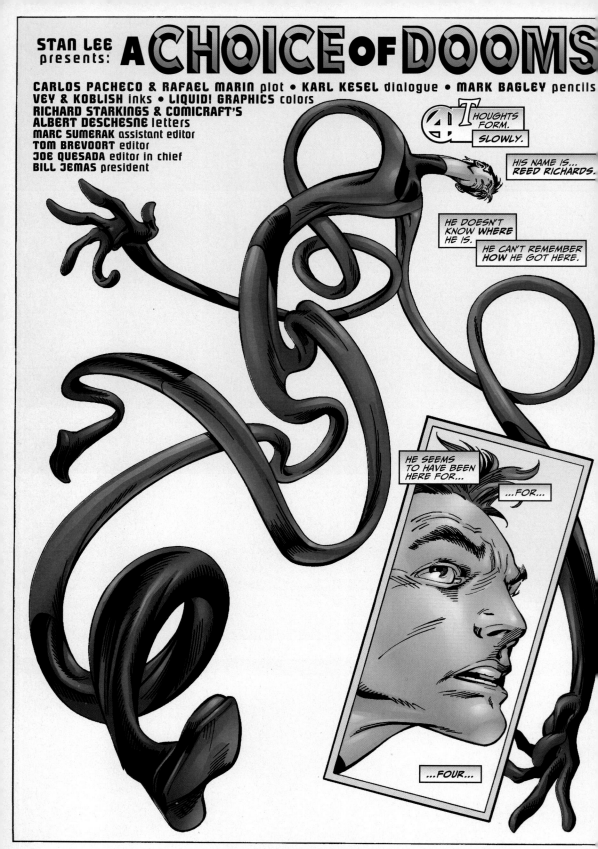

STAN LEE presents: A CHOICE OF DOOMS

CARLOS PACHECO & RAFAEL MARIN plot • **KARL KESEL** dialogue • **MARK BAGLEY** pencils
VEY & KOBLISH inks • **LIQUID! GRAPHICS** colors
RICHARD STARKINGS & COMICRAFT'S
ALBERT DESCHESNE letters
MARC SUMERAK assistant editor
TOM BREVOORT editor
JOE QUESADA editor in chief
BILL JEMAS president

THOUGHTS FORM. SLOWLY.

HIS NAME IS... REED RICHARDS.

HE DOESN'T KNOW WHERE HE IS.

HE CAN'T REMEMBER HOW HE GOT HERE.

HE SEEMS TO HAVE BEEN HERE FOR...

...FOR...

...FOUR...

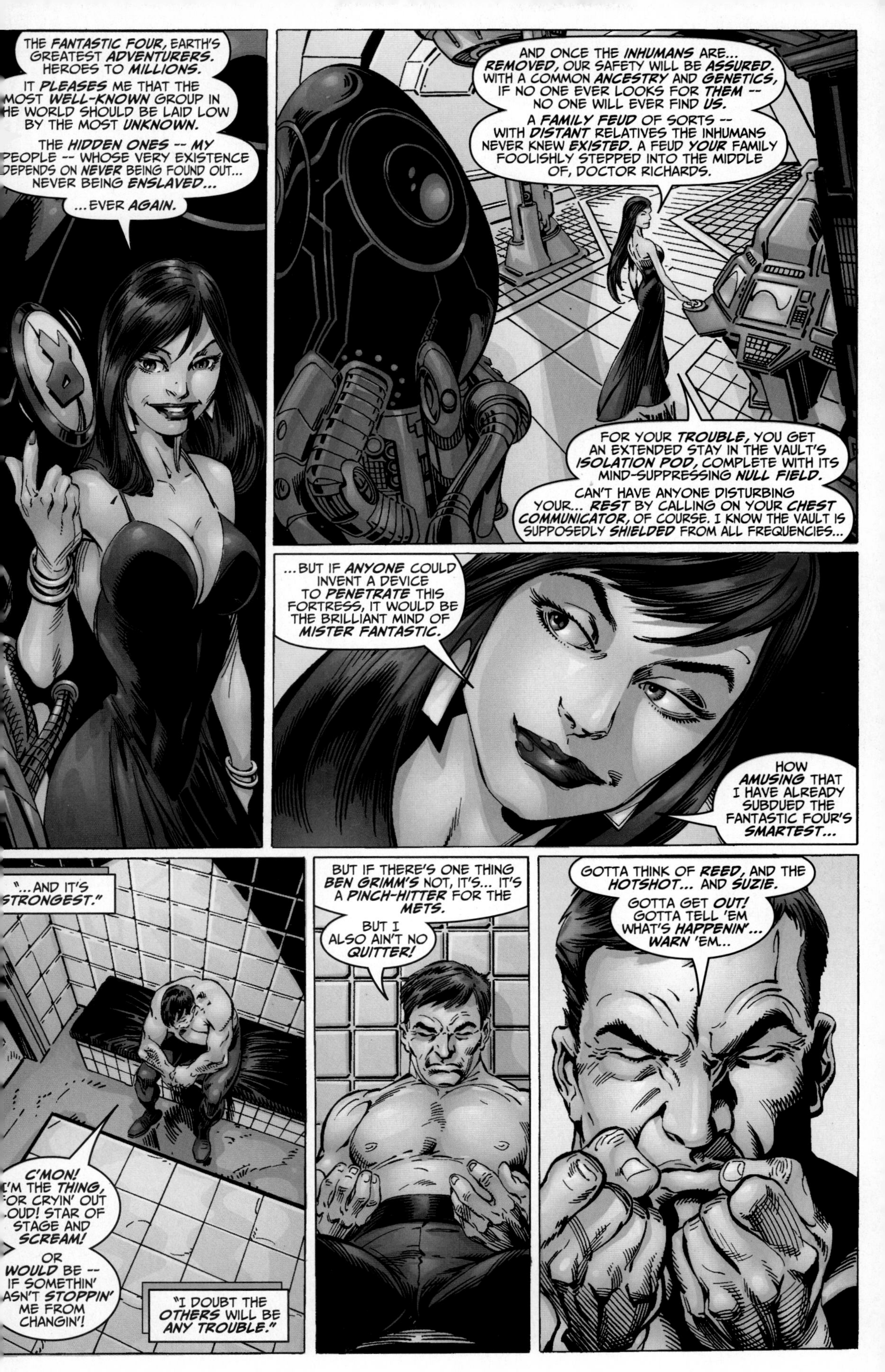

THE FANTASTIC FOUR, EARTH'S GREATEST ADVENTURERS. HEROES TO MILLIONS.
IT PLEASES ME THAT THE MOST WELL-KNOWN GROUP IN THE WORLD SHOULD BE LAID LOW BY THE MOST UNKNOWN.
THE HIDDEN ONES -- MY PEOPLE -- WHOSE VERY EXISTENCE DEPENDS ON NEVER BEING FOUND OUT... NEVER BEING ENSLAVED...
...EVER AGAIN.
AND ONCE THE INHUMANS ARE... REMOVED, OUR SAFETY WILL BE ASSURED. WITH A COMMON ANCESTRY AND GENETICS, IF NO ONE EVER LOOKS FOR THEM -- NO ONE WILL EVER FIND US.
A FAMILY FEUD OF SORTS -- WITH DISTANT RELATIVES THE INHUMANS NEVER KNEW EXISTED. A FEUD YOUR FAMILY FOOLISHLY STEPPED INTO THE MIDDLE OF, DOCTOR RICHARDS.
FOR YOUR TROUBLE, YOU GET AN EXTENDED STAY IN THE VAULT'S ISOLATION POD, COMPLETE WITH ITS MIND-SUPPRESSING NULL FIELD.
CAN'T HAVE ANYONE DISTURBING YOUR... REST BY CALLING ON YOUR CHEST COMMUNICATOR, OF COURSE. I KNOW THE VAULT IS SUPPOSEDLY SHIELDED FROM ALL FREQUENCIES...
...BUT IF ANYONE COULD INVENT A DEVICE TO PENETRATE THIS FORTRESS, IT WOULD BE THE BRILLIANT MIND OF MISTER FANTASTIC.
HOW AMUSING THAT I HAVE ALREADY SUBDUED THE FANTASTIC FOUR'S SMARTEST...
"...AND IT'S STRONGEST."
C'MON! I'M THE THING, FOR CRYIN' OUT LOUD! STAR OF STAGE AND SCREAM!
OR WOULD BE -- IF SOMETHIN' WASN'T STOPPIN' ME FROM CHANGIN'!
"I DOUBT THE OTHERS WILL BE ANY TROUBLE."
BUT IF THERE'S ONE THING BEN GRIMM'S NOT, IT'S... IT'S A PINCH-HITTER FOR THE METS.
BUT I ALSO AIN'T NO QUITTER!
GOTTA THINK OF REED, AND THE HOTSHOT... AND SUZIE.
GOTTA GET OUT! GOTTA TELL 'EM WHAT'S HAPPENIN'... WARN 'EM...

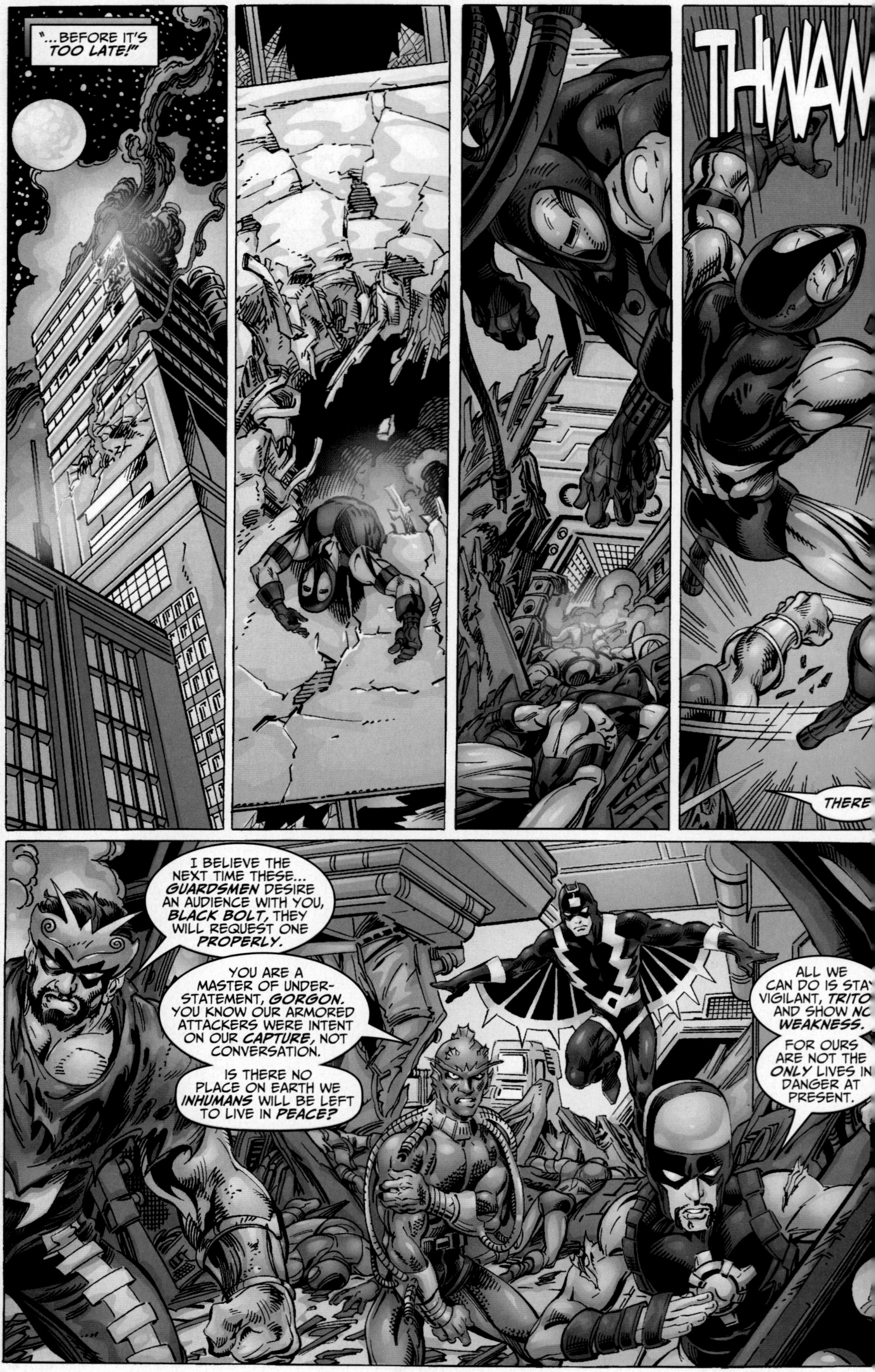
"...BEFORE IT'S TOO LATE!"
THWAM
THERE
I BELIEVE THE NEXT TIME THESE... GUARDSMEN DESIRE AN AUDIENCE WITH YOU, BLACK BOLT, THEY WILL REQUEST ONE PROPERLY.
YOU ARE A MASTER OF UNDER-STATEMENT, GORGON. YOU KNOW OUR ARMORED ATTACKERS WERE INTENT ON OUR CAPTURE, NOT CONVERSATION.
IS THERE NO PLACE ON EARTH WE INHUMANS WILL BE LEFT TO LIVE IN PEACE?
ALL WE CAN DO IS STAY VIGILANT, TRITO AND SHOW NO WEAKNESS.
FOR OURS ARE NOT THE ONLY LIVES IN DANGER AT PRESENT.

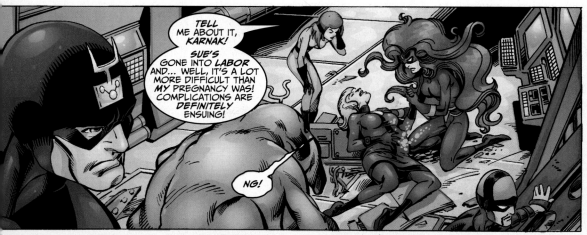

TELL ME ABOUT IT, *KARNAK!*

SUE'S GONE INTO *LABOR* AND... WELL, IT'S A LOT MORE DIFFICULT THAN *MY* PREGNANCY WAS! COMPLICATIONS ARE *DEFINITELY* ENSUING!

NG!

YOUR CHILD WASN'T... CONCEIVED IN THE... *NEGATIVE ZONE,* CRYSTAL...

LUCKY *YOU...*

BEEN THROUGH THIS *BEFORE...* DON'T WANT THE BABY... TO DIE *AGAIN!*

WHAT CAN WE *DO* FOR YOU, SUSAN? YOU HAVE BUT TO *NAME* IT!

GET REED!

DON'T KNOW WHY HE... ISN'T *ANSWERING* HIS... CHEST COMMUNICATOR! GET *REED,* GET --

AAA⁻!

GET *BACK!*

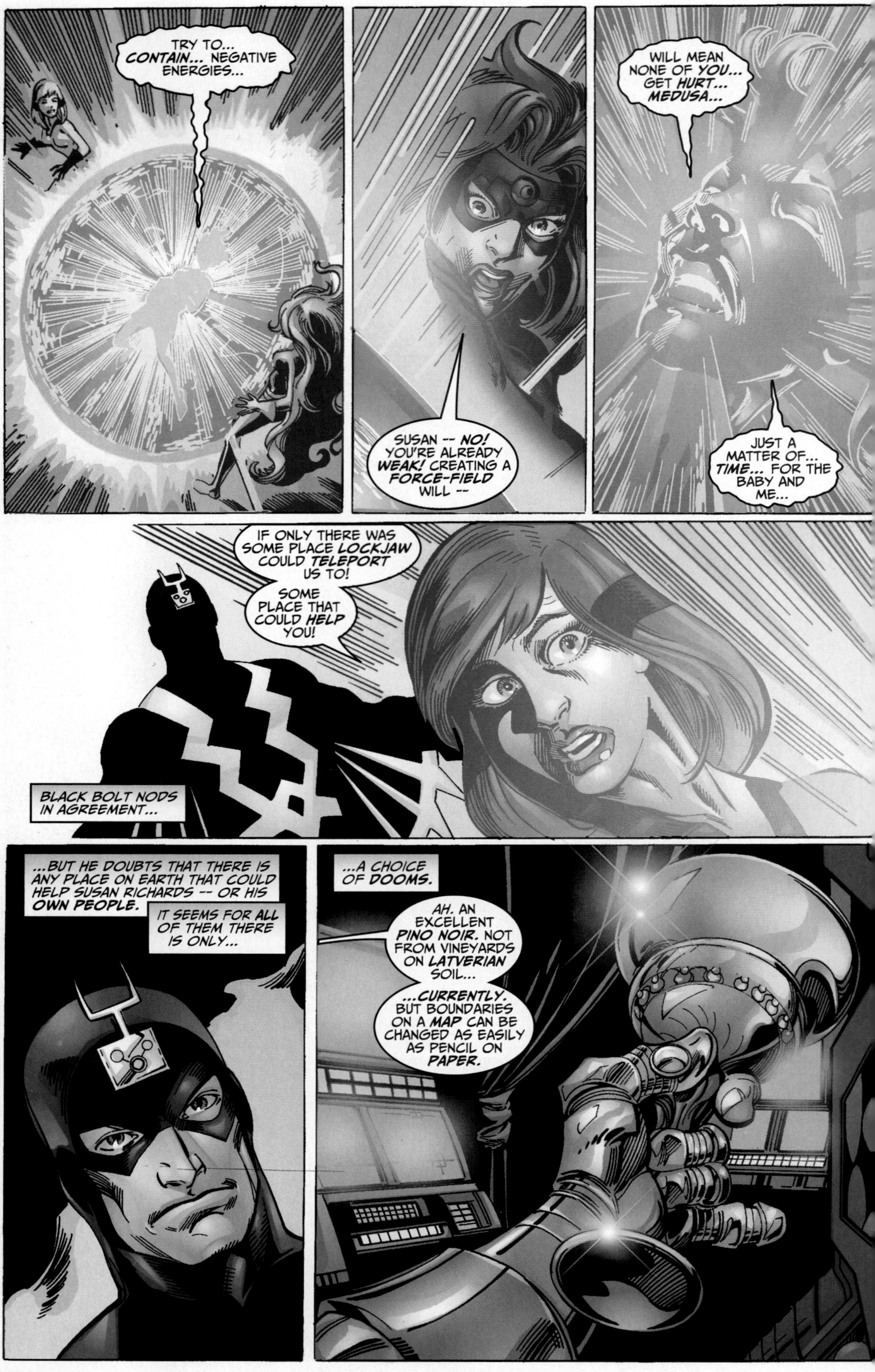
TRY TO... CONTAIN... NEGATIVE ENERGIES...
SUSAN -- NO! YOU'RE ALREADY WEAK! CREATING A FORCE-FIELD WILL --
WILL MEAN NONE OF YOU... GET HURT... MEDUSA...
JUST A MATTER OF... TIME... FOR THE BABY AND ME...
IF ONLY THERE WAS SOME PLACE LOCKJAW COULD TELEPORT US TO!
SOME PLACE THAT COULD HELP YOU!
BLACK BOLT NODS IN AGREEMENT...
...BUT HE DOUBTS THAT THERE IS ANY PLACE ON EARTH THAT COULD HELP SUSAN RICHARDS -- OR HIS OWN PEOPLE.
IT SEEMS FOR ALL OF THEM THERE IS ONLY...
...A CHOICE OF DOOMS.
AH. AN EXCELLENT PINO NOIR. NOT FROM VINEYARDS ON LATVERIAN SOIL...
...CURRENTLY. BUT BOUNDARIES ON A MAP CAN BE CHANGED AS EASILY AS PENCIL ON PAPER.

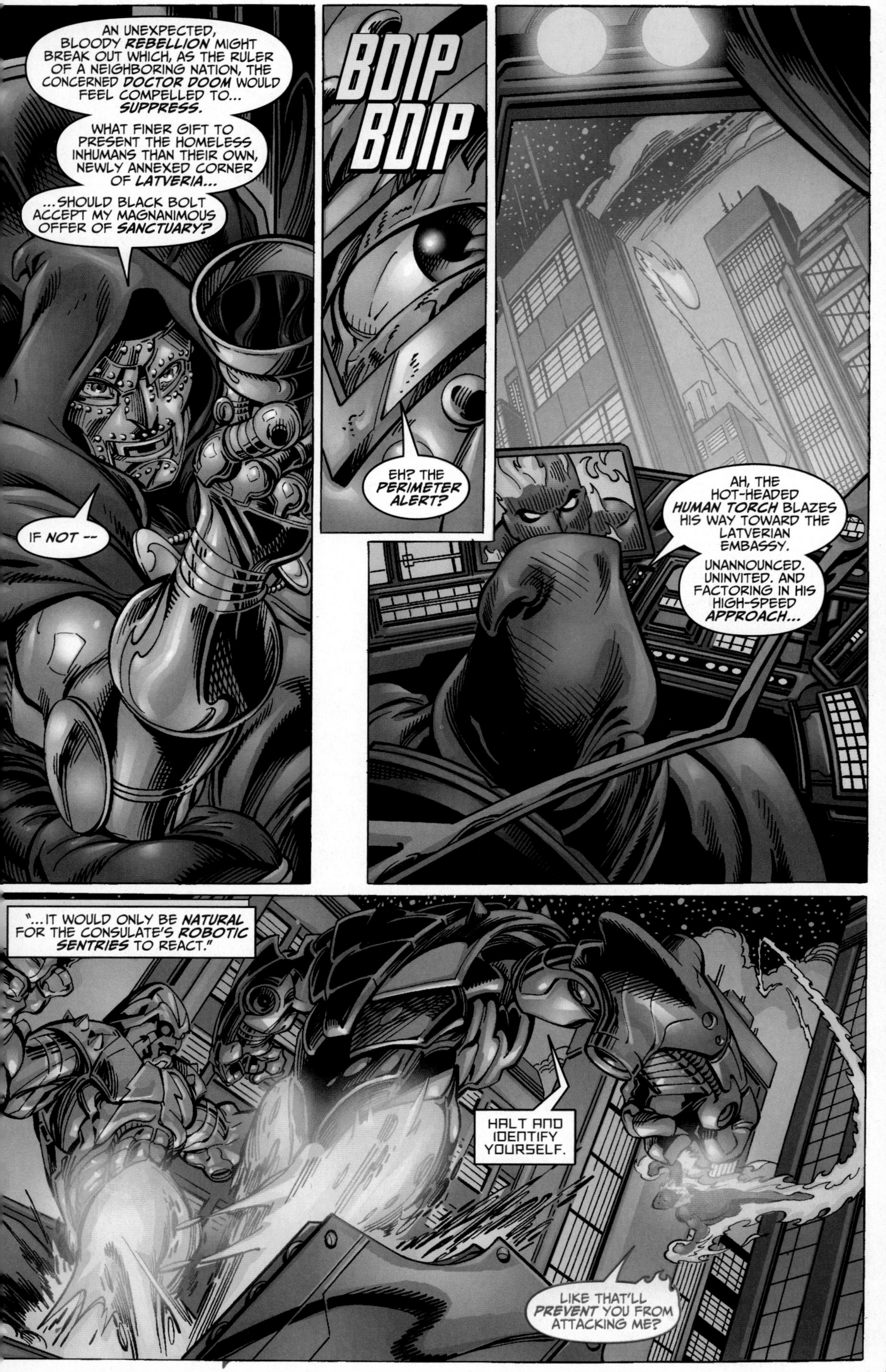

AN UNEXPECTED, BLOODY REBELLION MIGHT BREAK OUT WHICH, AS THE RULER OF A NEIGHBORING NATION, THE CONCERNED DOCTOR DOOM WOULD FEEL COMPELLED TO... SUPPRESS.
WHAT FINER GIFT TO PRESENT THE HOMELESS INHUMANS THAN THEIR OWN, NEWLY ANNEXED CORNER OF LATVERIA...
...SHOULD BLACK BOLT ACCEPT MY MAGNANIMOUS OFFER OF SANCTUARY?
IF NOT --
BDIP BDIP
EH? THE PERIMETER ALERT?
AH, THE HOT-HEADED HUMAN TORCH BLAZES HIS WAY TOWARD THE LATVERIAN EMBASSY.
UNANNOUNCED. UNINVITED. AND FACTORING IN HIS HIGH-SPEED APPROACH...
"...IT WOULD ONLY BE NATURAL FOR THE CONSULATE'S ROBOTIC SENTRIES TO REACT."
HALT AND IDENTIFY YOURSELF.
LIKE THAT'LL PREVENT YOU FROM ATTACKING ME?

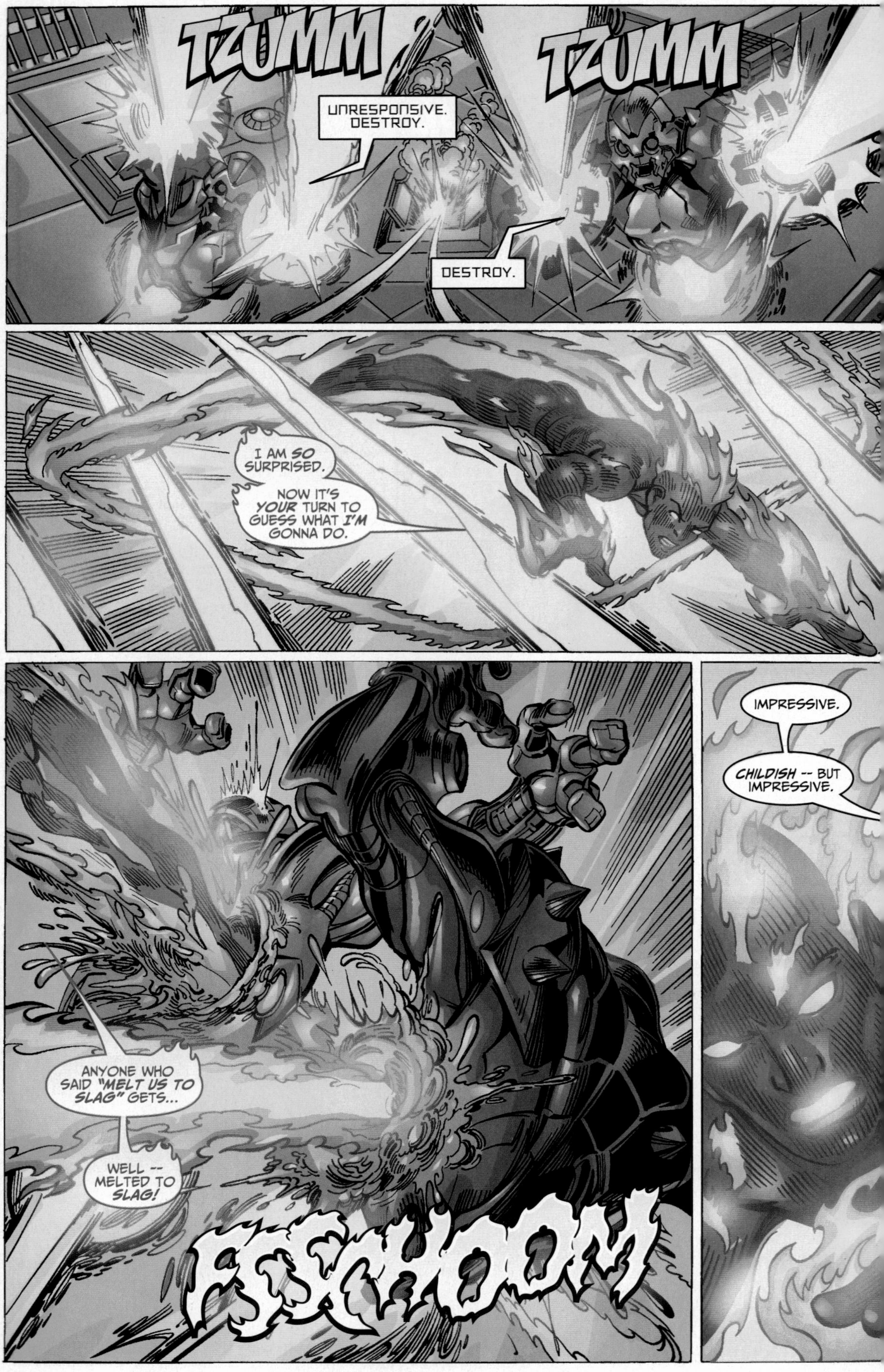
TZUMM
TZUMM
UNRESPONSIVE. DESTROY.
DESTROY.
I AM SO SURPRISED.
NOW IT'S YOUR TURN TO GUESS WHAT I'M GONNA DO.
ANYONE WHO SAID "MELT US TO SLAG" GETS...
WELL -- MELTED TO SLAG!
FSSHOOM
IMPRESSIVE.
CHILDISH -- BUT IMPRESSIVE.

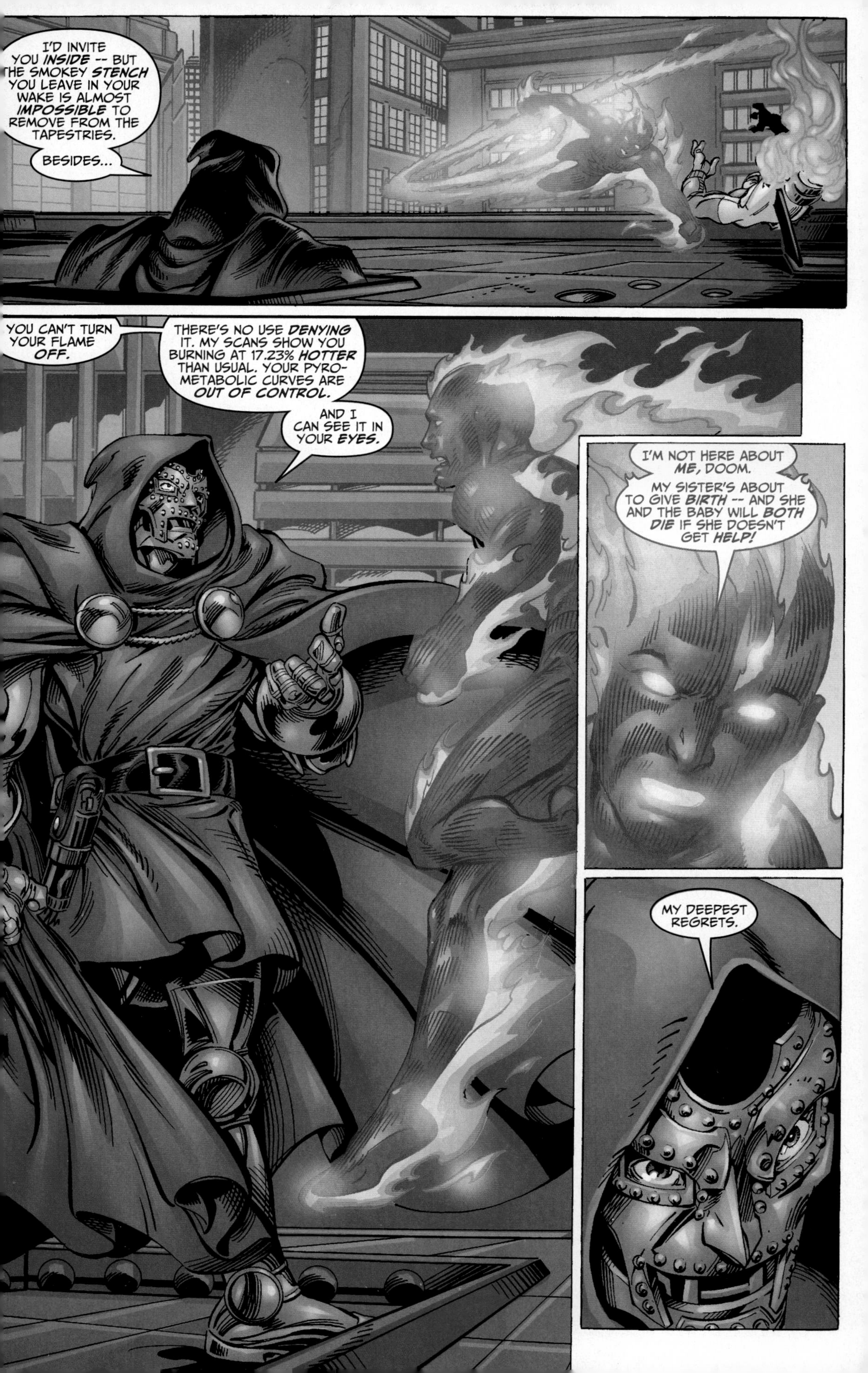
I'D INVITE YOU INSIDE -- BUT THE SMOKEY STENCH YOU LEAVE IN YOUR WAKE IS ALMOST IMPOSSIBLE TO REMOVE FROM THE TAPESTRIES.
BESIDES...
YOU CAN'T TURN YOUR FLAME OFF.
THERE'S NO USE DENYING IT. MY SCANS SHOW YOU BURNING AT 17.23% HOTTER THAN USUAL. YOUR PYRO-METABOLIC CURVES ARE OUT OF CONTROL.
AND I CAN SEE IT IN YOUR EYES.
I'M NOT HERE ABOUT ME, DOOM.
MY SISTER'S ABOUT TO GIVE BIRTH -- AND SHE AND THE BABY WILL BOTH DIE IF SHE DOESN'T GET HELP!
MY DEEPEST REGRETS.

I'M SURE *RICHARDS* WILL --

REED'S *MISSING!*

LOOK, DOC -- THE *LAST* TIME THIS HAPPENED, IT TOOK REED *AND* A COUPLE OTHER BIG-BRAINS TO SAVE SUE...

...BUT THE *BABY* DIDN'T MAKE IT.

I KNOW WE'VE HAD OUR... *DIFFERENCES...*

OKAY -- WE'VE BEATEN EACH OTHER *BLOODY.* *LOTS.* BUT THIS KID'S GOT *NOTHING* TO DO WITH THAT.

YOU GOTTA *HELP,* DOC. THERE'S NO ONE ELSE WHO *CAN.*

YOU'RE THE *BEST* CHANCE WE GOT.

THE *ONLY* CHANCE WE GOT.

PLEASE.

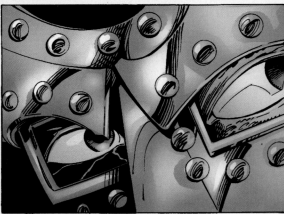

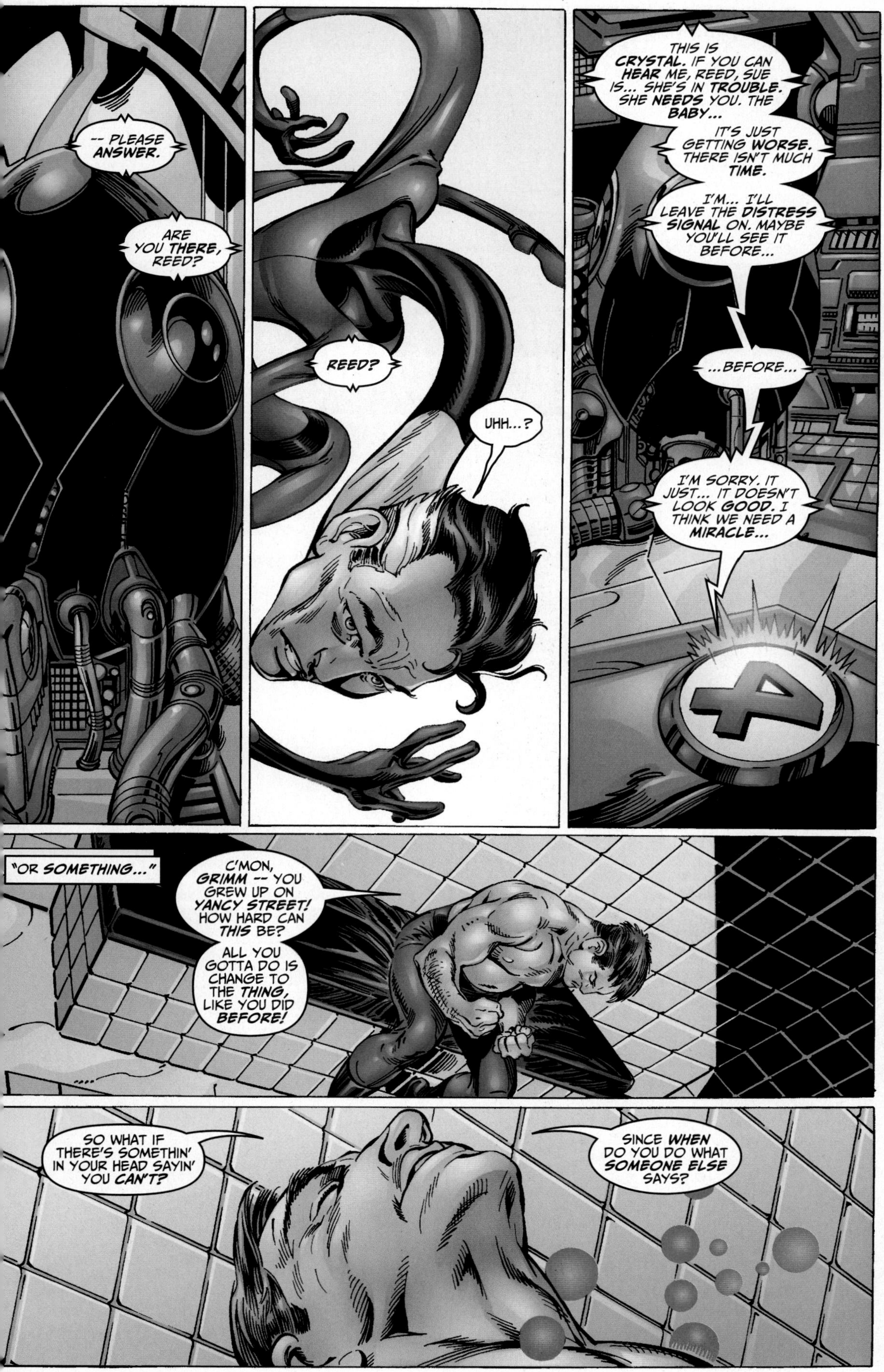
-- PLEASE ANSWER.
ARE YOU THERE, REED?
REED?
UHH...?
THIS IS CRYSTAL. IF YOU CAN HEAR ME, REED, SUE IS... SHE'S IN TROUBLE. SHE NEEDS YOU. THE BABY...
IT'S JUST GETTING WORSE. THERE ISN'T MUCH TIME.
I'M... I'LL LEAVE THE DISTRESS SIGNAL ON. MAYBE YOU'LL SEE IT BEFORE...
...BEFORE...
I'M SORRY. IT JUST... IT DOESN'T LOOK GOOD. I THINK WE NEED A MIRACLE...
"OR SOMETHING..."
C'MON, GRIMM -- YOU GREW UP ON YANCY STREET! HOW HARD CAN THIS BE?
ALL YOU GOTTA DO IS CHANGE TO THE THING, LIKE YOU DID BEFORE!
SO WHAT IF THERE'S SOMETHIN' IN YOUR HEAD SAYIN' YOU CAN'T?
SINCE WHEN DO YOU DO WHAT SOMEONE ELSE SAYS?

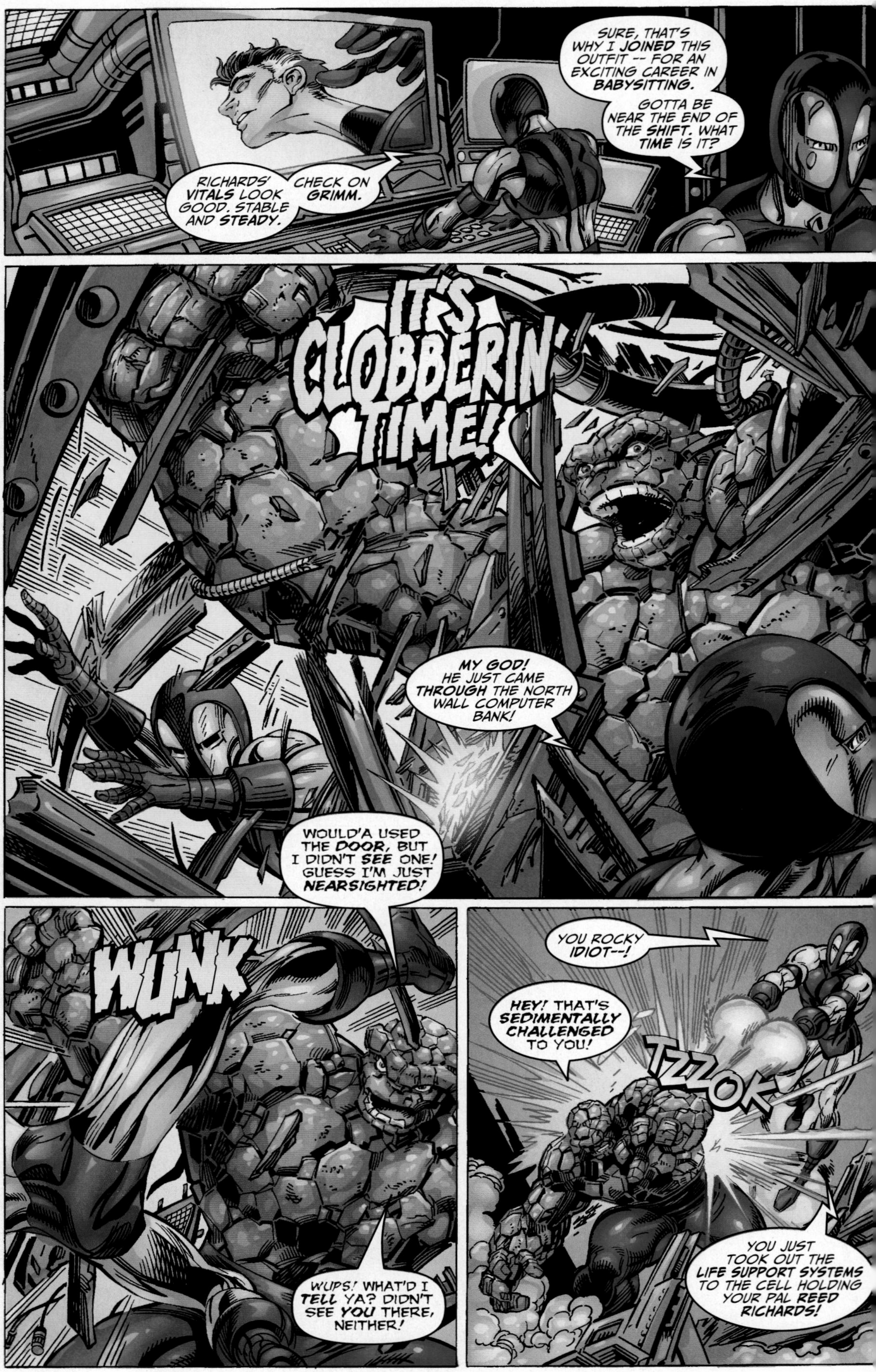
RICHARDS' VITALS LOOK GOOD. STABLE AND STEADY.
CHECK ON GRIMM.
SURE, THAT'S WHY I JOINED THIS OUTFIT -- FOR AN EXCITING CAREER IN BABYSITTING.
GOTTA BE NEAR THE END OF THE SHIFT. WHAT TIME IS IT?
IT'S CLOBBERIN' TIME!
MY GOD! HE JUST CAME THROUGH THE NORTH WALL COMPUTER BANK!
WOULD'A USED THE DOOR, BUT I DIDN'T SEE ONE! GUESS I'M JUST NEARSIGHTED!
WUNK
WUPS! WHAT'D I TELL YA? DIDN'T SEE YOU THERE, NEITHER!
YOU ROCKY IDIOT--!
HEY! THAT'S SEDIMENTALLY CHALLENGED TO YOU!
TZZOK
YOU JUST TOOK OUT THE LIFE SUPPORT SYSTEMS TO THE CELL HOLDING YOUR PAL REED RICHARDS!

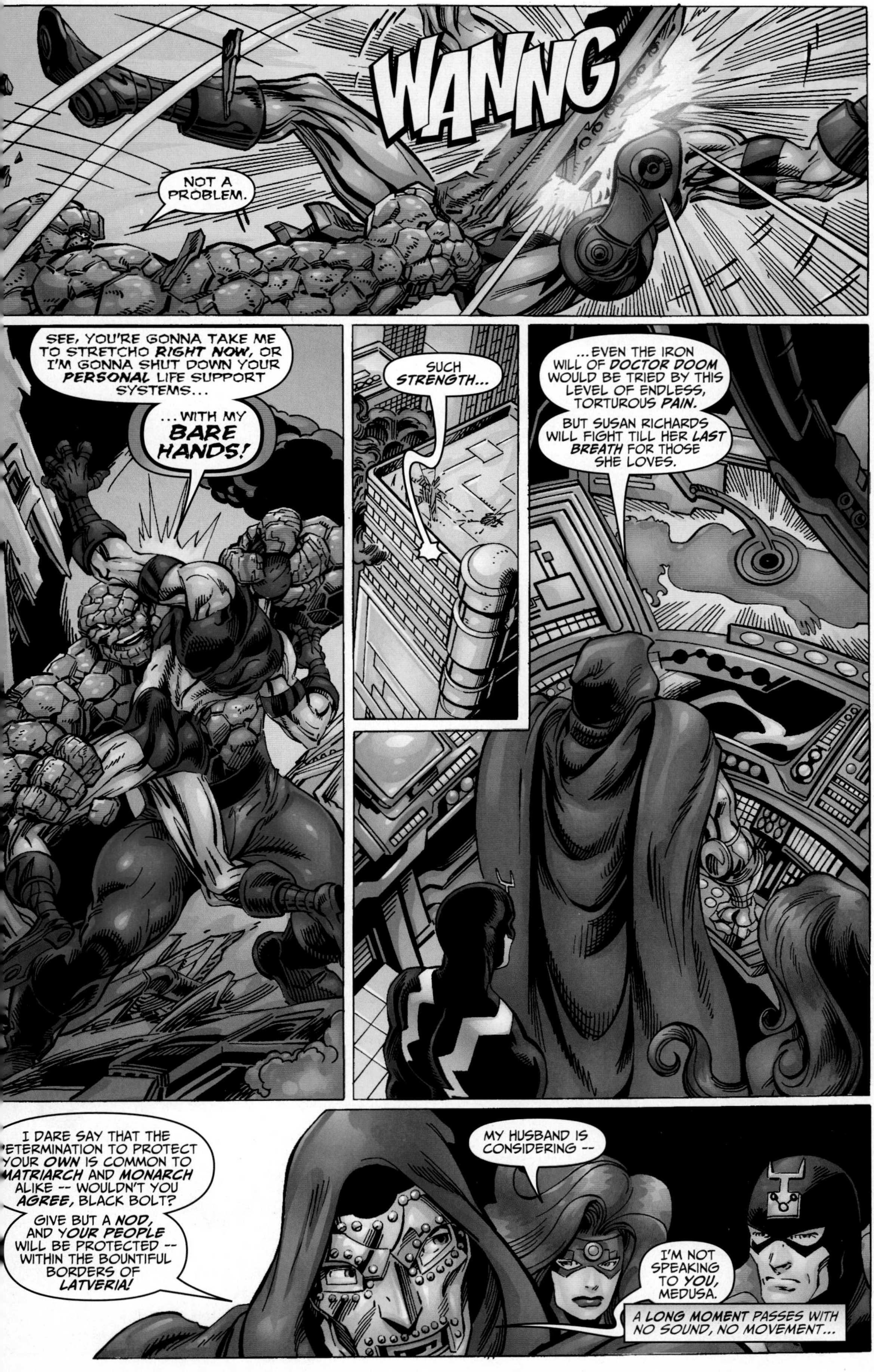
WANNG
NOT A PROBLEM.
SEE, YOU'RE GONNA TAKE ME TO STRETCHO RIGHT NOW, OR I'M GONNA SHUT DOWN YOUR PERSONAL LIFE SUPPORT SYSTEMS...
...WITH MY BARE HANDS!
SUCH STRENGTH...
...EVEN THE IRON WILL OF DOCTOR DOOM WOULD BE TRIED BY THIS LEVEL OF ENDLESS, TORTUROUS PAIN.
BUT SUSAN RICHARDS WILL FIGHT TILL HER LAST BREATH FOR THOSE SHE LOVES.
I DARE SAY THAT THE DETERMINATION TO PROTECT YOUR OWN IS COMMON TO MATRIARCH AND MONARCH ALIKE -- WOULDN'T YOU AGREE, BLACK BOLT?
GIVE BUT A NOD, AND YOUR PEOPLE WILL BE PROTECTED -- WITHIN THE BOUNTIFUL BORDERS OF LATVERIA!
MY HUSBAND IS CONSIDERING --
I'M NOT SPEAKING TO YOU, MEDUSA.
A LONG MOMENT PASSES WITH NO SOUND, NO MOVEMENT...

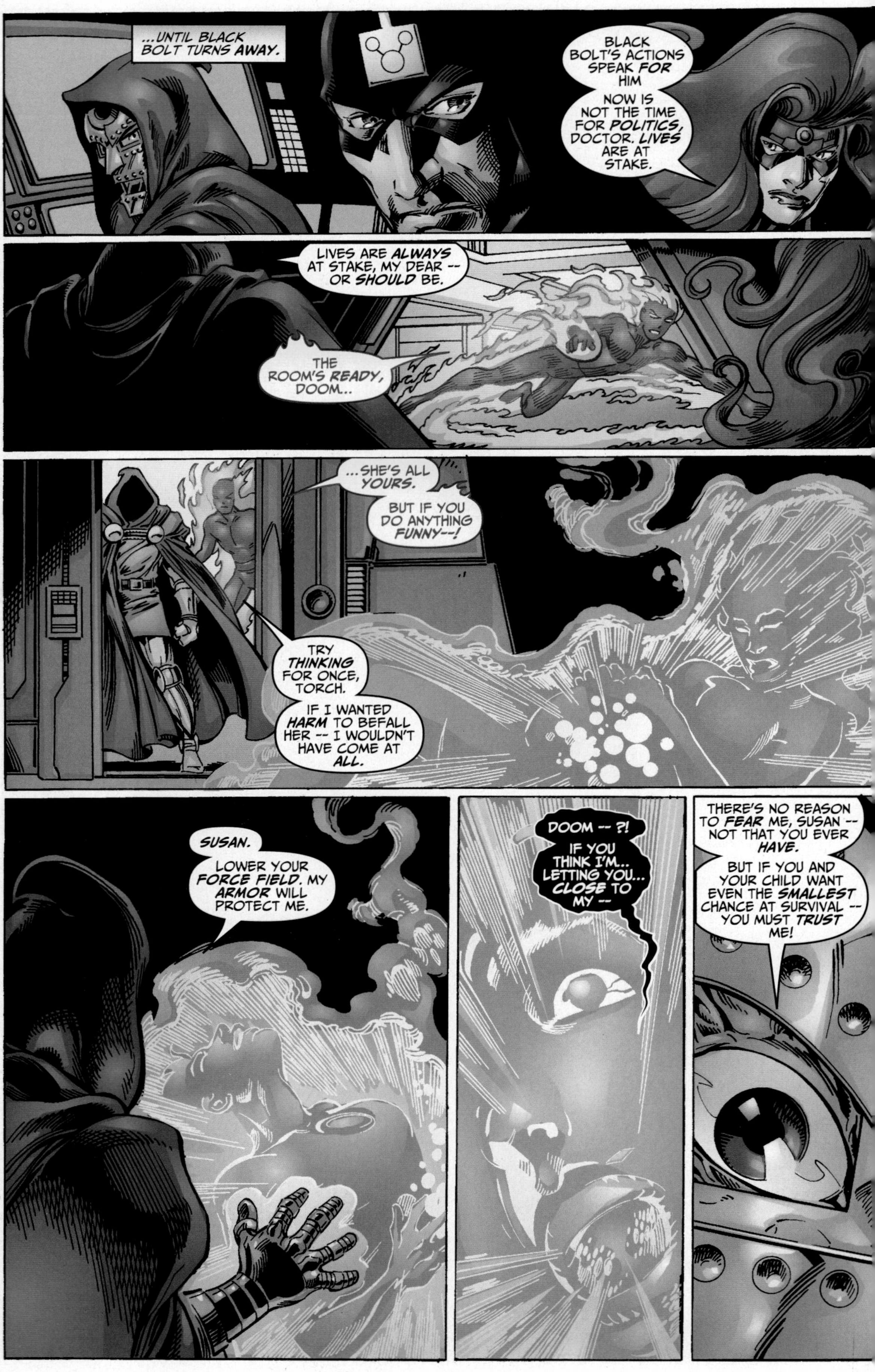
...UNTIL BLACK BOLT TURNS AWAY.
BLACK BOLT'S ACTIONS SPEAK FOR HIM
NOW IS NOT THE TIME FOR POLITICS, DOCTOR. LIVES ARE AT STAKE.
LIVES ARE ALWAYS AT STAKE, MY DEAR -- OR SHOULD BE.
THE ROOM'S READY, DOOM...
...SHE'S ALL YOURS.
BUT IF YOU DO ANYTHING FUNNY--!
TRY THINKING FOR ONCE, TORCH.
IF I WANTED HARM TO BEFALL HER -- I WOULDN'T HAVE COME AT ALL.
SUSAN.
LOWER YOUR FORCE FIELD. MY ARMOR WILL PROTECT ME.
DOOM -- ?!
IF YOU THINK I'M... LETTING YOU... CLOSE TO MY --
THERE'S NO REASON TO FEAR ME, SUSAN -- NOT THAT YOU EVER HAVE.
BUT IF YOU AND YOUR CHILD WANT EVEN THE SMALLEST CHANCE AT SURVIVAL -- YOU MUST TRUST ME!

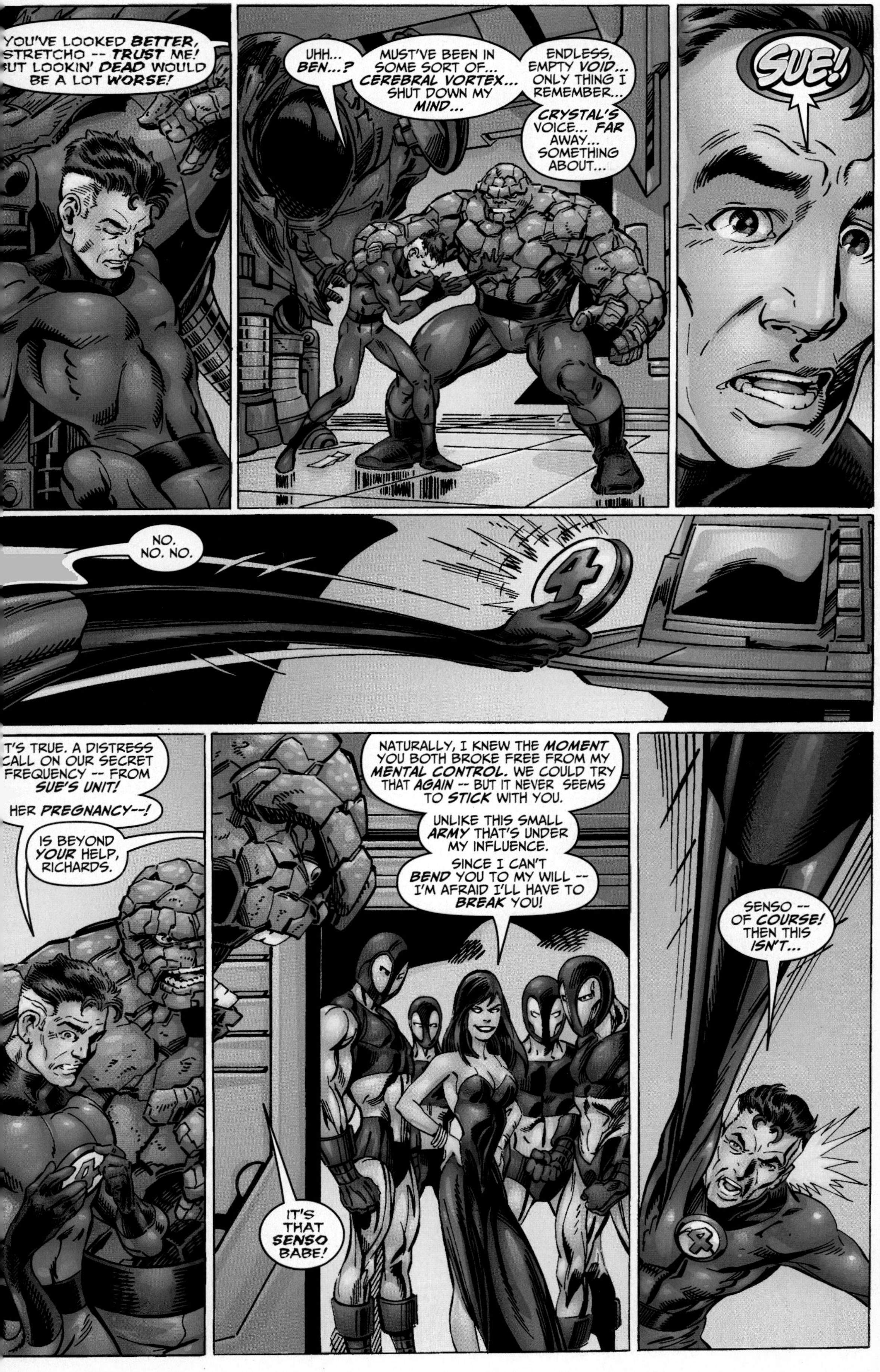
YOU'VE LOOKED BETTER, STRETCHO -- TRUST ME! BUT LOOKIN' DEAD WOULD BE A LOT WORSE!
UHH... BEN...?
MUST'VE BEEN IN SOME SORT OF... CEREBRAL VORTEX... SHUT DOWN MY MIND...
ENDLESS, EMPTY VOID... ONLY THING I REMEMBER...
CRYSTAL'S VOICE... FAR AWAY... SOMETHING ABOUT...
SUE!
NO. NO. NO.
IT'S TRUE. A DISTRESS CALL ON OUR SECRET FREQUENCY -- FROM SUE'S UNIT!
HER PREGNANCY--!
IS BEYOND YOUR HELP, RICHARDS.
NATURALLY, I KNEW THE MOMENT YOU BOTH BROKE FREE FROM MY MENTAL CONTROL. WE COULD TRY THAT AGAIN -- BUT IT NEVER SEEMS TO STICK WITH YOU.
UNLIKE THIS SMALL ARMY THAT'S UNDER MY INFLUENCE.
SINCE I CAN'T BEND YOU TO MY WILL -- I'M AFRAID I'LL HAVE TO BREAK YOU!
IT'S THAT SENSO BABE!
SENSO -- OF COURSE! THEN THIS ISN'T...

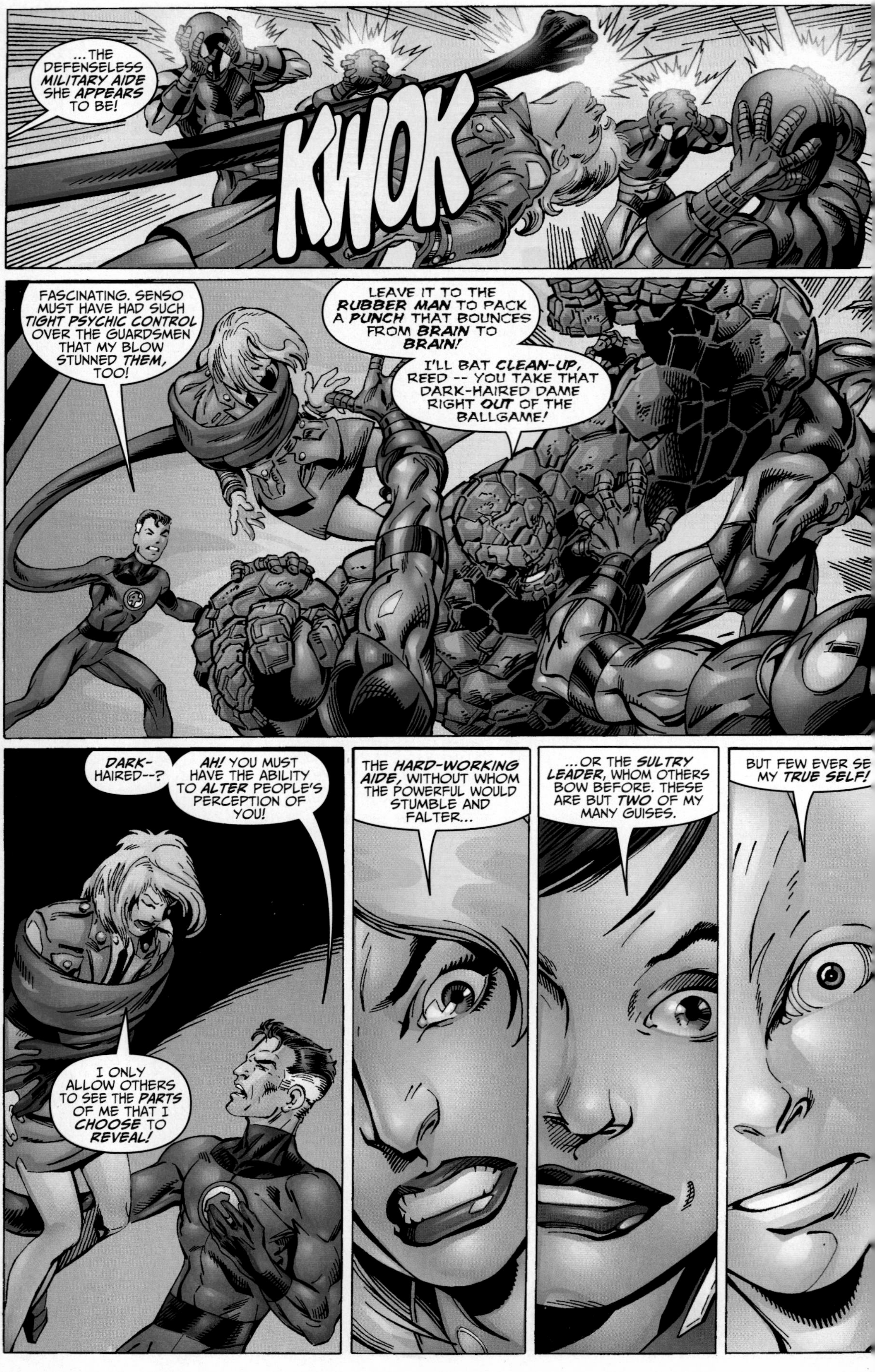
...THE DEFENSELESS MILITARY AIDE SHE APPEARS TO BE!
KWOK
FASCINATING. SENSO MUST HAVE HAD SUCH TIGHT PSYCHIC CONTROL OVER THE GUARDSMEN THAT MY BLOW STUNNED THEM, TOO!
LEAVE IT TO THE RUBBER MAN TO PACK A PUNCH THAT BOUNCES FROM BRAIN TO BRAIN!
I'LL BAT CLEAN-UP, REED -- YOU TAKE THAT DARK-HAIRED DAME RIGHT OUT OF THE BALLGAME!
DARK-HAIRED--?
AH! YOU MUST HAVE THE ABILITY TO ALTER PEOPLE'S PERCEPTION OF YOU!
I ONLY ALLOW OTHERS TO SEE THE PARTS OF ME THAT I CHOOSE TO REVEAL!
THE HARD-WORKING AIDE, WITHOUT WHOM THE POWERFUL WOULD STUMBLE AND FALTER...
...OR THE SULTRY LEADER, WHOM OTHERS BOW BEFORE. THESE ARE BUT TWO OF MY MANY GUISES.
BUT FEW EVER SE MY TRUE SELF!

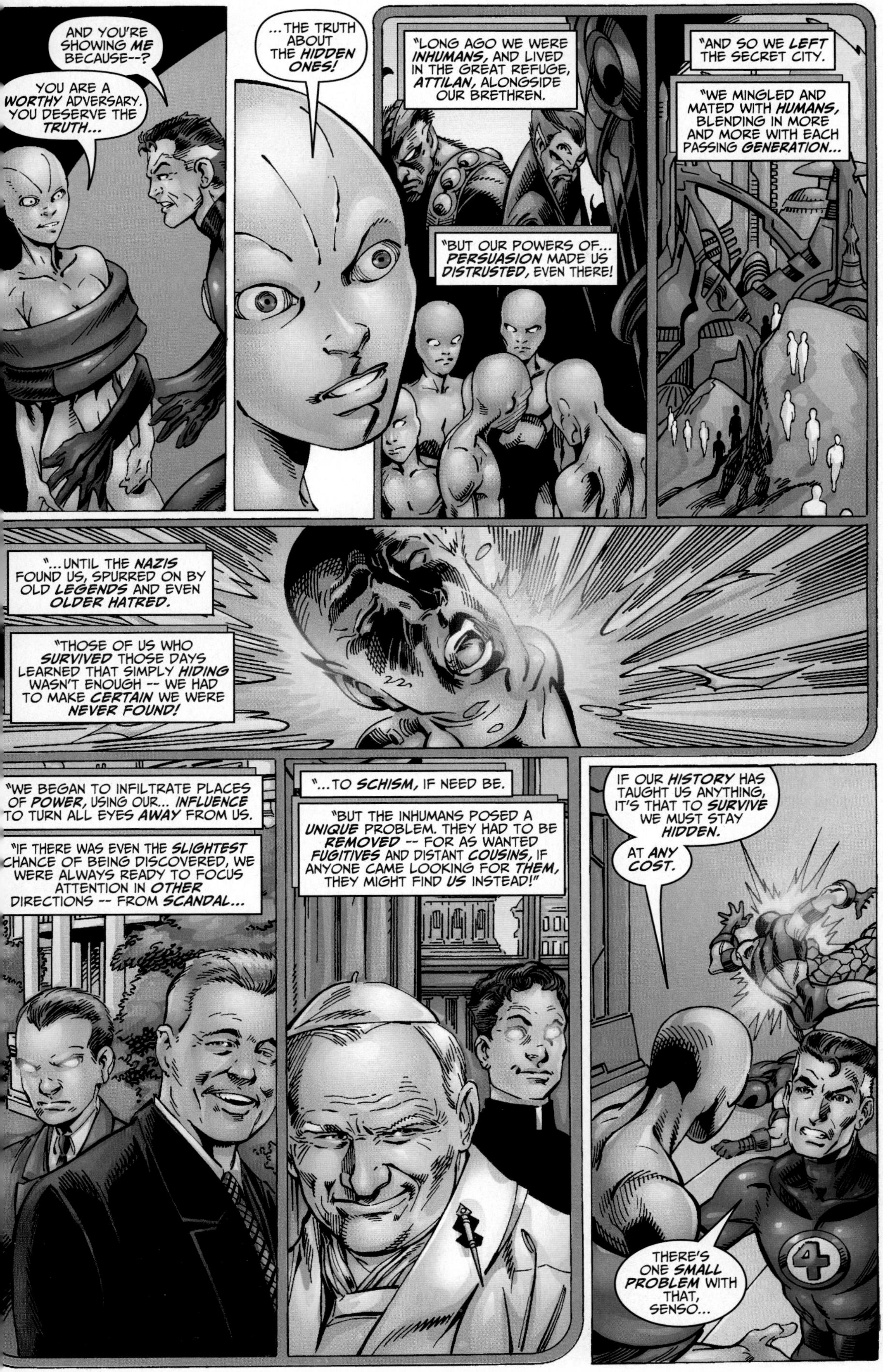
AND YOU'RE SHOWING ME BECAUSE--?
YOU ARE A WORTHY ADVERSARY. YOU DESERVE THE TRUTH...
...THE TRUTH ABOUT THE HIDDEN ONES!
"LONG AGO WE WERE INHUMANS, AND LIVED IN THE GREAT REFUGE, ATTILAN, ALONGSIDE OUR BRETHREN.
"BUT OUR POWERS OF... PERSUASION MADE US DISTRUSTED, EVEN THERE!
"AND SO WE LEFT THE SECRET CITY.
"WE MINGLED AND MATED WITH HUMANS, BLENDING IN MORE AND MORE WITH EACH PASSING GENERATION...
"...UNTIL THE NAZIS FOUND US, SPURRED ON BY OLD LEGENDS AND EVEN OLDER HATRED.
"THOSE OF US WHO SURVIVED THOSE DAYS LEARNED THAT SIMPLY HIDING WASN'T ENOUGH -- WE HAD TO MAKE CERTAIN WE WERE NEVER FOUND!
"WE BEGAN TO INFILTRATE PLACES OF POWER, USING OUR... INFLUENCE TO TURN ALL EYES AWAY FROM US.
"IF THERE WAS EVEN THE SLIGHTEST CHANCE OF BEING DISCOVERED, WE WERE ALWAYS READY TO FOCUS ATTENTION IN OTHER DIRECTIONS -- FROM SCANDAL...
"...TO SCHISM, IF NEED BE.
"BUT THE INHUMANS POSED A UNIQUE PROBLEM. THEY HAD TO BE REMOVED -- FOR AS WANTED FUGITIVES AND DISTANT COUSINS, IF ANYONE CAME LOOKING FOR THEM, THEY MIGHT FIND US INSTEAD!"
IF OUR HISTORY HAS TAUGHT US ANYTHING, IT'S THAT TO SURVIVE WE MUST STAY HIDDEN.
AT ANY COST.
THERE'S ONE SMALL PROBLEM WITH THAT, SENSO...

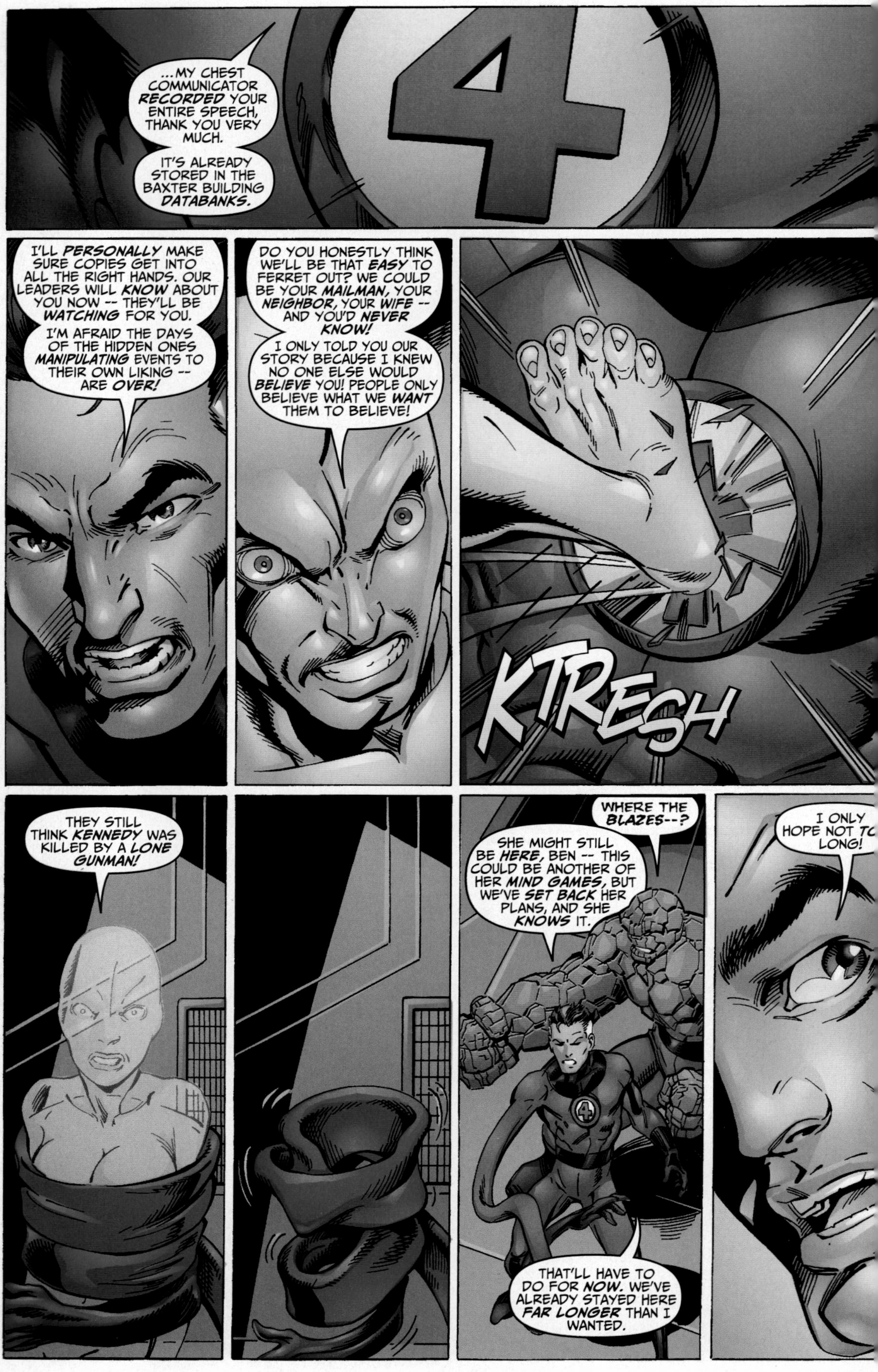
...MY CHEST COMMUNICATOR RECORDED YOUR ENTIRE SPEECH, THANK YOU VERY MUCH.
IT'S ALREADY STORED IN THE BAXTER BUILDING DATABANKS.
I'LL PERSONALLY MAKE SURE COPIES GET INTO ALL THE RIGHT HANDS. OUR LEADERS WILL KNOW ABOUT YOU NOW -- THEY'LL BE WATCHING FOR YOU.
I'M AFRAID THE DAYS OF THE HIDDEN ONES MANIPULATING EVENTS TO THEIR OWN LIKING -- ARE OVER!
DO YOU HONESTLY THINK WE'LL BE THAT EASY TO FERRET OUT? WE COULD BE YOUR MAILMAN, YOUR NEIGHBOR, YOUR WIFE -- AND YOU'D NEVER KNOW!
I ONLY TOLD YOU OUR STORY BECAUSE I KNEW NO ONE ELSE WOULD BELIEVE YOU! PEOPLE ONLY BELIEVE WHAT WE WANT THEM TO BELIEVE!
KTRESH
THEY STILL THINK KENNEDY WAS KILLED BY A LONE GUNMAN!
WHERE THE BLAZES--?
SHE MIGHT STILL BE HERE, BEN -- THIS COULD BE ANOTHER OF HER MIND GAMES, BUT WE'VE SET BACK HER PLANS, AND SHE KNOWS IT.
THAT'LL HAVE TO DO FOR NOW. WE'VE ALREADY STAYED HERE FAR LONGER THAN I WANTED.
I ONLY HOPE NOT

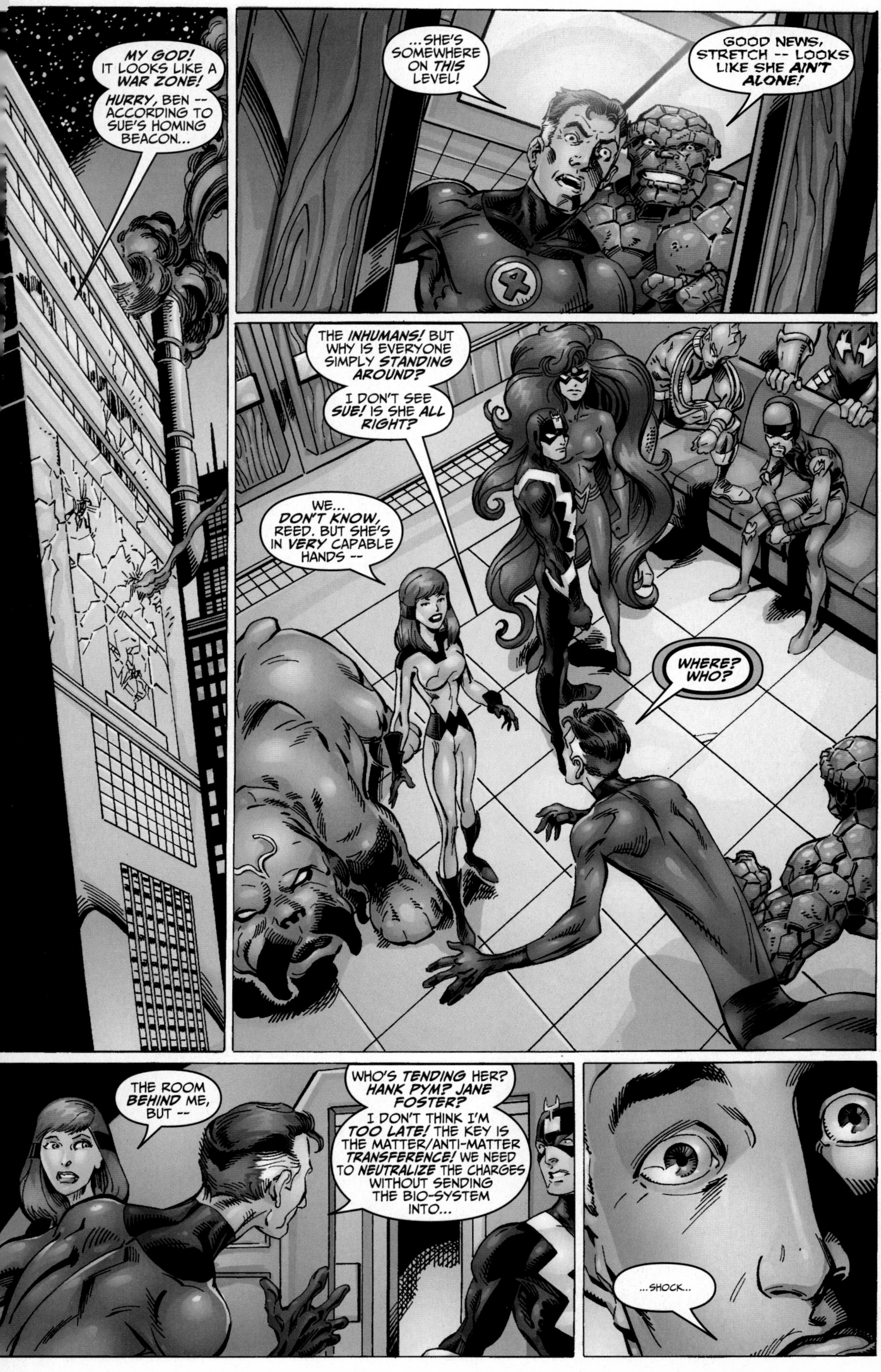
MY GOD! IT LOOKS LIKE A WAR ZONE!
HURRY, BEN -- ACCORDING TO SUE'S HOMING BEACON...
...SHE'S SOMEWHERE ON THIS LEVEL!
GOOD NEWS, STRETCH -- LOOKS LIKE SHE AIN'T ALONE!
THE INHUMANS! BUT WHY IS EVERYONE SIMPLY STANDING AROUND?
I DON'T SEE SUE! IS SHE ALL RIGHT?
WE... DON'T KNOW, REED. BUT SHE'S IN VERY CAPABLE HANDS --
WHERE? WHO?
THE ROOM BEHIND ME, BUT --
WHO'S TENDING HER? HANK PYM? JANE FOSTER?
I DON'T THINK I'M TOO LATE! THE KEY IS THE MATTER/ANTI-MATTER TRANSFERENCE! WE NEED TO NEUTRALIZE THE CHARGES WITHOUT SENDING THE BIO-SYSTEM INTO...
...SHOCK...

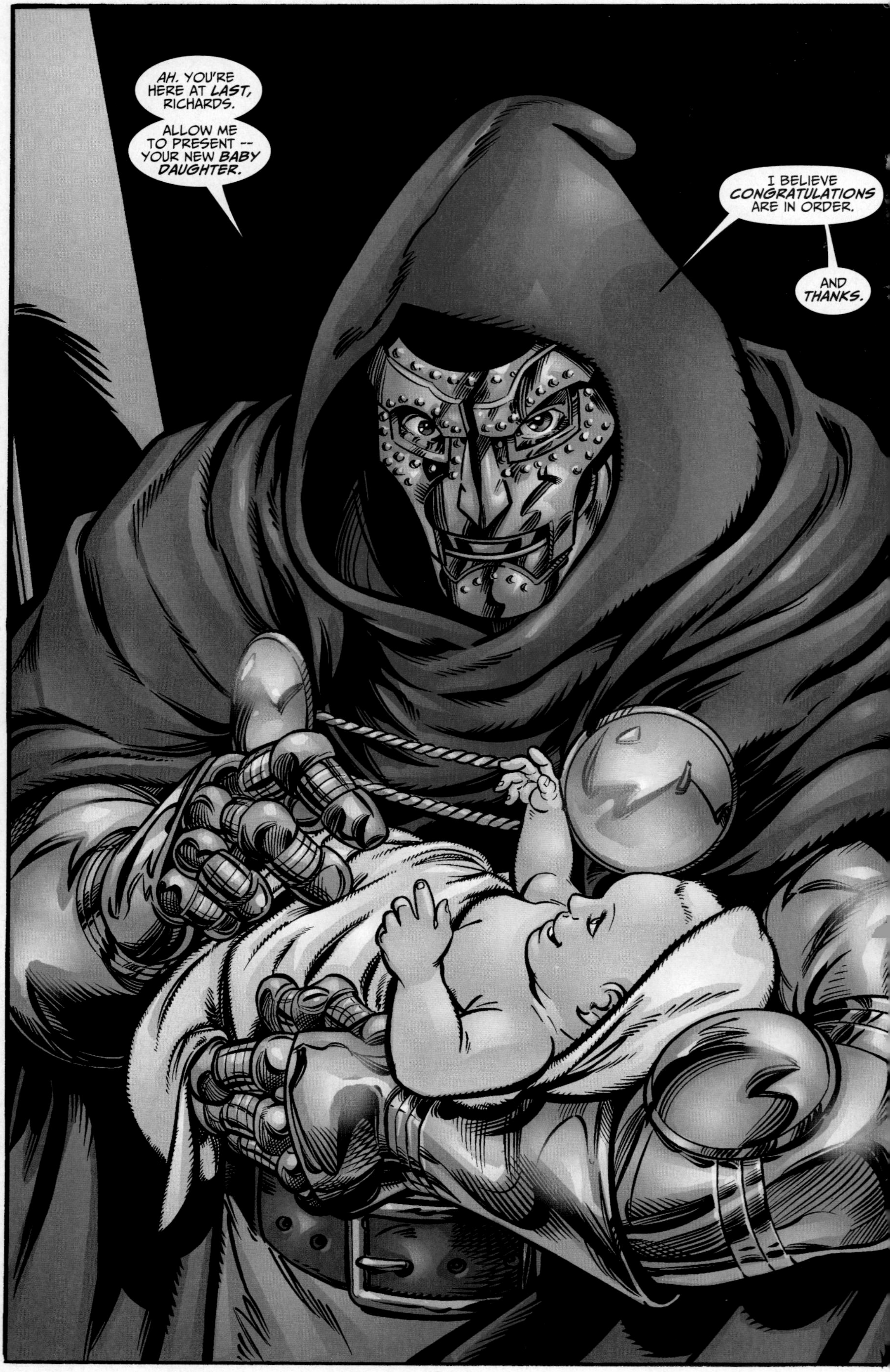
AH. YOU'RE HERE AT LAST, RICHARDS.
ALLOW ME TO PRESENT -- YOUR NEW BABY DAUGHTER.
I BELIEVE CONGRATULATIONS ARE IN ORDER.
AND THANKS.

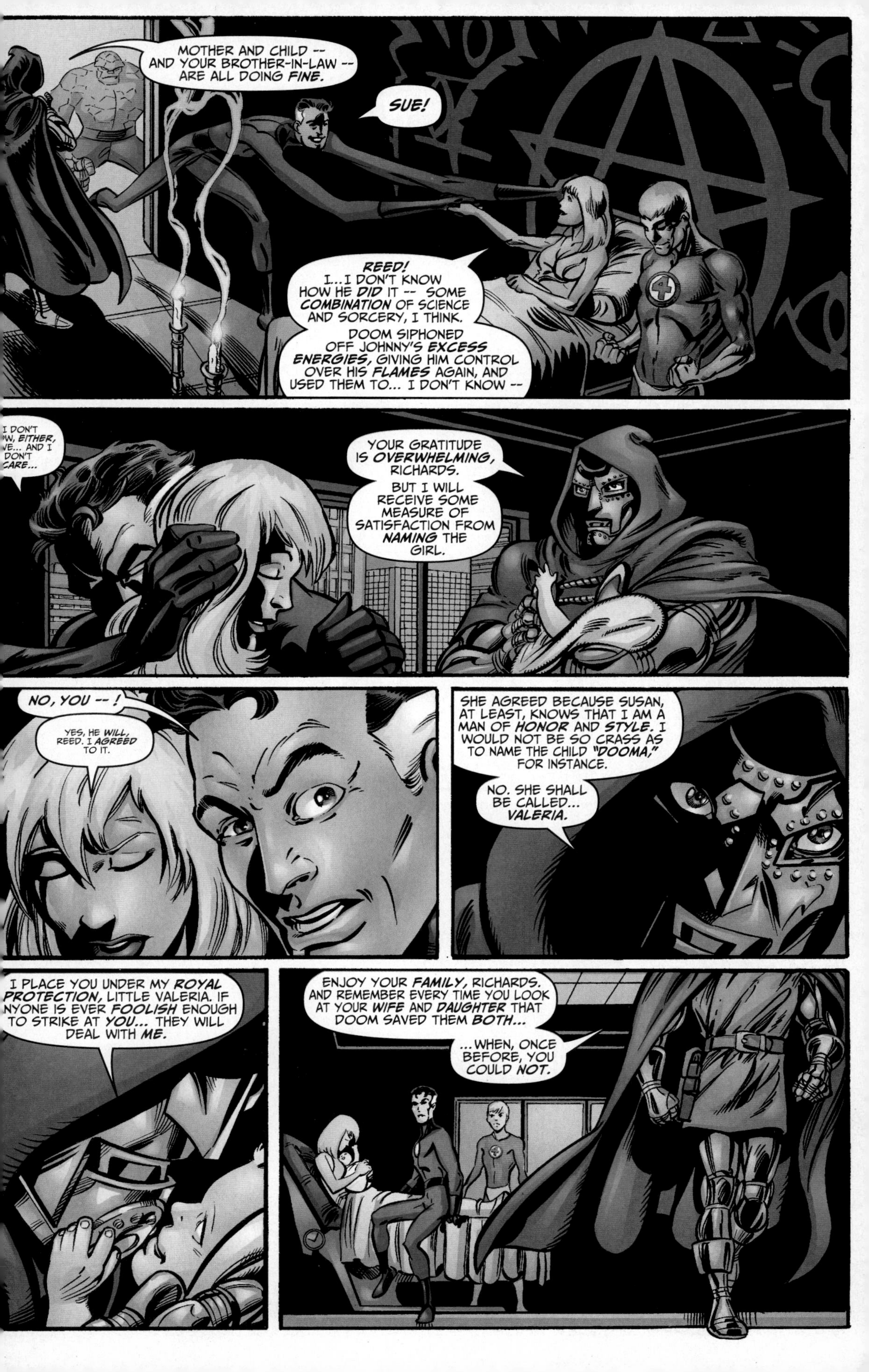

MOTHER AND CHILD -- AND YOUR BROTHER-IN-LAW -- ARE ALL DOING FINE.
SUE!
REED! I...I DON'T KNOW HOW HE DID IT -- SOME COMBINATION OF SCIENCE AND SORCERY, I THINK.
DOOM SIPHONED OFF JOHNNY'S EXCESS ENERGIES, GIVING HIM CONTROL OVER HIS FLAMES AGAIN, AND USED THEM TO... I DON'T KNOW --
I DON'T ...W, EITHER, ...VE... AND I DON'T CARE...
YOUR GRATITUDE IS OVERWHELMING, RICHARDS.
BUT I WILL RECEIVE SOME MEASURE OF SATISFACTION FROM NAMING THE GIRL.
NO, YOU -- !
YES, HE WILL, REED. I AGREED TO IT.
SHE AGREED BECAUSE SUSAN, AT LEAST, KNOWS THAT I AM A MAN OF HONOR AND STYLE. I WOULD NOT BE SO CRASS AS TO NAME THE CHILD "DOOMA," FOR INSTANCE.
NO. SHE SHALL BE CALLED... VALERIA.
I PLACE YOU UNDER MY ROYAL PROTECTION, LITTLE VALERIA. IF NYONE IS EVER FOOLISH ENOUGH TO STRIKE AT YOU... THEY WILL DEAL WITH ME.
ENJOY YOUR FAMILY, RICHARDS. AND REMEMBER EVERY TIME YOU LOOK AT YOUR WIFE AND DAUGHTER THAT DOOM SAVED THEM BOTH...
...WHEN, ONCE BEFORE, YOU COULD NOT.

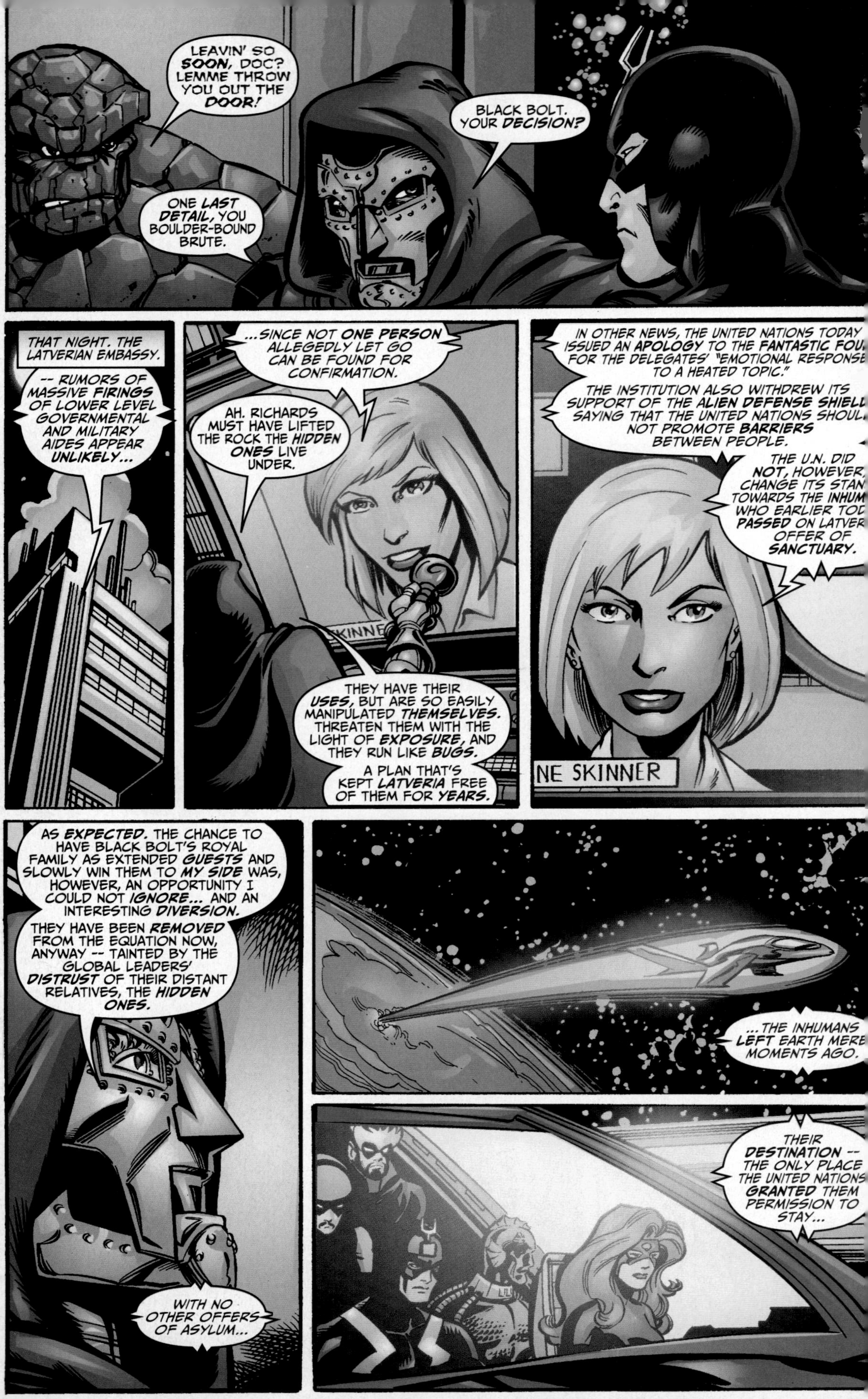

LEAVIN' SO SOON, DOC? LEMME THROW YOU OUT THE DOOR!
ONE LAST DETAIL, YOU BOULDER-BOUND BRUTE.
BLACK BOLT. YOUR DECISION?
THAT NIGHT. THE LATVERIAN EMBASSY.
-- RUMORS OF MASSIVE FIRINGS OF LOWER LEVEL GOVERNMENTAL AND MILITARY AIDES APPEAR UNLIKELY...
...SINCE NOT ONE PERSON ALLEGEDLY LET GO CAN BE FOUND FOR CONFIRMATION.
AH. RICHARDS MUST HAVE LIFTED THE ROCK THE HIDDEN ONES LIVE UNDER.
SKINNE
THEY HAVE THEIR USES, BUT ARE SO EASILY MANIPULATED THEMSELVES. THREATEN THEM WITH THE LIGHT OF EXPOSURE, AND THEY RUN LIKE BUGS.
A PLAN THAT'S KEPT LATVERIA FREE OF THEM FOR YEARS.
IN OTHER NEWS, THE UNITED NATIONS TODAY ISSUED AN APOLOGY TO THE FANTASTIC FOU FOR THE DELEGATES' "EMOTIONAL RESPONSE TO A HEATED TOPIC."
THE INSTITUTION ALSO WITHDREW ITS SUPPORT OF THE ALIEN DEFENSE SHIEL SAYING THAT THE UNITED NATIONS SHOUL NOT PROMOTE BARRIERS BETWEEN PEOPLE.
THE U.N. DID NOT, HOWEVER, CHANGE ITS STAN TOWARDS THE INHUM WHO EARLIER TOD PASSED ON LATVER OFFER OF SANCTUARY.
NE SKINNER
AS EXPECTED. THE CHANCE TO HAVE BLACK BOLT'S ROYAL FAMILY AS EXTENDED GUESTS AND SLOWLY WIN THEM TO MY SIDE WAS, HOWEVER, AN OPPORTUNITY I COULD NOT IGNORE... AND AN INTERESTING DIVERSION.
THEY HAVE BEEN REMOVED FROM THE EQUATION NOW, ANYWAY -- TAINTED BY THE GLOBAL LEADERS' DISTRUST OF THEIR DISTANT RELATIVES, THE HIDDEN ONES.
WITH NO OTHER OFFERS OF ASYLUM...
...THE INHUMANS LEFT EARTH MERE MOMENTS AGO.
THEIR DESTINATION -- THE ONLY PLACE THE UNITED NATIONS GRANTED THEM PERMISSION TO STAY...

...THE MYSTERIOUS BLUE AREA OF THE MOON, WHERE THEIR PEOPLE LIVED *ONCE* BEFORE.

AN UNNAMED UNITED NATIONS SOURCE STRESSED THIS IS NOT RELOCATION -- THIS IS RESETTLEMENT.

OH, THAT'S *GREAT!* YEAH, A *GREAT* BIG PILE OF --

JOHNNY -- ?

DON'T MIND ME, REED -- I'M JUST A WASHED-UP *HAS-BEEN!* ONE DAY YOU'RE *HOT* -- THE NEXT YOU'RE *NOT!*

THAT WAS THE *STUDIO.* THEY'RE FINISHING THE *RAWHIDE KID* MOVIE WITHOUT ME. USING A *LOOK-ALIKE.*

SHOULD'A READ THE FINE PRINT! I AM *SUCH* A *LOSER!*

IT'S ONLY A *MOVIE,* JOHNNY -- NOT THE *NOBEL PEACE PRIZE!*

IT'S NOT *JUST* THE MOVIE, REED, IT'S...

LOOK -- I KNOW IT'S *GREAT* THAT SIS AND THE KID ARE OKAY... AND NO ONE'S HAPPIER THAN *ME* THAT MY FLAME'S UNDER A *CONTROLLED BURN* AGAIN...

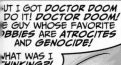

...UT I GOT *DOCTOR DOOM* DO IT! *DOCTOR DOOM!* E GUY WHOSE FAVORITE OBBIES ARE *ATROCITES* AND *GENOCIDE!*

WHAT WAS I THINKING?!

YOU WERE THINKING *FAST,* JOHNNY -- UNDER *TREMENDOUS* PRESSURE. AND, YES, YOU GOT *DOOM* -- BUT YOU *GOT DOOM!* HE CAME!

YOU *SAVED* THE LIVES OF THE TWO MOST IMPORTANT WOMEN IN THE *WORLD* TO ME. DON'T *FORGET* THAT -- *I* NEVER WILL.

AND THAT'S WHY SUE AND I WANT YOU TO BE VALERIA'S *GODFATHER.*

GODFATHER. WOW.

THAT'S, LIKE, AN OFFER I CAN'T REFUSE.

THEN WHAT'RE WE *WAITING* FOR?

LET'S GO SEE THE *FAMILY!*

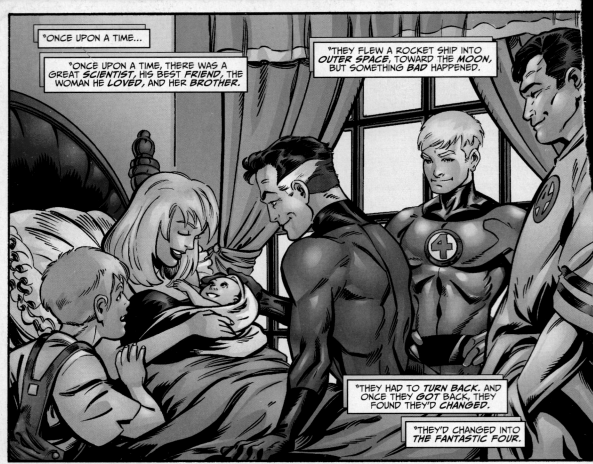

"ONCE UPON A TIME...

"ONCE UPON A TIME, THERE WAS A GREAT *SCIENTIST*, HIS BEST *FRIEND*, THE WOMAN HE *LOVED*, AND HER *BROTHER*.

"THEY FLEW A ROCKET SHIP INTO *OUTER SPACE*, TOWARD THE *MOON*, BUT SOMETHING *BAD* HAPPENED.

"THEY HAD TO *TURN BACK*. AND ONCE THEY *GOT BACK*, THEY FOUND THEY'D *CHANGED*.

"THEY'D CHANGED INTO *THE FANTASTIC FOUR*.

"WHEREVER THEY WENT AFTER THAT, WHATEVER *DANGERS* THEY FACED -- THEY FACED *TOGETHER*. THEY FACED AS A *FAMILY*.

"THEY BECAME THE MOST *FAMOUS* HEROES ON EARTH.

"LOVED BY *MILLIONS*."

THEY'RE *LUCKY*, BABY LUNA.

THEY'RE LUCKY THEY NEVER *REACHED* THE MOON.